BRITISH GEOLOGICAL SURVEY
Natural Environment Research Council

R. S. ARTHURTON
E. W. JOHNSON
and D. J. C. MUNDY

Geology of the country around Settle

Memoir for 1:50 000 geological sheet 60 (England and Wales)

LONDON: HER MAJESTY'S STATIONERY OFFICE 1988

iv

© Crown copyright 1988

First published 1988

ISBN 0 11 884403 2

Bibliographical reference

ARTHURTON, R. S., JOHNSON, E. W. and MUNDY, D. J. C. 1988.   Geology of the country around Settle.   Mem. Br. Geol. Surv., Sheet 60 (England & Wales).

Authors

R. S. ARTHURTON, BSc
British Geological Survey, Keyworth

E. W. JOHNSON, BSc
British Geological Survey,
Newcastle upon Tyne

D. J. C. MUNDY, BSc, PhD
BP Canada Inc.,
333 Fifth Avenue SW
Calgary, Alberta
Canada T2P 3B6

Contributors

J. D. Cornwell, BSc, PhD, A. D. Evans, BSc
M. Mitchell, MA, B. Owens, BSc, PhD
J. Pattison, MSc, N. J. Riley, BSc, PhD
A. W. A. Rushton, BA, PhD and
D. E. White, MSc, PhD
British Geological Survey, Keyworth

L. C. Jones, BSc
Marian, Esgyryn Road, Llandudno Junction,
Gwynedd LL31 9QE

W. H. C. Ramsbottom, MA, PhD
Brow Cottage, Kirkby Malzeard, Ripon,
North Yorkshire HG4 3RY

R. B. Rickards, BSc, PhD
Department of Earth Sciences
Downing Street, Cambridge CB2 3EQ

A. R. E. Strank, BSc, PhD
BP Research Centre, Chertsey Road,
Sunbury-on-Thames, Middlesex TW16 7LN

Printed in the United Kingdom for HMSO

Dd 240408   C20   3/88   398/2   12521

Other publications of the Survey dealing with this district and adjoining districts

BOOKS
British Regional Geology
The Pennines and adjacent areas (3rd Edition)
Sheet Memoirs
Geology of the country around Clitheroe and Nelson (sheet 68)
Geology of the country between Bradford and Skipton (sheet 69)

Economic Memoir
Geology of the Northern Pennine Orefield: Volume 2, Stainmore to Craven

Mineral Assessment Reports
The limestone resources of the Craven Lowlands
The limestone and dolomite resources of the country around Settle and Malham, North Yorkshire
Mineral Reconnaissance Programme Reports
Mineral reconnaissance surveys in the Craven Basin

MAPS
1:625 000
Sheet 2 Geological
Sheet 2 Quaternary
Sheet 2 Aeromagnetic

1:250 000 (Solid geology, Quaternary, Aeromagnetic and Gravity sheets)
Lake District
Liverpool Bay

1:100 000
Hydrogeological map of southern Yorkshire and adjoining areas

1:50 000 (and one inch to one mile)
Sheet 50 Hawes
Sheet 51 Masham
Sheet 67 Garstang (in preparation)
Sheet 68 Clitheroe
Sheet 69 Bradford

Geology of the country around Settle

The district described in this memoir extends from the Askrigg Block in the north to the Craven Basin in the south. The Askrigg Block is a structurally stable area; a thin sequence of gently inclined Carboniferous sedimentary rocks rests unconformably on strongly folded Lower Palaeozoic strata, seen in the Craven Inliers. The Craven Basin includes a much thicker Carboniferous sequence that is cut by major NW-trending faults and deformed in the ENE-trending Ribblesdale Fold Belt.

The transition zone at the block–basin hinge eastwards from Settle is marked by the Middle Craven Fault and the Craven Reef Belt. Marginal reef limestones in this zone define the southern limit of the karst-forming shelf limestones that characterise the block and form the spectacular scenery of Malham Cove and Gordale Scar.

Geophysical data indicate that the Bowland Fells form part of another structural block, named the Bowland Block; this is tilted northwards against the South Craven Fault and preserves the Millstone Grit and some Lower Coal Measures.

Limestones of the Askrigg Block and transition zone have formed hosts to vein minerals, notably baryte and galena. Elsewhere in the transition zone, and in parts of the Basin, limestone has been replaced by dolomite or silica.

Much of the district is covered by glacial deposits of Devensian age; Ipswichian interglacial deposits, including mammalian faunas, are recorded from Victoria Cave, near Settle.

Frontispiece
Malham
Formation,
Gordale Scar
[9153 6404]; a
popular locality
for field studies
and visitors to
the limestone
country in the
northern part of
Settle district
(L 2706)

CONTENTS

FIGURES

PLATES

TABLES

NOTES

In this memoir, the word 'district' means the area included in the 1:50 000 geological sheet 60 (Settle).

Numbers in square brackets are National Grid references within the 100 km square SD.

Numbers preceded by the letter E refer to the Sliced Rock Collection of the British Geological Survey.

Numbers preceded by the letter A or L refer to the Geological Survey Photograph Collection.

Numbers preceded by ARE, DEY, RSA, RU, ZAY or Zw refer to the Survey's Palaeontological collection.

PREFACE

The district covered by the Settle (60) sheet of the 1:50 000 Geological Map of England and Wales was originally surveyed on the scale of six inches to one mile by W. T. Aveline, T. McK. Hughes, W. Gunn, R. H. Tiddeman and W. H. Dalton and published on the one-inch scale as Old Series Sheet 92 NW (Solid and Drift) in 1892.

In 1975–81 the district was resurveyed on the six inch scale by Mr R. S. Arthurton, Drs E. W. Johnson and D. J. C. Mundy and Mrs L. C. Jones. A list of six inch maps and surveyors is given in Appendix 1. The solid edition of the 1:50 000 map of the district is in press and the drift edition is in preparation.

This memoir has been written by R. S. Arthurton, E. W. Johnson and D. J. C. Mundy, and incorporates information from Mrs L. C. Jones. Dr A. R. E. Strank contributed to the chapter on the Lower Carboniferous and Dr J. D. Cornwell and Mr A. D. Evans wrote the chapter on geophysical investigations.

Ordovician faunas were identified by Dr A. W. A. Rushton; Silurian faunas by Drs D. E. White and R. B. Rickards (graptolites); Lower Carboniferous shelly faunas by Messrs J. Pattison, M. Mitchell and Dr D. J. C. Mundy (macrofauna from the Craven Reef Belt); Carboniferous goniatites and shelly faunas by Drs W. H. C. Ramsbottom and N. J. Riley; Lower Carboniferous foraminifera and algae by Dr A. R. E. Strank, and Carboniferous miospores by Dr B. Owens.

Petrographical descriptions were written by E. W. Johnson (Ordovician) and D. J. C. Mundy (Carboniferous). Mr B. Humphreys carried out XRD analyses. The photographs were taken by Mr K. Thornton except where otherwise indicated. Much new data has accrued from the Survey's mineral assessment and mineral reconnaissance surveys; the co-operation of Messrs D. J. Harrison and D. W. Murray and Dr A. J. Wadge is acknowledged. The memoir was edited by M. Mitchell.

We gratefully acknowledge information and assistance generously provided by the Lancashire Naturalists Trust, North Yorkshire County Council (on road works) and the North West and Yorkshire water authorities (on boreholes for existing and proposed reservoirs); also the willing co-operation of local landowners and quarry operators, in particular Redland Aggregates, Tarmac Roadstone Holdings, Imperial Chemical Industries, Steetley Industries, Halton East Quarries and Tilling Construction Services. We acknowledge the provision of confidential borehole information by Amey Roadstone Corporation and the release of stratigraphical data by Cominco S.A. from their boreholes between Settle and Malham which has made an invaluable contribution to this work.

The resurvey and the production of this memoir were supported by the Department of Industry.

F. Geoffrey Larminie, OBE
Director

British Geological Survey
Keyworth
Nottinghamshire

10th December 1987

CHAPTER 1

Introduction

This memoir describes the geology of the district covered by the Settle Sheet (New Series 60) of the 1:50 000 Geological Map of England and Wales, together with a small area of the Hawes Sheet (New Series 50) on the northern margin (Figures 1 and 2).

Settle is situated on the northern margin of the Craven lowlands; the district extends northwards onto the northern Pennines (including much of Fountains Fell) and westwards onto Burn Moor which forms the eastern flank of the Bowland Fells. The district straddles the main (north–south) watershed of northern England; central and western areas drain to the Irish Sea by the rivers Wenning, Hodder and Ribble, and eastern areas to the North Sea by the rivers Wharfe and Aire. Most of the district lies within North Yorkshire, the remainder in Lancashire. The ground to the north of the A65 trunk road is largely included within the Yorkshire Dales National Park, and part of the south-west of the district is designated an area of outstanding natural beauty.

Limestone is quarried in Ribblesdale and Wharfedale to supply the construction industry and, to a lesser extent, the chemical industry. Lower Palaeozoic rocks are quarried for roadstone in Ribblesdale. Mining, mainly for lead, was formerly active between Settle and Malham and in the High Mark – Kilnsey Moor area. Coal was mined up to the early part of the twentieth century on Threshfield Moor and Boss Moor. The district supplies water to Lancashire from Stocks Reservoir and to West Yorkshire from Winterburn Reservoir. Groundwater is pumped from limestones in the Eshton–Hetton area to meet local demand.

The district is of considerable importance as a centre for field studies. The Field Studies Council maintains a research station at Malham Tarn House, and the Lancashire Naturalists Trust have their Bowland Field Station at Dale Head, Slaidburn. Every year many students visit the classic rock sections of Malham Cove, Gordale and Crummack Dale. Visitors should note that most exposures are on private land and permission should always be requested for access.

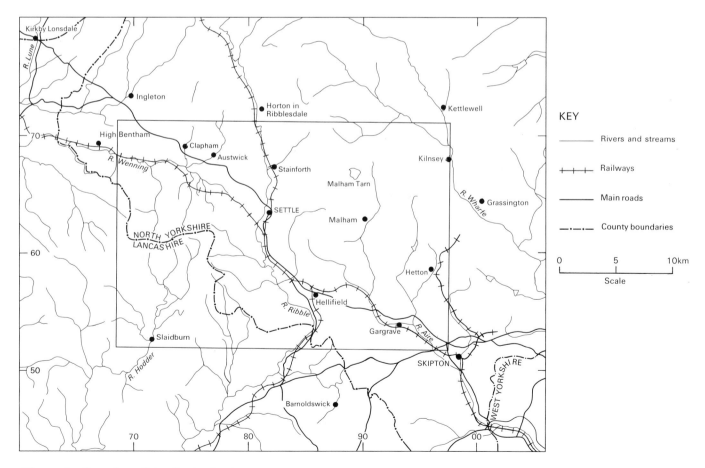

Figure 1 Location of the Settle district

OUTLINE OF GEOLOGICAL HISTORY

The geological history begins in early Ordovician times when Ingleton Group sediments were deposited on the margin of a 'European' continent which was separated from an 'American' continent to the north–west by the Iapetus Ocean. These sediments were tightly folded in pre-Ashgill times, the deformed Ingleton Group forming part of a belt of magnetic basement rocks on the north-eastern margin of an English microcraton. Erosion, in the Llanvirn–Caradoc interval, preceded the onlap of late Ashgill shelf sediments on to the Ingleton Group. Contemporaneous, though distant, volcanism is indicated by interbedded tuffs in the Ashgill Series.

Silurian sediments are mostly turbiditic, and were derived from the 'European' continent during the Wenlock but from the 'American' continent in Ludlow times. At the close of the Silurian the two continental plates collided, and the Lower Palaeozoic rocks were deformed in open folds. Subsequently the Wensleydale Granite pluton was emplaced (400 ± 10 Ma) in the adjoining Hawes district.

The interval end-Silurian to early Dinantian is unrepresented in the known succession. In late Devonian or early Dinantian times, however, the Craven Basin became established, bounded to the north by the Middle and North Craven faults which separate it from the Askrigg Block, an area of relatively high crustal buoyancy (Figure 2). A thick, predominantly argillaceous Dinantian sequence accumulated in the basin but, by contrast, the sequence on the Askrigg Block was relatively thin, with limestones dominating the succession.

From mid-Dinantian to early Namurian times strata in the Craven Basin were folded in a series of anticlines and synclines—the Ribblesdale Fold Belt—and were cut by major faults including the South Craven and Knotts fault-systems. In mid-Dinantian times the basin was transformed from one of widespread shallow water sedimentation to one of considerable bathymetric relief, with relatively deep water 'slope' and 'floor' environments, as well as areas of emergence marked by local unconformities within the succession.

In later Dinantian times, a belt of reef limestone—the Craven Reef Belt—developed in the transition zone between the Askrigg Block and Craven Basin, and defined the southern limit of shelf sedimentation represented by the Malham Formation and the lower part of the Wensleydale Group. Before the close of the Dinantian, however, the strata in this transition zone were strongly faulted and eroded following displacements on the Middle and North Craven faults. At about the same time the Bowland Block, in the north-western part of the district, began to subside and tilt northwards in relation to the Askrigg Block.

In early Silesian times deltaic and fluvial sediments prograded southwards across the Askrigg and Bowland blocks into the Craven Basin. The early Namurian Grassington Grit (or Brennand Grit) represents the first widespread shallow-water sedimentation in the basin since the mid-Dinantian, and is of particular interest because its base is unconformable not only in the southern part of the Askrigg Block but in many parts of the Craven Basin as well, indicating post-Dinantian–pre-Grassington Grit tectonism.

Deltaic and fluvial conditions persisted, although interrupted by numerous marine trangressions, through the Namurian and into Westphalian times when the highest strata in the district were deposited, the Coal Measures of the Ingleton Coalfield. The Silesian strata were displaced along the South Craven Fault at about the close of the Carboniferous and then again in post-Permian times. During the late Carboniferous to Permian interval hydrothermal mineralisation affected Dinantian limestones mainly in the Askrigg Block and transition zone.

There is a hiatus in the geological record between the Westphalian strata and the Quaternary (Pleistocene and Recent) drift deposits. The oldest known deposit above this break is a cave-earth of Ipswichian age which represents an interglacial interval during which elephant, rhinoceras, hippopotamus and hyaena roamed the country around Settle. Later, during the Devensian glaciation, the district was covered by a south and south-eastward moving ice-sheet, partly originating in the northern Pennines and partly having a Howgill Fells–Lake District provenance. An extensive blanket of boulder clay (till) was deposited by the ice sheet which moulded much of it into drumlin landforms. Melt waters from the stagnant ice-sheet established a subglacial drainage system with channels cut into till and solid rock, and deposited sand and gravel. In post-glacial times, as the climate ameliorated, vegetation became re-established and peat formed as a blanket over high ground and in ill drained areas on low ground where some was associated with lacustrine deposits. As the present-day drainage system became established, alluvium was deposited adjacent to streams and rivers, and in the larger valleys this formed terraces.   RSA

Figure 2   The major structures and generalised outcrops of the Settle district

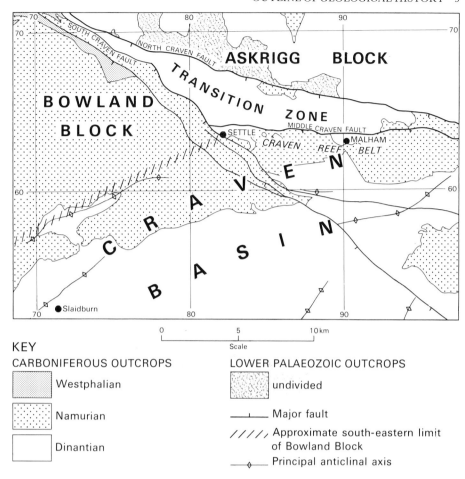

KEY

CARBONIFEROUS OUTCROPS

Westphalian

Namurian

Dinantian

LOWER PALAEOZOIC OUTCROPS

undivided

Major fault

Approximate south-eastern limit of Bowland Block

Principal anticlinal axis

CHAPTER 2

Ordovician and Silurian

Lower Palaeozoic rocks underlie Carboniferous strata on the Askrigg Block, and crop out in a series of inliers, known collectively as the Craven Inliers, along its southern margin (Figure 3). Both Ordovician and Silurian strata are present and are disposed in ESE-plunging folds. The small areas of the Austwick–Ribblesdale Inlier which lie within the adjoining Hawes district are included in this account.

Sedgwick (1852) first recognised that Phillips' Slate Series (1828) was of Lower Palaeozoic age. Since then the Craven Inliers have been the subject of numerous studies, notably by Marr (1887), Dakyns and others (1890), Hughes (1902 and 1907) and King and Wilcockson (1934). Specialised aspects of their stratigraphy and sedimentology have been researched by Reynolds (1894), King (1932), McCabe (1972), McCabe and Waugh (1973) and O'Nions and others (1973).

ORDOVICIAN

Ordovician strata crop out in the Austwick–Ribblesdale and Clapham Beck inliers. Their stratigraphy has been revised in the resurvey (Figure 4).

INGLETON GROUP

The Ingleton Group crops out in the Ribblesdale and the Chapel le Dale inliers (Figure 3), and probably underlies the Carboniferous rocks in much of the intervening area. The Group has been proved beneath Carboniferous cover at Ribblehead, by drilling in 1986, and also at Beckermonds Scar (Wilson and Cornwell, 1982) in upper Wharfedale, about 10 km north-east of Horton in Ribblesdale (Figure 33). The group comprises an interbedded succession of grey-green turbiditic sandstones, siltstones and conglomerates. Radiometric dating (O'Nions and others, 1973) suggested a late Tremadoc to early Arenig age; acritarchs from similar strata in the Beckermonds Scar Borehole indicate an Arenig age (Wilson and Cornwell, 1982). The strata are isoclinally folded and many siltstones within the succession are cleaved. At Horton in Ribblesdale the Ingleton Group outcrop is bounded by unconformably overlying Upper Ordovician and Silurian strata to the south, and elsewhere by Carboniferous rocks. The thickness of the group is unknown; neither its top nor its base are exposed but at least 600 m are known at outcrop.

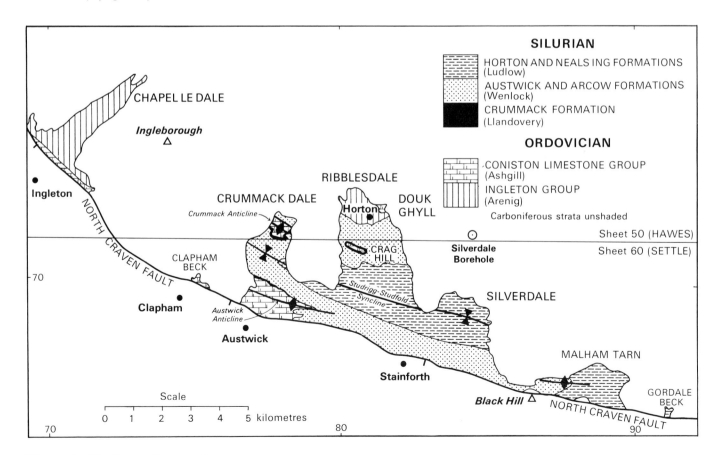

Figure 3 The Lower Palaeozoic Craven Inliers

The Ingleton Group is believed to have been derived from the English Microcraton (Wills, 1978) which lay to the south-east with its north-western margin extending from Skipton to Pembrokeshire. Rastall (1906) concluded that the group was derived from Precambrian igneous and metamorphic basement rocks. Leedal and Walker (1950) deduced, from contemporaneous slump-folds, that deposition took place on a palaeoslope inclined to the north-west. The proximal nature of the turbidite succession supports derivation from the English Microcraton. No determinable macrofossils have yet been found within the group, although Rayner (1957) has described a possible organically derived tool-mark from the Chapel le Dale Inlier.

DETAILS

The outcrop at Horton in Ribblesdale is mostly drift covered although there are several small exposures of the sandstones and siltstones, e.g. in the entrance to Horton Quarry and the nearby railway cutting [8040 7225 to 8045 7203], around the margins of a flooded, disused quarry [8015 7236 to 8031 7236] and in Douk Ghyll [8132 7233 to 8139 7237, and 8157 7243 to 8159 7247].

CONISTON LIMESTONE GROUP

A pre-Ashgill orogenic episode folded and uplifted the Ingleton Group; subsequent erosion produced a subdued topography which was gradually transgressed by an Ashgill sea in which shallow-water sediments were deposited. It is proposed that the Ashgill succession, referred to as the Coniston Limestone Group (King and Wilcockson, 1934), be subdivided into two formations; the Norber Formation, a mainly uniform succession of calcareous siltstones and argillaceous limestones, and the overlying Sowerthwaite For-

mation, a varied succession of siltstones and mudstones with interbedded tuffs, sandstones and conglomerates (Figure 4). As far as possible, the named lithological units of King and Wilcockson (1934) have been retained within the new formational divisions.

The zonal subdivision, based on shelly faunas, was established by Ingham (1966) in the Howgill Fells, some 25 km north-west of the district, where the Ashgill succession is most complete. Previously the oldest Ashgill strata at Austwick were thought to belong to zone 6 of the Rawtheyan (Ingham and Rickards, 1974), but beds belonging to zone 3 of the Cautleyan have been identified during the resurvey. Non-sequences are present within the succession; one separates the Cautleyan and Rawtheyan stages (zones 3 and 6), and others are present in zone 7 of the Rawtheyan and in the Hirnantian (Figure 4).

Norber Formation

The calcareous siltstones and argillaceous limestones that comprise the Norber Formation are up to 160 m thick. They crop out in the core of the Austwick Anticline between Norber Brow and Wharfe Gill, north-east of Austwick, and this section is designated as the type locality although exposures are discontinuous. This outcrop extends north-westward, beneath Carboniferous cover, to the small inlier of Clapham Beck. In Ribblesdale the formation crops out in Douk Ghyll (Figure 5), the only locality in the Craven Inliers where the unconformable relationship with the underlying Ingleton Group is exposed. The Crag Hill Limestone, which crops out at Crag Hill on the west side of Ribblesdale and in the Crummack Anticline (Figure 5), is considered to be a member of the Norber Formation. An irregular neptunian dyke of fossiliferous limestone in the Ingleton Group south of Horton in Ribblesdale station (King, 1932), is tentatively assigned to the formation.

The formation is generally poorly exposed. In Douk Ghyll 20–30 m of siltstones are preserved above the basal conglomerate; these yield a rich shelly fauna (Plate 2) assigned to the Rawtheyan Stage (zones 5 or 6) on the occurrence of *Tretaspis hadelandica brachystichus*. This is a revision of the Cautleyan age suggested by Ingham and Rickards (1974). The thickest succession occurs in the Austwick Anticline; there up to 160 m of strata are known and the base of the succession has not been proved. The lowest beds in this succession yield an abundant and varied Cautleyan fauna including corals, bryozoa, numerous brachiopods and trilobites (Plate 2) and, at one locality, *Tretaspis convergens deliqua* representative of zone 3. A non-sequence probably separates Cautleyan and Rawtheyan strata in the Austwick Anticline. Breaks in the succession at this stratigraphic level also occur in the Dent Inliers (Ingham and Rickards, 1974), the Lake District (Ingham and others, 1978) and the Cross Fell Inlier (Burgess and Holliday, 1979), suggesting a widespread regression.

CRAG HILL LIMESTONE

The Crag Hill Limestone comprises at least 30 m of nodular-bedded argillaceous limestones with siltstone partings. It crops out in a tight, asymmetrical (with a more steeply dip-

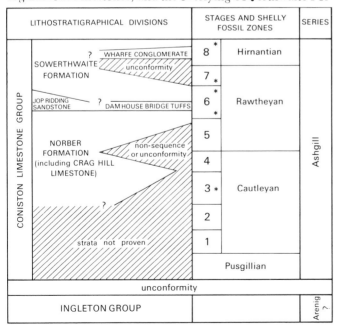

Figure 4 Classification of Ordovician strata. Shading indicates Ashgill strata that is locally absent or has not been proved; * indicates levels at which there is faunal control

ping northern limb), ESE-plunging anticline on the west side of Ribblesdale [8061 7097 to 8016 7155], north-west of the farm after which it is named (Figures 3 and 5). The anticline extends WNW, beneath the cover of Carboniferous rocks, into Crummack Dale, where the fold plunges WNW and the limestone is unconformably overlain by the Sowerthwaite Formation or by Silurian strata. The base of the limestone is not seen in any of the Craven Inliers. Decalcified patches of the limestone yield an abundant fauna of silicified corals, bryozoa, brachiopods (Plate 2) and a few trilobites. The fauna is not diagnostic of a particular Ashgill zone, but has a Cautleyan or Rawtheyan aspect.

DETAILS

In Douk Ghyll [8140 7237 to 8156 7243] there is a siliceous conglomerate up to 6 m thick at the base of the Norber Formation. It is thickly bedded, and fills irregularities in the surface of the Ingleton Group upon which it rests unconformably. Disseminated pyrite and galena are present in the conglomerate and there are irregular patches of hematite staining. There is a gradational passage upwards into strongly cleaved, calcareous siltstones which contain nodules of impure limestone. An abundant fauna including bryozoa, *Dalmanella sp.*, *Dolerorthis inaequicostata*, *Eoplectodonta rhombica*, *Eremotrema* cf. *paucicostellatum*, *Glyptorthis sp.*, *Laticrura sp.*, *Nicolella actoniae*, *Orthambonites* cf. *humilidorsatus*, *Platystrophia sp.*, *Reuschella sp.*, *Sampo ruralis*, *Skenidioides sp.*, various mollusca, *Atrac-topyge* cf. *scabra*, *Calymene* (s.l.) *sp.*, *Pseudosphaerexochus conformis* and *Tretaspis hadelandica brachystichus* has been recovered from weathered and decalcified patches of siltstone. The faunal list, enlarged by the labours of Mr John Worthington, has a Cautleyan aspect, but the *Tretaspis* indicates a Rawtheyan age. Selected fossils are shown on Plate 2.

Ashgill strata are also preserved in a neptunian dyke exposed on the eastern side of the railway cutting [8045 7206] at Horton in Ribblesdale. Little of the dyke, which attains a maximum width of 1.2 m, remains; all that was observed in the resurvey was a breccia of angular blocks of Ingleton Group sandstone in a limestone matrix. The dyke was described by King (1932), who collected a brachiopod and trilobite fauna which Ingham and Rickards (1974) interpreted as a 'facies fauna of Keisley type' probably of Cautleyan age.

The Norber Formation crops out in the core of the ESE-plunging Austwick Anticline, with the oldest strata in Wharfe Gill [7815 6914 to 7877 6912]. A small exposure [7815 6914] of decalcified siltstone on the southern limb of the anticline yielded a rich Cautleyan (zone 3) fauna including algae, corals, bryozoa, many brachiopods, bivalves, gastropods, cephalopods, trilobites (including *Tretaspis* cf. *moeldenensis*), ostracods and echinoderms. Two argillaceous limestones are present towards the top of the succession, stratigraphically some 30 m above the fossil locality. The upper limestone, about 20 m thick, contains calcite veinlets up to 5 mm wide with small amounts of galena. Towards the top of this limestone there is a patchily dolomitised calcirudite containing sparsely disseminated galena. Both this, and the lower limestone

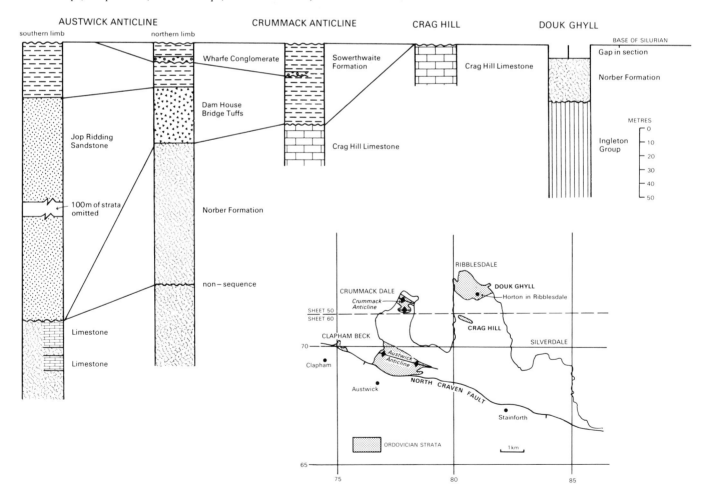

Figure 5   Comparative sections of Ordovician strata in the Craven Inliers

Figure 6 Ordovician outcrops in the Austwick Anticline

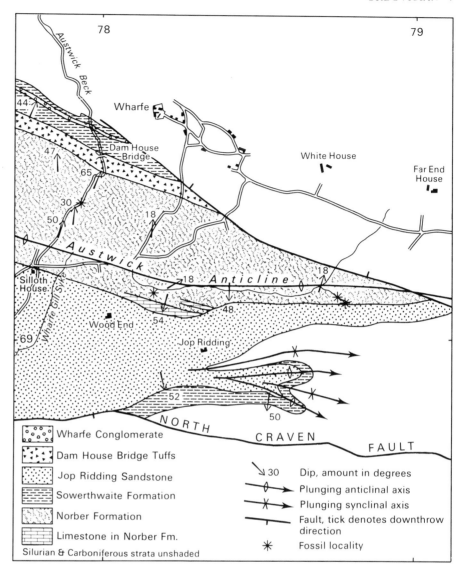

Wharfe Conglomerate

Dam House Bridge Tuffs

Jop Ridding Sandstone

Sowerthwaite Formation

Norber Formation

Limestone in Norber Fm.

Silurian & Carboniferous strata unshaded

↘30 Dip, amount in degrees

Plunging anticlinal axis

Plunging synclinal axis

Fault, tick denotes downthrow direction

✳ Fossil locality

strike into the base of the overlying Jop Ridding Sandstone [7829 6907 and 7835 6909 respectively], demonstrating that the latter is unconformable. Other fossiliferous localities in Wharfe Gill [7875 6913 and 7877 6912] have yielded Cautleyan (zone 3) faunas with bryozoa, brachiopods (including *Strophomena shallockiensis* and *Sampo ruralis*) orthocones, trilobites (including *Tretaspis convergens deliqua*), ostracodes and echinoderm fragments (Plate 2).

On the northern limb of the anticline, beds of argillaceous limestone, up to 0.5 m thick, lie towards the top of the succession and form a prominent scarp between Nappa Scars [7690 6977] and Austwick Beck [7795 6951]. Fossils occur locally, and the Rawtheyan Stage (zone 5 or 6) is indicated by *Tretaspis hadelandica brachystichus*, for example near Norber Brow [772 697] and in Austwick Beck [7792 6941]. The Norber Formation is overlain, probably conformably, by the Dam House Bridge Tuff Member of the Sowerthwaite Formation.

In the Clapham Beck Inlier calcareous siltstones of the Norber Formation are strongly cleaved, and contain a sparse fauna which suggests a Rawtheyan age, though no diagnostic forms were found.

Sowerthwaite Formation

The term Sowerthwaite Formation is introduced for the varied succession of up to 300 m of siltstones and mudstones

with interbedded tuff, sandstone and conglomerate members overlying the Norber Formation; the name is taken from Sowerthwaite Farm [7757 6988]. The formation crops out in the Austwick and Crummack anticlines (Figure 5), although it is mostly drift covered; the best exposed sections are in Austwick Beck [7798 6953 to 7795 6969]. Non-sequences are present within it, and one is succeeded by a conglomerate. A sparse fauna is locally present and is indicative of the Rawtheyan (zones 6 and 7) and Hirnantian stages of the Ashgill. Most of the argillaceous rocks in the formation are cleaved.

The Sowerthwaite Formation varies markedly across the axis of the Austwick Anticline (Figure 5). On the southern limb, the basal member of the formation is the Jop Ridding Sandstone, 40–250 m thick, which contains epiclastic volcanic debris. This sandstone is correlated with the Dam House Bridge Tuffs, an interbedded succession of tuffs and siltstones some 40 m thick which forms the basal member on the northern limb of the fold (Plate 1). These two members indicate a volcanic episode towards the close of the Rawtheyan Stage. Similar rhyolitic tuffs occur at the same stratigraphic level in the Ashgill successions in the Cautley

DAM HOUSE BRIDGE
[7799 6957]

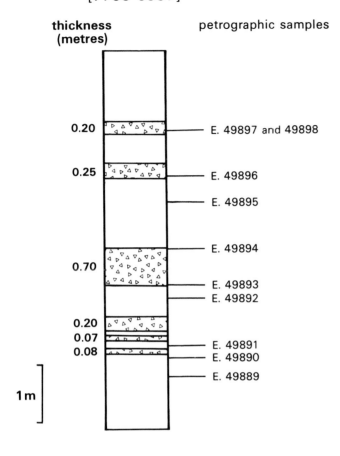

**thickness
(metres)**

petrographic samples

0.20 — E. 49897 and 49898

0.25 — E. 49896

— E. 49895

— E. 49894

0.70

— E. 49893
— E. 49892

0.20
0.07
0.08 — E. 49891
— E. 49890

— E. 49889

1 m

KEY

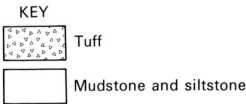

Tuff

Mudstone and siltstone

Figure 7 Section in upper part of Dam House Bridge Tuffs in Austwick Beck; tuffs less than 0.05 m thick are omitted

and Dent inliers (Ingham and Rickards, 1974) and in the Lake District (Ingham and others, 1978). Siltstones and mudstones overlie the Jop Ridding Sandstone and Dam House Bridge Tuffs. They vary in thickness from 40 m on the southern limb of the anticline to 50–60 m on the northern limb. They yield a sparse Rawtheyan (zone 6) fauna including *Dalmanella* and other brachiopods, and a few trilobites including *Tretaspis hadelandica brachystichus*.

A Rawtheyan (zone 6) fauna was also found in the Crummack Anticline (Figure 4), and at one locality a fauna with *Tretaspis latilimbus distichus* indicative of zone 7 strata was identified. Here, the thickness of Sowerthwaite Formation is difficult to ascertain because of minor folding and poor exposure; it is estimated that 50–60 m of strata are present.

A 2 m unit of well cemented pebble conglomerate with a sandy matrix (Plate 1), known as the Wharfe Conglomerate (King and Wilcockson, 1934), lies towards the top of the succession. Similar conglomerates occur in the Cautley and Dent inliers (Ingham and Rickards, 1974) and mark a widespread non-sequence and erosional event. In both anticlines the conglomerate is overlain by strongly laminated, sandy siltstones which become finer grained upwards. This 10–20 m siltstone succession contains a Hirnantian (zone 8) fauna, and the beds are correlated with the Ashgill Shales of the Lake District and Cautley Inliers. The Sowerthwaite Formation is overlain, in places unconformably, by Silurian strata.

DETAILS

Jop Ridding Sandstone

This name is introduced for the basal member of the Sowerthwaite Formation on the southern limb of the Austwick Anticline (Figures 5 and 6), an unbedded, well jointed sandstone with epiclastic volcanic debris that is best exposed around the type locality Jop Ridding Farm [6831 6897]. The thickness of the sandstone increases westwards, from 40 m to 250 m in little over 1 km. Some of this thickening may be caused by minor folding such as that seen in the overlying strata. The outcrop of the sandstone suggests that it has a lenticular cross-section.

The rock is generally greenish or purplish grey, mostly medium grained with larger crystals and clasts. It is a poorly sorted tuffaceous sandstone, and a weak lamination is locally defined by crystal-rich laminae. Clasts of lava are common, including aphyric and plagioclase-phyric types (Plate 1). It also contains elongate, subangular fragments of pumice that are mostly altered to quartz-sericite-chlorite aggregates with relict filamentous and vesicular textures. A few ignimbrite fragments are present; these are well rounded, and some contain shards that have ghostly outlines and are devitrified, the original glass being replaced by microcrystalline aggregates of quartz. Crystals of anhedral to euhedral quartz are common in the sandstone and some have embayed margins indicative of their volcanic origin. Plagioclase is present as altered anhedral to euhedral crystals some with multiple twinning preserved. Rounded crystals and aggregates of sphene, rutile and opaque oxides are present in accessory quantities. Clasts of sedimentary rocks are generally small and less abundant than volcanoclasts. Subrounded siltstones and mudstones, some laminated, are the most common; quartzite and calcareous siltstones also occur. Angular and subangular intraclasts are also present; most have poorly defined margins, suggesting that they are locally derived. The matrix is a microcrystalline intergrowth of quartz, sericite and chlorite. Some veinlets of quartz up to 0.5 mm wide may contain minor chlorite and/or calcite. Where present, cleavage is outlined by a non-penetrative alignment of phyllosilicate-rich folia, oblique to the sedimentary lamination.

Dam House Bridge Tuffs

The basal member of the Sowerthwaite Formation on the northern limb of the Austwick Anticline (Figures 5 and 6) is named after Dam House Bridge which crosses Austwick Beck at the top of the best natural section [7798 6953 to 7799 6957]. The outcrop extends WNW beneath superficial deposits, and the member is poorly exposed [771 699] west of Sowerthwaite Farm. Tuffs are interbedded with the siltstones and mudstones that form the dominant part of the succession. The tuff at the base of the succession is 4 m thick, but overlying beds are thinner, ranging from a few millimetres to 0.7 m. The upper part of the succession is well exposed (Figure 7). The tuffs are pale grey or buff, and contrast with the darker inter-

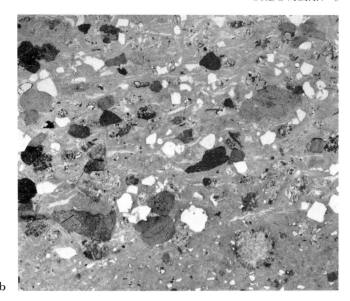

a

b

c

d

Plate 1 Sowerthwaite Formation lithologies near Wharfe [784 695]

A. Graded bed of air-fall tuff from Dam House Bridge Member. E 49897

B. Photomicrograph of Dam House Bridge Member, the tuff contains a variety of clasts, crystals and shards in a recrystallised matrix and has a eutaxitic fabric. Field of view 12 mm. E 49896

C. Photomicrograph of Jop Ridding Member, the poorly sorted tuffaceous sandstone contains a variety of volcanic rock fragments and crystals. Field of view 12 mm. E 49460

D. Wharfe Conglomerate, a variety of older Ordovician clasts, including abundant Ingleton Group pebbles are set in a sandy matrix. E 60519

bedded sediments. They vary from fine to coarse grained. The thicker beds are generally coarser grained, and many beds are graded (Plate 1).

The interbedded siltstones and mudstones are calcareous in part. Some of the beds are extensively bioturbated. Some of the burrows are reddened, suggesting deposition within shallow oxygenated water. Towards the top of the succession, where the tuffs are fewer and thinner, there is a gradational passage upwards from pale grey, calcareous siltstones and mudstones into darker grey, non-calcareous rocks. A sparse Ashgill fauna is present in the interbedded sediments within the Dam House Bridge Tuffs, but is not zonally diagnostic. Faunas from the underlying and overlying strata indicate that the tuff member is of Rawtheyan (zone 6) age. The

Dam House Bridge Tuffs are classified as lithic crystal tuffs and are probably rhyolitic in composition as are their correlatives in the Cautley Inlier and the Lake District (Ingham and Rickards, 1974). The widespread distribution suggests that the tuffs are air-fall, probably the product of a distant Plinian-type eruption. Grading in individual tuff beds supports an air-fall origin, and the interbedded marine strata indicate that they are waterlain.

The tuffs consist of shards, crystals and clasts, in a fine-grained matrix of quartz, sericite and chlorite (Plate 1). Coarsely crystalline calcite obliterates primary textures and fabrics in the most extensively altered tuffs. In less altered tuffs, devitrified cuspate shards (up to 1.2 mm) are preserved. Rounded and embayed quartz crystals are common; some are fractured and others less commonly

Plate 2 Selected Ashgill fossils from the Coniston Limestone Group

All the illustrated specimens are in the Palaeontological Collection of the BGS. Specimens with numbers prefixed by Zw were donated by Mr John Worthington. Photographs by T. Cullen

a. *Strophomena shallockiensis* Davidson, RU7767, ×1. Norber Formation, Wharfe Gill Sike [7875 6913]

b,c,d. *Reuschella* sp., all ×1. b. Internal mould of brachial valve, Zw7719. c. External (rubber cast), Zw7768. d. Internal mould of pedicle valve, Zw7715. Norber Formation, Douk Ghyll [c.814 724).

e,f,g. *Eremotrema* cf. *paucicostellatum* Mitchell, all ×3. e and f. Internal mould and external (rubber cast) of brachial valves, ZAY 172, Zw7546. g. Internal mould of pedicle valve, Zw7541. Norber Formation, Douk Ghyll [c.814 724]

h. *Haplosphaeronis multifida* Paul, rubber cast of RX130, ×3. View of oral surface showing cover-plates and brachiole facets. Norber Formation, 250 m SSE of Jop Ridding [785 688]

i. *Eoplectodonta rhombica* (McCoy), external mould of brachial valve, Zw7551, ×1.5. Norber Formation, Douk Ghyll [c.814 724]

j,m,n. *Platystrophia* sp., all ×1.5. j. Exterior of brachial valve, d2834. m and n. Internal moulds of brachial value and pedicle valve, Zw7497, Zw7491. All Norber Formation, Douk Ghyll [c.814 724].

k,l. *Dolerorthis inaequicostata* Wright, ×2, internal mould of pedicle valve and brachial valve, Zw7462, Zw7480. Norber Formation, Douk Ghyll [c.814 724]

o,r,s. *Christiania* sp., silicified shells (formerly conjoined), ×2. o. Interior of brachial valve, DEY245a. r and s. Ventral and side views of pedicle valve, DEY245b. Crag Hill Limestone, railway cutting NW of Crag Hill [805 710].

p. *Laticrura* sp., internal mould of brachial valve, Zw7596, ×3. Norber Formation, Douk Ghyll [c.814 724]

q. Dasycladacean alga, side view of mould of decorticated thallus. RU7873, ×2. Norber Formation, Wharfe Gill Sike [7815 6914]

t. *Atractopyge scabra* Dean, internal mould, RU7945, ×2. Norber Formation, Wharfe Gill Sike [7815 6914]

are intergrown with plagioclase or form equant aggregates up to 3 mm. Plagioclase occurs mostly as euhedral laths, up to 1.5 mm, with multiple or, more rarely, simple twinning. Alteration to sericite is variable, and may be confined to the margins of compositionally zoned plagioclases. Flakes of secondary mica up to 1.5 mm long are present in some specimens. Pyrite occurs as euhedral cubes and aggregates. In one specimen it is associated with titanomagnetite and occurs as pseudomorphs after mafic minerals; the majority of these pseudomorphs are anhedral, but a few are euhedral and these suggest replacement of amphibole. Rutile and zircon are present in accessory quantities in some specimens.

Clasts of sedimentary origin, mostly less than 1 mm, form up to 10 per cent of the tuffs. They are mostly rounded siltstones and mudstones; some are laminated, and many contain rotted pyrite crystals. Quartzite clasts up to 0.3 mm occur rarely. Pumice clasts are also present; these have recrystallised, but relict filamentous and vesicular fabrics are still discernible. Most have ragged, diffuse margins that are difficult to distinguish from the groundmass.

The matrix forms up to 70 per cent of the tuffs, and is a fine-grained intergrowth of quartz, calcite, sericite and chlorite; a secondary cement of polygonal calcite occurs locally. Where cleavage is developed, phyllosilicates in the matrix are aligned parallel to a non-penetrative anastomosing foliation.

Both the Jop Ridding Sandstone and the Dam House Bridge Tuffs are succeeded by siltstones and mudstones of the Sowerthwaite Formation. On the northern limb of the Austwick Anticline, the Dam House Bridge Tuffs pass gradationally upwards into mudstones and siltstones which contain a few tuffaceous laminae. Towards the top of this succession the Wharfe Conglomerate forms a marker bed. The sequence is exposed in Austwick Beck [7799 6957 to 7795 6969] and in an adjoining field to the west. The succession below the Wharfe Conglomerate consists mostly of dark grey, weakly bedded siltstones and mudstones. These are locally bioturbated, and many of the burrows are pyritised. Scattered phosphatic nodules are present towards the top. A fauna of brachiopods and trilobites, including dalmanellids, *Leptestiina* sp., *Arthrorhachis tarda*, *Dindymene* cf. *hughesiae*, *Phillipsinella parabola*, *Stenopareia* sp. and *Tretaspis* sp., suggests a Rawtheyan age.

The Wharfe Conglomerate attains its maximum thickness of 2 m on the northern limb of the Austwick Anticline where it forms a small scarp [7755 6983 to 7796 6965]. The base of the conglomerate rests on an erosion surface marking a non-sequence. Most of the clasts in the conglomerate are pebble-sized and make up most of the rock. They are mainly rounded or subrounded, and are set in a well-cemented sandy matrix (Plate 1). Most are grey-green sandstones and siltstones, and their colour suggests derivation from the Ingleton Group. Other pebbles include limestones and siltstones from the Norber Formation, and dark grey silty mudstone and phosphatic nodules from the immediately underlying part of the Sowerthwaite Formation. Pebbles of vein-quartz and vesicular lava are also present, but their provenance is not known. There are a few thin laterally impersistent beds of coarse sand. Indeterminate and fragmentary fossils, including algal pellets, bryozoa, crinoid columnals, brachiopods, trilobites and molluscs, occur in the conglomerate, both in the matrix and in some of the limestone clasts.

Laminated sandy siltstones overlie the Wharfe Conglomerate. In Austwick Beck [7797 6968] they are 5 m thick and yield *Eostropheodonta hirnantensis*. The succession thickens along strike, and King and Wilcockson (1934) recorded 15 m of strata in a trench section [7760 6984] south of Sowerthwaite Farm. In this section the siltstones fine upwards, and towards the top of the succession there is 0.1 m of tuff. A Hirnantian (zone 8) fauna, including well preserved *Dalmanella testudinaria*, *Eostropheodonta hirnantensis*, *Hindella crassa*, *Plectothyrella crassicostis* and tentaculitids, was collected from the upper part of the succession in the trench.

Overlying the Jop Ridding Sandstone on the southern limb of the Austwick Anticline [7809 6878 to 7863 6894] the upper part of the Sowerthwaite Formation is about 40 m thick, cleaved, poorly exposed, with a few thin argillaceous limestones. The limestones are mostly decalcified, and some [e.g. 7847 6884] contain a sparse Ashgill fauna including *Dalmanella* sp., *Eremotrema* cf. *paucicostellatum*, *Leptestiina* sp., *Nicolella* sp., *Orthambonites* sp., *Atractopyge* cf. *scabra* and *Haplosphaeronis multifida* (Plate 2). Tuff laminae up to 3 mm thick occur [7853 6880] within the mudstones; red and green Leisegang rings are also present in the mudstones here, indicating subaerial weathering before deposition of Carboniferous strata, presumably in the end-Silurian to early Dinantian interval.

In the Crummack Anticline minor folding, poor exposure and limited lithological variation of the Sowerthwaite Formation below the Wharfe Conglomerate prevent the establishment of the stratigraphic position of many of the small exposures. However, near Austwick Beck Head [7764 7186] argillaceous limestones underlying the Wharfe Conglomerate are exposed, and a sparse fauna, including *Dalmanella* sp., *Dicoelosia* sp., *Leptestiina* sp., ostracods and *Tretaspis latilimbus distichus*, was collected from decalcified patches [7764 7185 and 7763 7185]. The last-named species suggests, by analogy with the Cautley succession, that these beds are high Rawtheyan (zone 7); they lie 3 m below the Wharfe Conglomerate.

The Wharfe Conglomerate is exposed at Austwick Beck Head [7764 7186] in a synclinal flexure. A little to the east [7777 7194] it is succeeded by laminated sandy siltstones that have distinctive polygonal joints which developed contemporaneously with the cleavage. These siltstones are exposed at Austwick Beck Head [7764 7186], in a minor anticline in Austwick Beck [7779 7136], and on Hunterstye [7808 7142]. Younger strata are exposed above the siltstones on Hunterstye, and consist of some 15 m of greenish grey, partly calcareous siltstones and mudstones with thin argillaceous limestone interbeds. A fauna of late Ashgill age was recorded by King and Wilcockson (1934), and includes the type-material of *Stephanocrinus ramsbottomi* (Donovan and Paul, 1985).

SILURIAN

The Silurian rocks in the Craven Inliers are mainly turbiditic sandstones and siltstones; their classification is presented in Figure 8. A marine transgression in the Llandovery coincided with the development of the Silurian 'geosyncline'. During the Wenlock a deepening trough, aligned approximately E–W, developed across the area and turbiditic sandstones were introduced from the south. The close of the Wenlock marked an episode of widespread stability with the deposition of calcareous siltstones. These conditions persisted for a short time into the Ludlow before progressive deepening of the geosyncline occurred. Initially the sediments comprised distal siltstones but turbiditic sandstones of northern provenence were later deposited in the syncline.

The closure of the Iapetus Ocean and the collision of the 'American' and 'European' continents, or 'Laurentia' and 'Cadomia' (Soper and Hutton, 1984), occurred in late Silurian or early Devonian times. Thus sedimentation at this time represents the concluding phase of marine deposition in the remnant ocean before continental conditions were established.

Crummack Formation

The Crummack Formation is the name proposed for the thin and varied succession of mudstones and siltstones at the base of the Silurian (Figure 9). The name is taken from the farm [772 713] south-west of the outcrop in the Crummack Anticline. It replaces the Lake District term Stockdale Shales introduced in the Settle area by Marr (1887) and used by King and Wilcockson (1934). The outcrops in the Crummack, Austwick and Crag Hill anticlines are mostly obscured by superficial deposits, and there are no continuous sections through the formation which attains a maximum thickness of 35 m, though locally it is absent. Two members, Hunterstye and Capple Bank, respectively up to 15 m and 20 m thick, have been identified and named in the resurvey. The basal Hunterstye Member is present only locally and is named after the spur on the east side of Crummack Dale where King and Wilcockson excavated a trench [7794 7130] that revealed 15 m of black, graptolitic mudstone. This trench is proposed as the type section. The overlying Capple Bank Member is named from the hillside above the outcrop [7773 7206 to 7820 7179] on the northern limb of the Crummack Anticline which is proposed as its type locality. This member consists of about 20 m of partly calcareous siltstones.

The mudstones at the base of the Hunterstye Member are calcareous with a shelly fauna. Graptolite faunas in the Hunterstye Member indicate the Rhuddanian and Aeronian

stages of the Llandovery Series. Not all the graptolite zones have been proved; this may indicate non-sequences but is more likely due to poor exposure. The calcareous siltstones of the Capple Bank Member contain nodules and thin beds of limestone. Towards the top of the succession the siltstones are lithologically uniform, greenish grey, commonly with dendritic growths of manganese oxide, and are generally cleaved. The more calcareous parts of the Capple Bank Member yield a shelly fauna including trilobites, presumably of latest Aeronian or Telychian age.

Hiatuses in the Crummack Formation, caused either by non-deposition or by subsequent erosion, imply a shallow water environment associated with uplift and variable rates of sedimentation, but this is difficult to reconcile with the occurrence of dark graptolitic shales. It is suggested that the area lay close to a shoreline throughout the Llandovery, with a low ridge of the Ingleton Group forming a landmass to the north.

Ingham and Rickards (1974) suggested that the apparent hiatuses in the Craven Inlier Llandovery succession may be caused by faulting in poorly exposed ground. However, in Austwick Beck upstream of Dam House Bridge, the section displays a non-sequence; here 0.10 to 0.15 m of argillaceous limestone of latest Aeronian or Telychian age separate Ordovician strata with a Hirnantian fauna from laminated siltstones of the Austwick Formation that contain basal Wenlock graptolites less than 1 m above the base.

LITHOSTRATIGRAPHY		SERIES	STAGES	GRAPTOLITE ZONES
NEALS ING FORMATION		Ludlow	Gorstian	*Cucullograptus (Lobograptus) scanicus*
STUDFOLD SANDSTONE				
HORTON FORMATION				and
				Neodiversograptus nilssoni
ARCOW FORMATION		Wenlock	Homerian	*Monograptus ludensis*
				Gothograptus nassa
				Cyrtograptus lundgreni
AUSTWICK FORMATION			Sheinwoodian	*Cyrtograptus ellesae*
				Cyrtograptus linnarssoni
				Cyrtograptus rigidus
				Monograptus antennularius
				Monograptus riccartonensis
				Cyrtograptus murchisoni
				Cyrtograptus centrifugus
CRUMMACK FORMATION	CAPPLE BANK MEMBER	Llandovery	Telychian	*Monoclimacis crenulata*
				Monoclimacis griestoniensis
				Monograptus crispus
				Monograptus turriculatus
	HUNTERSTYE MEMBER		Aeronian	*Monograptus sedgwickii*
				Monograptus convolutus
				Monograptus argenteus
				Diplograptus magnus
				Monograptus triangulatus
			Rhuddanian	*Coronograptus cyphus*
				Lagarograptus acinaces
				Atavograptus atavus
				Parakidograptus acuminatus
				Glyptograptus persculptus

Figure 8 Classification of Silurian strata. Following the decision of the Subcommission on Silurian Stratigraphy (Holland, 1985), the base of the Silurian System is now coincident with the base of the *Parakidograptus acuminatus* Zone

DETAILS

The most complete sections occur in the Crummack Anticline. The oldest strata are the calcareous mudstones at the base of the Hunterstye Member with exposures [7776 7204] west of Capple Bank and [7794 7131, 7809 7156 and 7812 7162] north of Hunterstye. Abundant shell debris is present, consisting mainly of small brachiopods, including indeterminate dalmanellids, *Dolerorthis sp.* (costate and costellate forms), *Leangella* cf. *scissa*, *Cryptothyrella sp.*, *Eoplectodonta sp.*, *Resserella?*, *Skenidioides sp.*, *Ygerodiscus?* and *Ravozetina sp.*, as well as crinoid columnals and indeterminate ostracods. North of Hunterstye the calcareous mudstones dip beneath the dark grey graptolitic mudstones. In the Howgill Fells and the Lake District similar calcareous strata 'Basal Beds' occur at the base of the Llandovery Series, and are there considered to be equivalent to the *Glyptograptus persculptus* and locally the *Parakidograptus acuminatus* graptolite zones of the Rhuddanian Stage (Rickards *in* Moseley, 1978). The overlying graptolitic mudstones are mostly drift covered and the only exposures occur in a stream [7814 7131 and 7794 7130] on Hunterstye. At the second locality the mudstones yield poorly preserved graptolite fragments, with *?Monograptus sandersoni*, *M. triangulatus* (s.l.) and *?M. triangulatus major*, indicating the *Monograptus triangulatus* Zone of the Aeronian Stage. In the trench excavated by King and Wilcockson (1934) between the stream and exposures in the overlying Capple Bank Member, six graptolite-bearing layers were identified in the 15 m of black mudstones of the Hunterstye Member. Four graptolite zones were identified: *Dimorphograptus* (approximately equivalent to the *Atavograptus atavus* Zone), *M. triangulatus*, *M. convolutus* and *M. sedgwickii*; these indicate an age ranging from within the Rhuddanian to the Aeronian Stage. In the trench the graptolitic mudstones are conformably overlain by paler siltstones, here placed in the Capple Bank Member, and which are presumably of latest Aeronian or Telychian age.

At the base of the Capple Bank Member the siltstones are mostly calcareous and contain a distinctive fauna dominated by trilobites; towards the top of the succession they are less calcareous and less fossiliferous. On Hunterstye the member can be traced across numerous minor fold axes within the envelope of the main anticline. Decalcified limestone nodules within the siltstones [7814 7129] yielded a varied trilobite fauna including *Acernaspis elliptifrons* (formerly *Phacops elegans*), *Scotoharpes* cf. *willsi*, *Astroproetus* aff. *pseudolatifrons*, *Octillaenus?* and *Proromma sp.* (*?P. bregmops*), together with indeterminate solitary corals, the brachiopods *Dicoelosia* aff. *biloba*, *Hyattidina?* and *Skenidioides sp.* and the ostracod *Beyrichia* (s.l.). There is a similar fauna in the Sedgwick Museum Collection at Cambridge that has been obtained from an exposure [7782 7202] of the Capple Bank Member on the northern limb of the Crummack Anticline. In the Austwick Anticline the succession is much thinner and has been recognised only on the northern limb of the fold. This outcrop is mostly drift covered although there is a well exposed section in Austwick Beck [7795 6969]. Here the only strata that can definitely be assigned to the member comprise a 0.1–0.3 m bed of argillaceous limestone with abundant trilobite debris which King and Wilcockson (1934) called the *Phacops elegans* Limestone. The limestone is pale greenish grey and near the base contains dark grey siltstone clasts. It is richly fossiliferous with the best preserved specimens occurring in decalcified patches. Trilobites are most abundant and include: *Acernaspis elliptifrons*, *Astroproetus* aff. *pseudolatifrons*, *Encrinurus spp.*, *Harpidella sp.*, *Proromma* cf. *bregmops*, *Staurocephalus sp.*, *Stenopareia?*, *Whittingtonia sp.* and *Youngia* cf. *moroides*. Indeterminate solitary corals, the brachiopods *Dicoelosia* aff. *biloba*, *Leangella?* and *Toxorthis?*, crinoid columnals, smooth ostracods and a possible example of the dendroid graptolite *Koremagraptus* are also present. Along strike to the WNW, King and Wilcockson noted that the limestone lay 18 inches (0.45 m) above the base of the Llandovery siltstone which they recorded as being 'a few feet thick'.

In Ribblesdale the Crummack Formation is poorly exposed and probably less than 10 m thick in the Crag Hill Anticline [806 710]. The mudstones are mostly greenish grey, weakly laminated and strongly cleaved. The lithology and juxtaposition of the overlying Austwick Formation suggest that only the Capple Bank Member is present here, although no identifiable fossils have been found.

Austwick Formation

McCabe (1972) introduced the term 'Austwick Formation' to replace the 'Austwick Flags and Grits' of King and Wilcockson (1934). He defined the formation in Crummack Dale as 'units of turbidites alternating with units of mudstones; its base is defined by the incoming of carbonaceous silty mudstones and its upper boundary at the base of the calcareous beds of the Arcow Formation'.

The formation has an extensive outcrop in the Austwick–Ribblesdale Inlier on the flanks of the Studrigg–Studfold Syncline, the beds on the southern limb forming a prominent escarpment (Figures 3 and 9). In Crummack Dale it also crops out on the northern limb of the Crummack Anticline and on the southern limb of the Austwick Anticline. In Ribblesdale the formation is best exposed in Arcow Wood Quarry (Plate 3), near Sherwood Brow, and north of Stainforth. East of Ribblesdale the drift cover is extensive, although there are exposures as far east as Black Hill. The formation attains a maximum thickness of about 600 m in the southern part of Ribblesdale where the succession is mostly sandstone. It thins northwards to about 300 m in the northern part of this valley where siltstones are dominant. Mapping in Ribblesdale suggests that the Austwick Formation oversteps the Crummack Formation and Ashgill strata northwards, to rest unconformably on the ridge of Ingleton Group that persisted as a positive area during the Wenlock. In the south of Crummack Dale the formation is about 400 m thick. Here, the basal part of the succession, best exposed on the southern limb of the syncline, comprises laminated argillaceous siltstones up to 80 m thick; locally these contain an abundant graptolite fauna indicative of the *Cyrtograptus centrifugus* Zone at the base of the Sheinwoodian Stage of the Wenlock Series. The remaining part of the succession comprises alternating units of turbiditic sandstone and laminated siltstone, the latter locally containing graptolite faunas that indicate an age ranging from within the Sheinwoodian into the Homerian Stage (Figure 8).

The sandstones are parallel-bedded turbidites that show the internal subdivisions as described by Bouma (1962). Individual beds are generally 0.7–1.0 m thick and are separated by siltstone partings, the pelitic subdivision E in Bouma's classification. Where exposure permits, some of the sandstone units with a regular geometry can be traced for several kilometres along strike. However, other sandstones and some of the siltstone interbeds are impersistent and less regular. These variations, as McCabe and Waugh (1973) suggested, were most likely caused by internal migration of the Austwick Formation turbidite fan; this would account for the increase in thickness and number of turbidite units southwards. The thicker and more persistent siltstone interbeds, as these authors suggest, represent southward migrations of the fan; the thinner, less persistent siltstones are caused by local variations in sediment supply during the growth of the turbidite fan. The sandstones are fine to medium grained, and consist of an ill sorted assemblage of quartz, feldspar and rock fragments in a clay matrix. Sole-structures, mostly flute-casts, indicate that the sandstones were deposited under the influence of ESE–WNW currents (McCabe and Waugh, 1973). The northward thinning of the formation, first recognised by King and Wilcockson (1934), is caused by a reduction in number and thickness of the sandstone units. McCabe and Waugh (1973) suggested that the source area of the turbidites was the Midland Block landmass and that the currents were deflected by a ridge of basement rocks in the Austwick region. It is proposed that this ridge was probably formed by the Ingleton Group.

Details

The laminated siltstones at the base of the formation are exposed on the flanks of the Austwick, Crummack and Crag Hill anticlines. On the northern limb of the Austwick Anticline some 40 m of siltstones are exposed in Austwick Beck [7796 6968 to 7780 6999], and many of the contained graptolites are pyritised probably indicating an anaerobic environment at the time of deposition. An exposure [7796 6968] of the siltstones stratigraphically 3 m above the *Phacops elegans* Limestone of King and Wilcockson (1934) contains a *Cyrtograptus centrifugus* Zone fauna including *C. centrifugus?*, *Monoclimacis linnarssoni*, *M. vomerinus* (s.l.), *M. vomerinus basilica* and *Monograptus*

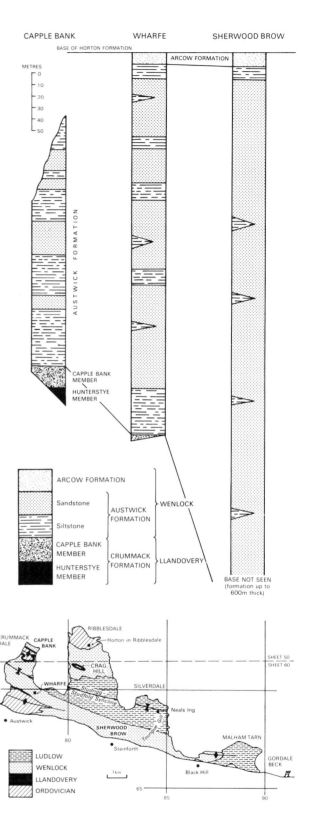

Plate 3 Austwick Formation, Arcow Wood Quarry [803 703]. Parallel bedded turbiditic sandstones up to 2 m thick, separated by laminated siltstone. (L 2351)

Figure 9 Comparative sections of Llandovery and Wenlock strata in the Craven Inliers, showing the northward thinning of sandstones in the Austwick Formation

priodon. In the succeeding 3 m of strata a similar fauna is present, with the addition of *Retiolites geinitzianus geinitzianus.* Higher in the succession the graptolites are fragmentary and poorly preserved; no zonal indices have been recognised. To the NW [7791 6975] indeterminate cyrtograptids, *?Monoclimacis flumendosae* and *Monograptus sp.,* have been collected, and at another exposure [7786 6989] the siltstones yielded *Monograptus* cf. *minimus* and *M. priodon.* On the southern limb of the Austwick Anticline the siltstones are poorly exposed and the succession is thinner and locally absent [7843 6892].

In the Crummack Anticline the basal part of the succession is 50–80 m thick, partly drift-covered and poorly exposed. Indeterminate species of *Monoclimacis* were found in Austwick Beck [7792 7124].

The siltstones are 50–80 m thick in Ribblesdale, and exposures south [8015 7113] and west [8010 7122] of the Crag Hill Anticline contain graptolites indicative of the *centrifugus* Zone.

The interbedded turbiditic sandstones and siltstones that form the major part of the Austwick Formation are best exposed on the southern limb of the Studrigg–Studfold Syncline in a prominent escarpment between White Stone Wood [780 703] and Newfield House [795 694]. Sole-structures are well displayed on the bases of many of the turbiditic sandstones that form small crags along the outcrop. Only the highest units of sandstone can be traced across the axis of the Studrigg–Studfold Syncline with certainty. As McCabe and Waugh (1973) demonstrated, there are fewer sandstones in the succession on the northern limb of the syncline. The reduction takes place close to the fold axis and may have influenced its position. On the northern limb of the syncline, parts of the formation are well exposed in old quarries [7825 7115 to 7813 7090] below Studrigg Scars where the siltstone units contain poorly preserved graptolites. One quarry [7816 7100] yielded *Pristiograptus dubius* and *P.* cf. *meneghinii,* indicative of a horizon somewhere within the *Monograptus riccartonensis* to *Cyrtograptus linnarssoni* zones. A more abundant probable *Cyrtograptus rigidus* Zone fauna including *Cyrtograptus* cf. *rigidus, Monograptus flemingii, P. dubius* and *P.* cf. *meneghinii* was collected from the southern part of the quarry [7813 7091].

On the northern limb of the Crummack Anticline [7825 7182], the formation has distinctive red and green Liesegang rings. It was called the 'Moughton Whetstones' by King and Wilcockson (1934) who concluded that graptolite faunas from this area indicated an age range from the *Cyrtograptus lundgreni* Zone of the Wenlock to the *Neodiversograptus nilsonni – Cucullograptus scanicus* zones of the Ludlow Series, and suggested that the distinctive rocks were part of the Horton Formation. However, McCabe (1972) concluded that the Moughton Whetstones differed from the Austwick Formation on Capple Bank only in exhibiting Liesegang rings, and that the Ludlow elements in the faunas were probably collected from loose boulders, a conclusion supported by the present survey.

In Ribblesdale the formation is well exposed between Gillet Brae [8004 7193] (where there are poorly developed Leisegang rings) and Arcow Wood Quarry [803 703] (Plate 3). On the eastern side of the valley the formation is less well exposed. Between Dry Beck [8150 7146] and Hardlands Plantation [8158 7186] it is much deformed by minor folding. King and Wilcockson (1934) mapped an area of down-faulted Horton Formation and Studfold Sandstone between White Sike Barn [8181 7092] and Higher Studfold [814 705]. The identification of *Cyrtograptus rigidus* Zone graptolites in this down-faulted area (Furness and others, 1967) indicates that the succession is part of the Austwick Formation. Farther south, the dominantly sandstone succession is exposed between Bargh House [8173 6850] and Rains Barn [8200 6768]. Some 400 m of strata are exposed in a discontinuous section in Tongue Gill [8252 6756 to 8332 6807], but farther east the formation is extensively drift-covered. The easternmost outcrop occurs in a melt-water channel [8626 6643 to 8666 6657] north of Black Hill.

Arcow Formation

McCabe (1972) defined the Arcow Formation as 'dominantly calcareous, unstriped mudstones, medium-light grey in colour, with thin silty laminations', and designated the 9 m succession in Arcow Wood Quarry as the type locality. Previously these calcareous mudstones were not distinguished as a separate unit and were included in the Horton Flags (Hughes, 1907; King and Wilcockson, 1934). McCabe (1972) described the formation as thinning and dying out westwards, but later (McCabe and Waugh, 1973) considered this thinning to be caused either by subsequent erosion or by deposition on an undulating sea floor. During the resurvey the formation was identified throughout the Austwick – Ribblesdale Inlier and its outcrop mapped on both limbs of the Studrigg – Studfold Syncline (Figures 3 and 9). The lithology was found to be calcareous siltstone rather than mudstone as originally defined.

The formation is generally about 10 m thick, although locally a maximum of 35 m has been recorded. It has a sharp base and conformably overlies laminated siltstones of the Austwick Formation. The calcareous siltstones are mottled, pale to medium grey, and thickly bedded. Bedding is poorly defined although locally the lowest metre is laminated or cross-laminated. The siltstones are extensively bioturbated, and McCabe (1972) recognised two types of burrow. The commonest type is vermicular, with 1–2 mm diameter *Chondrites*-like cylindrical burrows that are frequently pyritised; the second type superficially resembles *Phycodes,* but is smaller and branches downwards. A sparse shelly fauna is present but no identifiable graptolites have been found. The siltstones are generally cleaved with well defined, widely spaced, major cleavage planes that separate closely spaced, less well developed crenulate partings.

Lithologically the Arcow Formation correlates with the Middle Coldwell Beds of the Howgill Fells which Ingham and others (1978) concluded are offshore, relatively deep-water deposits. The widespread occurrence and the uniform lithology indicate a quiet depositional environment. The benthonic faunas and bioturbation suggest aerobic bottom conditions. Interbedded laminated siltstones within the Middle Coldwell Beds in the Lake District are of youngest Wenlock (*Monograptus ludensis* Zone) and earliest Ludlow age (*Neodiversograptus nilssoni – Cucullograptus scanicus* zones) (Rickards, 1970).

Details

The formation is exposed in Arcow Wood Quarry [8012 7051 and 8039 7041]. The base is sharp, and in the lowest 1.1 m there are thin beds, up to 0.05 m, of argillaceous limestone that are ripple cross-laminated. The overlying part of the formation is thickly bedded. The top is gradational over 2 m, and is intercalated with laminated siltstones of the overlying Horton Formation. A fauna that includes *Cardiola sp.* and *Delops sp.,* but is dominated by indeterminate orthocones, was collected from a bedding surface [8039 7041] 6.7 m above the base of the formation. To the east of the River Ribble the formation is exposed in parasitic folds on the northern limb of the Studrigg – Studfold Syncline, and near Higher Studfold [814 705] 8 m are exposed.

West of Arcow Wood Quarry [8005 7053] the formation strikes

beneath the unconformably-overlying Carboniferous Limestone and reappears [7810 7072] south of Studrigg Scar in Crummack Dale, where it is well exposed in the axial region of the Studrigg–Studfold Syncline [779 706]. On the southern limb of the fold [7811 7042] the formation is 10–11 m thick, well exposed and traceable to crags [8029 6916] west of Swarth Moor. North-east of Far End House [7926 6957] an upper leaf splits from the formation and is separated from it by laminated, carbonaceous siltstones that thicken westwards. The upper leaf is 4.5 m thick; its outcrop extends WNW to the sub-Carboniferous unconformity [7875 6975]. The laminated siltstones separating the two leaves attain a maximum thickness of about 50 m, and include 5 m of fine-grained, calcareous, turbiditic sandstone. They are lithologically similar to the succeeding Horton Formation, and are interpreted as the most distal part of a turbidite fan that has a southern provenance similar to the underlying Austwick Formation. The Arcow Formation is 7.5 m thick in a railway cutting [8126 6874] near Sherwood House, but an estimated 35 m of strata occur in small crags [8155 6866]. This increase in thickness is anomalous, and is probably caused by minor folding in the weakly bedded, strongly cleaved siltstone. In Tongue Gill [8333 6810] the formation is 12 m thick.

Horton Formation

McCabe (1972) introduced the term Horton Formation to describe the laminated siltstones that lie between his Arcow Formation and the Studfold Sandstone of King and Wilcockson (1934). These siltstones were formerly part of King and Wilcockson's 'Horton Flags'. During the resurvey however, 250 m of siltstones were recognised above the Studfold Sandstone, the youngest unit identified by King and Wilcockson, and have been included in the Horton Formation. In Tongue Gill (Silverdale valley) the redefined Horton Formation is 710 m thick, and includes the 40 m Studfold Sandstone as a member (Figures 8 and 9). Hughes (1907) and McCabe and Waugh (1973) correlated the Studford Sandstone (*sensu* King and Wilcockson) with a sandstone in Silverdale, now known to lie above the Studfold Sandstone Member and to be separated from it by 250 m of Horton Formation siltstones. The sandstone in Silverdale is here named the Neals Ing Formation (Figures 8 and 9).

The Horton Formation crops out in the centre of the Studrigg–Studfold Syncline, broadening ESE from Crummack Dale towards Tongue Gill along the plunge of the fold. It consists of medium to dark grey, laminated, micaceous and partly calcareous sandy siltstones, containing carbonaceous debris. Near the base calcareous nodules occur commonly in layers. Sole-structures, mainly bounce- and groove-marks of variable trend, are present on some bedding planes, and low amplitude ripple-marks on others. The siltstones are generally cleaved parallel to the WNW-trending fold axes and the intensity of the cleavage varies locally.

The Studfold Sandstone Member is a succession of turbiditic sandstones, cropping out south-east of Studfold where it illustrates minor folding in the axial region of the Studrigg–Studfold syncline. Near Studfold the sandstone is about 80 m thick and thins southeastwards to only 40 m in Tongue Gill. The south-eastward thinning suggests derivation from the northwest. The sandstone is mostly thick-bedded, with individual beds up to 1.6 m thick showing Bouma subdivisions to varying degrees of completeness. The sandstone is arkosic, fine grained, poorly sorted and slightly calcareous; some beds contain calcareous nodules.

The formation contains a sparse and poorly preserved fauna including graptolites indicative of the *nilssoni–scanicus* zones of the Gorstian Stage of the Ludlow Series. Some of the calcareous nodules in the siltstones contain brachiopods and orthocone fragments.

Laminated siltstones, penetrated by two boreholes drilled through the Carboniferous Limestone cover north and east of the Craven Inliers, are considered to belong to the Horton Formation, suggesting that Ludlow strata extend eastwards towards Wharfedale. In the Silverdale Borehole [8435 7144], within the Hawes district, graptolite fragments, including a possible example of *Monograptus uncinatus orbatus* and *Saetograptus ?chimaera semispinosus*, confirm that the strata belong to the Ludlow Series. In the Chapel House Borehole [9726 6647], however, only an indeterminate graptolite fragment was found, and microfossils yielded no reliable age.

On lithological and faunal criteria the Horton Formation correlates with the Upper Coldwell Beds of the Lake District and with unnamed mudstones below the Coniston Grit in the Howgill Fells (Rickards, 1978). Relatively tranquil conditions must have prevailed during its deposition. The thickness of the formation suggests that such conditions persisted longer in the Craven Inliers than to the north-west where the correlative strata are thinner. In the Lake District the siltstones are succeeded by the Coniston Grits, mostly fine-grained turbiditic sandstones that show a dominantly northwesterly derivation (Rickards, 1978). In the Craven Inliers, the incursion of turbiditic sandstones into the Ludlow succession took place much later, possibly delayed by the ridge formed by the Ingleton Group which lay to the north of the area. It is suggested that this ridge was a barrier to the southward migrating turbidites until the Studfold Sandstone entered the area, either across the ridge or along its southern flank. The thickness of the Studfold Sandstone and the overlying part of the Horton Formation suggests that this incursion was relatively brief.

DETAILS

The most complete section of this formation occurs on the southern limb of the Studrigg–Studfold Syncline in Tongue Gill [8330 6810 to 8387 6879] where some 670 m of siltstones are present. In addition, 40 m of Studfold Sandstone occur 420 m above the base of the formation, and are exposed in small crags [8335 6862 to 8376 6852] on the sides of the valley. The lower part of the succession is exposed also in Catrigg Beck [8450 6783 to 8451 6832]. The Horton Formation is believed to underlie the drift-covered area around Malham Tarn where a stream section [8749 6641 to 8759 6633] reveals about 80 m of laminated siltstones. The formation is exposed also in a small inlier [911 656] where Gordale Beck and one of its tributaries have eroded through the cover of Carboniferous Limestone. No diagnostic fossils were found at the time of the resurvey, but indeterminate monograptids have been recorded (Williamson, 1958).

On the east side of Ribblesdale, a continuous section in a railway cutting [8126 6876 to 8121 6929] dips uniformly northwards and exposes 400 m of siltstones that are repeated in minor folds in the axial region of the Studrigg–Studfold Syncline. The base of the conformably overlying Studfold Sandstone is exposed [8157 6953 to 8179 6991] east of Helwith Bridge. The top of the Studfold Sandstone and the overlying part of the Horton Formation are concealed beneath boulder clay. On the northern limb of the syncline, the lower part of the formation is exposed in small crags and in a disused quarry [8134 7014], north and east of Studfold respectively.

West of the River Ribble in Arcow Wood Quarry [8012 7050 to 8029 7045], the base of the siltstone succession is exposed, conformably overlying the Arcow Formation. The lower part of the Horton Formation is seen also in Combs Quarry [8002 7017]. On the southern limb of the syncline, the lower part of the formation is exposed in Dry Rigg Quarry [799 695 to 805 695], to the west in small crags on the south-facing escarpment [799 695 to 786 699], and in Sunny Bank Quarry [801 692]. In Crummack Dale the basal beds of the formation crop out [780 705] along the axis of the syncline south of Studrigg Scar.

Neals Ing Formation

The Neals Ing Formation is here defined as the succession of turbiditic sandstones, at least 250 m thick, that conformably overlies the Horton Formation and crops out in Tongue Gill (Silverdale) around the farm of Neals Ing [8410 6905]. The formation comprises the youngest Ludlow strata identified in the Craven Inliers (Figure 8). Its top has not been seen, and it is unconformably overlain by Carboniferous Limestone.

The sandstone is arkosic in composition; it is thick and parallel bedded, with individual beds up to 1 m thick. It is mostly of medium grain-size and is noticeably coarser than the Studfold Sandstone. No fauna has been found. The conformable base is exposed east and north of Sannet Hall [8393 6872 and 8352 6909]. In Rough Lands Gill [8442 6932 to 8453 6945] the sandstones are green-weathering, the discolouration probably being caused by weathering predating the deposition of Carboniferous cover.

The Neals Ing Formation is correlated on lithology with the Lower Coniston Grits of the Lake District and Howgill Fells. The coarse-grained sandstones are interpreted as proximal turbidites, and demonstrate the gradual southward migration and progressive filling of the Silurian geosyncline during the Ludlow. Their presence may also indicate that the supposed Ingleton Group ridge had been overwhelmed and was no longer a barrier for sediments with a northerly provenence.   EWJ

CHAPTER 3

Lower Carboniferous: Dinantian

Dinantian strata of the Carboniferous Limestone Series dominate the subdrift outcrop of the district (Figure 2). On the Askrigg Block they form a largely flat-lying succession of predominantly carbonate rocks up to 500 m thick, resting unconformably on Lower Palaeozoic rocks and overlain by Silesian. In the Craven Basin they form a much thicker, more argillaceous, succession and some 3 km are known in the adjoining Clitheroe district (Earp and others, 1961; Charsley, 1984), although their base neither crops out, nor has been penetrated in boreholes. In contrast to their simple structure on the Askrigg Block, the Dinantian strata of the basin are disposed in tight anticlines and broad intervening synclines—part of the Ribblesdale Fold Belt—and are cut by major faults including those of the north-west-trending South Craven and Knotts fault systems. The boundary between the Askrigg Block and the Craven Basin is marked by a fault-belt coinciding with a transition zone of major Dinantian facies change.

Estimates of the thickness of the concealed Dinantian sequence in the Craven Basin are speculative, although gravity data (Chapter 8) suggest that there may be at least an additional 3 km of strata with a density similar to that of the lowest known Dinantian resting on Lower Palaeozoic rocks (Cornwell in Arthurton, 1984).

Dinantian strata remain unproved beneath the Silesian cover of the Bowland Block (Figure 2), but their existence there is surmised in this account.

PREVIOUS RESEARCH

The Dinantian stratigraphy of the region was dealt with in the classic accounts of Yorkshire geology by Phillips (1836) and Kendall and Wroot (1924). It was also the subject of comprehensive reviews by Rayner (1953), Earp and others (1961) and Ramsbottom (1974).

Tiddeman mapped the Dinantian rocks during the Primary Survey of the district (published at one inch to one mile in 1892) but no accompanying memoir was published. Subsequent papers on the stratigraphy of the Craven Basin (or 'Craven Lowlands') include that of Wilmore (1910). Papers describing the sequences in the various anticlines include those on the Eshton–Hetton Anticline (Booker and Hudson, 1926), the Slaidburn and Catlow anticlines (Parkinson, 1936), the Skipton Anticline (Hudson and Mitchell, 1937), the Broughton Anticline (Hudson, 1944a), the Swinden Anticline (Hudson and Dunnington, 1944), and part of the Airton Anticline (Hudson, 1949).

The Dinantian succession of the Askrigg Block and the transition zone (Figure 2) was the subject of papers by Johns (1908), Garwood and Goodyear (1924) and Hudson (1930a, b); the stratigraphy of the Askrigg Block has been recently reviewed by Dunham and Wilson (1985).

PALAEOGEOGRAPHY

In late Devonian to Dinantian times northern England lay within a rift province in which, as a result of crustal stretching, basins formed between stable blocks of relatively buoyant crust (Leeder, 1982).

A marine transgression which began in early Dinantian times gradually invaded a land surface composed of uplands and intermontane basins (Johnson, 1967). The Craven Basin was one of these basins. It was bounded to the north (in the eastern part of the district) by the Askrigg Block, parts of which remained land until Holkerian times to the north-west the basin extended as far as the Bowland Block.

A comparatively thick succession of shallow-water marine sediments accumulated in the Craven Basin from Tournaisian times. Tectonism in late Chadian to Arundian times caused a varied marine bathymetry in the basin, with extensive 'deeper water' and 'slope' environments which persisted throughout the remainder of the Dinantian. The basin became a receptacle for turbidites and debris-flow deposits, with syndepositional deformation, including slumping and dislocation of slope sediments. Sabkha conditions, in which anhydrite and dolomite formed, were established in the block–basin transition zone during the Tournaisian to early Chadian. In Arundian times, the Askrigg Block landmass became progressively inundated, with a temporary recurrence of sabkha conditions, and was completely submerged during the Holkerian.

In Holkerian to Asbian times the Craven Reef Belt produced a sharp divide between shallow-water 'shelf' sedimentation on the Askrigg Block and transition zone, and deeper-water 'slope' sedimentation in the basin. In early to mid-Brigantian times the Reef Belt formed the southern limit of Yoredale sedimentation. This divide ceased to be effective following a tectonic episode in late Brigantian times when deeper-water conditions extended northwards across much of the transition zone.

CLASSIFICATION

Lithostratigraphy

Reviews of the lithostratigraphical classification of the Dinantian strata of the Askrigg Block and Craven Basin were given by Rayner (1953) and Ramsbottom (1974), and of the Craven Basin alone by Fewtrell and Smith (1980).

The classification of the Askrigg Block and transition zone successions has been revised in this resurvey to accord with the chosen mapping criteria and new borehole information, and has been listed in Figure 10. The term 'Great Scar Limestone Group', applied by George and others (1976) to all the Dinantian strata in the Settle–Horton area beneath the limestones and shales of Yoredale facies (Wensleydale Formation of George and others, 1976), is not used; nor are the subdivisions of that group—the 'Kingsdale Limestones' and the 'Horton Limestone' (Ramsbottom, 1974), or the 'Gastropod Beds' and the 'Michelinia grandis Beds' (Garwood and Goodyear, 1924). In their place four new formations are introduced. The oldest of these—the Stockdale Farm Formation—is known only in boreholes; the remainder, in upward sequence, comprise the Chapel House Limestone, the Kilnsey Formation and the Malham Formation (Mundy and Arthurton, 1980). The term Wensleydale Group is preferred for the overlying strata of Yoredale facies, on the grounds that the division contains many extensive rock units, including the named Yoredale limestones, for which formational status is considered appropriate.

The lithostratigraphy in the Craven Basin (Figure 15) follows the broad framework established by Tiddeman in the Primary Survey. It incorporates some of the named divisions employed by later workers (see below), although some of the divisional boundaries have been adjusted. The principal divisions recognised at crop are, in order of superposition, the Chatburn Limestone (Parkinson, 1926), the Thornton Shales-with-Limestone and Thornton Limestone (Hudson, 1944a), the Worston Shales (Parkinson, 1936), the Pendleside Limestone (sensu Fewtrell and Smith, 1980) and the Lower Bowland Shales (Booker and Hudson, 1926). The classification into five formations proposed by Fewtrell and Smith (1980) is considered to be only partly appropriate to the Settle district (Figure 16). In particular their use of 'Clitheroe Formation' to include units separately recognised by previous workers is not supported by the evidence of the resurvey. Compared with the Askrigg Block and the transition zone, the stratigraphy in the Craven Basin is less precise because of the structural complexity of these strata, and poor exposure. With certain exceptions the thicknesses quoted for the major lithostratigraphical divisions are calculated using the recorded structural data. There is, however, scope for error resulting from the non-recognition of possible tectonic structures in poorly exposed ground, and from tectonic thickening or attenuation, particularly in mudstone dominated parts of the succession. RSA,DJCM

Biostratigraphy

The coral–brachiopod zonation of the British Dinantian proposed by Vaughan (1905) was applied to the Askrigg Block in the Settle and adjoining Hawes districts by Johns (1906, 1908) and to the Craven Basin by Wilmore (1910). Garwood and Goodyear (1924) worked out and mapped a faunal sequence of coral-brachiopod zones in the succession of the Askrigg Block–Craven Basin transition zone. The Vaughanian zonal scheme was also adopted for the basin and transition zone by Hudson (1930a), and used in later basinal studies by Hudson and his co-workers, and by Parkinson (1936).

The zonation of Vaughan was more appropriate to limestone dominated shelf sequences. For the late Dinantian mudstone sequences, Parkinson (1936) and Hudson and his co-workers (e.g. Hudson and Mitchell, 1937) used a goniatite zonal scheme modified from Bisat (1924, 1928), and this scheme has served as the basis for the zonation of these mudstones in this resurvey. Goniatites are also the

principal means of dating the marginal reef limestones in the transition zone.

Microfossil zonations that have been applied to the Dinantian rocks of the region include those based on conodonts (Rhodes and others, 1969; Metcalfe, 1981), miospores (Neves and others, 1972), and algae and foraminifera. The zonal scheme using foraminifera developed by Belgian workers (Conil and others, 1977) has been applied to the Craven Basin (Charsley, 1984).

Ramsbottom (1973) erected a chronostratigraphical classification of the British Dinantian, utilising Major Cycles of eustatic transgression and regression which he defined on sedimentological criteria. Individual cycles were recognised by their contained fossils. George and others (1976) divided the British Dinantian into six regional stages which they considered to coincide approximately with Ramsbottom's Major Cycles. This regional stage classification has been adopted in this resurvey, with the amendments of Ramsbottom and Mitchell (1980) concerning the replacement of the Courceyan Stage by the Ivorian and Hastarian stages following the redefinition of the Tournaisian and Viséan series (Conil and others, 1977), although this recommendation is not widely accepted (Varker and Sevastopulo, 1985).

The Dinantian stages of George and others (1976) were defined in stratotype sections and correlated mainly on palaeontological criteria. The base of each stage is defined at the first lithological change below the lowest occurrence of certain taxa considered diagnostic of that stage. Recent studies by Strank (1981) and Fewtrell and others (1981) have produced a detailed analysis of the characteristic foraminifera and algae, both for the stratotypes and for other sections of known age. These authors have achieved microfaunal subdivision of the stages, and have suggested several anomalies in the published palaeontological stage definitions: their results are summarised below.

The Courceyan Stage stratotype section at the Old Head of Kinsale, Co. Cork, has yielded no foraminifera because of the unfavourable facies, and strata of equivalent age in the Settle region have produced only an impoverished fauna with few useful taxa. Marchant in Charsley (1984) has described the foraminifera from the Swinden No. 1 Borehole and correlated them with the Belgian foraminiferal zonation scheme (Conil and others, 1977).

The Chadian Stage is defined in the Chatburn road cutting, within the adjoining Clitheroe district; it is recognised by George and others (1976) at the first change in lithology below the entrance of the foraminifer Eoparastaffella. Studies by one of us (Strank) and Fewtrell and others (1981) could not substantiate the presence of this genus, and the original material could not be traced for the purposes of confirmation. The lowest record of the Chadian brachiopod Levitusia humerosa is 180 m above the defined base of the Chadian in the stratotype section. As it has not yet proved possible to verify the published microfossil criteria used to define the basal Chadian boundary in the stratotype, only the faunal criteria observed by the writer in the stratotype have been used to recognise the stage in this account. Typical Chadian assemblages include Biseriella bristolensis, Brunsia spp., Dainella sp., Eblanaia michoti, Endochernella sp., Endospiroplectammina syzranica, Eotextularia diversa, Mediocris sp., Palaeospiroplectammina tchernyshinensis, P. mellina, Spinoendothyra sp., Valvulinella

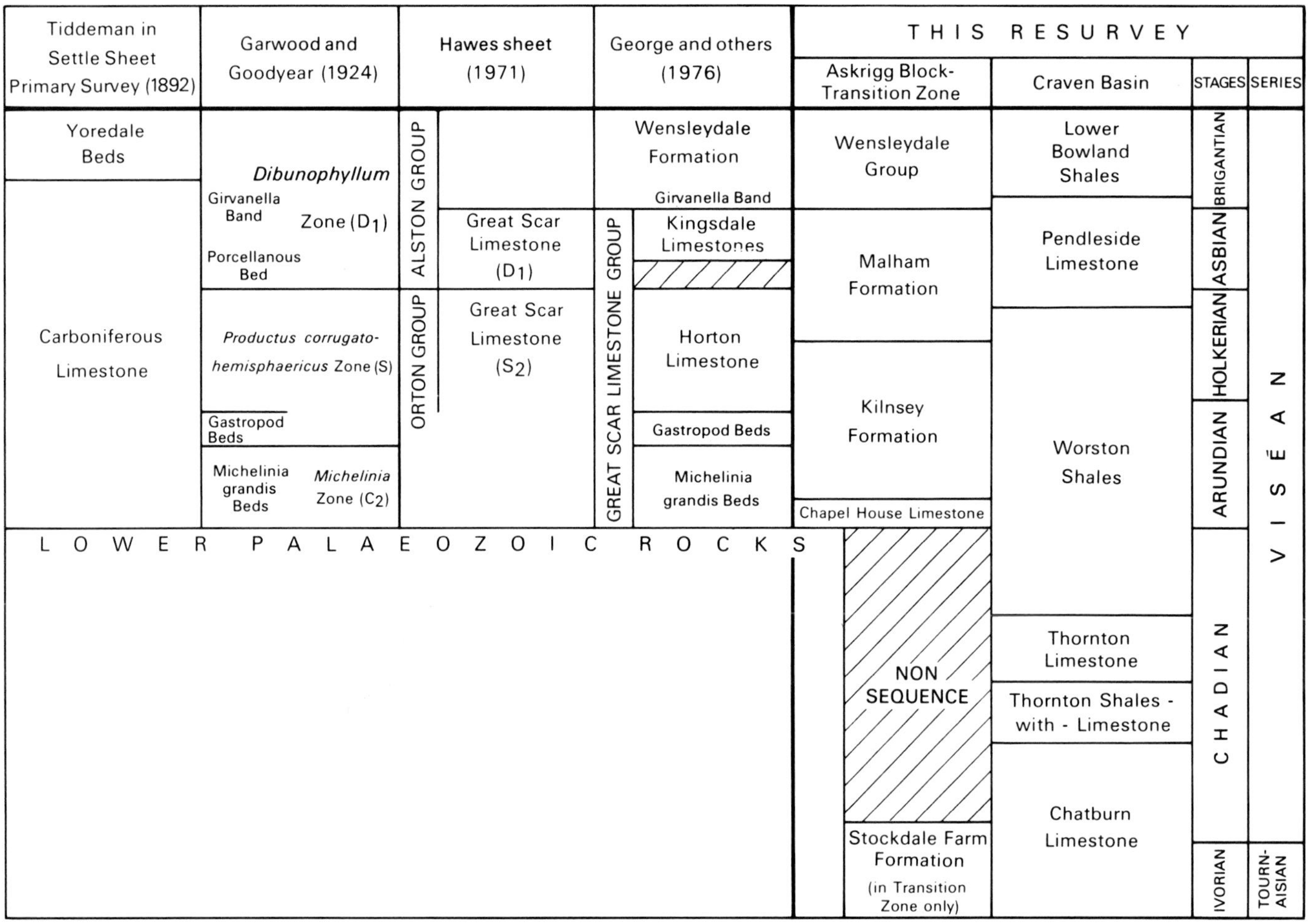

Tiddeman in Settle Sheet Primary Survey (1892)	Garwood and Goodyear (1924)	Hawes sheet (1971)	George and others (1976)	THIS RESURVEY			
				Askrigg Block-Transition Zone	Craven Basin	STAGES	SERIES
Yoredale Beds	*Dibunophyllum* Zone (D₁) — Girvanella Band / Porcellanous Bed		Wensleydale Formation — Girvanella Band	Wensleydale Group	Lower Bowland Shales	BRIGANTIAN	
Carboniferous Limestone		Great Scar Limestone (D₁)	Kingsdale Limestones	Malham Formation	Pendleside Limestone	ASBIAN	
	Productus corrugato-hemisphaericus Zone (S)	Great Scar Limestone (S₂)	Horton Limestone			HOLKERIAN	VISÉAN
	Gastropod Beds		Gastropod Beds	Kilnsey Formation	Worston Shales	ARUNDIAN	
	Michelinia grandis Beds / *Michelinia* Zone (C₂)		Michelinia grandis Beds	Chapel House Limestone			
LOWER PALAEOZOIC ROCKS				NON SEQUENCE	Thornton Limestone	CHADIAN	
					Thornton Shales - with - Limestone		
					Chatburn Limestone		
				Stockdale Farm Formation (in Transition Zone only)		IVORIAN	TOURN-AISIAN

Figure 10   Classifications of Dinantian strata on the Askrigg Block

sp. and abundant Endothyridae and Tournayellidae.

The base of the Arundian Stage is readily recognisable by the appearance of Archaediscidae foraminifera, and the dasycladaean alga *Koninckopora*, exhibiting a double wall. The stage can be subdivided by successive evolutionary stages of the Archaediscidae. These divisions are locally recognisable in the Settle district (Strank, 1981), and have been described in Fewtrell and others (1981) and Conil and others (1977). Typical Arundian assemblages include *Ammarchaediscus bucullentus, Eblanaia michoti, Eoparastaffella simplex, Eotextularia diversa, Glomodiscus miloni, Latiendothyranopsis menneri, Plectogyranopsis moraviae, Pseudolituotuba hibernica, Rectodiscus sp.*, *Tubispirodiscus settlensis*, and the algae *Koninckopora inflata* and *K. mortelmansi* are also very abundant.

The Holkerian Stage is defined by George and others (1976) at the entrance of *Archaediscus* at the 'concavus' stage together with double-walled palaeotextulariids. Detailed work on British Holkerian sections (Strank, 1981; Fewtrell and others, 1981) has shown, however, that *Archaediscus* at the 'concavus' stage also occurs in the underlying Arundian and overlying Asbian stages, and that double-walled palaeotextulariids do not appear in the British sequences until the middle part of the Asbian (when they are rare), and that they are common only in the late Asbian or Brigantian.

The brachiopod *Davidsonina carbonaria*, considered to be a diagnostic Holkerian marker by George and others (1976), has since been found in the lowest limestone of the Asbian as currently defined in the stratotype at Little Asby Scar, Cumbria (J. Pattison, personal communication; Strank, 1981), but it is not known below the base of the Holkerian. The prolific and diverse Holkerian foraminiferal assemblages on the Askrigg Block include the diagnostic forms *Bogoshella ziganensis, Holkeria avonensis, H. daggari, Koskinotextularia cribriformis, Nibelia nibelis, Palaeospiroplectammina paprothae* and *Septabrunsiina tynanti*. The algae *Konickopora inflata, K. tenuiramosa* and *K. mortelmansi* occur even more abundantly, and reach their acme in this stage. The Holkerian faunas from the Craven Basin contrast markedly and tend to be stunted, with many stratigraphically useful taxa including *Holkeria* and *Nibelia* missing due to unfavourable facies. The base of the stage is commonly recognisable only by the identification of the top of the underlying Arundian strata as, for example, in the Chapel House Borehole and the Cominco boreholes S2 and S7.

Throughout the Settle district the Asbian Stage displays an abundant and diverse foraminiferal fauna. Early, middle and late Asbian faunas have been recognised in the stratotype at Little Asby Scar (Strank, 1981). Generally these divisions persist into the Settle district and are used in the present account. According to George and others (1976) the Asbian Stage is recognised by a change in wall structure of *Eostaffella* compared with that in the Holkerian, together with the appearance of *Howchinia sp*. Recent work shows that no such change in wall structure of *Eostaffella* occurs, and that *Howchinia* does not appear until the latest Asbian (Strank, 1981; Fewtrell and others, 1981). Amongst the brachiopods, *Daviesiella llangollensis*, quoted by George and others (1976) as an early Asbian marker, has been found in Holkerian strata in Derbyshire (Cope, 1940) and North Wales (Somerville and Strank, 1984a). A rare example of the the late Asbian marker *Davidsonina septosa* has now been found in dark limestones in the basal Brigantian (Chisholm and others, 1983).

The Brigantian Stage was defined by George and others (1976) at Janny Wood, Cumbria, with its base at the base of the Peghorn Limestone, a lithological and palaeontological boundary which can be recognised over a wide area of northern England including the Settle district (Burgess and Mitchell, 1976). The microfossils and macrofossils from the latest Asbian and earliest Brigantian strata have also been studied in detail in Derbyshire (Chisholm and others, 1983) and North Wales (Somerville and Strank, 1984b). In these two areas, some anomalies occur with relict Asbian fossils being recorded from the lowest Brigantian beds. Of the fossils listed as characteristic of the Brigantian (George and others, 1976), the macrofossils are still considered to indicate this stage, but the foraminifera *Neoarchaediscus* and *Bradyina* both occur first in the late Asbian, and *Asteroarchaediscus* is confined to the late Brigantian. Characteristic Brigantian microfossils include *Asperodiscus stellatus*, *Bradyina rotula*, *Howchinia bradyana*, *Loeblichia parammonoides* and *Neoarchaediscus occlusus*.   ARES

Petrographical classification and description

The petrographical description of limestones follows the scheme, based on depositional textures, proposed by Dunham (1962) combined with the grain-size classification of Leighton and Pendexter (1962). The advantages of this scheme are that it is practical and that it can be used both in the field for hand specimens and for microscope descriptions of thin sections.

The colour of limestones is commonly a distinguishing factor. Fresh, dry surfaces of samples have been compared with the 'Rock-Color Chart' of the Geological Society of America and the appropriate colour name used in the limestone description.

ASKRIGG BLOCK AND TRANSITION ZONE

Stockdale Farm Formation (?Tournaisian to early Chadian)

The Stockdale Farm Formation (here proposed) occurs at depth at Stockdale, east of Settle, and has been cored in two boreholes—Stockdale Farm (Cominco Borehole S7) [8541 6378] and Cominco Borehole S2 [8491 6345] at Halsteads—which together prove a sequence of strata in excess of 165 m. The formation is defined by the limits of the three constituent members which are recognised on lithological characters (Figure 11). These rocks are the oldest Dinantian strata known north of the Craven Basin. A Tournaisian age is suggested for most of the Stockdale Farm Formation though foraminifera from limestones in the highest 11 m indicate an early Chadian age. The top of the formation is a deeply fissured surface marking a significant nonsequence which is overlain by the Arundian Chapel House Limestone.

HALSTEADS SHALES-WITH-ANHYDRITE

This member occurs in the basal 37 m of the Cominco Borehole S2 (the type section), where it is thrown against Scaleber Force Limestone (Arundian) by the Middle Craven Fault. Compensation for a dip up to 45° gives the true thickness for the cored interval at about 26 m. These rocks lie stratigraphically below the sequence in the Stockdale Farm Borehole, but their contact relations are unknown. They are placed in the Stockdale Farm Formation because they show lithological and environmental continuity with the Stockdale Farm Sandstones and Shales.

The Halsteads Shales-with-anhydrite consist of a variable sequence of dolostones, dolomitic-siliciclastic silts, mudstones and, in the lower part, laminated anhydrite (Plate 4a). These lithologies are characteristically fissile and split along organic-rich films. Secondary gypsum occurs throughout as veins and cavity fills. The dolostones are laminated but tend to be more compact than the other interbedded lithologies; individual 'beds' rarely exceed 0.5 m, although a single unit 1.5 m thick occurs at the top of the member. These dolostones vary from fine and medium subhedral mosaics to dolomicrites, and typically contain abundant detrital grains, particularly quartz. Vermiform voids (possibly rhizoliths) lined with dolomite euhedra and filled by gypsum are present in two of the dolostones. The siliclastic siltstones are composed largely of quartz, feldspar, micas and chlorite; they are commonly finely interlaminated with mudstone, dolostone or anhydrite and exhibit small scale ripple cross-lamination.

STOCKDALE FARM SANDSTONES AND SHALES

An alternation of sandstones, siltstones, mudstones and thin limestones characterises this member. It is known only from its type section in the Stockdale Farm Borehole where 67 m were proved. The member extends from the base of the borehole to the base of the succeeding Stockdale Farm Limestones and Shales. The sandstones make up approximately 40 per cent of the sequence and occur in beds varying in thickness from 0.1 to 4 m. They are light grey, fine grained, commonly micaceous and carbonaceous, and are cemented by dolomite and quartz. Petrographically they are arkosic in type with the feldspars showing crystal overgrowths. Many beds are bioturbated and some are ripple cross-laminated. The shales consist of dark grey micaceous siltstones and subordinate mudstones which are pyritic, carbonaceous, plant-bearing and commonly bioturbated. Some of the siltstones are markedly dolomitic and are similar to the siltstones in the underlying member. Limestone interbeds are present in the siliclastics; these are rarely more than 1 m thick and make up 13 per cent of the

Figure 11 Borehole provings in the Stockdale Farm Formation

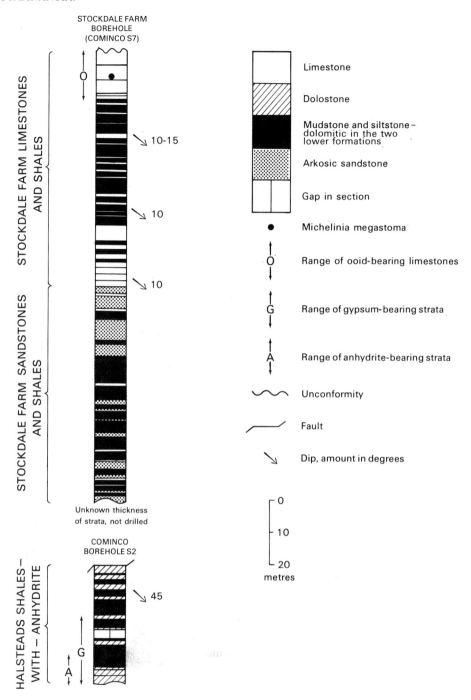

succession. The limestones are largely dark grey lime-mudstones, but fine and medium calcarenite packstones and wackestones also occur. The lime-mudstones have a very restricted biota, with ostracods, calcispheres and small gastropods being the only recognisable bioclasts. However, a thin fenestral wackestone near the top of the succession contains abundant lumps of the filamentous codiacean alga *Garwoodia*. Sand- and silt-grade terrigenous components (largely quartz) are abundant throughout the limestone units.

STOCKDALE FARM LIMESTONES AND SHALES

In the type-section (Stockdale Farm Borehole) this member is about 73 m thick. Its base is taken at the top of the youngest sandstone in the Stockdale Farm Sandstones and Shales, and its top at a deeply fissured surface of a limestone which is overlain by conglomeratic units of the Chapel House Limestone. The member comprises an alternation of limestones, siltstones and mudstones, with the limestone–shale ratio being approximately equal throughout the succession, apart from in the highest 12 m where limestones make up over 80 per cent of the sequence. The limestone beds are generally less than 0.5 m thick and few exceed 2 m. They are medium-dark grey to dark grey in colour, and are dominated by lime mudstones some of which pass into fine and medium calcarenite wackestones and packstones, commonly argillaceous and bioturbated. In the highest 12 m of the member, however, the limestones include fine and medium calcarenite grainstones.

The siltstones and mudstones, composed largely of quartz, chlorite, mica and feldspsar, are commonly carbonaceous and calcareous but, unlike the shales in the preceding member, are not dolomitic. The lime-mudstones are typically fenestral, with cavities filled by calcite spar and geopetal calcisiltite. Bioclasts are generally restricted to ostracods, foraminifera, calcispheres and gastropods, with some units having only ostracods (Plate 4b). These lime-mudstones pass into fine calcarenite wackestones and packstones; these have a greater diversity of bioclasts, with the addition of brachiopod and molluscan fragments, crinoid plates, and algae (kamaenids and *Girvanella*). Non-bioclastic components include peloids and rare limestone lithoclasts. The fine and medium calcarenites in the topmost 12 m are packstones and grainstones; these contain a wide range of bioclasts as well as peloids (usually micritised grains), limestone lithoclasts and ooids. In some of the grainstone units ooids are the dominant grains. As with the preceding member, terrigenous components in the limestones, particularly angular quartz grains, are ubiquitous, and are commonly amongst the most abundant grains. Minor replacement of matrix and grains by dolomite and pyrite is common throughout.

The macrofauna of the member is poor save for the highest 12 m where *Delepinea sp.* and *Michelinia megastoma* occur. Foraminifera from these topmost strata include the typical early Chadian forms *Palaeospiroplectammina mellina*, *Endothyra danica*, *Lugtonia monilis* and *Spinoendothyra mitchelli*.

Chapel House Limestone (Arundian)

The term Chapel House Limestone is introduced here for the sequence which underlies the Kilnsey Formation and either unconformably overlies the Stockdale Farm Formation, or lies directly on Lower Palaeozoic rocks (Figure 12). In the type section, the Chapel House Borehole, the formation is 33.6 m thick. Elsewhere to the north of the North Craven Fault, the formation onlaps, and is locally absent over topographic highs in the Lower Palaeozoic basement. The limestone is thickest adjacent to the Middle Craven Fault where 56 m are present in the Stockdale Farm Borehole. Within the district the limestone crops out only in three small inliers; in Gordale Beck, at Stainforth Force on the River Ribble, and at Barrel Sykes, north of Settle. In addition parts of the succession have been proved in the Lower Winskill and Cominco S8 boreholes.

In the lower part of the succession the dominant lithologies are medium to medium-light grey, medium and coarse calcarenite grainstones, which commonly contain Lower Palaeozoic lithoclasts and are notably oolitic (Plate 4c). Interbedded with the grainstones are conglomerates of Lower Palaeozoic lithoclasts (with either carbonate or siliciclastic matrix), 'mixed laminites' (interbedded fissile siltstones, commonly with sandstone and mudstone laminae) (Plate 4e), dolomicrites (some with calcite pseudomorphs after evaporite minerals) (Plate 4d) and lime-mudstones (fenestral or algal). Argillaceous wackestones are present in the upper part of the succession in the Kilnsey area. The contact of the Chapel House Limestone (grainstones) with the darker argillaceous packstones of the overlying Kilnsey Limestone-with-mudstone is sharp in all sections. The Chapel House Limestone is equivalent to the beds mapped

by Garwood and Goodyear (1924) as the lower part of their *Michelinia* Zone (C$_2$), and described by them as 'limestone often, false-bedded, containing layers of pebbles'.

No macrofauna was collected from this limestone within the district. *Michelinia megastoma* was noted, however, in Stainforth Beck [8198 6700] near the top of the limestone and *Palaeosmilia murchisoni* was recovered from the base of the Chapel House Limestone at 191 m in the Silverdale Borehole [8435 7143], within the adjoining Hawes district, and these indicate an Arundian age. Foraminifera from the Chapel House and Stockdale Farm boreholes and from Gordale Beck confirm this age, the diagnostic taxa being *Ammarchaediscus bucullentus*, *Eoparastaffella simplex*, *Glomodiscus miloni*, *Latiendothyranopsis menneri solida* and *Rectodiscus sp.*   DJCM

DETAILS

In the Chapel House Borehole [9726 6647], there are 33.6 m of Chapel House Limestone overlying 3.1 m of conglomerate which separate it from the Horton Formation (Silurian). The conglomerate is succeeded by 4 m of 'mixed laminites' which include a fenestral wackestone with mudstones above and below, overlain by 3.5 m of dolostone and dolomitic siltstone, laminated in parts, with thin mudstone partings. The dolostone consists of a finely crystalline euhedral to subhedral mosaic with laminae of angular quartz and other detrital grains and abundant pyrite. Overlying the dolostone is 1.6 m of grainstone which in turn is succeeded by 11.9 m of totally dolomitised limestone; evidence from other measured sections suggests that these rocks were originally grainstones. The non-dolomitised grainstones are medium grey, medium calcarenites and are notably oolitic; mixed bioclasts and abundant detrital quartz (generally less than 0.1 mm) occur with the ooids. Overlying the dolomitised limestone are 11.5 m of medium-dark grey argillaceous wackestones which are generally bioturbated. These wackestones are poorly sorted and bioclastic with the dominant grains being foraminifera, crinoid plates, molluscan fragments, algae (particularly kamaenids) and ostracods. The highest 3.8 m of the Chapel House Limestone are coarse calcarenite grainstones, medium-light grey in colour which contrast strongly with the overlying medium-dark grey argillaceous Kilnsey Limestone-with-mudstone. The grainstones are mixed bioclastic and peloidal (the latter being micritised grains), with common bioclasts being crinoid plates, algae (*Koninckopora*), foraminifera, and shell fragments (molluscan and brachiopod).

An inlier of Chapel House Limestone occurs in the upper part of Gordale Beck [910 658], resting unconformably on Horton Formation. Here the discontinuously exposed succession is about 24 m thick, and consists dominantly of medium calcarenite grainstones. Some beds contain Lower Palaeozoic pebbles and much of the sequence is dolomitised.

A small inlier of Chapel House Limestone crops out in the River Ribble and Stainforth Beck, near Stainforth Force [8185 6716]. The gently dipping north limb of an anticline provides a section through some 19 m of strata. The limestone is thin- and medium-bedded, commonly with undulate bedding planes. Apart from a few dolomitised posts, it is a uniform, medium grey, medium to coarse calcarenite grainstone, composed of a mixture of peloids (micritised grains), and bioclasts (commonly crinoid plates, foraminifera and *Koninckopora*), with small, scattered Lower Palaeozoic lithoclasts (mostly less than 5 mm), as well as detrital quartz grains and disseminated ooids.

Medium-light grey, medium to coarse calcarenite (bioclastic grainstone), containing Arundian foraminifera, occurs in an isolated exposure [8211 6423] near Barrel Sykes, north of Settle, and is assigned to the Chapel House Limestone.

The Lower Winskill Borehole [8259 6670] proved 35 m of Chapel House Limestone without penetrating its base. The lowest 7 m consist of 'mixed laminites'; an interbedded succession of these comprises fissile siliciclastics (a variable interlamination of mudstone, siltstone and sandstone), dolomicrites, and thin limestones (lime mudstones and dolomitic calcisiltites). The beds of dolomicrite are 5 to 30 cm thick, and show dessication fracturing, calcite pseudomorphs after halite (with individual crystals from 2 to 15 mm), and nodular sulphates. Overlying the 'mixed laminites' are 28 m of partially or totally dolomitised limestone. Despite this alteration it is clear that the dominant lithology is a medium grey, medium to coarse calcarenite grainstone which is peloidal and bioclastic, with ooids near the base of the unit. Lower Palaeozoic lithoclasts, generally less than 5 mm in diameter, occur over an 11 m interval 12 m above the base of the grainstone.

The greatest known thickness of Chapel House Limestone occurs immediately north of the Middle Craven Fault in the Stockdale Farm Borehole [8541 6378], where 55.6 m of these strata are present. At the base of the formation are 8 m of conglomerate which rest on the fissured surface of the Stockdale Farm Limestones and Shales. The conglomerate, composed of Lower Palaeozoic lithoclasts set in a sandstone or siltstone matrix, is thick-bedded and contains interbeds of grainstones and subordinate silty mudstones. The grainstones are medium grey to medium-light grey and composed of peloids, ooids and mixed bioclasts. Grainstones dominate the succeeding 10 m of the sequence; these are conspicuously oolitic, fine and medium calcarenites which contain scattered Lower Palaeozoic lithoclasts and disseminated angular detrital quartz grains. The overlying 7.45 m of strata are 'mixed laminites' similar to those in the Lower Winskill Borehole, consisting of siliciclastic units alternating with dolomicrites, grainstones, and fenestral and algal laminated lime-mudstones. The dolomicrites vary from 0.9 m

to less than 5 cm, and differ from those in the Lower Winskill Borehole in that they have no obvious pseudomorphs after evaporite minerals. Angular clasts of these dolomicrites and Lower Palaeozoic lithoclasts occur in some of the siltstone units. The grainstones are also oolitic and contain Lower Palaeozoic lithoclasts. The 'mixed laminites' are succeeded by 1.7 m of conglomerate similar to that at the base of the formation; this has a siltstone matrix at the base and a grainstone matrix above. The overlying 28.45 m of the formation consist of medium and medium-light grey, fine and medium calcarenite, bioclastic and peloidal grainstones and packstones. These form a conspicuous contrast with the succeeding darker argillaceous packstones of the Kilnsey Limestone-with-mudstone.

The Cominco Borehole S8 [8562 6352], drilled at the foot of High South Bank, intersected a branch of the Middle Craven Fault at 156 m depth. The fault throws the Malham Formation against 6.5 m of grainstone with conglomeratic units (Lower Palaeozoic lithoclasts) and siltstone interbeds, lithologies that correlate with the lower part of the Chapel House Limestone in the Stockdale Farm Borehole. DJCM, LCJ

Kilnsey Formation (Arundian and Holkerian)

The Kilnsey Formation (Mundy and Arthurton, 1980) is the sequence of essentially dark limestones that occurs between the Chapel House Limestone and the Malham Formation (Figure 12); it is defined by the limits of its two constituent members (see below). The Kilnsey Formation occurs as a series of inliers flooring many of the valleys, and has a discontinuous outcrop bordering the Lower Palaeozoic Craven Inliers. At its maximum, south of the Middle Craven Fault (Cominco boreholes S2, S10), the formation is

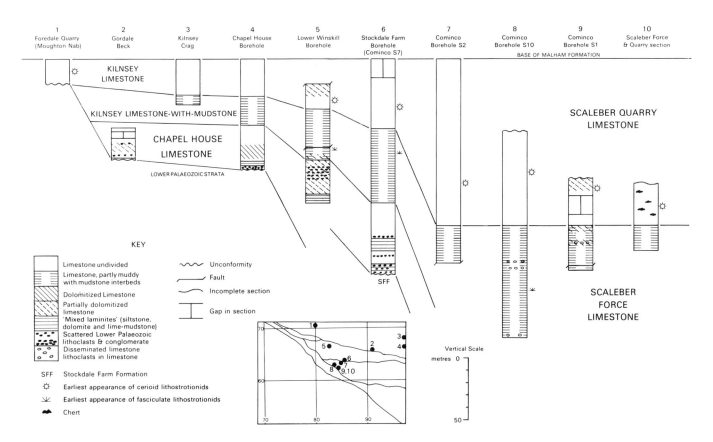

Figure 12 Comparative sections of the Chapel House Limestone and Kilnsey Formation

224 m thick, but it thins rapidly northwards and only some 53 m are present in the Kilnsey area. Over topographic highs on the irregular Lower Palaeozoic surface it is absent. Locally the Kilnsey Formation has been divided into a lower Kilnsey Limestone-with-mudstone Member where mudstone intercalations are present, and an upper Kilnsey Limestone Member of essentially cleaner, albeit dark, limestones. South of the Middle Craven Fault near Scaleber Bridge, Hudson's (1930a) local names Scaleber Force Limestone and Scaleber Quarry Limestone are retained. They are recognised on the same criteria as the divisions of the Kilnsey Formation north of the Middle Craven Fault, the Scaleber Force Limestone being equivalent to the Kilnsey Limestone-with-mudstone and the Scaleber Quarry Limestone to the Kilnsey Limestone. Use of these local names is apt because of modifications in this marginal sequence, a substantial thickness increase, the prolific nature of the local lithostrotionid fauna, and the introduction of chert layers in the Scaleber Quarry Limestone.

The Kilnsey Limestone-with-mudstone is approximately equivalent to the upper part of the *Michelinia* Zone (C_2) of Garwood and Goodyear (1924), described by them as 'an upper darker and more earthy limestone from which (Lower Palaeozoic) pebbles are usually absent', and the lowest unit (the Gastropod Beds) of their *Productus corrugato-hemisphericus* Zone (S), described as 'hard dark limestone with earthy and shaley partings'. The Kilnsey Limestone is the equivalent of the *Cyrtina carbonaria* Subzone (S_2) of Garwood and Goodyear, together with the lower part of their *Nematophyllum minus* Subzone (S_2) the latter described as a 'dark grey limestone'. The Kilnsey Limestone is also equivalent to the lowest part of the Horton Limestone, a term proposed by Ramsbottom (1974) for the sequence between the Gastropod Beds of Garwood and Goodyear (1924) and the Porcellanous Band. The type section for this limestone was the quarry at Horton Limeworks, where 58 m (this resurvey) of the 'Horton Limestone' occur. The lowest 10 m of this sequence, however, are dark grey limestones, referable to the Kilnsey Limestone, and they rest directly on Lower Palaeozoic rocks.

KILNSEY LIMESTONE-WITH-MUDSTONE (ARUNDIAN)

The Kilnsey Limestone-with-mudstone consists of a medium-dark grey limestone with mudstone beds and partings. The member is 22 m thick in its type section in the Chapel House Borehole; the thickness varies considerably elsewhere in the district. Locally it is absent over the highest parts of the Lower Palaeozoic basement, and its maximum is of about 58 m in the Stockdale Farm Borehole (Figure 12). Where the member rests on Chapel House Limestone the contact is sharp, and its dark limestones contrast with the paler grainstones of the Chapel House Limestone. The Kilnsey Limestone-with-mudstone is poorly exposed within the district, and the base of the unit is exposed only in Gordale Beck and the River Ribble just north of Stainforth Force. Elsewhere (Cowside Beck, around Hawkswick and Kilnsey), only the upper few metres of the succession are exposed.

The limestones are bioclastic, fine to coarse calcarenites, packstones and subordinate wackestones, generally argillaceous with common detrital quartz throughout (Plate 4f). Bioclasts are variable, and include crinoid plates, foraminifera, algae (*Koninckopora*, aoujgaliids and kamaenids), calcispheres and shell fragments (molluscan and brachiopod). Peloids (micritised bioclasts) are normally present. The mudstone beds do not exceed 1.8 m, and their thickness varies laterally; in many sections they are present only as thin interbeds (less than 0.3 m), partings or films. Bioturbation is common throughout the sequence.

The macrofauna is quite diverse; an Arundian age is confirmed by the presence of *Delepinea carinata* at Mill Scar Lash [9796 6638] in the Pateley Bridge district, and by the incoming of *Lithostrotion martini* associated with *Palaeosmilia murchisoni*. Brachiopods are dominated by *Megachonetes spp.* Foraminifera from the Chapel House and Stockdale Farm boreholes confirm an Arundian age for the member, diagnostic taxa being *Ammarchaediscus bucullentus*, *Rectodiscus sp.* and *Tubispirodiscus settlensis*.

SCALEBER FORCE LIMESTONE (ARUNDIAN)

This limestone is broadly equivalent to, and petrographically similar to, the Kilnsey Limestone-with-mudstone (Figure 12). It is a bioturbated sequence of dark grey, well bedded, unevenly grained packstones up to 90 m thick (Plate 4g) with mudstone partings and interbeds (the latter up to 2 m thick). The only outcrops are at Scaleber Force.

Common macrofossils include *Lithostrotion martini, L. sp. nov.* aff. *pauciradiale*, *Megachonetes spp.* and *Schizophoria resupinata*. The presence of abundant fasciculate *Lithostrotion* and the absence of cerioid forms suggest an Arundian age. Foraminiferal assemblages from the Cominco Borehole S10 include *Brunsiarchaediscus sp.*, *Glomodiscus miloni*, *Plectogyranopsis moraviae*, *Pseudolituotuba hibernica* and *Rectodiscus sp.* which confirm an Arundian age.   DJCM

DETAILS

Kilnsey Limestone-with-mudstone crops out, but is poorly exposed, in the valley floors of Cowside Beck, the River Skirfare and the River Wharfe. There is an 8 m section in Cowside Beck [9220 7096] and a comparable thickness at the base of Kilnsey Crag [9735 6846] (Plate 5). A 13 m section of the lower part of the member occurs in the River Wharfe at Mill Scar Lash [9796 6638] just within the Pateley Bridge district, some 1.5 km SSE of Kilnsey. However, the full sequence in the Kilnsey area (22.2 m) was cored in the Chapel House Borehole [9726 6647], which proved the thickest mudstone beds known in the member (individual beds up to 1.8 m) and showed that the limestones are dominated by wackestones rather than packstones.

The Kilnsey Formation has not been divided in the Ribble valley, although the members can be differentiated locally. In the river section [8182 6717] north of Stainforth Force, 26 m of thin-bedded fetid medium-dark grey packstones and wackestones occur, and are referable to the Kilnsey Limestone-with-mudstone. There are no significant mudstone beds, but the presence of undercut posts and seepages indicate the presence of argillaceous partings. *Lithostrotion martini* makes its appearance 6 m above the base of the member and is present in the beds exposed beneath Stainforth Bridge [8178 6724]. A bed containing abundant *Composita ficoidea* [8174 6737] is present 18 m above the base. *Delepinea notata* has also been recorded. In the Stainforth railway cutting [8220 6682], the upper part of the member and the contact with the overlying Kilnsey Limestone is exposed in the core of an anticline.

In the Lower Winskill Borehole [8259 6670] the member is

represented by about 41 m of strata. Discrete mudstone beds are absent here, although the succession is conspicuously argillaceous. A 20 cm unit of angular limestone lithoclasts in an argillaceous matrix occurs 4.5 m below the top of the member. The Kilnsey Limestone-with-mudstone also occurs in the Stockdale Farm Borehole [8541 6378]. The 58 m sequence consists of medium-dark grey and medium grey packstones and wackestones, commonly with argillaceous partings and films, but mudstone beds are uncommon and do not exceed 30 cm in thickness.

At Scaleber Force [8407 6256] a 22 m section of the Scaleber Force Limestone is the only natural section of the member. The sequence weathers as a series of limestone posts, the 'shaley' interbeds forming prominant undercuts. The fullest known sequence of Scaleber Force Limestone occurs in Cominco Borehole S10 where 90.4 m were proved. Three 10 to 20 cm thick beds of conglomerate, composed of limestone lithoclasts of local derivation, occur 0.9 m, 57 m and 62 m above the local base. Fasciculate lithostrotionids (*Lithostrotion martini*, *L. sp. nov.* aff. *pauciradiale*) make their appearance 40 m above the base and are common throughout the upper part of the member.

KILNSEY LIMESTONE (HOLKERIAN)

This member is 29 m thick in the type section at Kilnsey Crag (Figure 12, Plate 5). The thickness varies within the district from about 56 m in the Stockdale Farm Borehole to about 30 m in the Cowside Beck – Kilnsey area. The member thins out and is locally absent over the highest parts of Lower Palaeozoic basement. The contact of the Kilnsey Limestone with the underlying Kilnsey Limestone-with-mudstone is taken at the conspicuous reduction in argillaceous content. The passage into the overlying Malham Formation is gradational and taken at the change from darker to paler lithologies.

The member consists of well bedded, thin and thick beds of medium-dark grey to medium-light grey limestones, with characteristic lithologies being fine to coarse calcarenite packstones and grainstones (Plate 4h). Medium-dark grey packstones characterise the lower part of the sequence, and these pass up into medium grey and medium-light grey packstones and grainstones. These limestones are dominantly bioclastic, common grains being crinoid plates, foraminifera, algae (*Koninckopora*, kamaenids and aoujgaliids) and shell fragments. Peloids, generally micritised bioclasts, are common throughout.

The macrofauna is dominated by corals, brachiopods and molluscs. It includes both cerioid and fasciculate lithostrotionids, including *Diphyphyllum smithii*, *Lithostrotion martini*, *L. sociale*, *L. vorticale* (*L. minus* auctt.), and *Composita ficoidea*, rare *Davidsonina carbonaria*, *Linoprotonia ashfellensis*, *L. corrugatohemisphericus*, *L. hemisphaerica* and *Megachonetes spp.* The appearance of cerioid lithostrotionids together with *C. ficoidea*, *D. carbonaria*, *Linoprotonia ashfellensis* and *L. corrugatohemispherica* confirm the Holkerian age. The foraminifera are dominated by small 'involutus' and partial 'angulatus' stage *Archaediscus* and *Nodosarchaediscus*. Such restricted assemblages are typical of the Holkerian in this province. The Holkerian age is confirmed, however, by the presence of *Koskinotextularia cribriformis* and *Nibelia nibelis*.

Plate 4 Photomicrographs of Stockdale Farm Formation, Chapel House Limestone and Kilnsey Formation limestones

a. Halsteads Shales-with-anhydrite, Cominco Borehole S2 [8491 6345], at 425.3 m. Enterolithically folded anhydrite-lath laminae. Field of view 1 mm E 60522

b. Stockdale Farm Limestones and Shales, Stockdale Farm Borehole [8541 6378] at 240.8 m. Bioclasts in the lime mudstone matrix are confined to ostracods and calcispheres. Fine-grained detrital quartz is disseminated throughout the rock. Field of view 5 mm ARE 1614

c. Chapel House Limestone, Stockdale Farm Borehole [8541 6378], at 167.6 m. Grainstone composed of moderately well sorted peloids, bioclasts (crinoid plates and foraminifera), ooids, limestone intraclasts and Lower Palaeozoic extraclasts. Field of view 5 mm ARE 1593

d. Chapel House Limestone, Lower Winskill Borehole [8259 6670] at 215.3 m. Calcite pseudomorphs ?after nodular anhydrite forming a layer in dolomicrite; part of the 'mixed laminites' subdivision of the Chapel House Limestone. Field of view 5 mm E 60523

e. Chapel House Limestone, Lower Winskill Borehole [8259 6670] at 218 m. Sandstone-mudstone laminite. This lithology alternates with dolostone (shown in d) in the 'mixed laminites' of the Chapel House Limestone. Field of view 5 mm E 60524

f. Kilnsey Limestone-with-mudstone, Stockdale Farm Borehole [8541 6378] at 85.7 m. Unevenly grained packstone consisting of crinoid plates, peloids and brachiopod fragments, with disseminated detrital quartz grains. Field of view 5 mm ARE 1561

g. Scaleber Force Limestone, Cominco Borehole S10 [8360 6304] at 206.6 m. Packstone with mixed grains including algae (*Koninckopora*, kamaenids and aoujgaliids), foraminifera, calcispheres and peloids in a matrix partly altered to neomorphic spar. Field of view 5 mm ARE 1999

h. Kilnsey Limestone, Chapel House Borehole [9726 6647] at 5.7 m. Grainstone, unevenly grained, consisting of forminifera, algae (kamaenids), crinoid plates and peloids. Field of view 5 mm ARE 1625

SCALEBER QUARRY LIMESTONE (HOLKERIAN)

This member is broadly equivalent to the Kilnsey Limestone (Figure 12). It consists of well bedded medium and medium-dark grey bioclastic packstones (Plate 8a), similar in composition to the Kilnsey Limestone, with minor argillaceous partings and layers and nodules of black chert in the lowest 33 m. The contact of this limestone with the underlying Scaleber Force Limestone is gradational; it is marked by the increase in the siliciclastic content of the latter, and is taken for convenience at the highest prominent mudstone horizon. The full sequence is known only in Cominco Borehole S2 where 134 m are present, and where the top of the Scaleber Quarry Limestone is taken at a colour change to medium-light grey limestone which marks the base of the Malham Formation. The limestone crops out over a small area at Scaleber and has been cored in Cominco boreholes S1, S2 and S10. A small outcrop has been inferred west of Scaleber Quarry in the vicinity of Preston's Barn.

The Scaleber Quarry Limestone contains an abundant macrofauna (the *'ischnon'* fauna of Hudson 1930b) characterised by cerioid and fasciculate lithostrotionids, and

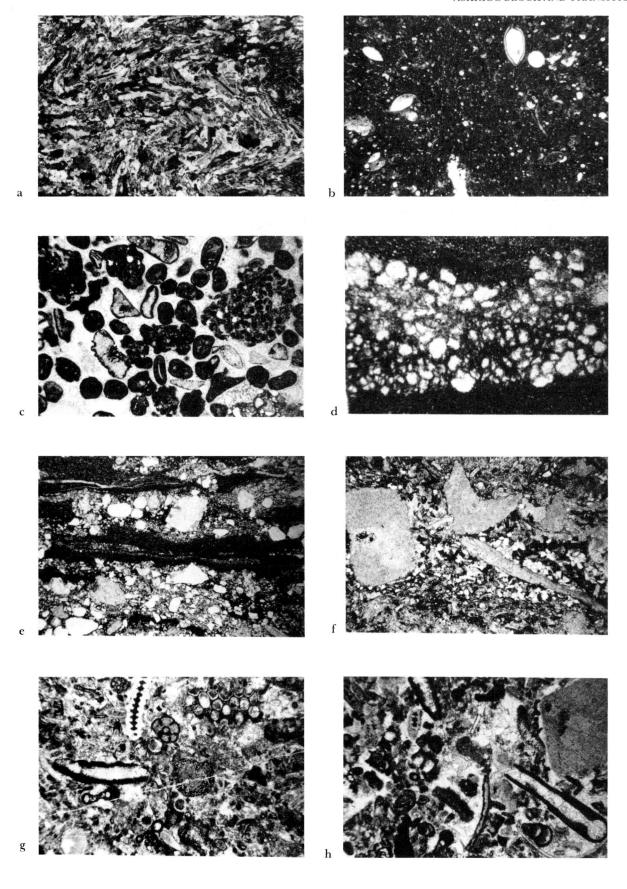

includes *Diphyphyllum smithii*, *Lithostrotion ischnon*, *L. martini*, *L. sociale*, *L. vorticale*, *Syringopora* cf. *reticulata*, *Leptagonia sp.*, *Linoprotonia spp.*, *Megachonetes spp.* and *Schizophoria resupinata*. The appearance of cerioid lithostrotionids some 20 m above the base of the limestone is again diagnostic of a Holkerian age, and this is confirmed by the foraminiferal assemblages from Cominco Borehole S10 where diagnostic taxa include archaediscids with 'concavus' and partial 'angulatus' stages, together with *Ammarchaediscus sp.*, *Koskinotextularia sp.*, *Leptodiscus sp.* and *Nodosarchaediscus sp.*

DETAILS

At Kilnsey Crag [9735 6846], the cliff section exposes the whole of the Kilnsey Limestone (29 m). The contact with the underlying Kilnsey Limestone-with-mudstone is exposed at the base of the cliff and that with the Cove Limestone (Malham Formation) occurs some 14 m above the prominent overhang (Plate 5).

At Yew Cogar Scar (Cowside Beck) [9220 7096] and in the Chapel House Borehole full sequences are 28 m and 30 m thick respectively. In the latter borehole the lowest 11 m of the member are dolomitised. Comparable sections occur at Newby Cote [7332 7072] and Clapham Beck [7510 7015 to 7523 7065].

In an old quarry [7998 7010] above Foredale Cottages, 20 m of Kilnsey Limestone rest unconformably on a near-planar surface of Silurian rocks. The limestone here is well bedded (bed thicknesses between 0.3 and 1.1 m), and contains scattered small Lower Palaeozoic pebbles at several levels. This section continues northwards, where the member is well exposed in the disused Foredale Quarry [799 704], the limestone containing an abundant macrofauna including *Lithostrotion vorticale* (*L. minus* auctt.), *Davidsonina carbonaria*, and common large bellerophontid gastropods.

The Kilnsey Limestone is 57 m thick in the Stockdale Farm Borehole adjacent to the Middle Craven Fault. The limestone here retains the typical character of the member, and contains a rich fauna including *Lithostrotion arachnoideum*, *L. martini*, *L. sociale*, *Megachonetes spp.* and *Linoprotonia ashfellensis*. Outcrops in the vicinity of the Middle Craven Fault occur to the east of the Ribble below Blua Crags [824 643], at the base of the Little Banks [8475 6388], and in the Malham Beck valley [8972 6388] immediately south of Malham Cove.

The Scaleber Quarry Limestone crops out in the Scaleber Bridge area where it is overlain unconformably by both limestone conglomerate (boulder beds) of Brigantian age and Upper Bowland Shales (Pendleian). The base of the limestone is exposed [8407 6257] in the waterfall section of Scaleber Force. A 12 m section, 18 m above the base of the member, is exposed in Scaleber Quarry [8407 6263], the type locality for *Lithostrotion ischnon*. Here the well bedded limestone (with individual posts between 0.3 and 1 m thick) contains colonies of fasciculate and cerioid *Lithostrotion* and conspicuous layers and nodules of light grey and black chert. Smaller exposures of the limestone occur 100 m NE of the quarry in Stockdale Beck, where the unconformable contact of the Scaleber Quarry Limestone with overlying limestone conglomerate is exposed in the stream bank [8416 6275]. This unconformity is also proved in the Cominco boreholes S1 and S10. In the latter, an incomplete sequence of 76 m is proved, and this reduces to 38 m in Borehole S1 because of the unconformable base of the conglomerate. In Borehole S10 the limestone carries the typical coral fauna with cerioid lithostrotionids (*Lithostrotion ischnon*) appearing 46 m above the base of the member. North of the reef limestone outcrop and adjacent to the Middle Craven Fault, the Scaleber Quarry Limestone was cored in Cominco Borehole S2 where 134 m were proved, with the limestone passing upwards conformably into the Malham Formation. The characteristic fauna was present in the borehole, the first appearance of the cerioid *L. ischnon* being some 36 m above the base of the member.   DJCM,LCJ

Malham Formation (Holkerian – Asbian)

The Malham Formation (Mundy and Arthurton, 1980) comprises the light grey limestone succession of Holkerian and Asbian age that overlies the Kilnsey Limestone and Scaleber Quarry Limestone (Figure 13). The formation has been subdivided in the Settle district into a lithologically variable Gordale Limestone Member (Asbian) and a more uniform Cove Limestone Member (Holkerian), with the

Plate 5 Kilnsey and Malham formations, Kilnsey Crag [974 683]. The type section of the Kilnsey Limestone Member forms the overhanging cliff and is overlain by Malham Formation at the top of the crag. (A 7574)

type sections at Gordale and Malham Cove respectively. The marginal reef limestones are included as a facies member within this formation. The Malham Formation is defined by the limits of its two constituent members, and has a maximum thickness of about 220 m south of the Middle Craven Fault, though here the Cove and Gordale limestones are poorly differentiated and pass southwards into marginal reef limestones. Between the North and Middle Craven faults the maximum known thickness is 190 m, and north of the North Craven Fault it is 140 metres. Garwood and Goodyear (1924) placed this interval of strata into their *Nematophyllum minus* Subzone—S_2 (less the lowest dark limestones which are included here in the Kilnsey Limestone) and their *Cyathophyllum murchisoni* Subzone—D_1, and used the Porcellanous Bed, a prominent lime-mudstone unit, as the mapping division between the two subzones. The Porcellanous Bed was also used by Ramsbottom (1974) to divide his proposed Horton and Kingsdale limestones. The Horton Limestone included the strata in the *Cyrtina carbonaria* and *Nematophyllum minus* subzones of Garwood and Goodyear, and the Kingsdale Limestone the strata corresponding to the *Cyathophyllum murchisoni* Subzone, with its top at the base of the Girvanella Band and its base resting on the Porcellanous Bed.

Within the Settle district the Porcellanous Bed occurs in the upper part of the Cove Limestone, but fails southwards and is absent 0.5 km south of the northern margin of the district (Figure 13). Farther south, its horizon is traceable only with difficulty, though its likely position has been estimated by various workers including Garwood and Goodyear (1924), Schwarzacher (1958), Doughty (1968) and Jefferson (1980). However, lime-mudstones lithologically similar to the Porcellanous Bed occur at two horizons some 18 m apart in the strata mapped as Cove Limestone in the Horton–Ingleton area, and this causes further confusion in correlation. Rather than map an inferred position for the absent Porcellanous Bed on the Settle sheet to accommodate the terms 'Horton Limestone' and 'Kingsdale Limestones',

the Malham Formation has been divided slightly higher in the sequence at a recognisable lithostratigraphical boundary.

COVE LIMESTONE (HOLKERIAN)

The Cove Limestone is 72 m thick in its type section at Malham Cove [8975 6411], up to 100 m thick between the North and Middle Craven faults, 45 to 74 m in the area north of these faults, and up to 114 m south of the Middle Craven Fault (Cominco Borehole S2). It overlies the darker grey Kilnsey Limestone in most sections but locally, as in Crummack Dale [781 707 and 767 710], rests unconformably on Lower Palaeozoic strata. The contact with the Kilnsey Limestone is gradational and slightly diachronous.

The Cove Limestone is represented in most sections by massive to weakly bedded, light grey to very light grey, medium and coarse calcarenite packstones and grainstones. In the Moughton–Long Scar area [790 710], south of Horton, there is a conspicuous increase in the proportion of grainstone. This coincides with a marked thinning of the sequence and the presence of the Porcellanous Bed. The base of the latter lies at 6 m and 15 m below the top of the member in the Horton and Yew Cogar Scar sections respectively. Clay beds have been detected at a number of sections, for example in Yew Cogar Scar, Cowside Beck (Figure 13), some overlying palaeokarstic surfaces. Comparable clays were detected in limestones of the same age north of Ingleton by Waltham (1971).

Petrographically the Cove Limestone consists of medium and coarse calcarenites, bioclastic and peloidal packstones and grainstones (Plate 8c). These are generally unevenly grained, but in the northern part of the district (Moughton–Long Scar) many of these are well sorted. The dominant bioclasts are crinoid fragments, foraminifera, algae (particularly *Koninckopora* but with kamaenids also present), and brachiopod fragments. Peloids (interpreted as micritised bioclasts) are ubiquitous. The Porcellanous Bed is a lime-mudstone, variably fenestral (Plate 8b), with calcisiltite geopetally filling many cavities. Bioclasts in the

Plate 6   Malham Formation, Yew Cogar Scar [918 710]. (L 2373)

lime-mudstone are restricted to calcispheres, ostracods and small gastropods.

The Cove Limestone generally produces a topography characterised by steep grassy slopes with few scar-forming features, although the uppermost 6 m of the limestone forms a continuous scar. The latter commonly has a well developed overhang, and its top is a conspicuous bedding-plane which is the contact with the Gordale Limestone.

The macrofauna of the Cove Limestone is poor apart from ubiquitous crinoid debris, and tends to be confined to bands with concentrations of single species of brachiopods and corals. Typical taxa include *Axophyllum vaughani*, *Lithostrotion sociale*, *Syringopora sp.*, *Linoprotonia ashfellensis* and *Megachonetes papilionaceous* group.

A restricted assemblage of foraminifera from the Gordale section, consisting essentially of *Archaediscus sp.* (non 'angulatus' stage) and *Koskinotextularia cribriformis*, is interpreted as a deeper water Holkerian fauna. A typical Holkerian (shallow water) assemblage was encountered, however, in the Cove Limestone of the Silverdale Borehole [8435 7143], where diagnostic taxa included *Archaediscus stilus*, *Holkeria daggeri*, *Nibelia nibelis*, *Palaeospiroplectammina paprothae* and *Septabrunsiina tynanti*.

GORDALE LIMESTONE (ASBIAN)

The Gordale Limestone is some 94 m thick in its type section at Gordale Scar [913 640] (Frontispiece and Plate 23), but elsewhere a thickness between 70 and 75 m is typical. Its base is taken at a prominant bedding plane at the top of the lowest scar-forming unit, and the upper limit at the contact with the Lower Hawes Limestone. The member is a well bedded (varying from thick- to very thick-bedded), medium-light grey to very light grey limestone in which lithological alternations are conspicuous (Plate 6). Variations include fine and medium (more rarely coarse) calcarenite packstones, wackestones and subordinate grainstones, with thin conglomerate units at several levels adjacent to the Middle Craven Fault (Figure 13). Spotting and pseudobrecciation locally characterise the wackestone and packstone units, and the grainstones are commonly cross-bedded. Palaeokarstic surfaces punctuate the sequence at intervals; these are generally undulate, and some carry thin clays (Figure 13). The latter are conspicuous in the northern part of the outcrop but become less obvious southwards, being poorly developed south of the Middle Craven Fault. A few of the limestone surfaces immediately below the palaeokarsts have laminated crusts, but more commonly rhizoliths are present. Concentrations of macrofossils (excepting ubiquitous crinoidal debris) are confined to discrete beds including the *Davidsonina (Cyrtina) septosa* bands of previous authors. These beds are characterised by a mixed fauna of brachiopods and corals which are generally drifted and commonly have oncolitic coatings.

Petrographically the limestones consist of fine to medium, and some coarse, calcarenite bioclastic packstones, wackestones and grainstones (Plate 8d and e). Principal grains in these are foraminifera, calcispheres, crinoid fragments, algae, ostracods and peloids. Kamaenids dominate the algae, and at some levels are the most dominant grains, *Koninckopora* being less abundant than in the underlying Cove Limestone. Partial or complete matrix neomorphism to spar is almost ubiquitous in the packstones and wackestones.

Typical Asbian macrofossils in the Gordale Limestone include *Dibunophyllum bourtonense*, *Davidsonina septosa* and *Delepinea comoides*, with other common taxa being *Axophyllum vaughani*, *Chaetetes depressus*, *Lithostrotion junceum*, *L. pauciradiale*, *Palaeosmilia murchisoni*, *Gigantoproductus maximus* and *Linoprotonia hemisphaerica*. Foraminifera from the Gordale Scar section confirm an Asbian age with diagnostic taxa being *Archaediscus karreri*, *Cribrostomum lecomptei*, *Endothyra* aff. *excellens*, *Endothyranopsis crassa*, *Florennella stricta* and *Pseudoendothyra* aff. *sublimis*.

Topographically the limestone forms conspicuous scar-features (many scree-covered in their lower parts), bounded by bedding planes, and with prominent limestone pavements (Plate 7). Schwarzacher (1958) divided the Settle district sequence between the top of the Porcellanous Bed and the base of the Girvanella Band into nine cycles, each bounded by correlatable 'master bedding planes' which occurred at regular intervals (about 10 m). The latter strongly controlled the topography produced by the limestones, giving rise 'to the stepped nature of the scarp face'. The cycles he suggested had fossil concentrations and increased current activity near to the master bedding planes. Doughty (1968), in an independent study of the density of conjugate joints, found nine rhythms of joint pattern within these D_1 limestones. Each rhythm was characterised by high joint density at the

Plate 7   Malham Formation above Malham Cove [896 642]. Typical pavement-forming, thick bedded, pseudobrecciated Gordale Member limestones. (L 2402)

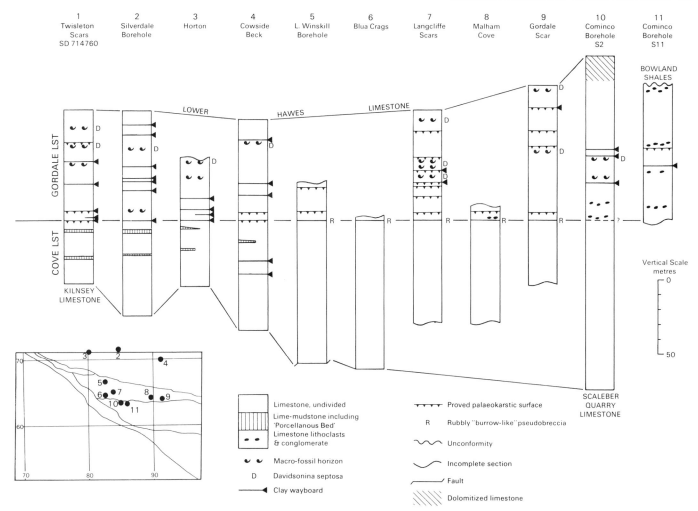

Figure 13   Comparative sections of the Malham Formation

base and low joint density at the top, with the density being related directly to lithological variation. The nine rhythms were found to correspond 'exactly with the cycles described by Schwarzacher'. These rhythms were later mapped by Doughty (1974) in the Settle area, where he suggested that their continuity proved that previously mapped faults in this area were not present.

Waltham (1971) recognized up to 14 shale units in these same limestones north of Ingleton, some of which directly overlay the master bedding planes of the 'Schwarzacher cycles', but he also found that significant shale beds occurred within many of the cycles. The lithological variation observed in underground exposures, together with the numerous shale beds, indicate that sedimentation of the D_1 limestones is more complex than the simple cyclical scheme that Schwarzacher suggested. Walkden (1972) studied the 'clay wayboards', comparable to the shale beds, in the Dinantian limestones of Derbyshire, and found that they were potassium bentonites of probable volcanic origin. This view was supported by work in North Wales by Somerville (1979), who considered the 'clay wayboards' to be palaeosols derived from decomposition of wind-blown volcanic material which accumulated subaerially on palaeokarst surfaces.

Evidence from the resurvey allows a reappraisal of the cyclic nature of sedimentation. North of the North Craven Fault, where thicker shales occur presumably on palaeokarsts, they have a marked influence in defining feature-forming units which are traceable for some distance (e.g. the section of Yew Cogar Scar (Plate 6) can be correlated with a section at Twistleton Scars 23 km to the WNW (Figure 13)). In these sections, however, other palaeokarstic surfaces are present *within* the feature-forming units. Between the North and Middle Craven faults however, where the shale beds are thin or absent, thick-bedded wackestones and packstones appear to be the main factor controlling the units, with most of the proved palaeokarstic surfaces occurring within individual scars. This makes correlation with the area north of the North Craven Fault, and even in the area between the North and Middle Craven faults, difficult if based solely on master bedding planes and feature-forming units.

The link between joint density and changes in lithology emphasised by Doughty (1968) is very apparent, with high joint densities in grainstone units and low densities in packstones and wackestones. Observations during the survey, however, have shown that the frequency of joint pattern change is far more complex than this, and does not fall into nine simple rhythms. Crude sedimentary cyclicity is present in the Gordale Limestone, but is more complicated than envisaged by Schwarzacher and Doughty, and requires further definition.   DJCM

DETAILS

At Malham Cove [8975 6411] 72 m of the Cove Limestone are exposed. The underlying Kilnsey Limestone crops out in isolated crags 160 m south of the section, and the contact with the Cove Limestone is taken at the base of the cliff. The member here is a massive, uniform packstone with only four bedding-planes of any significance, and closely spaced joints are characteristic. An overhang is developed in the uppermost 4 to 6 m of the section and the character of the unit changes in the highest 3 m where rubbly pseudobreccia occurs. Macrofauna apart from crinoid debris is rather sparse, but sections at Gordale Scar [914 640] have yielded *Axophyllum vaughani*, *Lithostrotion sociale*, *Linoprotonia sp.* and *Megachonetes sp.*

Between the Middle and North Craven faults, the thickest section of the Cove Limestone is on the east side of the Ribble valley at Blua Crags [826 644], where at least 100 m are present. A similar thickness occurs in the Lower Winskill Borehole [8259 6670]. At Blua Crags and on the lower slopes of Attermire Scar [824 640] the Cove Limestone exhibits weak bedding with many beds, commonly between 0.5 and 2 m thick, defined by horizontal stylolites. The uniform nature of the member is well illustrated at Giggleswick Quarry [8092 6488] and at the old Craven Limeworks quarry [825 664]; at the latter locality, however, petrographic studies by Jefferson (1980) have revealed a cryptic cyclicity. Although the macrofauna are sparse, bands crowded with *Megachonetes* occur at several localities, for example on In Moor [7951 6776], near Feizor.

North of the North Craven Fault the Cove Limestone varies in thickness from 45 m in the Moughton–Long Scar area [790 710] to 74 m at Cowside Beck (Yew Cogar Scar) [918 706]; this attenuation is not solely caused by overlap onto the Lower Palaeozoic basement as both sections are underlain by Kilnsey Limestone. In the Moughton–Long Scar area, grainstone, which is conspicuously cross-bedded at several horizons, is more abundant. The fauna here is again sparse, but *Megachonetes* bands are present, and at one exposure [7985 7101] there is a conspicuous bed of *Linoprotonia* shells (all showing convex-up current orientation) in a laminated packstone-grainstone. The Porcellanous Bed is some 6 to 8 m below the top of the Cove Limestone in this area. It has a maximum thickness of 2.85 m but dies out between 100 and 500 m south of the northern margin of the district. The progressive southward thinning is well exposed on the east side of Crummack Dale.

At Yew Cogar Scar [9224 7087] the Porcellanous Bed is 15 m below the top of the Cove Limestone. It is 1 m thick but again dies out rapidly southward. Between the Porcellanous Bed and the base of the member, zones of seepage testify to the presence of mudstone beds probably comparable to those exposed overlying pot-holed palaeokarstic surfaces in the Cove Limestone at Skythorns Quarry [975 644].

The Gordale Limestone at Gordale Scar [913 640] is up to 94 m thick, the maximum thickness known north of the Middle Craven Fault. However, within the Gordale Scar exposures, individual beds change rapidly in thickness over a few tens of metres. The base of the member is taken at a conspicuous bedding plane at the top of the lowest scar (5 m above a prominent overhang). This level marks the change from uniform lithologies below (Cove Limestone) to more variable limestones above (Gordale Limestone). The scar-forming nature of the Gordale Limestone is extremely well shown in the gorge, where the 'master-bedding planes' defining these scars are, in most instances, developed on thick-bedded packstones and wackestones which are commonly pseudobrecciated. Good examples of palaeokarstic surfaces are present at 6 m, 50 m, 60 m and 76 m above the base, but they all occur within individual scar-forming units. Cross-bedded grainstones are present at three horizons (2 m, 19 m and 74 m above the base). The lowest unit is partly oolitic (the only oolitic limestone recognised in the Malham Formation), and is capped by a palaeokarstic surface. The macrofauna is concentrated at a few horizons, but does not at any level take on the typical nature of a *Davidsonina (Cyrtina) septosa* Band (auctt). Common taxa include *Axophyllum vaughani*, *Chaetetes depressus*, *Dibunophyllum bourtonense*, *Lithostrotion spp.* (including *L. junceum*, *L. maccoyanum*, *L. martini*, *L. pauciradiale*, *L.portlocki*), *Palaeosmilia murchisoni*, *Davidsonina septosa*, *Gigantoproductus maximus* and *Linoprotonia sp*. *Davidsonina septosa* makes its appearance about 22 m above the base of the member.

In the Langcliffe Scar–Attermire Scar area the contact with the Cove Limestone is the same as that at Gordale Scar, but the overall thickness of the Gordale Limestone is reduced to 73 m The ground here is highly faulted, and the base of the Gordale Limestone provides a datum for mapping these faults. Concentrations of macrofossils occur at two levels, the lower one (which ranges over some 11 m) 29 m above the base, and the upper one (2 m thick) 67 m above the base. Seven palaeokarstic surfaces are recognisable but again they do not coincide with the feature-forming 'master-bedding planes'. A fine cliff section through 17 m of the Gordale Limestone is exposed [8385 6505] at Victoria Cave where four palaeokarstic surfaces, from 1.6 m to 8 m apart, are present. Just south of the cave, conspicuous cross-bedded grainstones are present both above and below a palaeokarst.

West of the River Ribble, south of the North Craven Fault, the Gordale Limestone retains a thickness of about 72 m, and the two fossil horizons recognised at Langcliffe Scar are again present. The lower one is exposed over a thickness of 10 m at Riseber Wood [8089 6791] where common taxa include *Axophyllum vaughani*, *Chaetetes depressus*, *Lithostrotion pauciradiale*, *Palaeosmilia murchisoni*, *Davidsonia septosa* and *Delepinea comoides*. The upper fossil bed, sampled at an exposure [8055 6723] NW of Riseber Wood, is some 7 m below the top of the member, and has a similar fauna to the lower one, but with conspicuous oncolites.

North of the North Craven Fault, the Gordale Limestone has the same general character, its thickness being about 70 m. The contact with the Cove Limestones is well seen in most sections and commonly carries a thin 'shale'. A feature of the Gordale Limestone in this area is the increased number and the conspicuous nature of the shale horizons. These were found at eight levels in the Silverdale Borehole [8435 7143], and Waltham (1971) recorded many more north of Ingleton. Fossil bands occur at several intervals.

Conglomeratic (limestone lithoclasts) grainstone units indicating 'shelf' marginal conditions, occur at several stratigraphical levels in the Gordale Limestone both immediately north and south of the Middle Craven Fault. A prominent conglomerate in the few metres of strata above the base of the member is traceable in exposures [e.g. 9064 6365] near Strideout Edge (west of Gordale Scar), and continues westward in several exposures to the east side of Malham Cove. The same bed is traceable west of Malham Cove in an exposure [8896 6378] below Jorden Scar. The conglomerate consists of well rounded 5 mm to 10 cm lithoclasts in a coarse calcarenite grainstone. Similar conglomerate occurs near the top of the Gordale Limestone south of the Middle Craven Fault at High Hill [8353 6355] and at Halsteads [8477 6346], and up to four horizons have been proved in the Cominco boreholes S2, S3, S8 and S11. DJCM,LCJ

MARGINAL REEF LIMESTONES (?HOLKERIAN TO BRIGANTIAN)

Marginal reef limestones occur in a roughly west–east tract extending for 15 km from Settle to the eastern margin of the district, and form part of the Craven Reef Belt of Hudson (1930a). The principal outcrops, at Settle, Malham, and Swinden near Linton Moor, represent the exposed parts of a continuous facies belt which are isolated by Namurian cover. The limestones are complex build-ups that form a marginal facies to the 'shelf' successions of the Malham Formation and the Lower Hawes Limestone at the southern margin of the Askrigg Block (Figure 29).

The reef limestones were first described by Tiddeman (1889) and have been the subject of many subsequent studies. For the history of research concerning these limestones and the 'knoll-reef' theory see Tiddeman (1889), Marr (1899), Hudson (1930a, 1932), Bond (1950a) and the reviews of Rayner (1953), Black (1954), Parkinson (1957), Ramsbottom (1974), and Miller and Grayson (1982).

The Settle–Malham section of the Craven Reef Belt is considered here to be part of a once continuous apron reef (*sensu* Eden and others, 1964; *non* Bond, 1950b), rather than several discrete knolls (*sensu* Tiddeman, 1889). Dislocation of this apron reef into fault-slices (related to concomitant movements of the Craven faults), and substantial erosion has severely modified the build-ups (Hudson, 1932). The eroded reef topography was subsequently buried by the onlapping Namurian Bowland Shales (Hudson, 1930a, 1932) and the present-day outcrops represent an exhumed pre-Namurian surface.

The marginal reef limestones consist of medium and medium-light grey limestones ranging from organic bound-stones to packstones and wackestones, with variable grain size depending on the nature of the bioclastic components. Conspicuous fabrics involving radial fibrous calcite ('reef tufa' auctt.), interpreted as marine cements, are common. The biota is characteristically diverse and includes brachiopods and molluscs together with bryozoa, corals, cephalopods, arthropods and echinoderms. Ecological division of these limestones into algal-reef, fore-reef and back-reef, as mapped in Staffordshire and Derbyshire (Wolfenden, 1958; Stevenson and Gaunt, 1971), is not feasible because of the considerable dissection which the build-ups have undergone. Remnants of these biotopes have, however, been recognised and are documented below.

The exposed sections of the reef limestones in the Settle district are wholly of Asbian (B_2) age, with separate goniatite assemblages being characterised by, in stratigraphically younging order, *Goniatites hudsoni*, *G. wedberensis*, *Bollandites castletonensis* and *G. moorei*. The fact that reefs were present in P_{1a} times is indicated by blocks of reef limestones containing *Goniatites crenistria* (ss) in a limestone conglomerate at Scaleber [8415 6284]. Foraminifera from P_{1a} reef limestones at Cracoe [Pateley Bridge district] were recently examined by A. R. E. Strank (personal communication); these contain a restricted fauna characterised by stellate archaediscids and *Howchinia bradyana*, confirming a Brigantian age. Thus reef limestones equivalent in age to the Lower Hawes Limestone of the shelf succession were once present in the Settle–Malham area, and have been subsequently stripped off by late-Dinantian or later erosion.

Field relationships indicate that both the Cove Limestone (Holkerian) and the Gordale Limestone (Asbian) pass laterally into reef facies, but no reef limestones of Holkerian age have yet been verified at outcrop. Foraminiferal studies of the marginal reef limestones have not yet been undertaken.

DETAILS

The main reef limestone outcrops near Settle are at High Hill [833 633] and Scaleber [840 630]; there are small outcrops [823 634] near Albert Hill, immediately ESE of Settle, and exposures [8595 6300] on the south side of High South Bank. The reef limestones in these localities occur together with the Malham Formation and Wensleydale Group in fault-bounded slices on the downthrow side of the Middle Craven Fault.

The reef limestones form the impressive exposures on the steep southern slopes of High Hill (Figure 29, sections 1 and 2). The northern side of the hill is a dip-slope in Gordale Limestone, with northward dips of up to 26° (more generally 15°), passing laterally into and overlapping the reef limestone to the south. This relationship is well demonstrated at an exposure [8367 6338] on the east side of High Hill. The northward tilt of the reef limestone is confirmed by 16 to 20° dips in geopetal fabrics in an exposure [8346 6331] on the southern side of the hill.

The Scaleber outcrop projects southwards as a low mound some 230 m beyond that of the main High Hill mass. Geopetal fabrics in these exposures give no indication that the outcrop is allochthonous, and so structural continuity with the High Hill outcrop is presumed. Banked against the southern side of the outcrop is a limestone conglomerate composed largely of reef-derived boulders.

Erosion of the reef 'front' at High Hill was considerable, with little evidence left for any fore-reef palaeoslope. Many of the exposures at the western end of the outcrop [8319 6345, 8306 6350] consist of unbedded limestone with conspicuous large gigantoproductoids, and several exposures [e.g. 8300 6355] contain abundant drifted coral colonies, particularly *Lithostrotion pauciradiale*. These exposures have a back-reef aspect, and it is possible that erosion through the reef-front has cut to such a level as to expose the transitional beds. Part of an algal reef is exposed [8362 6326] on the middle part of the eastern slopes of High Hill; this facies is a boundstone composed of stromatolitic algae, lithistid sponges (particularly '*Radiotospongia*' *carbonaria*), and the bryozoa *Fistulipora incrustans*, *Tabulipora* and '*Thamniscus*'.

All the in-situ reef limestones in the High Hill–Scaleber area appear to be Asbian in age. Stratigraphically useful fossils from High Hill include the characteristic Asbian brachiopod *Davidsonina septosa* from a number of localities [8377 6335, 8356 6329] on the eastern side of the hill, and the B_2 *Goniatites wedberensis* from an exposure [8329 6336] on the middle slopes of the central part of the hill. At Scaleber, one exposure [8394 6302] yielded the upper B_2 *Bollandites castletonensis*, and another exposure [8406 6316] *Bollandoceras sp. nov.*, a tumid form conspecific with specimens occurring at Cracoe and Malham in upper B_2 assemblages.

A small area of reef limestone crops out on Albert Hill [823 634] in a narrow fault slice between the Malham Formation of Castlebergh and Low High Hill. The tilts of geopetal fabrics in these unbedded reef limestones give a southerly component up to 20°; this conforms to the general dip of the adjacent bedded limestones, and thus suggests that the reef limestones are in situ rather than a displaced block (olistolith). No faunal collections have been made from this outcrop.

Reef limestones are present on the southern side of High South Bank (Figure 29, section 3), where four sink-holes at the base of the Upper Bowland Shales expose small crags of shelly reef limestones. Immediately north of these sinks the reef limestones pass into Gordale Limestone dipping northward at approximately 15°. No diagnostic fossils were present in collections from the reef exposures, but the brachiopod assemblages are typical of an upper B_2 Zone age.

The reef limestones at Malham crop out on the hills of Burns [895 631], Cawden [905 630] and Wedber Brow [912 628], and there is a small outcrop between Burns and Cawden (north of King House). The reef limestones again occur on the southern side of fault-bounded slices which have Gordale Limestone on the northern side and are tilted towards the Middle Craven Fault. The structure shown by the reef limestones is consistent with their being part of a dissected marginal complex rather than discrete knolls.

A substantial outcrop of reef limestone occurs on the southern half of Cawden; the rest of the hill being Gordale Limestone, dipping north between 16 and 20°, and producing a marked feature as it locally overlaps the reef limestone to the south. The quarries at the base of the hill on its southern side expose fore-reef limestones dipping at 30° to the south. One of these quarries [9037 6301] has yielded the upper B_2 goniatites *Bollandoceras micronotum*, *B. sp.* (tumid form), *Goniatites moorei* and *G.* aff. *crenistria* (early form) from the youngest reef limestones now exposed on the hill. Older reef limestones (both upper and lower B_2) crop out on the western side of the hill and separate exposures have yielded *Bollandites castletonensis* [9137 6312] and *Goniatites wedberensis* [9034 6313]. Bisat (1934, p.303) has recorded the lower B_2 form *Goniatites hudsoni* from Cawden, but this specimen was unlocalised. An algal reef some 75 m in length by 40 m wide produces a prominent feature [9053 6307] near the summit of the hill. This algal boundstone is composed of stromatolitic algae, lithistid sponges ('*Radiotospongia*' *carbonaria*) and bryozoans, particularly the encrusting form *Tabulipora* and the fenestrates *Fenestella*, *Levifenestella* and '*Thamniscus*'. It also contains an unusual brachiopod fauna including *Palmerhytis stebdenensis*, "*Productus*" *griffithianus*, *Proboscidella proboscidea*, *Rugicostella nystiana*, *Stipulina deshayesiana*, *S. sp. nov.*, *Streptorhynchus anomalus* and *Undaria erminea*.

Wedber Brow has the same general structure as Cawden. Exposures in the gorge of Gordale Beck show Gordale Limestone which makes up much of the central and northern parts of the hill; the dip of these limestones, up to 26° to the north, is tectonic in origin. Minor intercalations of shelly limestones which resemble the reef phase occur in these bedded limestones. At an exposure [9106 6319] to the east of Gordale Beck such a shelly intercalation contains abundant *Gigantoproductus spp.* and large diameter *Koninckopora inflata*, and is thought to represent a 'back-reef' limestone interbedded with the Gordale Limestone. Towards the southern end of the gorge section, the dips of the limestone become southward, and this reversal of dip direction is associated with an abrupt change in lithology to typical shelly reef-limestone. The 'turn-over' of the dip, well seen at an exposure [9095 6312] in the eastern bank of the stream, marks a 'hinge' zone between originally horizontal bedded limestone and the southward-dipping marginal reef palaeoslope. An exposure [9093 6307] of the stratigraphically lowest reef limestone has yielded the lower B_2 goniatite *Goniatites antiquatus-hudsoni* group. No other goniatites have been found in the re-survey. The holotype and paratype of *Goniatites wedberensis* (Bisat, 1934) were obtained from a stone wall on Wedber Brow, but this species has still to be located on the hill. On the southern slopes of Wedber Brow shelly limestones containing limestone lithoclasts are exposed [9106 6294] resting on older reef limestones. The shelly fauna includes numerous *Productus productus*, *Schizophoria connivens* and *Striatifera striata*, brachiopods that are very common in P_{1a} assemblages from the Cracoe reefs (Mundy, 1978, 1980), but unfortunately at Wedber Brow there is no goniatite control.

Reef limestone is seen in small exposures on the low hill centred around Burns Barn [8953 6312] to the west of Malham, but little indication can be gained of its structure. The outcrop extends over a substantial north–south distance with exposures occurring within 120 m of the Middle Craven Fault. The wide outcrop may reflect a deeper level of erosion that has intersected an early part of the reef; alternatively the erosional level may have intersected an extended 'back-reef' environment which had regressed over the bedded Malham Formation limestones. Faunal assemblages are of B_2 aspect, but the only goniatite find was *Goniatites wedberensis-hudsoni* group indicating a low B_2 Zone age. A limestone boulder bed with a substantial content of reef-derived blocks occurs in Head Beck (Hudson, 1944b) [8930 6300], and is interpreted as being banked against in situ reef limestones. A down-faulted outcrop of reef limestone is present in the valley of Malham Beck between Burns and Cawden. A small exposure [9017 6307] immediately behind King House has yielded the upper B_2 goniatite *Bollandites castletonense*.

The extreme south-western part of the reef limestone outcrop of Swinden [975 610] lies within the Settle district. Swinden is an elongate, south-west-trending hill, some 750 m in maximum width and 1.9 km in length (of which 1.65 km lies within the Pateley Bridge district), that is surrounded by Bowland Shales on all but its southwestern side. Dips in these shales attain a maximum of 50° in Eller Beck to the west of the hill. This large reef limestone outcrop is anomalous in its orientation, and is also south of the main east–west trend of the reef belt which continues from Malham through into the Pateley Bridge district as the outcrops of Elbolton, Thorpe Kail and Hartlington Kail. Swinden was regarded by Bond (1950c) as an anticline, and this view was supported by Black (1958) who further suggested that it was a 'post-shale' (Bowland Shales) fold because of the dip of the shales and 'the general shale distribution'. Swinden hill is on the same alignment as the Eshton-Hetton Anticline, but recent quarrying has opened up the centre of the hill and this has revealed strikes and dips of a northward-younging sequence with no indication of an anticlinal axis. A large, south-east-trending fault cuts the south-central part of the hill and south-west of this, beds with tectonic dips of up to 75° dip into the axis of the hill. Most of the limestones exposed on Swinden are of reef facies, but the oldest strata in the quarry are medium and medium-dark grey bedded crinoidal packstones which probably pre-date the reef limestone. These pass up into light grey wackestones which show signs of undulatory bedding-planes and incipient bank development. Tracing this younging sequence northwards through the quarries the bedding characters diminish and a large carbonate bank consisting of light grey and very light grey wackestones is present. Bedded crinoidal packstones cap the massive wackestones at the north-eastern end of the quarry. The sequence is further complicated by zones of megabrecciation and neptunian dykes, the latter filled with dark crinoidal packstones and mudstones (presumably of Bowland Shales origin). Some exposures [e.g. 9783 6102] on the sides of the hill consist of typical flank facies, but an algal-boundstone framework has been located [9753 6132] at surface and in a borehole on the lower south-western side of the hill. The facies relations in the Swinden outcrop are difficult to interpret; they suggest a complex hybrid build-up with the coincidence of the orientation of Swinden and the trace of the Eshton–Hetton Anticline indicating an obvious explanation for the production of reef limestones in this position. Furthermore the zones of megabrecciation, the disposition of tectonic dips within the hill (some of which are related to fractures with a north-easterly orientation), and the abrupt lateral termination of the facies, suggest that faulting strongly influenced the present expression of the build-up.

Most of the reef limestones at Swinden are regarded as of B_2 Zone age. *Goniatites hudsoni* (lower B_2), *Beyrichoceras* aff. *vesiculiferum* and *Bollandoceras micronotoides* were recorded by Bisat (1934), from the old south quarry (Hudson and Cotton, 1945). Upper B_2 limestones are presumed to be present, but no diagnostic goniatites have been recorded. A small exposure [9849 6189] on the north-eastern part of the hill contains a shelly fauna which closely resembles P_{1a} assemblages from Elbolton and Stebden, and *Goniatites striatus* was recovered from Swinden (Bisat, 1934), a record which suggests that limestones of P_{1b} age are also represented. The age of the bedded sub-reef limestone at the base of the quarry has not been determined.

DJCM

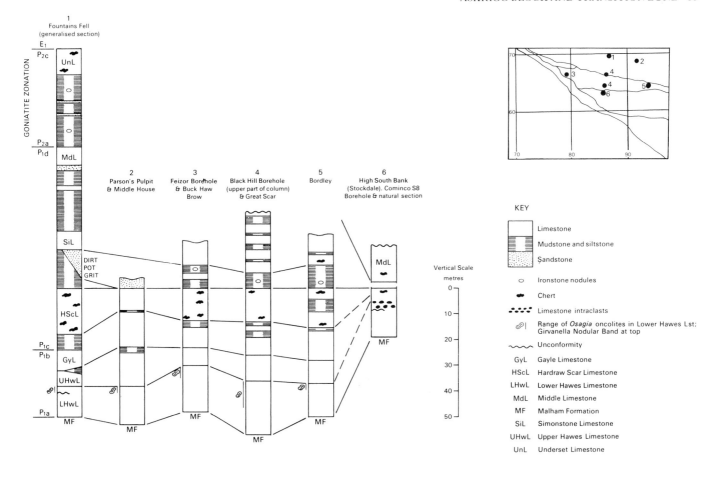

Figure 14 Comparative sections of the Brigantian part of the Wensleydale Group

Wensleydale Group (part) (Brigantian)

The term Wensleydale Formation was applied by George and others (1976, table 1) to the Dinantian strata of Yoredale facies (the 'Yordale Series' of Phillips, 1836); these consist of an alternation of limestones and siliciclastics (mudstones, siltstones and sandstones), with or without coals. In the type area of the northern Askrigg Block, these beds show cyclothemic alternations with the following idealised upward lithological succession: limestone – mudstone – siltstone – sandstone – seatearth – coal (Hudson, 1924; Moore, 1958). Group rather than Formation status is considered to be appropriate to this succession, because of the persistence of its contained lithostratigraphical units, in particular the named Yoredale limestones, which are best regarded as formations.

The succession of the Wensleydale Group varies greatly from the northern and central Askrigg Block to the marginal areas (Hicks, 1959; Black, 1950; Black and Bond, 1952; Dunham and Stubblefield, 1945; Dunham and Wilson, 1985). In the Settle district the sequence is much thinner than in the type area, sandstones are reduced or absent, no coals or seatearths are present and certain of the limestones are absent, particularly in the upper part of the sequence (Figure 14). On Fountains Fell [870 710], the full local development of the Brigantian part of the Wensleydale Group is 146 m, compared with 315 m for a similar interval in Wensleydale. A striking attenuation of the sequence also occurs within the Settle district, where 105 m of strata (base of the Lower Hawes Limestone to the top of the Middle Limestone) on Fountains Fell is reduced to 36 m on High South Bank [857 632] 7.5 km to the south, a thinning due to attenuation and local non-sequences that are related to movements on the Middle Craven Fault and concomitant structures.

The named lithological units are mostly limestones which bear the names of their correlatives in Wensleydale (Figure 14). The base of the sequence is taken at a lithological change (generally from lighter to darker grey limestone) at the base of the Lower Hawes Limestone. This change lies between 10 and 21 m below the top of the Girvanella Nodular Band which was taken by Garwood and Goodyear (1924, p.200) and later workers as the local base of the Upper *Dibunophyllum* (D$_2$) Zone. The lithological change marking the base of the Lower Hawes Limestone (= Peghorn Limestone of the Alston Block) is coincident with the earliest occurrence of Brigantian (D$_2$) faunas in the Brough and Penrith districts (Burgess and Mitchell, 1976). In the Settle district no diagnostic macrofauna has been recovered from the basal beds of the limestone identified as the Lower Hawes, although a Brigantian macrofauna occurs half way up the unit. Foraminifera from the Great Scar section [8580

6423] north of Stockdale, however, confirm an early Brigantian age for the basal Lower Hawes limestones, with *Climacammina* and stellate archaediscids being diagnostic taxa. The top of the Dinantian part of the Wensleydale Group is taken below the incoming of Pendleian goniatites. During this survey *Cravenoceras leion* was located in exposures [8738 7173] of decalcified siltstones and cherts immediately above the Underset Limestone in a tributary of Darnbrook Beck (on the eastern side of Fountains Fell, just within the Hawes district). The base of the Namurian is thus taken at a slightly lower horizon from that hitherto taken in this region.

The limestones and certain mudstones of this part of the Wensleydale Group contain a rich biota including diagnostic asssemblages of Brigantian corals and brachiopods as well as trepostome bryozoans, algae (generally 'skeletal' oncolites) and ubiquitous crinoids.

The Wensleydale Group crops out in a number of outliers north of the North Craven Fault, the main outcrops occurring on Fountains Fell and Out Fell, around Parson's Pulpit, and on High Mark and Hawkswick Clowder. Between the North Craven and Middle Craven faults, separate crops occur near Feizor; in a broad tract between Overclose, Grizedales and Dean Moor; in the Malham Lings area; and between Gordale Scar and Bordley. South of the Middle Craven Fault small outcrops occur on High Hill and High South Bank. DJCM

DETAILS

The Lower Hawes Limestone is a variable unit with conspicuous facies variation; it is present throughout the area and varies from about 12 m thick in the Fountains Fell – Out Fell area to 21 m at its maximum in the Great Scar section [8580 6432 to 8579 6431]. South of the North Craven Fault the base of the Lower Hawes Limestone is marked by the onset of medium-dark grey bioclastic packstones which commonly carry thin oncolites. The latter are well seen in the cliff [8846 6532] at Long Scar, in the roadside quarry [9067 6487] at Malham Ings, at Jubilee Cave [8376 6552], and in exposures [8359 6372] west of Sugar Loaf Hill. The colour change to darker limestones is less obvious in sections north of the North Craven Fault, but the base of the formation here can usually be recognised on gross lithological changes from the preceding Gordale Limestone.

The top part of the Lower Hawes Limestone consists of dark grey, fetid, unevenly grained, bioclastic wackestones and packstones (Plate 8f) with prominent skeletal oncolites (many in excess of 2 cm diameter and containing *Girvanella* filaments and a few *Aphralysia* 'cells', referable to the form-genus *Osagia*); this is the Girvanella Nodular Band of Garwood and Goodyear (1924) and later authors. In the Fountains Fell, Middle House and Bordley areas this oncolite-bearing unit is generally less than 2 m thick and, in places such as Gingling Hole [8557 7019], Fountains Fell, rests on an eroded limestone surface, a feature noted by Burgess and Mitchell (1976) and Ramsbottom (1974). Between the North Craven and Middle Craven faults no such erosion surface has been recorded, and in the Great Scar section dark limestones with oncolites extend over an interval of 10 m (the maximum thickness recorded anywhere in the district) and are interbedded with crinoidal packstones (coarse calcarenites and calcirudites). In Cominco boreholes S4 [8606 6470] and S5 [8701 6432] 2 m of medium-light grey, coarse calcarenite bioclastic and oolitic grainstone are intercalated with the oncolite-bearing limestones. In the Great Scar section a conspicuous shelly unit also occurs within the dark limetones in the upper part of the Lower Hawes. It contains abundant

Plate 8 Photomicrographs of Scaleber Quarry Limestone, Malham Formation and Wensleydale Group.

a. Scaleber Quarry Limestone, Cominco Borehole S10 [8360 6304] at 109.2 m. Unevenly grained bioclastic packstone consisting of brachiopod fragments, crinoid plates, foraminifera and calcispheres. Field of view 5 mm ARE 1947
b. Cove Limestone, 'Porcellanous Bed', Horton Quarry No. 4 Borehole [7955 7171], at 21.1 m. The lime-mudstone with laterally connecting spar-filled fenestrae, locally develops a peloidal fabric. Bioclasts are largely confined to calcispheres. Field of view 5 mm E 60520
c. Cove Limestone, Gordale Scar [9150 6403]. Unevenly grained packstone-grainstone consists of crinoid plates, algae (*Koninckopora* and aoujgaliids), foraminifera and peloids. Note the micrite envelope around the crinoid fragment. Field of view 5 mm E 60525
d. Gordale Limestone, Gordale Scar [9134 6392]. Moderately well sorted bioclastic-oolitic grainstone. Bioclasts include foraminifera, crinoid plates and molluscan fragments. This lithology occurs locally some 3 m above the base of the Gordale Limestone and is the only oolitic unit recognised in the Malham Formation. Field of view 5 mm E 60527
e. Gordale Limestone, Gordale Scar [9134 6392]. Bioclastic wackestone consisting of foraminifera, calcispheres, algae (kamaenids) and molluscan fragments in a matrix partially altered to neomorphic spar. Field of view 5 mm E 60526
f. Lower Hawes Limestone, 'Girvanella Band', near Bordley Hall [9434 6425]. Bioclastic packstone consisting of crinoid plates, brachiopod and molluscan fragments, bryozoa, foraminifera and oncolitic algae. The bored brachiopod fragment in centre field has a thin oncolitic coating (black) composed of *Girvanella* filaments and *Aphralysia* cells (not discernable in this field). Field of view 5 mm E 60530
g. Gayle Limestone, Parson's Pulpit [9180 6847]. Unevenly grained bioclastic packstone, composed mostly of crinoid plates and brachiopod fragments. Field of view 5 mm E 60521
h. Hardraw Scar Limestone, Great Scar [8630 6438]. Unevenly grained bioclastic packstone composed of bryozoan fragments and crinoid plates. Field of view 5 mm E 60528

brachiopods including *Gigantoproductus* cf. *gaylensis*, *G. okensis*, *Latiproductus latissimus* and *Pugilis pugilis*, as well as colonies of *Lithostrotion spp*. This horizon is widespread, and is well seen in an exposure [8837 6456] on the eastern side of Grizedales and in another [8392 6558] ENE of Jubilee Cave. In the Feizor area, the horizon of this fossil band is represented by a prolific coral bed (largely composed of lithostrotionids) which is well exposed in Blackriggs Quarry [7926 6606]. The coral bed is traceable over several square kilometres and forms limestone pavements at an exposure [8007 6629] north of Buck Haw Brow and at another [7850 6680] WNW of Brunton House. The Brunton House locality was described in detail by Rayner (1946) and was regarded by Hill (1938) as 'probably the best example' of a Dinantian 'reef-coral fauna'. The coral fauna at these localities includes *Dibunophyllum bipartium*, *D. konincki*, *Diphyphyllum lateseptatum*, *Lithostrotion spp*. and *Lonsdaleia floriformis*. South of the Middle Craven Fault, these beds at the top of the Lower Hawes Limestone are correlated with a lithoclast-bearing shelly coquina (calcirudite packstone) which is 2 m thick on Low South Bank, and is well exposed in a stream [8531 6316] and adjacent sinkhole [8532 6317]. In the High Hill area the typical oncolite-bearing lithofacies is present in an isolated exposure [8378 6356] immediately south of Sugar Loaf Hill.

Between the lowest dark beds of the Lower Hawes Limestone and the upper beds containing '*Girvanella*' oncolites, an intervening unit

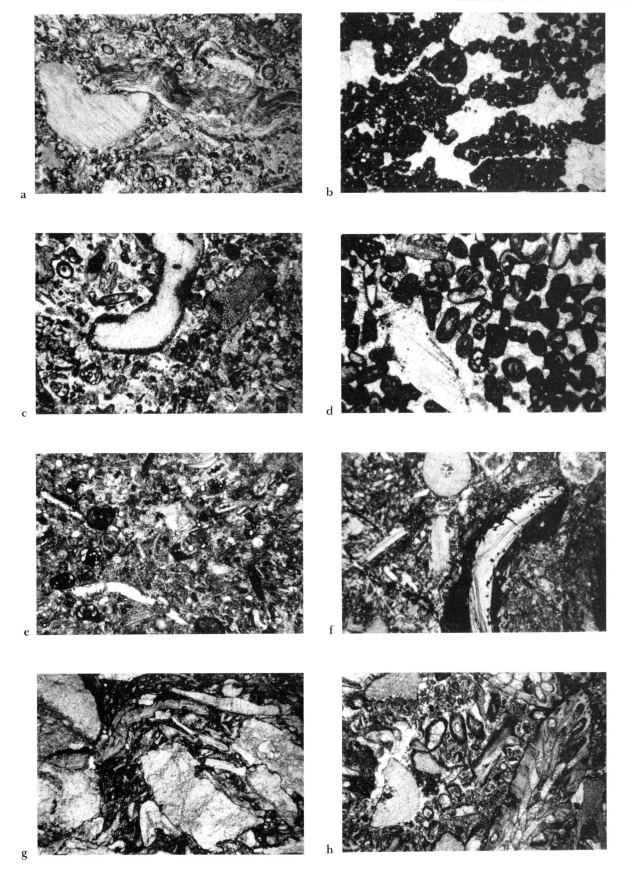

of light grey grainstone up to 4 m thick is present at many sections, and is the equivalent of the 'White Post' of Burgess and Mitchell (1976).

Over much of their outcrop the Upper Hawes and Gayle limestones are lithologically similar, and are separated only by a thin siliciclastic unit. They are difficult to subdivide in many sections and have been mapped as a single lithostratigraphic unit. In the best sections and in borehole cores, however, it is possible to detect thin mudstone partings or more argillaceous limestones which represent the mudstone below the Gayle Limestone; these are used to separate the two limestones on the comparative sections (Figure 14). The Upper Hawes Limestone is a thin, 'platy' bedded, medium to medium-light grey coarse calcarenite to calcirudite, crinoidal and bryozoan packstone. It generally varies from 7 to 10 m in thickness, but is 6 m on Fountains Fell and 13 m on Parson's Pulpit. It contains a poor macrofauna, apart from ubiquitous crinoid and bryozoan debris. The Gayle Limestone is also a thin-bedded, crinoidal and bryozoan packstone (Plate 8g) in most areas, but tends to be slightly darker (medium grey). At Bordley, however, exposures in Cow Gill [9364 6428] and Bordley Beck [9432 6423 to 9433 6425] show cross-bedded medium and coarse calcarenites (medium grey) at the base and top of the limestone, with a conspicuous nodular, medium-dark grey, fine to medium calcarenite containing abundant *Gigantoproductus spp.* in the middle of the unit. The Gayle Limestone is generally 7 to 8 m thick, but is thicker at Bordley (12 m) and Parson's Pulpit (14 m). At the latter locality abrupt thickness variations are present on the southwestern side of the hill and have the form of lenticular swellings. The macrofauna shows a marked areal variation. North of the North Craven Fault, the limestone commonly contains a rich shelly fauna with gigantoproductids and this fauna is well developed in the High Mark and Hawkswick Clowder area. South of the North Craven Fault, the shelly fauna is not conspicuous except in the Bordley section where it assumes more of the character of the northern area, and includes *Diphyphyllum lateseptatum*, *Lithostrotion pauciradiale*, *Gigantoproductus* cf. *gaylensis*, *G. sp. gigantoides* group and *G.* cf. *okensis*.

A dark grey calcareous mudstone separates the Gayle from the Hardraw Scar Limestone and is the oldest persistant mudstone unit in the Wensleydale Group within the district. On Fountains Fell this mudstone is up to 6 m thick, but it thins on Parson's Pulpit to less than 1 m. In Cominco Borehole S4 [8606 6470] 6 m of mudstone are present with thin limestone interbeds, the mudstones containing *Eomarginifera cambriensis*, *Plicochonetes buchianus*, *Rhipidomella michelini* and abundant bryozoans.

The Hardraw Scar Limestone crops out on Fountains Fell and Out Fell, in the Parson's Pulpit – High Mark area, at Feizor, in a continouous outcrop from Overclose through Back Scar and Grizedales to Haw Knab, at Bordley, and on High South Bank. It varies in thickness from 18 m on Fountains Fell to 13 m at Great Scar and in the Feizor Borehole [7870 6722]. On Parson's Pulpit only 8 m are present, but here the limestone is directly overlain by the Dirt Pot Grit which may rest on an erosion surface. Chert-bearing limestone referable to the Hardraw Scar Limestone occurs on Low South Bank [8537 6319] and High South Bank [8555 6327] south of the Middle Craven Fault, but here it cannot be separated from the Gayle and Upper Hawes, and the three limestones form a condensed sequence only 5 m thick. The Hardraw Scar Limestone is represented by a single unit of limestone in most sections, but at Cow Gill [9316 6454 to 9325 6446], Bordley, a 15 m sequence is separated into two leaves by 5 m of mudstone, a feature of this limestone in Wensleydale (Moore, 1958) and at Whernside and Ingleborough (Hicks, 1959). The lithology of the limestone is variable. Generally it is medium-dark grey and argillaceous at its base and near its top, where it consists of coarse calcarenites, packstones and wackestones, grading to calcisiltite. Light grey limestones generally occur in the middle part of the sequence and

are represented by coarse calcarenite and calcirudite crinoidal packstones and grainstones (Plate 8h). Some of the latter exhibit large scale cross-bedding, as for example at High Scar [9171 6884] on the western side of Parson's Pulpit, and contain discrete buildups (up to 6 m high) which are well seen in an exposure [8657 6470] on the western side of Grizedales and in the Great Scar section [8593 6452]. Chert occurs as bands or nodules throughout, and fossils are generally silicified.

The Hardraw Scar Limestone carries a rich fauna of corals and brachiopods. In the Great Scar section the fauna includes *Diphyphyllum lateseptatum*, *Lithostrotion junceum*, *L. pauciradiale*, *Londsdaleia floriformis*, *Palaeosmilia murchisoni*, *Antiquatonia sulcata* and *Pugilis pugilis*. Outcrops in this vicinity, including an old quarry [8630 6438], also contain abundant *Actinoconchus lamellosus*, which are generally silicified and are conspicuous on weathered surfaces, with abundant trepostome bryozoans (Plate 8H). In an exposure [7960 6680] ENE of Brunton House cherty Hardraw Scar Limestone contains a similar coral–brachiopod fauna, but here *Orionastraea edmondsi* and *O. phillipsi* occur. Similar rich faunas were obtained from the Gingling Hole section [8573 7016] on the western side of Out Fell.

A variable thickness of siliciclastics separates the Hardraw Scar Limestone from the Simonstone Limestone. These include dark grey mudstones (calcareous and non-calcareous) with abundant ironstone nodules (well exposed in Clattering Sike [8698 6498] in the Grizedales area), and a sandstone, the Dirt Pot Grit, on the eastern side of Fountains Fell and on the summit of Parson's Pulpit [9184 6875]. On the north-east side of Fountains Fell, this sandstone is 10 m thick and is separated from the Hardraw Scar Limestone by at least 4 m of mudstone, but it thins and passes laterally southwards into mudstone. On Parson's Pulpit 4 m of the Dirt Pot Grit rest directly on the Hardraw Scar Limestone; here the sandstone is fine and medium grained and is pinkish grey in colour.

Younger Wensleydale Group strata occur on Fountains Fell and Out Fell, at Feizor, in the Gorbeck – Black Hill area (north of Back Scar), at Bordley, and on High South Bank. Although it is possible to divide this part of the sequence into named units on Fountains Fell, calibration in the other areas is somewhat tentative because of facies variations, and is based largely on the order of superposition.

The Simonstone Limestone is represented on Fountains Fell by about 15 m of strata and is split into two leaves by a mudstone unit up to 4 m thick. The limestone is a medium to dark grey, unevenly grained calcarenite packstone, locally crinoidal, which is thin- and thick-bedded. The Feizor Borehole [7870 6722] was sited on a small outcrop of Simonstone Limestone and proved 9.5 m of the unit consisting of a dark grey calcisiltite which contained *Lithostrotion junceum* and latissimoid productoids. In the Gorbeck area [860 657] and in the Black Hill Borehole [8630 6628] about 20 m of limestone with interbedded thin mudstones have been referred to this formation. The limestone here is medium to medium-dark grey, and varies from coarse calcarenite and calcirudite (crinoidal packstone and wackestone) to calcisiltite; *Lithostrotion junceum* is recorded. The correlative in crags [9316 6459] at Bordley is 12 m of limestone which is chert-bearing and medium-dark grey at its base, overlain by 8 m of medium grey grainstone which contains conspicuous lithoclasts (both limestone and sandy limestone), ooliths and scattered algal nodules. The lowest dark limestones yielded productoids, including *Gigantoproductus edelbergensis* and *G. sp. giganteus* group, *G. okensis*, and foraminifera of early Brigantian type.

The Middle Limestone on Fountains Fell and Out Fell is represented by about 7 m of medium and medium-light grey, medium and coarse calcarenite crinoidal packstone, which are underlain by 2 to 4 m of thinly bedded fine-grained sandstone. This sandstone is separated from the underlying Simonstone Limestone by about 15 m of siltstone and silty mudstone which contain 2 m of interbedded and unnamed limestone (medium calcarenite packstone-wackestone with disseminated crinoid plates and shell fragments). Wensleydale Group strata equivalent to, or younger than, the Middle Limestone are preserved in the other outcrops within the district only on High South Bank, Stockdale, where about 14 m of medium grey, fine to medium calcarenite grainstone are present in the Cominco Borehole S8 [8562 6352] and are well exposed in old quarries [e.g. 8565 6344] on the northern flanks of the hill. This limestone contains a late Brigantian foraminiferal fauna including the genus *Asteroarchaediscus* which is typical of the Cockleshell Limestone (the middle leaf of the Middle Limestone in Wensleydale). On High South Bank, the Middle Limestone is separated from the condensed Upper Hawes to Hardraw Scar sequence by a thin mudstone.

Outcrops of beds above the Middle Limestone are confined to the Fountains Fell area where the Underset Limestone (the youngest limestone unit in the Brigantian part of the Wensleydale Group) is separated from the Middle Limestone by about 28 m of micaceous siltstone, locally containing ironstone nodules and two thin (about 1 m) sandstones. No representatives of the Five Yard or Three Yard limestones are present. On Fountains Fell the Underset Limestone is 10 m thick-bedded medium grey, fine calcarenite packstone which is fetid and contains lenticular chert nodules.

DJCM,LCJ,RSA,EWJ

CRAVEN BASIN

Chatburn Limestone (Chadian) and older strata

Some 240 m of limestones in the core of the Slaidburn Anticline, classified as Chatburn Limestone following Parkinson (1936), are the oldest Dinantian strata at outcrop within the district (Figure 15). The detailed lithostratigraphical equivalence to the succession at Chatburn (Parkinson, 1926; Earp and others, 1961) has not been determined, and the algal layers characteristic of much of the Chatburn sequence (Figure 16) are not known at Slaidburn although *Solenopora* has been identified in thin section.

The limestones are well bedded with muddy partings, and comprise medium-dark grey, bioclastic and peloidal wackestones and packstones; grain-size ranges from fine calcarenite to calcirudite. The principal grains are crinoid plates, calcispheres, foraminifera, peloids and kamaenid algae. Crinoid plates tend to be partially replaced by chalcedonic quartz. In places the matrix is partially or completely neomorphosed to spar (Plate 9a and b).

Individual beds range in thickness from a few centimetres to more than 0.8 m, the bedding planes being flat or wavy. Some of the limestones in the lower part of the sequence show crude lamination, cross-lamination or cross-bedding, and chert layers or nodules occur through most of the sequence. Layers of micaceous silty mudstone are present in the lowest strata, and higher in the formation there are muddy layers up to 3 m thick. Foraminifera from the middle and upper parts of the succession include *Brunsia* cf. *spirillinoides*, cf. *Dainella sp.* and *Eblania michoti* and indicate an early Chadian age.

The Haw Bank Limestone of the Skipton and Broughton anticlines (Hudson and Mitchell, 1937; Hudson, 1944a) has been widely regarded as an equivalent of the Chatburn Limestone (see Tiddeman, 1891; Hudson, 1933; Fewtrell and Smith, 1980), though this view was not supported by Ramsbottom (1974). The equivalence is, however, accepted here (Figure 16), and it is probable that the Chatburn Limestone/Haw Bank Limestone occurs extensively at depth in the basinal area of the Settle district.

Tiddeman in Settle Sheet Primary Survey (1892)	Parkinson (1936)	Hudson and Mitchell (1937)	Hudson (1944a)	Earp and others (1961)		Fewtrell and Smith (1980)	THIS RESURVEY			
							Craven Basin	Askrigg Block - Transition Zone	STAGES	SERIES
Bowland Shales (part)	Lower Bowland Shales	Middle Bowland Shales / Nettleber Sandstone / Lower Bowland Shales / Draughton Shales		Lower Bowland Shales		Bowland Formation (part)	Lower Bowland Shales	Wensleydale Group	BRIGANTIAN	
Pendleside Limestone	Pendleside Limestone	Draughton Limestone Series		Pendleside Limestone		Pendleside Formation	Pendleside Limestone	Malham Formation	ASBIAN	VISÉAN
	B. hodderense Band			*B. hodderense* Beds					HOLKERIAN	
Shales - with - Limestones	Worston Series	Skibeden Shales	Skibeden Shales - with - Limestone	Worston Shales		Worston Formation	Worston Shales	Kilnsey Formation	ARUNDIAN	
		Embsay Limestone	Broughton Beds	Salt Hill Knoll Limestones				Chapel House Limestone		
		NON SEQUENCE	Butterhaw Limestone / Butterhaw Shales-with-Limestone					(rests on Lower Palaeozoic rocks on Askrigg Block)	CHADIAN	
			Thornton Limestone	Peach Quarry Limestone		Clitheroe Formation	Thornton Limestone			
Clitheroe Limestones	Clitheroe Limestone	Halton Shales-with-Limestones	Thornton Shales - with - Limestone	Coplow Knoll Limestones			Thornton Shales - with - Limestone	NON SEQUENCE		
		Haw Bank Limestone	Haw Bank Limestone	Chatburn Limestone		Chatburn Formation	Chatburn Limestone	Stockdale Farm Formation	IVORIAN	TOURNAISIAN
Black Limestone of Chatburn etc.			Haw Bank Limestone-with-Shales	Gisburn Cotes Beds				(in Transition Zone only)		

Figure 15 Classifications of Dinantian strata in the Craven Basin

Muddy and silty limestones, mudstones, siltstones and fine-grained sandstones of the Haw Bank Limestones-with-Shales (Hudson, 1944a) underlie the Haw Bank Limestone at Skipton and Broughton, and 657 m (corrected for dip) of lithologically similar strata of Tournaisian age were proved in the Swinden No.1 Borehole [8597 5051] to the south of the district (see Figure 16 and Charsley, 1984). The latter strata are equivalent to the Gisburn Cotes Beds of the Clitheroe district (Earp and others, 1961). Gravity data (Chapter 8) suggest the existence of perhaps an additional 3 km of Tournaisian or ?late Devonian strata in the Craven Basin, and it is probable that this thick layer of Tournaisian strata extends at depth into the basinal part of the Settle district.

There is no clear equivalent of the Chatburn Limestone in the block-marginal sequence proved in the Stockdale Farm Borehole (Figure 17); however, the interbedded limestones and mudstones, forming the upper part of the Stockdale Farm Formation have yielded early Chadian foraminifera and may be a marginal counterpart.

DETAILS

The lowest exposed Chatburn Limestone at Slaidburn consists of about 3 m of micaceous silty mudstone and is seen in a ditch [7003 5236] south-west of Pages. The mudstone is partly calcareous and includes shells and crinoidal debris. In a stream [6989 5194 to 6995 5195] SE of Pain Hill, crinoidal mudstone with fenestellid bryozoans overlies crinoidal wackestone, and in the bank [6929 5245] of a stream north of Pain Hill slipped debris of micaceous silty mudstone is exposed. Limestones low in the sequence are seen in a 10 m quarry section [7057 5247] south-east of Pages where thick and wavy-bedded, medium-dark grey, cherty wackestones and packstones with muddy partings predominate. The limestones are sparsely to richly crinoidal, and lamination and cross-lamination are apparent.

Some 100 m of succeeding strata are partially exposed in Croasdale Beck [7063 5297 to 7105 5251], upstream from Slaidburn (Figure 17). They comprise thick- and thin-, wavy- and flat-bedded, medium to medium-dark grey crinoidal packstones and wackestones (Plate 9b) commonly with chert nodules, and with muddy wisps and partings. Foraminifera from these strata include *Brunsia* cf. *spirillinoides*, cf. *Dainella sp.*, *Eblania michoti* and *Glomospiranella dainae*, indicating an early Chadian age. The lower beds, up to a conspicuous 0.6 m mudstone, are poorly laminated in parts, and a thin-section [7068 5228] shows the packstone matrix to be completely neomorphosed to spar. A 2 m bed of partly calcareous mudstone lies some 10 m higher in the sequence, and includes well preserved crinoid stems and plates. A thin section from a sample [7092 5257] from the succeeding limestones shows bioclastic-peloidal packstone with the matrix substantially neomorphosed (Plate 9a); algal clasts include kamaenids and *Solenopora*. The upper part of the Chatburn Limestone is partially exposed downstream from the weir, and includes 3 m of mudstone, partly calcareous and with thin beds of limestone, lying 12 m below the top of the exposed section.

Higher beds, not exposed in Croasdale Brook, include thin- and wavy-bedded, crinoidal, cherty wackestones interbedded with crinoidal calcareous mudstones, and are exposed [7118 5265] ENE of Townhead. Similar strata, though without chert, crop out [7075 5223 to 7085 5233 and 7071 5216 to 7084 5212] on the hillside SW of Slaidburn village.

A quarry [6905 5253] north-east of New Biggin exposes 23.5 m of thin- and medium-bedded, flat- to wavy-bedded, medium-dark grey packstones and wackestones high in the sequence. Diffuse muddy partings, some shelly and crinoidal, are common, and chert nodules are present in some parts. Foraminifera from these limestones include *Eblania michoti*. A thin section shows bioclastic peloidal packstone of fine to medium calcarenite; the matrix is partially neomorphosed to spar.

Thornton Shales-with-Limestone (Chadian)

Hudson (1944a, p.201) applied this name to the poorly exposed strata between the Haw Bank Limestone (below) and the Thornton Limestone in the Broughton and Thornton anticlines (Figure 15); he estimated their thickness to be about 183 m. No satisfactory definition of this division applicable to the Settle district has been achieved during the resurvey because of lithological variation between the isolated outcrops, and the comparative sections in Figure 17 should be regarded as tentative.

The Thornton Shales-with-Limestone comprise mudstones and calcareous mudstones with differing amounts of limestone, mostly muddy and thinly bedded, but including some thick-bedded units. They also include knoll-reef limestones, and that at Newsholme (near Paythorne) is the largest at crop, with an estimated thickness of about 65 m. The Thornton Shales-with-Limestone are the oldest strata to crop out in those parts of the Swinden and Broughton anticlines within the district; at Swinden some 130 m are estimated from outcrop and borehole sections; and at Broughton at least 100 m are estimated at crop. Farther north, in the Airton Anticline, a faulted sequence of 96 m of mudstone and muddy limestone referred to the Thornton Shales-with-Limestone was proved under Thornton Limestone in the High Ings Barn Borehole.

In the Slaidburn Anticline the Thornton Shales-with-Limestone appear to form a much thinner, even impersistent, division. They are not mappable along part of the north-western limb of the anticline, and were not recorded in the Bowland Forest Tunnel (Earp, 1955). On the south-eastern limb 39 m of mudstones and muddy limestones capped by 41 m of knoll-reef limestones were proved in the Blue Butts Farm Borehole, just within the Clitheroe district, and there is a small outcrop of knoll-reef limestone at a similar stratigraphic level in Slaidburn village. The mudstones in the borehole have been classified as Thornton Shales-with-Limestone, but it is questionable whether the reef limestones should also be included in this division, and a grouping with the Thornton Limestone may be more appropriate.

The upper limit of the Thornton Shales-with-Limestone in the Broughton Anticline corresponds to that employed by Hudson (1944a) and is some 50 m below the '10 Feet Shale'. Similarly on the eastern limb of the Swinden Anticline, the upper limit is in accord with that of Hudson and Dunnington (1944), and is taken at the base of the limestone forming the 'Lower Scar' at Marton Scars. On the north-western limb, some 24 m of mudstones with subordinate muddy limestones, regarded as belonging to the Thornton Shales-with-Limestone, were proved under the Thornton Limestone in the High Laithe Borehole. Hudson and Dunnington (1944) took the boundary (on this limb) about 125 m below this junction and included the knoll-reef limestones [848 519 and 872 524] near Newsholme and Flambers Hill in the Thornton Limestone.

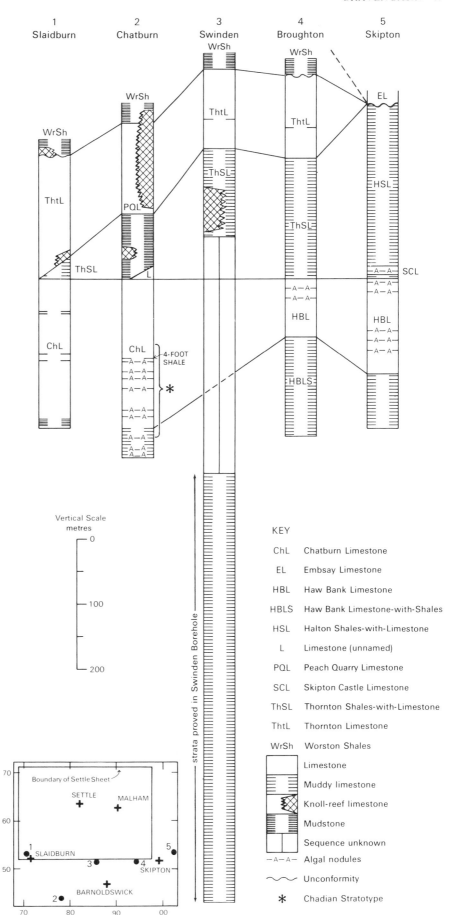

Figure 16 Generalised comparative sections of Tournaisian and early Viséan strata in the Settle district and adjoining parts of the Craven Basin.

Sources: 1; This resurvey. 2; Earp and others, 1961 and Chatburn By-pass section (this resurvey). 3; This resurvey and Charsley, 1984. 4; This resurvey and Hudson, 1944a. 5; Hudson and Mitchell, 1937 and Arthurton, 1983

Vertical Scale
metres

KEY

ChL   Chatburn Limestone

EL   Embsay Limestone

HBL   Haw Bank Limestone

HBLS   Haw Bank Limestone-with-Shales

HSL   Halton Shales-with-Limestone

L   Limestone (unnamed)

PQL   Peach Quarry Limestone

SCL   Skipton Castle Limestone

ThSL   Thornton Shales-with-Limestone

ThtL   Thornton Limestone

WrSh   Worston Shales

Limestone

Muddy limestone

Knoll-reef limestone

Mudstone

Sequence unknown

-A—A-   Algal nodules

〜〜〜   Unconformity

✳   Chadian Stratotype

In the extreme south-east of the district there is an outcrop of mudstones on the northern limb of the Skipton Anticline belonging to the Halton Shales-with-Limestone of Hudson and Mitchell (1937). Part of these mudstones may be the equivalent of the Thornton Shales-with-Limestone farther west.

No age-diagnostic fossils have been recovered from the Thornton Shales-with-Limestone.

DETAILS

Broughton Anticline

Limestones and muddy limestones of the Thornton Shales-with-Limestone are exposed sporadically WSW of Oxen Close. The lowest beds [9332 5177] are partly laminated muddy limestones. Higher in the sequence 6.7 m of thick- and thin-bedded limestones are exposed [9319 5177], the lowest 2 m being irregularly laminated calcisiltites, but higher beds are crinoidal and partly shelly packstones, with chert at the top. Muddy and partly platy calcisiltites are exposed in a small quarry [9320 5182] near the top of the sequence. The highest 5 m, comprising mudstones and muddy limestones with a 0.7 m limestone at the base, are exposed [9303 5175] under 8.9 m of mostly thick-bedded Thornton Limestone.

Swinden Anticline

On the north-western limb, fissile, crinoidal, calcareous siltstones and muddy limestones with nodules and bands of dolomitic limestone crop out in a ditch [8507 5196] near Slack. These are the lowest strata exposed, and appear to lie stratigraphically below the base of the Newsholme knoll-reef limestone, exposed some 200 m to the west. A disused quarry [8480 5194] in this build-up shows dolomitised, vughy and laminated wackestones overlying massive wackestone, and a section [8474 5196] nearby exposes dolomitised shelly packstone. In the Dobbers Quarry Borehole [8471 5194] knoll-reef limestone, consisting mainly of medium grey, vughy wackestone with sparse to abundant bryozoa, crinoid and shell debris, and disseminated dolomite, was proved from 1.15 m below surface to 56.90 m. Allowing for a tectonic dip of 30°, the thickness of knoll-reef limestone is about 48 m. Below this, some 9 m of calcareous mudstone and muddy limestone were proved to the base of the hole at 67.40 m. Interbedded fissile, partly micaceous mudstones, siltstones and flaggy calcisiltites, stratigraphically higher than the Newsholme knoll-reef, are exposed [8455 5219 to 8469 5214] in a stream some 200 m to the north. Mudstones and limestones at about this level were proved in a borehole [8438 5182] just within the Clitheroe district, from a depth of 0.9 m to 37.5 m; below this depth, there was limestone with a few muddy beds (knoll-reef limestone) to 105.5 m, and mudstone from there to the base of the hole at 106.7 m.

In the High Laithe Borehole [8606 5301] near Nappa, the Thornton Shales-with-Limestone were entered at 72.31 m and drilled to the base of the hole at 98.06 m; allowing for a dip of 22°, the thickness proved is about 24 m, mostly of micaceous, calcareous mudstones.

On the eastern limb, the Thornton Shales-with-Limestone are exposed south-east of Flambers Hill in ground forming part of the Marton Scar section described by Hudson and Dunnington (1944). A limestone partially exposed in a small quarry [8788 5181] is calculated to be about 40 m thick, with its top lying some 20 m below the base of the Thornton Limestone. Hudson and Dunnington described 4.6 m of 'black flaggy limestone and shales' underlying this limestone in nearby quarries along the strike to the south.

Slaidburn Anticline

Calcareous mudstones and subordinate dolomitic muddy limestones, regarded as Thornton Shales-with-Limestone, were entered below the knoll-reef limestone of Dunnow (see Parkinson, 1936; Earp and others, 1961) at 50.92 m in the Blue Butts Farm Borehole [7029 5123], just within the Clitheroe district. These mudstones were drilled to the base of the hole at 98.90 m, and allowing for a dip of 30° their proved thickness is about 39 m. They are generally fossiliferous, with crinoidal debris, brachiopods, caninioid and zaphrentoid corals, and bryozoa including *Fenestella sp.* The topmost 9 m are transitional to the knoll-reef limestone, and include thin beds and irregular lenses of medium grey dolomitic wackestone of reef facies.

Fossiliferous bryozoa-rich mudstones, probably not exceeding 5 m thick, occur between the Chatburn and Thornton limestones on the north-western limb of the anticline, and are taken to be Thornton Shales-with-Limestone; they are partially exposed in Lanshaw Brook [7043 5339] near Bridge End. Farther south-west similar fossiliferous mudstones are poorly exposed underlying the Thornton Limestone in the banks [6903 5255] of Eller Beck near New Biggin.

Airton Anticline

Calcareous mudstones, siltstones and muddy limestones of the Thornton Shales-with-Limestone were proved in the High Ings Barn Borehole [8867 6031] near Airton, from 97.94 m to the base of the hole at 221.90 m. Allowing for 40 to 50° dips, but not for the presumed small effects of three faults, the thickness proved is about 93 m. The mudstones and siltstones are slightly to richly micaceous, and generally bioturbated; the limestones are mostly thin bedded to nodular, dark or medium-dark grey, muddy or silty wackestones with fine to medium crinoidal debris. Corals including *Syringopora sp.*, and brachiopods are common in the lower part of the sequence. Less muddy limestone with some chert lies 23 to 30 m below the top. Partly muddy limestones with some chert presumed to lie within the top 30 m of the sequence are exposed in disused quarries [8851 6010 to 8850 6005] SSW of the borehole and in a pit [8885 5978] near Low Scarth Barn.

Thornton Limestone (Chadian)

A widespread limestone division of varied lithofacies conformably succeeds the Thornton Shales-with-Limestone. The name 'Thornton Limestone' was given to this division by Hudson (1944a) in the Thornton and Broughton anticlines, and in this account the use of this name is extended to lithostratigraphic equivalents in the Slaidburn, Airton and Eshton anticlines (Figure 15). Foraminifera including *Eblania michoti*, *Eoparastaffella sp.*, *E. restricta*, *E. simplex*, *Eotextularia sp.*, *E. diversa* and *Spinoendothyra mitchelli*, and coral-brachiopod faunas including *Levitusia humerosa* and *Siphonophyllia cylindrica*, show that the formation is of Chadian age. The Thornton Limestone has not been recognised in boreholes in the Craven Reef Belt nor in the Skipton Anticline.

There are three principal lithofacies and these occur in sequence (Figure 17). The lowest, absent from the Slaidburn Anticline and unproved in the Eshton–Hetton Anticline, comprises up to 80 m of limestones with subordinate mudstones and muddy limestones. This lithofacies includes units of thick-bedded to massive, medium to medium-light grey packstones and grainstones, and is the 'light coloured

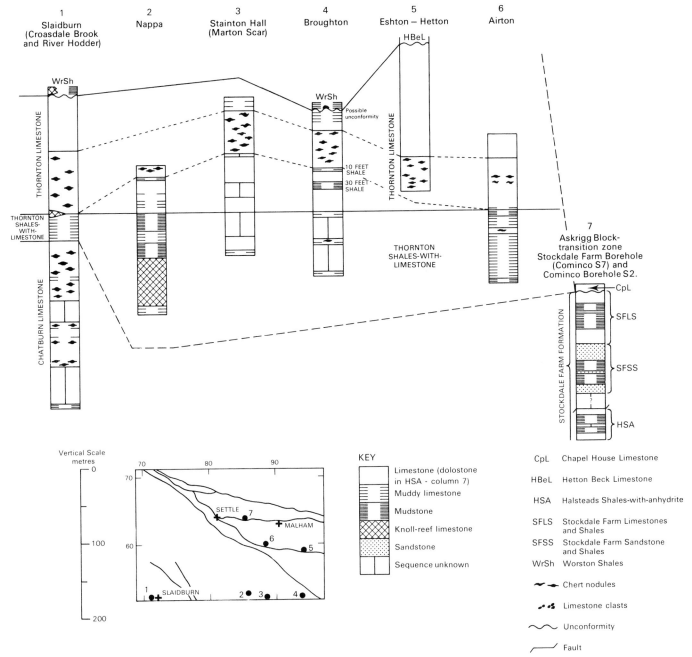

Figure 17 Comparative sections of Tournaisian–Chadian strata below the top of the Thornton Limestone. Sequence in transition zone is shown for reference

fragmental limestones' described by Hudson and Dunnington (1944) at Marton Scar in the Swinden Anticline and by Hudson (1944a) at Clints Rock, Broughton. It includes the '30 ft' and '10 ft' shales of Hudson (1944a), the latter marking the junction of his 'Lower' and 'Upper Thornton' limestones.

The succeeding lithofacies is up to 75 m thick and is present in all crops, though only poorly developed at Airton. It comprises thick- and thin-bedded limestones ranging from medium-dark grey wackestones to medium-light grey grainstones (Plate 9c and d) with pronounced wavy to lenticular bedding, and in some sections conspicuous cross-bedding; it is characterised by abundant chert bands and nodules.

The uppermost lithofacies is also present in all outcrops of the Thornton Limestone. It consists of uniform, flat- to wavy-bedded, medium-dark grey wackestones and packstones with subordinate lighter coloured grainstones; in most sections there are sops of the tabulate coral *Syringopora sp.* Mudstone is present locally either as partings or thicker beds, but chert is generally absent. Its thickness ranges from an estimated 150 m in the Eshton–Hetton Anticline to less than 30 m in parts of the Broughton Anticline. At the western end of the Eshton–Hetton Anticline near Bell Busk, the top of this lithofacies is an irregular erosion surface under the Worston Shales, and the Worston Shales rest on a particularly thin development of this unit in the Butterhaw Borehole in the Broughton Anticline, suggesting that there too the top of the formation may be an erosion surface. Pre-Worston Shales erosion is also apparent near Hammerton Hall on the south-eastern limb of the Slaidburn Anticline, where a knoll-reef limestone at the base of the Worston Shales rests with angular unconformity on the Thornton Limestone (Plate 10).

DETAILS

Slaidburn Anticline

Strata here classified as Thornton Limestone were referred to the upper part of the Clitheroe Limestone by Parkinson (1936). The lower lithofacies is absent from this area, but the cherty limestones of the middle lithofacies (75 to 85 m thick) are well exposed in natural and quarry sections north of Slaidburn, notably in Lanshaw Brook [7028 5362 to 7043 5340] near Bridge End, in the River Hodder [7168 5399 to 7179 5384] near Hammerton Hall, and in the numerous quarries around Wood House Gate. Thin sections of grainstones from one of these latter quarries [7111 5374] show the principal grains to be crinoid plates, foraminifera, ostracods, mollusc fragments and kamaenid algae; the matrix is slightly neomorphosed, and quartz occurs as a replacement of grains and cement (Plate 9c). The foraminiferal assemblages from these limestones include *Bessiella sp*, *Eblania michoti*, *Endothyra* aff. *paraspinosa*, *Eoparastaffella sp.*, *Eotextularia sp.*, *Florennella sp.*, cf. *Latiendothyranopsis sp.*, *Lugtonia monilis*, *Palaeospiroplectammina mellina* and *Spinoendothyra mitchelli*, and confirm a Chadian age which is further supported by the recovery of *Levitusia humerosa*, a diagnostic Chadian brachiopod, from one of the Wood House Gate quarries [7110 5383].

A small outcrop of knoll-reef limestone, comprising about 5 m of massive to crudely bedded medium grey, vughy wackestone, is present at what is taken as the base of the Thornton Limestone in the stream bank [7121 5248] at Old Bridge, Slaidburn. The relation of this knoll-reef to higher beds is not seen here, but in a section [7050 5176 to 7061 5175] in Dunnow Syke just within the Clitheroe district, the cherty grainstone-bearing lithofacies is intercalated with thick-bedded to massive (reefal) wackestones which form the basal part of the analogous Dunnow knoll-reef. A similar relationship was proved nearby in the Blue Butts Farm Borehole [7029 5123].

On the north-western limb of the anticline a stream section [6900 5256] near New Biggin exposes 13 m of a limestone at the base of the Thornton Limestone of a facies not known elsewhere. These beds are wavy-bedded to lenticular, medium-dark grey calcarenite wackestones and muddy wackestones, and are sparsely to richly crinoidal. They include coral biostromes forming mounds up to 0.3 m high and have yielded *Caninophyllum patulum*, a species known to range from Ivorian to Chadian.

The upper, non-cherty lithofacies at Slaidburn is best exposed around the north-eastern closure of the anticline where up to 70 m are calculated to be present. The topmost 7 m of limestone, in wavy beds up to 0.5 m thick and including *Syringopora sp.*, are exposed under Worston Shales in Phynis Beck [7151 5429 to 7155 5427], near Phynis. Similar well-bedded, medium-dark grey calcarenite wackestones with muddy wisps form a 4 m quarry section [7186 5412] north of Hammerton Hall where corals including silicified *Syringopora sp.* are common. Traced towards Slaidburn, this upper lithofacies thins, apparently due to erosion pre-dating the accumulation of the overlying Worston Shales, and at The Crag [7176 5320], south of Barn Gill, knoll-reef limestone (basal Worston Shales) rests with angular unconformity on about 30 m of the upper lithofacies (Plate 10).

Catlow Anticline

Farther north, in the core of the Catlow Anticline near Lamb Hill Farm, a quarry section [7072 5820] exposes thick- and thin-bedded, irregular- to wavy-bedded, medium to medium-dark grey wackestones and packstones with chert nodules and irregular muddy partings. These beds are tentatively classified as Thornton Limestone. A thin-section from this locality shows bioclastic-peloidal, fine to medium calcarenite packstone, with interclasts of wackestone and lime-mudstone. The principal grains are foraminifera, calcispheres, peloids, kamaenida and crinoid plates, some of which have minor internal replacement by quartz, and the matrix has been completely neomorphosed to spar. Foraminifera from this locality include cf. *Dainella sp.*, *Eoparastaffella simplex* and cf. *Eoparastaffella sp.*

Swinden Anticline

The resurvey confirms the Thornton Limestone succession described by Hudson and Dunnington (1944) in the outcrops on the eastern limb, but not that on the north-western limb. In the east the formation is best exposed south-east of Flambers Hill; the 'Marton Scar' section of Hudson and Dunnington. The lowest lithofacies, including about 80 m of well bedded, medium-light grey crinoidal packstones and grainstones, is exposed in small disused quarries [8804 5193; 8811 5200] in features extending northwards from the 'Marton Scar'; the overlying chert-rich lithofacies (about 55 m) is seen in numerous quarries [8832 5218; 8844 5210; 8848 5226] to the north-east. Limestones with interbedded mudstones of the topmost subdivision, up to 50 m thick, are exposed in a disused quarry [8802 5312] farther north, near Stainton Hall.

On the north-western flank of the Swinden Anticline, the lowest beds were proved in the High Laithe Borehole [8606 5301] near Nappa. The lower chert-free facies here comprises about 55 m of limestones with subordinate muddy limestones and calcareous, micaceous mudstone interbeds. The limestones range from medium-dark grey wackestones to medium grey grainstones. Some 9 m of the overlying cherty facies were proved in the top part of this borehole. A comparable but thinner sequence is partially exposed south-west of Nappa at Hull's Delf quarry [8463 5227] and in a nearby gully [8446 5228]; limestones from the quarry yielded *Levitusia humerosa*. Underlying mudstones and the Newsholme knoll-reef limestone are not included in the Thornton Limestone, though they were by Hudson and Dunnington (1944).

Broughton Anticline

The description of the Thornton Limestone given by Hudson (1944a) remains largely unmodified. The lowest 70 m or so of the sequence are partially exposed at Clints Delf [9303 5175], south-east of Pasture House. The basal 9 m of limestone consist of thin- and thick-bedded, medium to medium-dark grey packstones and subordinate grainstones, and are richly crinoidal with shelly layers. Higher in the sequence a section [9290 5176 – 9295 5178] exposes 26 m of strata including the '10 ft shale' of Hudson (1944a), which here consists of 2.1 m of crinoidal fissile mudstone with thin bands of limestone. Below this mudstone there are about 9 m of shelly, crinoidal packstones, and above it there are 3.5 m of medium grey, fine calcarenite packstones, followed by 10.9 m of thick- and thin-bedded, medium-dark grey packstones and wackestones with subordinate muddy limestone and interbeds of mudstone. These latter limestones include sparse to abundant medium to coarse crinoidal debris, and are partly wavy bedded towards the top.

Limestones in the overlying chert-rich facies are exposed in a disused quarry [9424 5205] west of Small House where wavy-bedded, medium to medium-dark grey, crinoidal packstones and wackestones with bands and nodules of black chert are present. The cherty facies was proved in the Butterhaw Borehole [9346 5259] from 72.8 m to the base at 99.9 m, and allowing for a dip of 30 to 35° the thickness proved is about 23 m. The topmost lithofacies of the Thornton Limestone was drilled in this borehole from 42.6 m to 72.8 m, a thickness, allowing for dips of 18 to 30°, of about 25 m; it comprises limestones with interbedded muddy limestones and mudstones, the limestones being medium to medium-dark grey, mostly wackestones and packstones but including some layers of grainstone. In the borehole the junction with the overlying Worston Shales is sharp but the basal mudstones are listricised and include clasts of Thornton Limestone. It is uncertain whether this junction represents a tectonic or an erosive break.

Eshton – Hetton Anticline

The base of the Thornton Limestone is not known at crop or in boreholes in this anticline. Even so the formation is calculated to be thicker than elsewhere in the district, although this may be exaggerated by unrecognised structural repetition. The lowest strata belong to the cherty limestone lithofacies and are best seen near Hetton. A disused quarry [9579 5901] north-west of the village exposes some 40 m of locally dolomitised thin-bedded fine calcarenite wackestones and packstones with scattered coarse crinoidal debris and chert nodules; the limestone beds are separated by muddy partings and have yielded *Siphonophyllia sp.* and *Syringopora catenata*. Farther west the cherty limestones are exposed in disused quarries [e.g. 9397 5878; 9388 5869] in the core of the anticline near Winterburn. They are not recorded, however, west of Eshton Beck.

The overlying largely chert-free lithofacies is well exposed in disused quarries [e.g. 9110 5708; 9114 5672 to 9118 5660] south of Eshton Moor. These show 16.5 m of thin- and thick-bedded (up to 0.7 m) mostly wavy-bedded, medium-dark grey, fine calcarenite packstone and wackestone, with sparse to abundant medium to coarse crinoidal debris and contain *Siphonophyllia cylindrica*, *Syringopora* cf. *ramulosa* and *S.* cf. *reticulata*. Similar limestones a little higher in the sequence are exposed at the southern end of Haw Crag Quarry [9135 5632] where they are capped by an irregular erosion surface under the Worston Shales. This erosion surface was encountered nearby in the Throstle Nest Borehole [9166 5660] at a depth of 28.6 m, below which Thornton Limestone was drilled to 137.3 m. The macrofauna from this sequence includes *Siphonophyllia cylindrica* and *Syringopora* cf. *reticulata*, and the microfauna *Dainella sp.*, *D. chomatica* and *Eoparastaffella sp.* The limestones are generally medium-dark grey wackestones and packstones, though 0.3 m of medium grey, foraminifera-rich grainstone was encountered at 80.60 m; a thin section of this grainstone shows crinoid plates, foraminifera, kamaenid algae and molluscan fragments to be the principal grains, and other bioclasts include lumps and strands of *Girvanella* and *Koninckopora*. Muddy limestone with the trace fossil *Zoophycos* and interbeds of mudstone feature particularly in the lower part of the borehole sequence, and dolomite occurs both as disseminated rhombs and as replacement of crinoidal debris. One nodule of white chert is recorded at a depth of 70.7 m. Limestones in this part of the sequence are exposed on both flanks of the anticline east of Winterburn; on the northern flank quarries [9395 5884; 9422 5903] have yielded *Siphonophyllia cylindrica*, *Syringopora* cf. *geniculata* and *S.* cf. *reticulata*. These beds are also exposed in disused quarries [e.g. 9549 5958; 9575 5986] north-west of Hetton and [9557 5826] on the southern flank, south-west of Hetton. The latter locality yielded the quadrate form of *Pustula pyxidiformis* which is thought to be restricted to the Chadian.

Boreholes have been drilled for water in the Thornton Limestone near Eshton and Hetton. The bore [9309 5703] at St Helen's Well proved limestone with shale partings from rock-head at 10.7 m to its base at 91.7 m, with an interruption of vein calcite from 74.7 to 80.8 m. The limestone yielded *Delepinea sp.* at 21.6 m, and *Siphonophyllia sp. cylindrica* group is recorded at intervals. The

Thornton Limestone was also proved in the Park Laithe Borehole [9629 5813], south of Hetton, from 164.38 m to the base of the hole at 199.96 m. The junction with the overlying Hetton Beck Limestone (Worston Shales) is interpreted as an unconformity.

Bell Busk

The uppermost, generally chert-free, lithofacies crops out in the core of a small anticline in the South Craven Fault system near Bell Busk. At least 11 m of flat- or wavy-bedded limestones with partings or layers of muddy limestone and mudstone are exposed in a disused quarry [8996 5671] and have yielded *Axophyllum simplex*, *Siphonophyllia cylindrica* and *Syringopora* cf. *reticulata*. These beds are overlain with a sharp junction [8995 5673] by poorly exposed medium-light grey crinoidal wackestone regarded as basal Worston Shales, and have yielded the Chadian reef brachiopod *Spirifer coplowensis*.

Airton Anticline

In this structurally complex anticline, there is no obvious division based on the incidence of chert as in the other outcrops. Instead the formation, previously referred to as the Airton Limestone (Hudson, 1949) in this anticline, comprises: a lower division characterised by thick-bedded to massive packstones and grainstones, mottled medium-dark to medium-light grey and including richly shelly layers, sops of *Syringopora sp.* and scattered nodules of white or grey chert; and an upper division of more uniform thick-bedded, medium-dark grey, fine to medium calcarenite wackestones and packstones with common *Syringopora sp.*

The lower beds were drilled in the High Ings Barn Borehole [8867 6031] from 1.1 m to 97.94 m; allowing for dips of 40 to 45° the proved sequence is about 72 m. The partially dolomitised limestones are muddy to very muddy towards their base, and rest on micaceous mudstones referred to the Thornton Shales-with-Limestone. Thin sections of grainstones at 58.55 m and 73.63 m showed them to be peloidal, bioclastic, medium calcarenites, with peloids, foraminifera, crinoid plates, calcispheres and kamaenid algae as the principal grains; intraclasts of wackestone and limemudstone are also present. The matrix in each sample shows slight neomorphism to spar, and crinoid plates show internal replacement by quartz (Plate 9D). The microfossils from samples between 37.70 and 89.50 m are typically Chadian and include *Bessiella sp.*, *Brunsia spirillinoides*, *Eoparastafella restricta*, *E. simplex*, *Eotextularia diversa*, *Palaeospiroplectammina syzranica* and *Pseudolituotubella multicamerata*. The presence of primitive *Koninckopora sp.* indicates a fairly late Chadian age. Limestones of the lower division are exposed in numerous disused quarries around Low Scarth Barn; one section [8891 5986] near the base exposes 16 m of thick-bedded to massive, partly mottled limestone with muddy layers in the basal metre; shelly layers are conspicuous, particularly at the base and top, and *Syringopora sp.* is common. The upper part of this section includes a low bank-like feature. These beds are also exposed in disused quarries [e.g. 8693 6008] north of Orms Gill Green, and at Airton Green an exposure [8749 5994] has yielded *Delepinea notata*. Airton Green is the type locality of this chonetid which is restricted to the Chadian.

The upper limestone division is exposed [8695 5991] north-west of Orms Gill Green and in the bed and banks of the River Aire at Airton where the outcrop is repeated by faulting. Some 30 to 35 m of these limestones are present in an exposure [9040 5936] near Foss Gill, and about 20 m [9028 5960] 250 m farther north.

Worston Shales (late Chadian to ?Asbian)

A complex division of mudstone and limestone termed Worston Shales succeeds the Thornton Limestone. It extends upwards to the base of the Pendleside Limestone, or where this is absent to the base of the Lower Bowland Shales. Its age ranges from Chadian to possibly Asbian.

The name Worston Shales (Figure 15) has been applied informally in the Slaidburn area (Parkinson, 1936) and in other parts of the Craven Basin (Earp and others, 1961, Miller and Grayson, 1972, George and others, 1976 and Fewtrell and Smith, 1980). It has also been used in other classifications as follows: 'Worston Shale Series' (Parkinson, 1926); 'Worston Series' (Parkinson, 1936); 'Worston Shale Group' (Earp and others, 1961); 'Worston Group' (Moseley, 1962); 'Worston Shale Formation' and 'Worston Formation' (Fewtrell and Smith, 1980). The relations of some of these various usages were illustrated in a table by Fewtrell and Smith (1980). The Worston Shales of the present account correspond to the 'Shales-with-Limestones' of the Primary Survey One-Inch Geological Map of the Settle district; also to the Worston Series of Parkinson (1936) with the inclusion of his 'Phynis Shales' at the base of the sequence. Earp and others (1961), however, used Worston Shale Group in a different sense and placed the lower boundary variously at the top of the Chatburn Limestone (Parkinson, 1926) in the Clitheroe Anticline, near the top of the Thornton Limestone (Hudson, 1944a) in the Broughton Anticline, and arbitrarily at the top of their 'Coppy Hill Limestone' in the Ribble valley section at Gisburn. They also included the Pendleside Limestone within the Worston Shale Group.

The Worston Shales have a widespread crop and may locally exceed 1400 m in thickness. They are not recognised on the Askrigg Block, the age-equivalent strata there comprising the Chapel House Limestone and the Kilnsey and Malham formations. Variations in their thickness and lithology, and those of the Pendleside Limestone, are illustrated in Figure 18.

The junction of Worston Shales with the Thornton Limestone is sharp in all recorded sections, and locally is known to be unconformable. Where mudstones form the basal beds, some are richly pyritic in the lowest metre or so. In the Eshton–Hetton Anticline, a basal conglomerate with Thornton Limestone clasts was proved, resting on an irregular surface of Thornton Limestone in the Park Laithe Borehole; the same relationship is present at the south-western end of this anticline in Haw Crag Quarry, near Bell Busk. On the south-eastern limb of the Slaidburn Anticline, near Hammerton Hall, there is an angular unconformity between knoll-reef limestone at the base of the Worston Shales and the Thornton Limestone (Plate 10), the upper part of which is cut out progressively towards the culmination of the fold.

The foraminifera assemblages indicate that the base of the Worston Shales is diachronous; in the central-southern part of the district there are several hundred metres of Chadian strata in the basal part of the division, but in parts of the Eshton–Hetton Anticline the basal beds are no older than Arundian. The top of the Worston Shales is likely to be diachronous also, though this has not been proved palaeontologically.

Plate 9 Photomicrographs of Chatburn Limestone, Thornton Limestone and Worston Shales limetones (knoll-reef, Hetton Beck and Rain Gill limestones).

a. Chatburn Limestone, Croasdale Brook, Slaidburn [7092 5257]. Unevenly grained packstone composed of crinoid plates, foraminifera and peloids in a matrix extensively altered to neomorphic spar. Field of view 5 mm RSA 2412

b. Chatburn Limestone, Croasdale Brook, Slaidburn [7095 5256]. Unevenly grained packstone consisting mostly of crinoid plates, foraminifera and calcispheres in a matrix largely altered to neomorphic spar. Note internal replacement of crinoid plate by chalcedonic quartz and dolomite (small euhedral rhombs). Field of view 5 mm RSA 2413

c. Thornton Limestone, Wood House Gate quarries [7111 5374] Slaidburn. Unevenly grained bioclastic grainstone composed of foraminifera, calcispheres and molluscan fragments. Field of view 5 mm E 60531

d. Thornton Limestone, High Ings Barn Borehole [8867 6031], at 58.55 m. Unevenly grained grainstone, composed of peloids, crinoid plates, foraminifera, calcispheres and algae (kamaenids). Field of view 5 mm E 60532

e. Knoll-reef limestone (bank facies), Worston Shales, The Crag [7179 5322], Hammerton Hall. Unevenly grained, bioclastic wackestone; crinoid plates and bryozoans are the dominant bioclasts. Field of view 5 mm RSA 2352

f. Hetton Beck Limestone, Worston Shales, Mill Laithe [9600 5796]. Unevenly grained crinoidal packstone with scattered bryozoan debris in a matrix replaced by dolomite euhedra. Note internal replacement of crinoid plate (lower left) by silica. Field of view 5 mm E 60533

g. Hetton Beck Limestone, Worston Shales, Park Laithe Borehole [9629 5813], at 153.55 m. Bioclastic grainstone with scattered ooids. Bioclasts dominated by crinoid plates but include kamaenid algae and bryozoa. Field of view 5 mm RSA 2451

h. Rain Gill Limestones, Worston Shales, Bell Sykes, Slaidburn [7201 5269]. Packstone composed of foraminifera, peloids and calcispheres in a matrix extensively replaced by neomorphic spar. Field of view 5 mm RSA 2324

In this account the Worston Shales are subdivided informally on the basis of the relative dominance of mudstone and limestone (Figure 18). A **lower mudstone-rich subdivision** (0 to 450 m plus) largely of late Chadian age is present in the southwestern and central-southern parts of the crop. This is overlain and overlapped by a complex **median limestone-rich subdivision** (100 to 500 m) of late Chadian to Arundian age, and this is in turn overlain by an **upper mudstone-rich subdivision** (0 to 400 m) of Arundian to ?Asbian age. The upper mudstones are thin or absent towards the north.

The **lower mudstone-rich subdivision** is best exposed in the Slaidburn Anticline, where the basal beds in part of this crop have been termed 'Phynis Shales' (Parkinson, 1936). The subdivision is seen also in Swinden Gill, south of Swinden on the north-western limb of the Swinden Anticline, in Monubent Beck, near Lower Flass, between Slaidburn and Paythorne, and rests on Thornton Limestone in the Butterhaw Borehole.

The lower part of the Slaidburn sequence is exposed in Phynis Beck and the River Hodder, near Phynis, and in Barn Gill. It comprises silty, micaceous and, in places, carbonaceous mudstones, containing calcareous layers, beds of mostly muddy limestones, and a few thin, evenly laminated beds of fine-grained sandstone. Clasts of medium-light grey

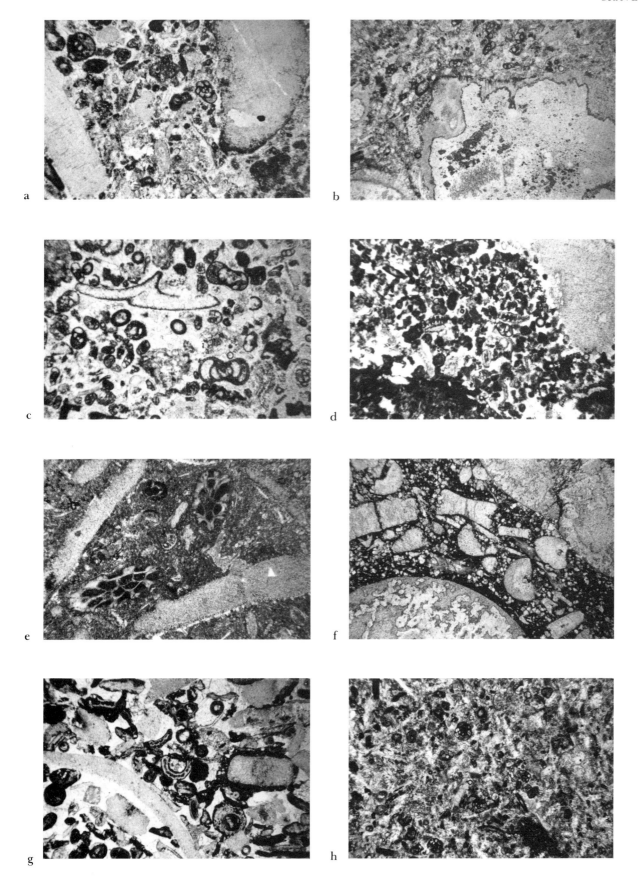

wackestone, presumed to be of reefal origin, are recorded at the top of the section in Phynis Beck. These lower beds have a fauna of crinoidal debris, brachiopods, fenestellid bryozoans, mollusca, zaphrentoid and caninioid corals including the Chadian species *Siphonophyllia cylindrica*. These beds were considered by Parkinson (1936) to be the lateral equivalents of the top part of the Clitheroe Limestone (Thornton Limestone of this account) and its associated knoll-reef limestones. The higher part of the subdivision is less well exposed, but in Barn Gill and adjacent sections it comprises 20 m of limestone overlain by about 80 m of mudstone with a further, though impersistent, limestone. The 20 m of limestone is composed of bioturbated fine calcarenite wackestones and packstones, but includes one bed of crinoidal calcirudite with clasts of limestone.

Knoll-reef limestone crops out south of Hammerton Hall (Plates 10 and 11) where it forms the basal member of the Worston Shales. It comprises massive to well bedded, medium to medium-light grey wackestone (Plate 9e), sparsely to richly crinoidal, includes impersistent mudstone partings, and is capped by crinoidal calcirudite. Its fauna compares with that of the Salt Hill reef-limestone of the Clitheroe district.

The section in Swinden Gill exposes fissile mudstones and siltstones, richly fossiliferous in part and interbedded with limestones and muddy limestones, including the 40 m-thick Nappa Limestone (Hudson and Dunnington, 1944). The latter comprises well bedded, medium to medium-dark grey, coarsely crinoidal packstones and wackestones, interbedded with thin mudstones and muddy limestones. The mudstones above and below the Nappa Limestone have been termed the 'Swinden Shales-with-Limestone' or 'Swinden Shales' and the 'Nappa Shales-with-Limestone' or 'Nappa Shales' respectively (Hudson and Dunnington, 1944).

The mudstones exposed in Monubent Beck are silty and calcareous, and contain thin beds of limestone and muddy limestone; fossils are generally sparse, though trilobite debris is recorded. The strata are involved in slump-folds, and one

of these has an amplitude of several metres. The mudstones here rest on 65 m of thick- and thin-bedded limestone which form the base of the exposed section. These limestones include sharp-based, graded beds of laminated, fine, medium and coarse calcarenite packstone. An estimated 500 to 700 m of additional strata referable to this subdivision may underlie the lowest exposed beds in this section (Figure 18).

The **median limestone-rich subdivision** includes three principal lithofacies. The lowest is a mainly limestone lithofacies comprising thick- and thin-bedded, medium-dark grey wackestones and packstones with subordinate mudstone as thin beds or partings; over most of the crop there follows interbedded, mainly laminated, medium-dark grey packstones and fissile mudstones (a lithofacies shown as 'limestone-with-mudstone' on the 1:50 000 scale maps); these in turn are succeeded by bioturbated muddy wackestones in the Eshton–Hetton area. All three lithofacies locally contain limestone lithoclasts and chert, and all are slump-folded in places. Such folds are, however, uncommon in the north-eastern parts of the crop.

Limestones of the lowest lithofacies in the south-west are referred to in this account collectively as the 'Rain Gill Limestones'. Various limestones in approximately this position farther east have been previously named, and include the 'Swinden Limestone' in the Swinden Anticline (Hudson and Dunnington, 1944), the 'Butterhaw' and the 'Broughton' limestones in the Broughton Anticline (Hudson, 1944a), and the 'Hetton Beck Limestones' in the Eshton–Hetton Anticline (Booker and Hudson, 1926).

The 'Rain Gill Limestones' are well exposed in the Slaidburn Anticline, where their foraminifera include *Glomodiscus miloni*, *G. oblongus*, *Rectodiscus sp.* and *Tubispirodiscus settlensis* and indicate an Arundian age. They comprise thick- and thin-bedded, medium-dark grey packstones (Plate 9h) and wackestones with thin beds and partings of mudstone, and they are mostly fine or medium calcarenites but include some coarse calcarenites and calcirudites. Instances of sharp-based, graded beds, and beds with groove-casts are record-

Plate 10 Knoll-reef limestone at base of Worston Shales unconformably overlying Thornton Limestone, Hammerton Hall [7176 5320]. (L 2776)

Plate 11 Knoll-reef limestone at base of Worston Shales, Hammerton Hall [7179 5322] (L 2777)

ed. Limestone and mudstone clasts and macrofossils are present in some of the coarser beds. Some of the limestones are laminated or cross-laminated and others are burrow-bioturbated. Slump-folds are a feature of the 'Rain Gill Limestones', and are particularly well displayed in quarries near Rain Gill and Black House (Plate 12) and in the section in Tosside Beck, near Ray Head. Slump-fold axial traces at the latter locality broadly conform to those in the overlying limestone-with-mudstone, trending N20 to 25°E; the folds are recumbent to the ESE. A contemporaneous dislocation surface is also exposed near Rain Gill.

The Swinden Limestone of the Swinden Anticline (Hudson and Dunnington, 1944) is taken to be an equivalent of the 'Rain Gill Limestones', and comprises thick-bedded, medium-dark grey crinoidal packstones and wackestones with muddy partings. Its coral–brachiopod fauna, including *Aulina horsfieldi*, *Siphonophyllia hettonensis* and *Schizophoria resupinata*, indicates an Arundian age. In the Broughton Anticline the equivalent beds comprise those previously named the 'Butterhaw' and 'Broughton' limestones (Hudson, 1944a), and form one limestone cropping out around the nose of the fold. Where exposed in Broughton Quarry, near Coppy Hill, this limestone comprises thick-bedded, medium to medium-dark grey, medium calcarenite packstones and wackestones, with interbedded mudstones and muddy limestones.

The limestone-rich subdivision is particularly variable around its crop in the Eshton–Hetton Anticline. In the south-east near Hetton, it comprises 250 to 300 m of strata characterised by bioturbated dolomitic wackestones, packstones and subordinate grainstones (Plate 9f); here there is no overlying limestone-with-mudstone. The lower part of this sequence is referred to in this account as the Hetton Beck Limestone (Booker and Hudson, 1926), and in the Park Laithe Borehole rests directly on Thornton Limestone without any intervening lower mudstone subdivision. It includes buff-weathering wackestones with angular clasts of medium-grey wackestones, and irregular, partially silicified lenses of medium grey wackestone, interpreted here as incipient knoll-reef limestone. Microfossils, including *Eoparastaffella simplex* and *Koninckopora inflata*, and macrofauna, in-

cluding *Levitusia humerosa*, indicate that this unit straddles the Chadian–Arundian boundary.

Traced south-westwards near Eshton, the Hetton Beck Limestone becomes separated from overlying bioturbated limestones by a wedge of laminated limestone-with-mudstone which thickens abruptly along strike. Besides thickening, the limestone-with-mudstone also becomes unconformable, cutting down firstly through the Hetton Beck Limestone, then into the Thornton Limestone. Lenses of limestone conglomerate, which underlie the limestone-with-mudstone on the unconformity at Haw Crag east of Bell Busk, include blocks and boulders of reef limestone and of the distinctive clast-bearing wackestone from the Hetton Beck Limestone (Plate 13) as well as debris from the Thornton Limestone. This debris deposit, proved also in the Throstle Nest Borehole, has a matrix of mudstone and muddy limestone. Despite the huge size of some of the reef limestone masses in this deposit (they include slabs measuring more than 50 m across) none of those exposed is regarded as autochthonous, as was supposed by Hudson (1927) and Hudson and Dunnington (1944). Where exposed in Haw Crag Quarry, the conglomerate fills a hollow in the lee of the north-westward facing scarp of the Thornton Limestone. An analogous limestone conglomerate including reef limestone debris is believed to rest unconformably on Thornton Limestone and Hetton Beck Limestone in a small anticline a little farther west at Bell Busk.

Units characterised by the laminated limestone–mudstone lithofacies (limestone-with-mudstone) (Plate 14) are dominant in the upper part of the subdivision over much of the crop. They include the 'Mallardale Shales-with-Limestone' and 'Toft Hill Limestone and Shales' of the Swinden Anticline (Hudson and Dunnington, 1944). Limestone-with-mudstone crops out in the core of the Catlow Anticline, where there are good sections in tributaries of the River Hodder near Lock Bridge. For example, in Flat Clough Beck 120 m of partly cherty, flaggy, laminated and cross-laminated fine calcarenite packstones and subordinate fissile mudstones are exposed, interbedded with sharp-based, thick beds of calcirudite or coarse calcarenite grading to fine calcarenite; the coarser beds include some shells, corals and crinoidal debris as well as clasts of limestone and mudstone, and nodules of chert. Some of the limestones are dolomitic. There are many similar sections with slump folding in the Slaidburn Anticline. Groove-casts are recorded in a few instances. Slump-folds, affecting thick-bedded limestones within the laminated lithofacies, are a feature of the sections farther east in Bond Beck and Tosside Beck. The axial traces of these folds trend N30 to 70°E, and most are recumbent towards the south-east. Mudstone makes up a larger proportion of the sequence in these sections than in the Catlow Anticline. East of the River Ribble there is less thick-bedded limestone than in the west and slump-folds are correspondingly fewer. The facies is exposed in many quarry and stream sections around Bell Busk and farther north in the vicinity of the Airton. In these more northerly sections mudstone is subordinate, and the limestones are commonly cross-laminated or, as at Foss Gill, cross-bedded.

The laminated limestone-with-mudstone facies is locally unconformable either on older Worston Shales or on Thornton Limestone. The unconformity is best displayed in the south-western part of the Eshton–Hetton Anticline (see below), and was described by Hudson (1944a) in a section (not seen during the resurvey) at the base of his Broughton Beds in the Broughton Anticline. Farther east, it was recognised by Hudson and Mitchell (1937) in the Skipton Anticline, at the base of their Embsay Limestone, regarded here as a lateral equivalent of the limestone-with-mudstone.

Lenses of limestone conglomerate are also known at the base of the laminated limestone-with-mudstone lithofacies in structurally complex ground at Coniston Cold, near Fogga and Pot Haw farms. These are regarded as age-equivalents of the Haw Crag deposit, following Hudson and Dunnington (1944), and, as at Haw Crag, none of the exposed masses of reef limestone is regarded as autochthonous. Unlike the Haw Crag conglomerates, however, those at Coniston Cold are separated from the Thornton Limestone by older Worston Shales which hereabouts appear to thicken abruptly south-westwards (Figure 18).

The source of the reef limestone debris is not known, though it is presumed to have been derived proximally from a contemporaneous outcrop within, or associated with, the Hetton Beck Limestone. Booker and Hudson (1926) described a small exposure of 'horizontal bedded reef limestone' in a quarry some 3 km ENE near Scarnber Laithe; in the resurvey, however, this section was interpreted as limestone conglomerate made up of jumbled blocks of reef limestone up to 1 m across.

Plate 12   Slump-folds in Rain Gill Limestones, Worston Shales, Black House [7224 5483]. Height of field of view 4 m (L 2785)

The Hetton Beck Limestone is not recognised on the northern limb of the Eshton–Hetton Anticline near Winterburn. In its place, under a thick sequence of laminated limestone-with-mudstone, there are well bedded, partly cherty packstones which are exposed in stream sections around Winterburn Wood Farm and include sharp-based, graded beds. Farther west, around Airton, bioturbated dolomitic wackestones and packstones with subordinate muddy limestones are again present, separated from the Thornton Limestone by some 50 to 100 m of richly micaceous mudstone and muddy limestone of the lower mudstone subdivision. Sections in streams and quarries near Park House provide good exposures of the bioturbated limestones which include clasts of wackestones at two levels.

The highest part of the limestone-rich subdivision around the Eshton–Hetton Anticline and on the northern flank of the Airton Anticline comprises bioturbated, partly dolomitic limestones and muddy limestones, mostly wackestones but including some packstones. These strata rest variously on laminated limestone-with-mudstone and Hetton Beck Limestone, locally with intervening mudstones; they were named 'Rylstone Limestone' by Booker and Hudson (1926), and 'Kirkby Malham Limestone' in the Airton Anticline by

Hudson (1949). There are good sections in Kirkby Beck, and in the railway cutting south-west of Rylstone.

The **upper mudstone-rich subdivision**, extending upwards to the Pendleside Limestone or locally to the Lower Bowland Shales, is widespread except near Kirkby Malham where the Pendleside Limestone rests directly on the limestone-rich subdivision. Some 300 m of these strata are present in the south-western part of the Eshton–Hetton Anticline, and thicker sequences may be present in poorly exposed ground farther west. In the Slaidburn Anticline, however, only about 100 m are present, and farther north in the Catlow Anticline, they thin to some 25 m.

The subdivision comprises silty mudstones that are generally calcareous and rather poorly fissile, with sparse to abundant interbedded limestones. The limestones include diffusely defined thick and thin beds of medium-dark grey muddy fine calcarenite wackestones and flaggy beds of laminated or cross-laminated fine calcarenite packstone. Limestone nodules and bullions are recorded in some sections.

These mudstones are well exposed in Otterburn Beck and its tributaries north and north-west of Otterburn. Here, as in the crop around the Slaidburn Anticline and in Bond Beck,

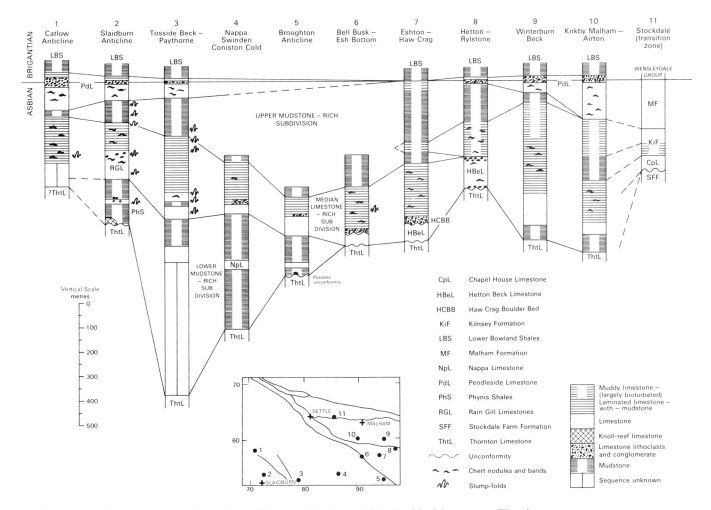

Figure 18 Comparative sections of the Worston Shales and Pendleside Limestone. The datum line is the Asbian–Brigantian boundary

Plate 13   Limestone conglomerate (Haw Crag Boulder Bed), Worston Shales, Bell Busk [9142 5637]. A large block of Hetton Beck Limestone with the bedding vertical, is present to the observer's right. (L 2802)

they are slump-folded. In sections at the top of the subdivision on the south-eastern limb of the Eshton–Hetton Anticline, interbedded wackestones are abundant and locally dominate the uppermost 50 m or so. Good exposures of these beds are seen in Washfold Beck, south of Rylstone, and in Flasby Beck, near Eshton Bridge.

DETAILS

Catlow Anticline

Some 120 m of laminated limestone-with-mudstone of the limestone-rich subdivision are intermittently exposed [7094 5759 to 7135 5847] in Flat Clough Beck, near Kenibus. The section comprises flaggy-weathering, thin-bedded, mostly even-laminated, medium-dark grey, fine calcarenite packstones with thin beds and partings of fissile mudstone. There are also sporadic thick (up to 0.6 m) beds of coarser calcarenite or calcirudite, some of which are sharp-based and show grading. These coarser beds are richly fossiliferous in places with partially silicified coarse crinoidal debris, shells and corals, and some include clasts of limestone and mudstone up to 6 cm across. Chert is common both as nodules and as bands. Slightly lower strata are exposed [7091 5776] in a disused quarry nearby, where some 5 m of extensively slumped cherty calcarenites and calcirudites rest on about the same thickness of mostly flaggy laminated limestones. A 1.3 m calcirudite lens in the slumped complex includes clasts of laminated fine calcarenite packstone up to 0.4 m across.

Slaidburn Anticline

Micaceous, crinoidal mudstones within a few metres of the base of the lower mudstone subdivision, are exposed on the north-western flank of the anticline in a ditch [6953 5365 and 6951 5372] near Procters Farm. The base is exposed farther south-west near New Biggin, just within the adjoining Lancaster district, where the section

[6843 5252] shows 0.3 m of silty mudstone with crinoid stems and fenestellid bryozoa resting sharply on an irregular surface of thick-bedded, cherty, medium and fine calcarenite (Thornton Limestone). The base was seen in the Bowland Forest Tunnel [6885 5301], and Earp (1955) recorded soft shaly mudstone on about 3 m of crinoidal calcareous shales with posts of cementstone and thin beds and lenses of crinoidal limestone resting in turn on massive crinoidal limestone.

About 110 m of the lower mudstone subdivision consisting mostly of micaceous mudstones are fairly well exposed [7135 5452 to 7151 5429] in Phynis Beck, near Phynis. They are in part richly fossiliferous and include brachiopods, *Siphonophyllia sp.*, zaphrentoids, *Fenestella sp.* and crinoidal debris. The lowest strata seen are 1.5 m of richly pyritic thin-bedded limestone, with partings and thin beds of crinoidal mudstone; these are separated from thick-, wavy-bedded Thornton Limestone by a 0.5 m unexposed interval. The section includes thin beds of even-laminated, fine-grained sandstone some 40 m above the base, and towards the top there are several metres of faulted, thick-bedded to massive, medium-dark grey crinoidal packstone to wackestone. The highest beds are thick- and thin-bedded limestones, including medium grey calcirudite packstone and muddy calcisiltite with angular clasts of medium-light grey crinoidal wackestone. A thin section of packstone [7135 5453] shows that crinoid plates and bryozoa are the principal grains, with subordinate spines; quartz occurs as an irregular matrix replacement and as internal replacement of crinoid plates. The matrix is almost completely neomorphosed to spar and there is syntaxial overgrowth of crinoid plates. The basal beds, including slump-folded limestones, are exposed nearby in the bed of the River Hodder just below Stocks Reservoir dam [7174 5432 to 7182 5441]. These beds have yielded *Siphonophyllia cylindrica*.

The lower mudstone subdivision is exposed on the southeastern limb of the anticline in Barn Gill [7210 5355 to 7240 5383]. The lowest beds there are partly calcareous, micaceous, silty mudstones with crinoidal debris, shells and fenestellid bryozoa, and they include thin beds of muddy or laminated calcisiltite. Higher strata in-

Plate 14 Limestone-with-mudstone in Worston Shales, Dunsop Brook [6935 5410]. Thin-bedded and laminated calcisiltites with mudstone interbeds typical of this facies. (L 2797)

clude laminae of siltstone and fine-grained sandstone. The top of the section exposes limestone about 20 m thick. This limestone is thick-and thin-bedded with mudstone partings, and includes slump-folds. It comprises medium-dark grey, bioturbated, fine calcarenite pack-wackestone, and also 0.1 m of crinoidal calcirudite with limestone clasts. The fauna from this unit include the trilobite *Gitarra gitarraeformis* and the goniatites *Ammonellipsites* aff. *kochi* and *Eonomismoceras sp.* (Riley, 1981).

Knoll-reef limestone, presumed to be the basal member of the Worston Shales, is exposed in a quarry [7179 5322] at The Crag, south of Hammerton Hall (Plate 11). The section shows up to 15 m of massive to crudely or well bedded, medium-light grey wackestone, richly crinoidal in part and with impersistent mudstone partings. A thin section from its lower part shows cavernous bioclastic wackestone, ranging from fine calcarenite to calcirudite (Plate 9e). The principal grains are crinoid plates, bryozoans and ostracods. Irregular connected cavities include calcisiltite geopetal infills and sparry cement. Chalcedony replaces some crinoid plates and spar. In a nearby exposure [7176 5320] crudely bedded wackestones at the base of the knoll-reef rest with angular unconformity on well bedded Thornton Limestone (Plate 10).

The 'Rain Gill Limestones' at the base of the limestone-rich subdivision are exposed on the north-western flank of the anticline in a stream [6962 5395] west of Dunsop Farm. The basal limestones include an irregular bed up to 0.4 m thick of coarse calcarenite and calcirudite, with clasts of wackestone, shells, and the coral *Caninia cornucopiae*, fining upwards to crinoidal calcisiltite. Higher beds [6948 5401 to 6956 5396] comprise thick- and thin-, mostly flat-bedded, medium-dark grey, fine calcarenite wackestones with a few lenses and layers of crinoidal coarse calcarenite packstone and sparse chert. Mudstone occurs as partings or thin beds. Similar limestones, but with conspicuous chert and slump-folds, form the highest part of the sequence [6939 5408].

The section [7036 5488 to 7051 5482] in Croasdale Brook southeast of Croasdale House provides further good exposures of the 'Rain Gill Limestones'. The upper part shows beds which are transitional to the limestone-with-mudstone facies, and is a slump-folded sequence of thin-bedded limestones with chert layers up to 0.1 m thick, interbedded with muddy limestones, mudstones and thick beds (up to 1 m) of cherty fine calcarenite wackestone to packstone with silicified corals and coarse crinoidal debris. Farther downstream [7056 5477], 7 m of thick- and thin-bedded fine calcarenite wackestone to packstone with sporadic chert nodules are exposed. These limestones are partly laminated and partly bioturbated, and are involved in major slump-folds. Microstylolites give a nodular appearance to the exposed rock in some beds.

Slumped limestones in this part of the sequence are well exposed [7224 5483] farther east in disused quarries west of Black House (Plate 12) and [7288 5417] south-west of Rain Gill where the 'Rain Gill Limestones' are 170 m thick. In another quarry [7290 5400] near Rain Gill, thin-bedded, burrow-bioturbated wackestones with layers of chert include lenses of calcirudite fining-upwards to laminated fine calcarenite packstone. The calcirudites are crinoidal, shelly and include angular clasts of dark limestone. A bedding discontinuity in the lower part of the section appears to be due to mass movement. A thin-section from this locality shows a bioclastic to intraclastic grainstone, with intraclasts up to 25 mm in a medium to coarse calcarenite. The grains comprise crinoid plates, foraminifera, intraclasts of fine calcarenite packstone, peloids, and algae including kamaenids and *Koninckopora sp.* Foraminifera include *Eoparastaffella simplex*, *Glomodiscus miloni* and *Tubispirodiscus settlensis*.

Farther south-eastwards the 'Rain Gill Limestones' are exposed in a gully [7197 5271 to 7222 5272] east of Bell Sykes where they are about 100 m thick. The section includes large slump-folds, and sharp-based, graded units of calcarenite are common. Interbedded mudstone is fissile in part, and carbonaceous plant fragments and an indeterminate goniatite are recorded. Thin sections of limestone from this gully [7207 5270 and 7201 5269] show medium calcarenite, bioclastic-peloidal-intraclastic packstone (Plate 9h). The grains are of foraminifera, kamaenid algae, *Koninckopora sp.*, calcispheres, ostracods, crinoid plates, peloids and intraclasts of wackestone and lime-mudstone. Quartz occurs as a replacement of shell fragments, and the matrix is completely neomorphosed to spar. Foraminifera include *Eblania michoti*, *Eoparastaffella simplex*, *Eotextularia diversa*, *Glomodiscus oblongus*, *Nudarchaediscus sp.*, *Rec-*

todiscus sp. and *Tubispirodiscus settlensis*, indicating an Arundian age. Similar heavily slumped limestones are exposed farther south-west in disused quarries [7154 5199 and 7154 5204] near Whiteholme.

The laminated limestone-with-mudstone lithofacies is exposed above 'Rain Gill Limestones' in Dunsop Brook [6933 5410 to 6937 5408] west of Dunsop Farm (Plate 14). The section shows thin-bedded, flaggy, laminated, fine calcarenite packstones interbedded with fissile mudstones and calcareous mudstones. It includes thicker, non-laminated limestones; some are slump-folded and some carry groove-casts. Farther north-east, about 80 m of limestone-with-mudstone are exposed in Phynis Beck [7114 5518 to 7119 5502], WSW of Hollins House. Here thin-bedded to flaggy, medium-dark grey, fine calcarenite packstones with mudstone and muddy limestone interbeds are dominant, and are interspersed with thick-bedded to massive slumped beds of limestone. Some of the slump-folds also involve the flaggy limestones and mudstones. The basal part of this section, below a waterfall, includes richly fossiliferous beds of limestone and mudstone and contains limestone pebbles and boulders. The fauna includes the coral *Koninckophyllum* aff. *cyathophylloides*.

Limestone-with-mudstone is exposed in strike sections on the shore of Stocks Reservoir near Black House, where thick beds of limestone, flaggy limestones and mudstones are slump-folded. At the western end of the section [7236 5514], a thick bed of medium calcarenite to calcirudite packstone includes angular clasts of fine calcarenite packstone up to 0.3 m across. Limestone-with-mudstone seen in a stream [7329 5412 to 7332 5403] on the south-eastern limb of the anticline south of Rain Gill also contains many thick to massive beds of slump-folded limestone. A richly fossiliferous bed of mudstone has yielded *Cummingella sp. nov.*, known from Arundian strata in the adjoining Clitheroe and Garstang districts. Southwestwards from this section the limestone-with-mudstone overlying the 'Rain Gill Limestones' appears to thin out.

In Croasdale Brook [7004 5500 to 7007 5495], 60 to 70 m of mudstones and calcareous mudstones with a few thin and thick beds of limestone constitutes the upper mudstone subdivision, and separates the Pendleside Limestone from limestone-with-mudstone. In a stream section [7222 5272 to 7260 5263] near High Field, on the south-eastern limb of the Slaidburn Anticline, the subdivision is about 145 m thick. It comprises partly calcareous mudstones with thick and thin beds of medium-dark grey calcisiltite as well as nodular calcisiltite, and includes slump structures.

Bond Beck, Tosside Beck, Monubent Beck

There are good exposures of mudstones and limestones within the lower mudstone subdivision in Monubent Beck, where some 12 m of partly calcareous, trilobite-bearing mudstones with a few beds of limestone crop in a meander-scar [7929 5238] near Lower Flass. The limestones are calcisiltites and fine calcarenites which are either sharp-based and laminated or diffusely defined and muddy; they are involved in a slump-fold several metres in amplitude. Slump-folds are recorded in other exposures nearby. An estimated 65 m of thick-bedded limestones underlying the mudstones are exposed in sections [7896 5189 to 7908 5222] farther downstream. These limestones include calcisiltites and sharp-based laminated calcarenite packstones, mostly fine but including some coarser, graded beds; they are separated by partings or interbeds of mudstone.

Thick- and thin-bedded, partly lenticular limestones grouped with the 'Rain Gill Limestones' are exposed in Tosside Beck (Skirden Beck), south-east of Ray Head. Medium-dark grey, calcarenite packstones are dominant, mostly laminated but some bioturbated; they are involved in major slump-folds with axial traces trending N20 to 30°E and recumbent towards the ESE. Some 180 m of laminated limestone-with-mudstone higher in the sequence are exposed in Bond Beck and Tosside Beck; in poorly exposed ground farther east this unit appears to thicken and incorporate a wedge of mudstone. The section in Bond Beck [7757 5346 to 7810 5296] shows thin-bedded to flaggy, medium-dark grey, laminated, fine calcarenite packstones interbedded with fissile and calcareous mudstones, and thick, generally slumped, beds of pack-wackestone. At the top of this section, thick-bedded, slumped limestones predominate and have been mapped as limestone. Slump-fold axial traces trend N30 to 50°E, and the folds are mostly recumbent towards the south-east. In Tosside Beck the unit is exposed in two sections. Of these, the stratigraphically lower section [7800 5466 to 7811 5434] comprises thin-, even- and lenticular-bedded, laminated, fine calcarenite packstones interbedded with calcareous mudstone. Slump-folds affect both limestones and mudstones, their axial traces trending N35 to 70°E, and are recumbent towards the south-east. The higher section [7793 5554 to 7787 5523] includes subordinate bioturbated limestones, and beds up to 0.3 m thick of sharp-based, pyritic coarse calcarenite packstone fining upwards to fine calcarenite; slumps are recorded in the lower part.

The upper mudstone subdivision is represented by about 150 m of mudstones and subordinate muddy and laminated limestones in Bond Beck and its tributaries east of Knotts. Exposures [7724 5396 to 7756 5346] in Bond Beck show slump structures, including one fold of several metres amplitude and recumbent towards the southeast, with its axial trace aligned N30°E; load-casts and groove-casts trending N70 to 100°E are recorded.

Swinden Anticline

The lower mudstone subdivision is exposed in a stream section [8691 5389] in Swinden Gill Wood. The lowest beds comprise thin-bedded dark grey crinoidal wackestones with interbedded siltstones and muddy limestones (Nappa Shales of Hudson and Dunnington, 1944), and include zaphrentoid corals and fenestellid bryozoa. Above these lie an estimated 40 m of thick- and thin-bedded limestone (Nappa Limestone of Hudson and Dunnington, 1944), typified by coarsely crinoidal wackestones with mudstone partings. A thin section from one exposure [8684 5393] shows crinoid plates, spicules and ostracods as the principal grains, with subordinate intraclasts of wackestone and lime-mudstone. Quartz internally replaces crinoid stems and spicules. Fossils from the limestone include *Sychnoelasma konincki*, *Lingula* aff. *lumsdeni*, *Pleuropugnoides* cf. *pleurodon*, *Orbiculoidea cincta*, *Parallelodon spp.* and *Spirifer furcatus*. The lowest 11 m of this limestone are exposed resting on fossiliferous mudstone in disused quarry [8620 5375] north of Cobers Laithe; the fauna includes *Amplexus coralloides*, *Siphonophyllia cylindrica*, *Acanthoplecta mesoloba*, *Pleuropugnoides pleurodon*, *Rhipidomella michelini*, *Schizophoria resupinata* and *Spirifer coplowensis*. The overlying strata comprise about 180 m of mudstones and siltstones with beds of medium-dark grey, partly muddy, wackestone; the mudstones are fossiliferous in part [e.g. 8672 5379] and include *Composita ambigua*, *Syringothyris* cf. *exoleta*, *Tylothyris laminosa*, bivalves and fenestellid bryozoa.

An equivalent of the 'Rain Gill Limestones' is exposed in the railway cutting [8624 5417] south of Swinden, and in the river bed and nearby disused quarries farther west. Thick-bedded partly dolomitic packstones and wackestones (Swinden Limestone of Hudson and Dunnington, 1944) in the cutting have yielded *Aulin horsfieldi*, *Siphonophyllia hettonensis* and *Schizophoria resupinata*. Farther east, this limestone is exposed in disused quarries [8820 5478; 9002 5414] near Haugh Field and Warrel Laithe respectively. The former exposure shows some 4 m of thick- and thin-bedded, medium to medium-dark grey, fine calcarenite packstones and wackestones with muddy partings. The limestones include silicified caninioid corals.

Limestone-with-mudstone higher in the sequence is exposed in small disused quarries [8693 5471; 8699 5466] near Mallardale

Laithe, east of Swinden; the latter locality shows interbedded flaggy limestone, fissile muddy limestone, and siltstone.

Broughton Anticline

In the Broughton Anticline the lower mudstone subdivision was drilled in the upper part of the Butterhaw Borehole [9346 5259], south-east of Butter Haw. The bore proved partly dolomitic, medium to medium-dark grey, bioturbated, fine calcarenite wackestone from rock-head at 2.39 m to 15.51 m, and beneath this micaceous silty mudstone and siltstone with subordinate muddy limestone to the top of the Thornton Limestone at 42.64 m. The mudstones are partly shelly and crinoidal and include laminae of fine-grained sandstone. Their basal 2.5 m comprise listricised and pyritic mudstone with clasts of Thornton Limestone.

Limestones broadly equivalent to the 'Rain Gill Limestones' are exposed in a disused quarry [9408 5308] ENE of Butter Haw (Butterhaw Quarry of Hudson 1944a) and in other quarries including Broughton Quarry [9465 5275]. A section in Broughton Quarry shows well bedded, medium to medium-dark grey, medium calcarenite pack-wackestones with partings and interbeds of calcareous mudstone and muddy limestone.

Limestone-with-mudstone higher in the sequence is exposed in a quarry [9225 5328] at Scaleber and in sections [9098 5450; 9115 5424; 9140 5415] in the banks of the River Aire.

Eshton – Hetton Anticline

The Hetton Beck Limestone at the base of the limestone-rich subdivision was proved in the Park Laithe Borehole [9629 5813], south of Hetton, from 38.55 m to 164.58 m below surface. At its base there is 0.3 m of conglomerate with clasts of Thornton Limestone resting on an irregular surface of dolomitised Thornton Limestone. The sequence comprises wackestones with subordinate packstones and grainstones, mostly fine to medium calcarenite but including some crinoidal, coarse calcarenite and calcirudite; interbedded mudstones are common in the lowest 20 m where there are slumps. Chert nodules are recorded between 61.0 and 68.0 m, and much of the sequence is bioturbated and dolomitic. A thin section of a grainstone (153.55 m) shows a bioclastic-oolitic medium to coarse calcarenite, the principal grains being crinoid plates, ooids and bryozoa (Plate 9g). Subordinate grains include kamaenid algae and *Koninckopora sp.*, peloids, and intraclasts. Quartz occurs as euhedra and as a minor internal replacement of crinoid plates. There is slight matrix neomorphism to spar and syntaxial overgrowth of crinoid plates. Muddy wackestones between 76.2 and 80.8 m include partly silicified, irregular nodules of clean medium-grey wackestone, interpreted as being of incipient reef facies. The highest 27 m of the sequence include scattered to abundant clasts of medium grey wackestone (probably of reef facies) in a dolomitic, bioturbated wackestone matrix. Clasts up to 5 cm across are recorded, and some are pyritic. The fauna includes *Emmonsia parasitica* (44.84 m), *Cladochonus sp.*, and the rostraconch *Conocardium hibernicum* (121.61 m).

Much of the Hetton Beck Limestone is exposed in Hetton Beck [9592 5793 to 9607 5828] (Plate 9f). It is also seen to the south-west in the banks [9346 5674] of Eshton Beck near Brockabank and in a nearby quarry [9351 5674], where the sequence comprises 56 m of thick- (up to 0.7 m) and thin-, mostly wavy-bedded, medium-dark to medium-light grey limestones, ranging from calcisiltite to fine and medium calcarenite wackestones, packstones and grainstones. Mudstone form partings and infills to wavy bed hollows. A thin section from one locality [9356 5670] shows bioclastic, fine to medium calcarenite wackestone with ostracods, spicules and crinoid plates, and quartz occurring as an internal replacement of crinoid plates. There is slight matrix neomorphism to coarse spar. Microfossils from this quarry include *Chernobaculites sp.*, *Dainella sp.*, *Eoparastaf-*

fella simplex, *Eotextularia diversa* and *Koninckopora inflata*, indicating an Arundian age. However, the macrofauna includes cf. *Levitusia humerosa* (from the quarry) and *Plicatifera plicatilis* (from the stream) and is of Chadian age, suggesting a correlation with the Salt Hill reef limestone of Clitheroe.

On the northern flank of the Eshton – Hetton Anticline, limestones which are probably equivalent to the Hetton Beck Limestone are exposed in Winterburn Beck and its tributaries near Winterburn Wood Farm. The best section [9337 5925 to 9347 5929] in Dog Kennel Gill shows thick- and thin-bedded, medium-dark grey, fine to medium calcarenite packstones with a few partings and interbeds of calcareous mudstone. The limestones are generally laminated and sharp-based, and some beds show grading. Higher beds in this stream [9367 5942] are similar, but conspicuously cherty, and they pass upwards into limestone-with-mudstone.

Farther west, limestones in a corresponding part of the sequence are well exposed in stream and quarry sections near Park House. The section [8844 5885 to 8840 5870] shows 38 m of mostly thick- and thin-bedded, medium-dark grey, fine calcarenite pack-wackestones, and subordinate calcareous silty mudstone and muddy limestone. The limestones are bioturbated and characteristically pale buff weathering. There are a few layers of medium and coarse calcarenite and calcirudite, some with shells and, in two instances, with clasts of wackestone.

Limestone-with-mudstone is exposed in Eshton Beck, apparently faulted against Hetton Beck Limestone. The section [9354 5665 to 9355 5655] shows flaggy, well-laminated fine calcarenite packstones interbedded with fissile mudstone, and includes beds of crinoidal coarse calcarenite with clasts of mudstone and wackestone. Farther west, these flaggy strata are exposed in disused quarries [e.g. 9166 5626] south of Throstle Nest, where the limestones include sparse chert and a thin slumped layer.

The basal beds of the limestone-with-mudstone are well exposed in the vicinity of Haw Crag, north-east of Crag Laithe; a section [9139 5636] at the southern end of Haw Crag Quarry shows them banked against and overlapping a north-west-facing scarp of Thornton Limestone. The strata immediately above the unconformity are 2 m of limestone conglomerate, comprising blocks and boulders of Thornton Limestone; these are succeeded by up to 2 m of flaggy, laminated limestone, interbedded with fissile calcareous mudstone; and these in turn by up to 7.5 m of partly micaceous silty mudstone with thick slumped beds of muddy limestone and more boulders of Thornton Limestone. Traced northwards along the quarry, the basal limestone conglomerate thickens to an estimated 20 m, and includes blocks and boulders of both Thornton Limestone and Hetton Beck Limestone and also of a medium-light grey wackestone yielding rich reef-faunas including *Plicatifera* cf. *plicatilis* (Plate 13). A block of bedded wackestones [9142 5637] yielded *Michelinia megastoma* and *Siphonophyllia* cf. *garwoodi*, and includes clasts of medium-grey wackestone and lime-mudstone. The lithology of this block can be matched in the upper part of the Hetton Beck Limestone of the Park Laithe Borehole. Blocks of reef limestone are dominant in the northern part of the quarry [9135 5642], though these are mixed with blocks of darker bedded limestones one of which, at the extreme northern end, forms a slab several metres across of coarsely crinoidal packstone, a lithology that can be matched in the Park Laithe sequence. Geopetal infills of the crinoid stems demonstrate inversion of this slab. The limestone blocks are in a matrix of mudstone and muddy limestone. The summit of Haw Crag and its northern spur are considered to be formed of detached slabs of reef limestone.

In the Throstle Nest Borehole [9166 5660], limestone-with-mudstone, comprising interbedded and interlaminated calcisiltites, fine calcarenite packstones and mudstones, partly dolomitic and with sporadic chert, were proved from rock-head at 2.0 m to 19.87 m below surface. These strata are interbedded with sharp-based, graded units of coarse calcarenite or calcirudite, including shells and mudstone clasts. Limestone conglomerate was proved below the limestone-with-mudstone, resting on the Thornton Limestone at 28.65 m. The clasts include some several metres across, and their lithologies can be matched locally in the Thornton Limestone. The conglomerate has a mudstone matrix, and this is dominant towards the base.

A disused quarry [9398 5788] near Scarnber Laithe, Hetton, exposes about 3 m of limestone conglomerate, comprising blocks of medium-light grey bioclastic wackestone. The conglomerate is capped by 0.1 m of bedded coarse calcarenite packstone with *Plicatifera plicatilis* and *Reediella stubblefieldi* resting on 6 cm of lime-mudstone coarsening upwards to coarse calcarenite packstone.

Some 200 m of limestone-with-mudstone are present on the northern limb of the Eshton–Hetton Anticline north of Winterburn, but no slump structures are recorded. A thin section from a sample from the banks [9404 5956] of Winterburn Beck shows alternating laminae of mudstone and fine calcarenite grainstone to calcisiltite. These beds are generally unfossiliferous, but exceptionally a locality [9359 5959] in Newton Bank Gill has yielded a rich fauna including *Brachythyris ovalis*, *Echinoconchus punctatus*, *Pustula pustulosa*, *Schizophoria resupinata* and *Spirifer striatus* group.

Farther west, near Airton, the limestone-with-mudstone is well exposed [9115 5954 to 9129 5976] in Foss Gill at Calton Spouts where it is about 68 m thick. Here mudstone is very subordinate, and most of the sequence comprises partly dolomitic, thin-bedded to flaggy, laminated calcisiltite and fine calcarenite packstone. Chert is abundant as lenses and bands up to 3 cm thick in the middle part of the sequence. No fossils are recorded other than scattered crinoidal debris in the thicker beds and trails on flaggy surfaces. Cross-lamination and cut-and-fill structures are recorded, as is cross-bedding with units up to 1 m thick. These strata overlie thick-bedded calcarenite pack-wackestones, some containing clasts of wackestone, and are overlain by at least 35 m of mudstone-dominated beds.

The highest limestones in the limestone-rich subdivision in the north-eastern parts of its crop are exposed in many disused quarries and a railway cutting near Rylstone. Some 44 m of these beds (Rylstone Limestone of Booker and Hudson, 1926) are exposed in the cutting [9631 5801 to 9635 5821], and they comprise thick- and thin-bedded, medium-dark grey, partly muddy and dolomitic, fine calcarenite packstones and wackestones, and include diffusely defined layers of calcareous mudstone. Chert is common at two levels, and the whole sequence is characterised by bioturbation. Beds of medium and coarse calcarenite packstone are interspersed, and some of these include shells and ostracods. These limestones were drilled in the Park Laithe Borehole [9629 5813] from 2.50 m to the top of the Hetton Beck Limestone at 38.55 m below surface. Higher in the sequence similar limestones with chert are exposed in disused quarries [e.g. 9648 5797] farther to the south-east. An exposure [9713 5871] of these limestones in a stream east of Manor House, Rylstone, has yielded a fauna including *Diploporana sp.*, *Penniretepora sp.*, *Dictyoclostus* cf. *multispiniferus* and *Schizophoria resupinata*. Fauna from a nearby exposure [9726 5865] of cherty limestones includes *Leptagonia analoga*, *Productina sp.* and *Schizophoria sp.* Analogous cherty bioturbated limestones are exposed [9440 5989] in Winterburn Beck below Winterburn Reservoir Dam; they have yielded a fauna including *Productina sp.*, *Schizophoria resupinata* and *S.* cf. *woodi*.

Diffusely interbedded mudstones and limestones of the upper mudstone subdivision are exposed south of Rylstone in Washfold Beck [9699 5773 to 9725 5789] and in Clints Rock Quarry [9669 5751]. The former section shows some 50 m of blocky calcareous mudstone, interbedded with thick- (up to 0.5 m) and thin-bedded fine calcarenite wackestone and muddy wackestone. The limestones are characteristically pale-weathering and bioturbated, with sparse shells and zaphrentoid corals. Their junction with the Pendleside Limestone is exposed in Clints Rock Quarry where *Pustula* cf. *pyx-idiformis* is recorded in the upper mudstone subdivision.

Farther south-west, limestone dominates the upper part of the upper mudstone subdivision, and interbedded bioturbated medium-dark grey wackestones and blocky calcareous mudstones are exposed up to the base of the Pendleside Limestone in Flasby Beck [9426 5598 to 9445 5617], south-west of Flasby Hall.

Airton Anticline

Bioturbated limestones are exposed in a stream [8677 6030] north of Orms Gill Green. These beds are incompletely exposed but are about 30 m thick, passing down into 27 m of well bedded calcarenite pack-wackestones with simple and fasciculate corals, gastropods, brachiopods, and coarse crinoidal debris including stems up to 10 cm long. These latter limestones rest sharply [8685 6021] on massive Thornton Limestone. Some 25 to 30 m of limestone-with-mudstone with a sharp base rest on the bioturbated limestones and comprise flaggy, laminated cherty limestones with subordinate mudstones. They include probable slumped units and several instances of cross-lamination.

Limestones higher in the sequence are exposed in a strike section [8839 6092 to 8949 6095] in Kirkby Beck. They are thin-bedded, medium-dark grey fine calcarenite packstones and wackestones, diffusely interbedded with calcareous mudstones.

Otterburn and Coniston Cold

Limestone believed to be equivalent to the Hetton Beck Limestone separates Thornton Limestone and limestone-with-mudstone on the eastern flank of a small anticline at Bell Busk. A section [9001 5609] in Esh Bottom Quarry exposes about 5 m of thickly bedded, medium to medium-dark grey, fine calcarenite packstones and wackestones with impersistent wavy mudstone partings. There are layers of coarse calcarenite; also one 0.4 m sharp-based bed which grades from calcirudite to fine calcarenite. *Koninckopora inflata* in samples from this locality indicates an Arundian age. South-westwards, limestones considered to be equivalent to the Hetton Beck Limestone are again exposed in quarries west of Coniston Cold, notably [8894 5516] east of Steeling Hill and [8923 5536] north-west of Fogger Rook. A thin section of a sample from the former locality included clasts of bioclastic wackestone that are cavernous with sparry fill and presumed to be of reefal origin.

Limestone conglomerate is locally present under limestone-with-mudstone in the anticline west of Bell Busk. In this area reef limestone debris is recorded directly overlying Thornton Limestone in the northern quarry [8995 5671] at Ravenflatt Rock, and in a section [9007 5616] overlying Arundian limestone within the Worston Shales near Esh Bottom Quarry (see also Hudson and Dunnington, 1944). The succeeding limestone-with-mudstone is exposed in stream and quarry sections farther south in Gill Plantation. A disused quarry [9006 5560] shows up to 2 m of well laminated, flaggy, fine calcarenite packstone and calcareous mudstone, with beds up to 0.6 m of cherty packstone; some of the thick beds have sharp bases and rest on erosion surfaces, and include shells and spicules as well as clasts of limestone and mudstone.

Limestone conglomerate is present at the base of the limestone-with-mudstone facies west of Coniston Cold. Sections at Dogber Rock [8973 5483 and 8959 5487], near Pot Haw Laithe, were described by Hudson and Dunnington (1944), but are now poorly exposed. They recorded a 12 m boulder bed at Dogber Rock, including 'angular, subangular and rounded boulders of both reef and bedded limestone'. Slabs of medium to medium-light grey wackestones up to 100 m long are present in a comparable deposit at Fogga Farm. The slabs include spar-filled vughs and patches of radial fibrous calcite, and are presumed to be of reefal origin. A thin section of a sample from one locality [8925 5526] shows bioclastic

Plate 15 Pendleside Limestone, Bottoms Beck [7453 5662]. Thin to medium-bedded calcisiltites and calcarenites with chert. (L 2814)

fine to medium calcarenite wackestone with disseminated' larger crinoid plates, bryozoa and ostracods. Geopetal infills in the northernmost slab [8931 5530] show that it is inverted. A temporary section [8930 5521] showed the largest slab resting on crinoidal mudstone with limestone boulders which included superficially pyritised, pale (reefal) wackestones, medium-dark grey, crinoidal pack-wackestones, and blocks of limestone conglomerate incorporating pale wackestone and darker packstone.

At least 120 m of mudstone-dominated strata higher in the sequence are calculated to be present in structurally complex sections [8827 5794 to 8827 5832] in Otterburn Beck and [8751 5829 to 8822 5796] its tributary Crook Beck. Mudstone is the main component, though thin beds of muddy or laminated to cross-laminated calcisiltite are locally common. Limestone also occurs as bullions, and slump-folds are recorded in the southern part of both sections. A 2 m layer of calcareous mudstone with nodular limestone in Crook Beck [8789 5820] has yielded a fauna including *Schizophoria resupinata*. Thicker-bedded limestones exposed farther downstream in Otterburn Beck [8825 5784 and 8831 5772] are considered to lie within the limestone-rich subdivision.

Pendleside Limestone (Holkerian – Brigantian)

The Pendleside Limestone generally succeeds the Worston Shales, extending upwards to the Lower Bowland Shales (Figure 15). In the extreme south-east, however, the formation is not present, the Worston Shales being succeeded directly by the Bowland Shales. Both its upper and its lower junctions are likely to be diachronous within the district, though this remains to be proved palaeontologically.

The term Pendleside Limestone was used by the Primary surveyors (Hull and others, 1875) in the Clitheroe district to denote the limestone strata separating the Shales-with-Limestone (below) from the Bowland Shales. Parkinson (1926) defined the 'Pendleside Limestone Series' in the Clitheroe district as the strata from the 'Hodderense Band' up to the base of P_1, the latter coinciding, according to him, with the base of the Bowland Shales, and the term was used in this sense by Parkinson (1936) and Earp (1955) in the Slaidburn area. Earp and others (1961) regarded the

Pendleside Limestone as an impersistent lithostratigraphical unit at the top of their Worston Shale Group, but George and others (1976) reinstated a partially biostratigraphical classification with a 'Pendleside Limestone Group' extending from the 'B. hodderense Beds' to the base of the Bowland Shale Group. Lithostratigraphical criteria were used by Fewtrell and Smith (1980) to define their proposed 'Pendleside Limestone Formation' or 'Pendleside Formation' for the Craven Basin as a whole. They placed the base 'at the oncoming of the characteristic turbidite limestones', and the top 'at the final disappearance of limestone beds of substantial thickness, at the corresponding change to the predominance of the characteristic Bowland Shale lithology'. The Pendleside Limestone of the present account corresponds to the Pendleside Limestone Formation of Fewtrell and Smith, and broadly to the Pendleside Limestone of the Primary Survey.

The Pendleside Limestone exhibits considerable variation in thickness. West of the River Ribble, it is some 140 m thick in the Catlow Anticline, though in the Bowland Forest Tunnel (Earp, 1955), on the north-western limb of the Slaidburn Anticline, strata here regarded as Pendleside Limestone are only 42 m thick. East of the River Ribble about 180 m are present near Hanlith and Kirkby Malham, but south of the South Craven Fault system near Orms Gill Green and in the east near Rylstone it is less than 10 m thick.

Three distinctive subdivisions can be recognised in the Pendleside Limestone. When seen in sequence they are: a **well bedded limestone subdivision** at the base; a **limestone conglomerate subdivision**; and a **limestone-with-mudstone subdivision** at the top. The relationships and thickness variations of these subdivisions are illustrated in Figure 19.

Limestones resting on Worston Shales, and classified as the **well bedded limestone subdivision** of the Pendleside Limestone, are 30 to 90 m thick west of the River Ribble, and about 150 m thick in the separate and geographically more restricted outcrop north-east of the South Craven Fault system near Hanlith and Kirkby Malham. These beds have not been recognised in the intervening ground, nor in the more eastern outcrops near Rylstone and Flasby. This subdivision consists of sharply defined, even beds, mostly less than 0.5 m thick (Plate 15). The beds include medium-dark to medium-light grey lime-mudstone, medium-dark grey calcisiltites, and fine to medium calcarenite packstones and grainstones; there are also subordinate coarse calcarenite and calcirudite packstones, some with limestone pebbles or boulders and derived shells and corals. The packstones and grainstones are commonly laminated, and both these and the finer-textured limestones tend to be conspicuously bioturbated by burrows (Plate 16). Bioturbation has imparted a characteristic mottled appearance to the lime-mudstones. Most sections contain sharp-based graded beds, fining upwards from calcirudite or coarse calcarenite to calcisiltite or even lime-mudstone. Disseminated dolomite is common, as is chert which is present either as nodules or bands, the latter commonly replacing the top part of individual beds (Plate 16). In the western part of the Catlow Anticline, the higher parts of the sequence are more extensively replaced by silica. Mudstones form partings and thin beds, particularly towards the base (which is locally transitional from Worston Shales) and towards the top (where bioturbation traces give them a marked streaky appearance in section).

At least 60 m of these strata can be seen in a faulted section in Croasdale Brook, in the Slaidburn Anticline. Mottled lime-mudstones near the base of the sequence carry the goniatite *Bollandoceras hodderense*. This unit was also proved at the base of a much thinner sequence in the Bowland Forest Tunnel (Earp, 1955). Some 50 m of the well bedded limestone subdivision are well exposed in Bottoms Beck,

Gisburn Forest; there the lowest 8 m are atypical, being slump-folded. Foraminifera in samples from this section, including *Archaediscus sp.*, *Earlandia moderata* and *Mediocris mediocris*, indicate that the strata are Holkerian to Asbian in age. Farther east, in the Snape House Borehole, a faulted sequence of about 70 m of this subdivision was drilled beneath limestone conglomerate; clasts of limestone and mudstone are recorded at intervals in the topmost 40 m. Foraminiferal assemblages in samples from 31.4 to 59.0 m, including *Archaediscus karreri vertens* and *Rectodiscus sp.*, indicate a late Asbian age, and this is supported by the presence of the trilobite cf. *Phillibole aprathensis*, which on Pendle Hill occurs below *Goniatites hudsoni*.

The well bedded limestone subdivision is not present in sections near Little Newton and Orms Gill Green, but farther north-east it attains an estimated thickness of 150 m at Hanlith. These strata, termed 'Hanlith Limestone' by Hudson (1949), are exposed in the banks of the River Aire and in numerous disused quarries, but thin south-eastwards and are absent at Rylstone or Flasby.

The **limestone conglomerate subdivision** succeeds the well bedded limestones except locally in the south-west and extreme south-east. It is also present near Little Newton and Orms Gill Green where the well bedded limestones are unrecorded, and overlaps the latter onto Worston Shales at Rylstone and Flasby. The subdivision is particularly well exposed in the Catlow Anticline (Plate 17), though there are many other good sections elsewhere. In the south-west, where the conglomerate was referred to as the 'Slaidburn Breccia' by Parkinson (1964), the thickest proving is 42 m in the How Hill boreholes near Halsteads in the Catlow An-

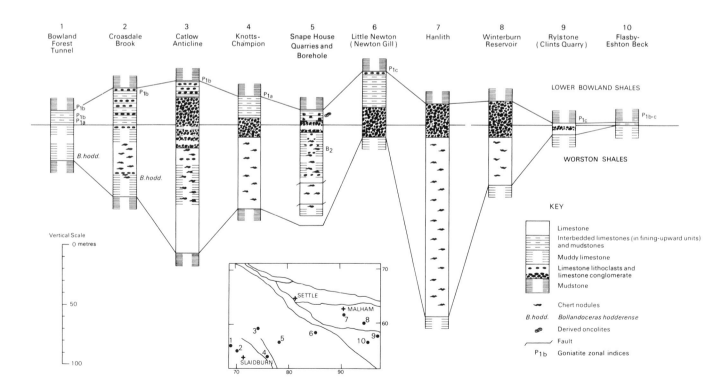

Figure 19 Comparative sections of the Pendleside Limestone showing faunal horizons. The datum line is the Asbian–Brigantian boundary

Plate 16   Bioturbated and dolomitic Pendleside Limestone, Bottoms Beck [7456 5667]. Beds of dolomitic calcarenite in the lower part of the formation are capped with nodules and layers of chert. (L 2816)

ticline (Wadge and others, 1983). The subdivision thins southwards; in the Snape House Borehole only about 10 m are present, but in sections in the extreme southwest, such as Croasdale Brook and the Bowland Forest Tunnel (Earp, 1955), it is absent. East of the Ribble about 25 m are present near Little Newton, and similar thicknesses are known from the Hanlith area (where the conglomerate was termed 'Black Hole Limestone' by Hudson, 1949) and around Winterburn Reservoir. On the southern flank of the Eshton–Hetton Anticline the subdivision is less than 10 m thick at Clints Quarry, south of Rylstone, where it was included in the 'Skelterton Limestone' of Booker and Hudson (1926); it thins out farther south-west at Flasby. The conglomerate is analogous to the sedimentary breccia recognised by Tiddeman (1891) in the Draughton Limestone of the Skipton Anticline, and later referred to as 'Tiddeman's Breccia' (see Hudson and Mitchell, 1937).

The subdivision comprises beds of limestone conglomerate up to 16 m thick interspersed with subordinate limestones or mudstones (Plate 17). In parts of the Catlow Anticline, however, bioturbated cherty limestones make substantial intercalations in the lower part of the sequence. The conglomerate tends to be polymict. The debris includes: medium-light grey bioclastic wackestones of reefal origin, typically carrying an irregular network of quartz; medium grey, medium and coarse calcarenite packstones and grainstones; and medium-dark grey, bioturbated and laminated fine calcarenite packstones. The clasts of reef limestones are generally angular to subangular, but those of other lithologies tend to be more rounded. The reef limestone clasts range from pebbles to blocks several metres across; other lithologies range from pebbles to boulders

generally less than 0.5 m across. No autochthonous masses of reef limestone have been noted during the resurvey, contrary to the view of Parkinson (1936). The bioturbated packstone clasts match lithologies common in the well bedded limestone subdivision of the Pendleside Limestone, and both these and at least some of the coarser packstones and grainstones are regarded as having been derived intraformationally. Other clasts comprise chert pebbles and boulders, as well as derived shells and masses of coral. The clasts are set in a matrix of buff-weathering, dolomitic calcarenite or calcirudite, commonly crinoidal and shelly, or more rarely of mudstone. Individual beds of conglomerate are generally sharp-based. In some sections the basal bed rests on an irregular erosion surface of well bedded limestones, but in others the basal conglomerate and the immediately underlying limestones are affected by similar minor folding.

Beds of limestone conglomerate, here classified as the Pendleside Limestone, are present under Lower Bowland Shales on the southern flank of the Craven Reef Belt near Scaleber Bridge. They rest with angular unconformity on marginal reef limestone of the Malham Formation, the Scaleber Quarry Limestone and the Scaleber Force Limestone. Boulders and blocks of reefal origin are dominant, and comprise medium-light grey bioclastic wackestone with radial fibrous calcite; there are also boulders of light grey coarse calcarenite packstone-grainstone, and dark grey, oncolitic-bioclastic wackestone derived from the Lower Hawes Limestone. Much of the deposit has a mudstone matrix, and there are interbeds of mudstone with limestone clasts.

The limestone conglomerate subdivision appears to span the Asbian–Brigantian boundary (see details), and both its base and its top are considered to be diachronous. Interbedded limestones in the Snape House Borehole yielded *Koninckopora inflata*, generally indicative of an age no younger than Asbian. An Asbian macrofauna was recovered at Winterburn Reservoir, though it may be derived. The same may be true of an occurrence of Asbian faunas in the limestone conglomerate at Clints Quarry, near Rylstone, for the highest posts there contain Brigantian corals and brachiopods. The limestone conglomerate in the Craven Reef Belt near Scaleber Bridge includes clasts of oncolitic limestone from the Lower Hawes Limestone which is of early Brigantian age, and the overlying Lower Bowland Shales have yielded a possible *Goniatites granosus* indicating a P_{2a} age: in view of the absence of recognisable clasts of younger limestones from the Wensleydale Group, an early Brigantian age is ascribed to this deposit.

The locally overlying **limestone-with-mudstone subdivision** consists of interbedded limestones, limestone conglomerates, mudstones and calcareous mudstones. This subdivision impersistently and transitionally overlies the limestone conglomerate in central and western areas where it is about 30 m thick, and rests directly on Worston Shales at Flasby in the south-east where it is probably less than 5 m thick. Good sections can be seen in Croasdale Brook near Croasdale House in the Slaidburn Anticline, and in streams near Dale House and Fair Hill in the Catlow Anticline. The subdivision forms a transition to the mudstone-dominated strata at the base of the Lower Bowland Shales, and there are considerable variations in the proportions of limestone, con-

Plate 17   Limestone conglomerate in Pendleside Limestone, Higher Clough [7290 5861], Slaidburn. The conglomerate overlies graded calcirudites and calcarenites. (L 2822)

glomerate and mudstone between individual sections. Thus, in Rig Gill Syke near Dale House, limestone conglomerates and subordinate limestones total about 11 m in a 20 m sequence, but in Croasdale Brook limestones with subordinate conglomerates total only about 9 m in a 32 m sequence. In a quarry near Snape House, limestone with subordinate conglomerate totalled 7.7 m in a 9.5 m section.

Sharp-based, beds of limestone conglomerate up to 1.3 m thick are recorded and locally rest on erosion surfaces. These are lithologically similar to those in the limestone conglomerate subdivision, with common clasts of reef limestone up to 0.3 m, and are characterised by silicified shells and corals. Sharp-based limestones are also present, ranging from crinoidal calcirudites to laminated fine calcarenite packstones and grainstones or calcisiltites (Plate 18). Some of these include limestone clasts, nodules or layers of chert and phosphatic concretions. There are many instances of fining-upwards beds, some ranging from limestone conglomerate to laminated or cross-laminated calcisiltite (Plate 18). The interspersed mudstones and calcareous mudstones are fissile or platy, and include layers of laminated calcisiltite, carbonaceous plant fragments, bivalves, goniatites and orthocones.

The limestone-with-mudstone subdivision is mainly of early Brigantian age. The thick sequence in Croasdale Beck includes beds with *Goniatites falcatus* of P_{1b} age at the top, but may extend down into the Asbian, poorly preserved goniatites of low P_{1a} or high B_2 age having been recovered from the middle part of the sequence. Farther east, in the Snape House Borehole, beds of limestone conglomerate and calcirudite include oncolites which may have been derived from the Lower Hawes Limestone (of P_{1a} age). In the section at Newton Gill, near Little Newton, the subdivision is overlain by Lower Bowland Shales of P_{1c} age.

DETAILS

Catlow Anticline

The well bedded limestone subdivision of the Pendleside Limestone is well seen [7152 5762 to 7184 5774] under limestone conglomerate in Copped Hill Clough near Collyholme. The limestones here form even and subordinate channel-fill beds up to 0.5 m thick, and have yielded *Koninckophyllum sp.*, *Lithostrotion sociale* and *Megachonetes* cf. *papilionaceous.* A section [7130 5887 to 7130 5882] in the River Hodder near Catlow displays intense bioturbation in well bedded (up to 0.5 m) fine calcarenite packstones and calcisiltites with chert nodules and bands up to 8 cm thick. Near Lamb Hill Farm, more than 30 m of the upper part of the sequence is extensively replaced by silica. The replacement is best exposed in White Syke [7047 5830], where white-weathering chert shows lamination and bioturbation traces typical of the normal limestone. The debris of a similar replacement is present on the hillside immediately west of disused quarry [7023 5783] south-west of Lamb Hill Farm where some 16 m of unsilicified, but partially dolomitised strata of the well-bedded limestone subdivision are exposed. This section includes unusually thick beds (up to 2.3 m) of calcirudite to coarse calcarenite packstone, one yielding *Lithostrotion sociale.*

There are many sections in the limestone conglomerate subdivision (Plate 17). The lowest 6.4 m are exposed in a disused quarry [7162 5893] north of Catlow. The basal bed is 3.1 m thick and includes a limestone block 1.8 m across. It has a locally discordant and undulating base that cuts out the top post of the well bedded limestone division, the top 0.9 m of which is folded. Above the massive basal bed there are three thin beds of calcirudite and calcarenite, two of which are graded, then a 0.7 m bed of limestone pebble conglomerate-calcirudite. A 2.0 m bed with limestone boulders caps the well exposed section, and this is succeeded by some 17 m of poorly exposed conglomerate.

The base of the conglomerate is well exposed farther east in a disused quarry [7271 5885] near Green Pike where 6 m of massive limestone conglomerate overlie 4.5 m of well bedded, bioturbated, cherty limestones (well bedded limestone subdivision) with an intervening 0.6 m sharp-based bed of coarse calcarenite to calcirudite packstone with limestone clasts. The clasts are mostly subangular to

Plate 18   Limestone-with-mudstone in Pendleside Limestone, Dob Dale Beck [7517 5955]. Sharp-based, graded limestone conglomerate and calcarenite with a mudstone interbed pass upwards into mudstones (at hammer) with bivalves and goniatites. (L 2839)

subrounded boulders (up to 0.2 m) of bioturbated, medium-dark grey, fine calcarenite packstone. They are associated with coral, crinoid and shell debris, and set in matrix of wackestone with an irregular network of silicification. The base of the limestone conglomerate subdivision appears to rest on an erosion surface in a section [7304 5889 to 7314 5885] of tightly folded strata in Huff Clough, north of Higher Clough, and some of the individual beds of conglomerate within the sequence also have sharp discordant bases, as seen in a disused quarry [7286 5867] west of Higher Clough.

The limestone conglomerate is again seen in quarries and stream sections near Halsteads and Fair Hill. In a quarry [7450 5941] at How Hill it includes a block of medium-light grey bioclastic wackestone of reefal origin that is 18 m wide; the wackestone carries a network of replacement silica. A similar block is exposed in the banks of Dob Dale Beck [7499 5945]. Other sections in Dob Dale Beck and its tributary Nursery Beck show that the limestone conglomerate is intercalcated with well bedded limestones; in one [7498 5940] the sequence includes 0.5 m of medium-dark grey, partly laminated but mostly intensely bioturbated, fine calcarenite packstone, with chert and subordinate mudstone.

The whole of the limestone conglomerate subdivision was proved

in the How Hill boreholes 1 and 2 [7469 5952 and 7469 5962]. Allowing for the steep dips encountered in these bores, its thickness is about 42 m. The clasts comprise medium-light grey bioclastic wackestone of reefal origin (dominant in the upper part of the sequence), medium-dark grey bioturbated fine calcarenite packstone, and subordinate medium grey coarse calcarenite packstone-grainstone. Boulders up to 3 m thick are recorded. The matrix is variously dolomitic or muddy. Beds of mudstone and limestone, including bioturbated fine calcarenite packstones, are present in the lowest 20 m of the sequence.

Bedded limestones intercalated in the lower part of the limestone conglomerate subdivision are exposed in the River Hodder [7185 5773 to 7192 5752], near Collyholme; the limestones are mostly cherty, intensely bioturbated, medium-dark grey, fine calcarenite packstones. The upper part of the limestone conglomerate, exposed farther downstream [7191 5761–7204 5743] is largely dolomitised and includes much dark limestone debris in clasts up to 16 cm where unaltered; towards the top interbedded calcirudite and calcarenite packstone-grainstone with subordinate beds and lenses of mudstone are present. The highest beds are slump-folded.

The limestone-with-mudstone subdivision is exposed in Rig Gill Syke [7350 5865 to 7359 5875], SE of Dale House, where it is about 20 m thick. Its base is transitional from the limestone conglomerate subdivision, and the sequence is overlain by Lower Bowland Shales. Sharp-based, commonly graded, beds of limestone conglomerate and limestone up to 1.3 m thick are interbedded with fissile mudstone and calcareous mudstone, some of these beds filling channels. Limestone clasts (up to 0.3 m) are mostly sub-angular, and tend to be associated with partially silicified coarse crinoid, shell and coral debris. A minor slump-fold affects laminated calcisiltite in the lower part of the sequence. Calcisiltites in the upper part of the sequence are associated with very dark grey layers composed of authigenic calcite. The highest beds have yielded *Posidonia becheri*, *P. corrugata*, *Goniatites falcatus*, *G. radiatus*, *G. striatus* and *G. spirifer*, indicative of a P_{1b} age. The *G. falcatus* band was also proved at the top of a similar limestone-with-mudstone sequence in the How Hill Borehole 2 [7469 5962], where it is also associated with layers rich in authigenic calcite. The total sequence, corrected for the steep dips, is about 18 m. *Nomismoceras sp.* and *G.* aff. *crenistria* or *G. concentricus* (P_{1a} or low P_{1b}) are recorded from the lower part of the sequence.

Some 13 m of similar beds are exposed under Lower Bowland Shales in Dob Dale Beck [7514 5955 to 7518 5955], SE of Fair Hill (Plate 18). Here again there are thin beds composed largely of authigenic calcite. The fauna from the top of this sequence includes *Posidonia becheri*, *P. kochi*, *Girtyoceras sp.*, *Goniatites elegans* and *Hibernicoceras carraunense*, indicating a P_{1c} age.

Slaidburn Anticline

In the Bowland Forest Tunnel, some 30 m of Pendleside Limestone were recorded, resting on Worston Shales (Earp, 1955), and are here referred to the well bedded limestone subdivision. At the base, 7.6 m of 'calcareous measures with beds (up to 0.46 m) of very hard porcellanous cementstone with purple and grey blotches' were present, and yielded *Bollandoceras hodderense*. These beds are exposed in a somewhat thicker but faulted sequence farther north-east in Croasdale Brook [7004 5501]. The base of the sequence is transitional from the underlying mudstones of the Worston Shales, and interbedded mudstone and limestone forms much of the lowest 17 m downstream from the fault. The base is taken at the lowest bed of bioturbated lime-mudstone, and *Bollandoceras hodderense* occurs some 12 m above this. A thin section of grainstone from a sharp-based graded bed in this part of the sequence [6998 5503] shows it to be bioclastic-peloidal, medium to coarse calcarenite (Plate 19d); principal grains are crinoid plates, peloids, foraminifera and *Koninckopora sp.*, and there are lithoclasts of wackestone. The sequence upstream from the fault [6998 5504] comprises 44 m of cherty, thin-bedded, medium to medium-dark grey, fine and medium calcarenite packstones and grainstones, with subordinate calcisiltites and lime-mudstones. Many of the coarser beds are laminated, and bioturbation is common throughout. A 1.7 m bed of limestone conglomerate, fining upwards to fine calcarenite, lies near the base. The clasts in this bed are pebbles and small boulders of fine and medium calcarenite packstone and are associated with coarse crinoidal and coral debris. There are partings and thin beds of poorly fissile streaky calcareous mudstone in the top 16 m of the sequence, which is overlain by fissile mudstones of the limestone-with-mudstone subdivision (see below). Bioturbated calcisiltites and lime-mudstones dominate in these uppermost 16 m.

About 50 m of the well bedded limestone subdivision are exposed in two sections in Bottoms Beck in Gisburn Forest. The lower sequence [7450 5657 to 7452 5659] includes thick-bedded, heavily slumped limestones, with mudstone clasts and shelly and crinoidal debris at the base, resting on mudstone. The upper [7456 5671 to 7454 5662] comprises 36 m of well bedded limestone (beds mostly less than 0.5 m), faulted near the top (Plate 15). The principal lithologies are partly dolomitic, medium-dark grey, fine calcarenite packstones and grainstones, mostly well laminated but partly bioturbated (Plate 16), and medium-dark grey calcisiltites. Subordinate lithologies are calcirudites and medium to coarse calcarenite packstones and grainstones, mostly in sharp-based, graded beds, and lime-mudstones occur at the tops of many of the graded beds in the uppermost part of the sequence. Chert nodules are common, and many limestone beds are capped by band of chert (Plate 16). A thin section of a laminated fine calcarenite grainstone from this sequence showed it to be peloidal and bioclastic, with peloids, calcispheres, foraminifera and crinoid plates as the principal grains. It included lithoclasts of wackestone and lime-mudstone, and showed slight matrix neomorphism. Foraminiferal assemblages in 22 samples from this stream section are restricted in both numbers of specimens and diversity of fauna. They include archaediscids at the *angulatus* and *concavus* stages, *Koskinotextularia cribriformis*, *Endostaffella sp.* and *Nodosarchaediscus sp.*, and are considered to be Holkerian to Asbian in age although several archaediscids at the *involutus* stage suggest some reworking of older Arundian sediments.

Slump-folds feature in a stream section [7261 5284 to 7277 5260] in the well bedded limestone subdivision near High Field, on the south-eastern flank of the Slaidburn Anticline. They occur not only at the base of the sequence but also near the top. In a nearby quarry section [7265 5256], some 15 m of the upper part of this sequence are exposed. Here the beds are partially dolomitised, and comprise thick- and thin-bedded, cherty, fine calcarenite packstones, calcisiltites, one bed of lime-mudstone, and subordinate crinoidal, coarse calcarenites and calcirudites including cerioid lithostrotionids (Parkinson, 1936, recorded *L. arachnoideum* from this locality, indicating a Holkerian age).

On the north-western limb of the anticline, a single 2 m thick dolomitised layer of limestone conglomerate, is exposed in a gully [7184 5545] near Hollins House; and 2.5 m of the same lithology crop out on the eastern bank of Bottoms Beck [7459 5673]. In disused quarry [7357 5332] near Standridge on the south-eastern limb, the conglomerate is represented by 1.4 m of massive calcirudite with limestone clasts up to 0.3 m across.

There is a good section through the limestone-with-mudstone subdivision in Croasdale Brook [6997 5514 to 6994 5507] where all but the lowest part is exposed. The sequence comprises typically sharp-based graded limestones up to 1 m thick interbedded with fissile mudstone, calcareous mudstone, and bands of calcisiltite. Many of the limestones contain lithoclasts or are conglomeratic, and they include partially silicified coarse crinoidal debris, shells and corals. The medium and fine calcarenite packstones and grainstones are commonly laminated, and the calcisiltites, which cap many of the graded beds, are laminated or cross-laminated. Fragments of fossilised wood and other coaly plant debris are

recorded, as are phosphatic nodules. Mudstones some 16 m below the top of the sequence have yielded indeterminate striatoid goniatites of probable high B_2 (Asbian) age; some 4 m higher in the sequence *Goniatites crenistria* and *Nomismoceras sp.* occur, indicating a P_{1a} or basal P_{1b} age. *G. falcatus* (P_{1b}) is known from two horizons within the top 5 m which are overlain by Lower Bowland Shales.

Knotts, Tosside, Wigglesworth

The well bedded limestone subdivision was entered under limestone conglomerate at 29.56 m in the Snape House Borehole [7794 5661], and drilled to the base at 100.28 m, but is faulted between 72 and 91 m. The sequence is dominated by medium-dark to medium grey fine calcarenite packstones and grainstones, some of which are laminated. These are interspersed with graded beds of calcirudites and coarser calcarenites. A thin-section of packstone at 46.15 m shows bioclastic-peloidal, medium to coarse calcarenite, the grains being crinoid plates, foraminifera, bryozoa, ostracods and peloids. There is complete matrix neomorphism to spar, as well as syntaxial overgrowth of crinoid plates. Streaky mudstones form much of the uppermost 6 m, and are common as partings or beds up to 0.5 m to a depth of 69.5 m. Muddy beds are common again below 94.7 m. Limestone lithoclasts up to 5 cm across are present down to 47.7 m, and between 66.0 and 69.0 m. They occur in conglomerates or as pebbly layers in finer lithologies. The trilobite cf. *Phillibole aprathensis* is recorded at 45.50 and 56.90 m, indicating a late Asbian age for these strata. Other macrofauna include *Koninckophyllum sp.*, *Lithostrotion portlocki* and *Rotiphyllum sp.* from 66.40 m. Foraminifera from four samples between 31.40 and 59.00 m include *Archaediscus karreri vertens*, *Endothyra tantala*, *Koskinobigenerina sp.* and *Rectodiscus sp.*, indicating a late Asbian age. The alga *Koninckopora inflata* is recorded in samples down to 46.15 m.

The limestone conglomerate subdivision extends to near the southern margin of the district at Knotts, where it is exposed in disused quarries. The best section [7645 5382] shows 2.30 m of limestone conglomerate, mostly massive, capped by 0.3 m of medium to coarse calcarenite packstone. The clasts in the conglomerate are up to 0.3 m across, and comprise dark bioturbated and pale reefal types.

Limestone conglomerate was proved under limestone-with-mudstone in the Snape House Borehole from 20.70 to 29.56 m where it rests on the well bedded limestone subdivision. Massive conglomerate, including clasts of dark bioturbated limestone and pale reefal limestone up to 23 cm across, forms most of the sequence, though calcarenite packstones and grainstones with limestone clasts occupy the mid-part. Much of the conglomerate matrix is muddy. A thin-section of a grainstone from 23.00 m shows it to be a peloidal and bioclastic, fine to coarse calcarenite, the grains including peloids, crinoid plates, foraminifera and algae (kamaenids and *Koninckopora sp.*). The alga *Koninckopora inflata*, which ranges up into the basal few metres of the Brigantian in Derbyshire (Chisholm and others, 1983), is abundant below 23.00 m. A comparable sequence is exposed in a disused quarry [7795 5644] nearby, where clasts up to 1 m are recorded.

Oncolites are recorded in the limestone-with-mudstone subdivision that was proved in the Snape House Borehole. These beds were drilled from rock-head at 10.68 m to the top of the limestone conglomerate subdivision at 20.70 m, mostly in limestones with subordinate limestone conglomerates. A Brigantian age is inferred for these limestones from the absence of *Koninckopora inflata* in any of the five thin sections studied for microfossils, in contrast to its presence in the underlying strata. Part of this sequence is exposed nearby in a disused quarry [7801 5654] where about 9.5 m of somewhat irregularly bedded limestone with interbedded mudstone are exposed. Fauna from the mudstone included specimens of a poorly preserved crenistriate goniatite and *Nomismoceras sp.*, indicating a B_2 or P_{1a} age.

An 11 m sequence of presumed limestone-with-mudstone is incompletely exposed in a quarry [7561 5520] near Brock Thorn (Plate 19a and c); here Parkinson (1936) recorded *Goniatites crenistria* and *Beyrichoceratoides truncatum* indicative of a P_{1a} age. Foraminifera from the lower part of the sequence include *Howchinia* cf. *bradyana* which, although it occurs in the late Asbian, is much more common in the Brigantian, and cf. *Neoarchaediscus sp.* indicative of the late Asbian. A thin section of a lithoclastic-bioclastic calcirudite within the lowest 2 m of the exposed section includes *Girvanella* oncolites which may have been derived from the Lower Hawes Limestone which is of Brigantian age.

An infilled quarry [8160 5720] at Teenley Hill near Wigglesworth worked pale-weathering cherty bioclastic limestones which are referred to the limestone-with-mudstone subdivision. A thin section of a typical sample shows lithoclastic-peloidal-bioclastic grainstone, variably grained, fine calcarenite to calcirudite (Plate 19b). Principal grains are lithoclasts, peloids, crinoid plates, foraminifera and *Koninckopora sp.* Quartz occurs as internal replacement of crinoid plates and molluscan fragments, as well as euhedra in lithoclasts. Foraminifera include *Endothyra spira*, *Neoarchaediscus sp.*, *Palaeotextularia ex gr. longiseptata*, *Planospiridiscus sp.* and *Rectodiscus sp.*, indicating a late Asbian age for these strata.

Little Newton, Orms Gill Green

East of the River Ribble the limestone conglomerate subdivision is exposed in a disused quarry [8520 5831] north of Little Newton, where about 25 m are present. The section shows up to 6 m of massive conglomerate with clasts mostly of medium-light grey bioclastic packstone; the matrix, which is crinoidal and includes shells and corals, is partially replaced by dolomite or silica. There are also beds of limestone, a thin section from one of these beds shows that it is a bioclastic-intraclastic grainstone, calcirudite. The lithoclasts include fine calcarenite grainstones and packstones, with peloidal and oolitic-bioclastic varieties. Quartz occurs as irregular silicification of intraclasts, and much of the matrix comprises clear spar.

The subdivision is represented by about 8 m of massive limestone conglomerate and limestone in a stream section [8704 5980] south of Orms Gill Green. Here it rests directly on calcareous mudstones of the Worston Shales and is overlain by mudstones with thin, graded limestones (Lower Bowland Shales). A thin section shows lithoclasts comprising mudstone and dolomitic siltstone, with grains of collophane disseminated throughout. RSA

Scaleber Bridge

On the southern flank of the Craven Reef Belt east of Settle, partly dolomitised limestone conglomerate, comprising blocks and boulders of reef limestone, is exposed in the banks [8414 6277 to 8417 6299] of Scaleber Beck upstream from Scaleber Bridge. Geopetals in many of these blocks are steeply inclined and in some they are inverted. In much of the section the conglomerate rests unconformably on marginal reef limestone (Malham Formation) but in one exposure [8417 6267] overlies Scaleber Quarry Limestone; it is overlain [8418 6295] by Upper Bowland Shales. Downstream from Scaleber Bridge, there is a section [8401 6243] in a slab of medium-light grey bioclastic wackestone (reef limestone) some 50 m long, resting unconformably on Scaleber Force Limestone and geopetals in the slab show it to be inverted. Crinoidal calcirudite of unknown age fills a fissure at the northeastern end of this slab, and the slab is covered by Upper Bowland Shales.

The limestone conglomerate of Scaleber Beck was proved in two boreholes nearby. The Cominco Borehole S1 [8421 6275] drilled the subdivision from rock-head at 1.88 m to the top of the Scaleber Quarry Limestone at 13.30 m. The sequence comprised blocks and boulders of medium-light grey wackestone (including many with

radial fibrous calcite), light grey coarse calcarenite packstone-grainstone, and (subordinate) dark grey muddy wackestone clasts with oncolites, apparently derived from the Lower Hawes Limestone. Mudstone is dominant in the lowest metre and forms the matrix at intervals above. In the Cominco Borehole S10 [8360 6304], the limestone conglomerate was proved (under Lower Bowland Shales of probable P_{2a} age) from 19.38 m to the top of the Scaleber Quarry Limestone at 58.64 m. The clasts are mostly of medium-light grey bioclastic wackestone, commonly with radial fibrous calcite; some are dolomitised. Muddy selvages separate many of the clasts, and mudstone dominates in places near the top of the sequence. RSA,DJCM

Hanlith (Airton Anticline)

The well bedded limestone subdivision crops out around Hanlith and Kirkby Malham and is about 150 m thick. It is exposed in a section [9003 6147 to 9020 6189] (presumed to be faulted) on the eastern bank of the River Aire, where it comprises well bedded (up to 0.4 m), medium-dark grey, fine and medium calcarenite packstones and wackestones. Some of the limestones are bioturbated, and chert is common as nodules and bands. Some 10 m of these beds are exposed in a disused quarry [9060 6132] south-east of Windy Pike where the fine calcarenite packstones are partly laminated. This section includes a sharp-based packstone grading from coarse calcarenite, and 0.5 m of medium grey wackestone, rich in silicified coral debris, near the top. Foraminifera from this quarry include the diagnostic Asbian forms of *Archaediscus* and *Gigasbia gigas* at the 'angulatus' stage.

There are many exposures of the limestone conglomerate subdivision in tightly folded strata to the east of the River Aire at Hanlith, for example in the river banks [9020 6189 to 9027 6209] and in disused quarries [9077 6120 and 9110 6051]. These show massive to crudely bedded limestone conglomerate with clasts mostly of medium-light grey bioclastic wackestone set in a matrix of medium-light grey crinoidal wackestone or packstone with shells and corals. The subdivision is here about 28 m thick. Its base is well exposed in a quarry [9105 6057] near Bark Laithe, where it rests sharply on well bedded, bioturbated, medium-dark grey, fine calcarenite packstones (well bedded limestone subdivision). A thin section of a sample from one locality [9028 6157] shows a variably grained lithoclastic-crinoidal packstone-wackestone; lithoclasts include lime-mudstone, foraminiferal-ostracod-brachiopod wackestone, and oolitic and bioclastic packstones. Irregular cavities contain calcisiltite.

Eshton – Hetton Anticline

Some 20 m of thick-bedded to massive pale-weathering limestone conglomerate and subordinate limestone of the limestone conglomerate subdivision are exposed in the banks [9459 6012] of Winterburn Reservoir at the eastern end of the dam. Clasts of medium-light grey bioclastic wackestone are dominant, set in a matrix of crinoidal, shelly wackestone and packstone. This locality has yielded a fauna of Asbian age including *Heterophyllia sp.*, *Siphonophyllia* cf. *benburbensis*, *Alitaria panderi*, *Avonia youngiana*, *Dictyoclostus* aff. *pinguis*, *D.* cf. *semireticulatus*, *Echinoconchus punctatus*, *Gigantoproductus* cf. *maximus*, *Overtonia fimbriata*, *Productina margaritacea*, *Productus productus* and *Spirifer sp. striatus* group.

On the south-eastern flank of the Eshton – Hetton Anticline, 8.7 m of the limestone conglomerate subdivision are exposed in Clints Rock Quarry [9670 5750] south of Rylstone. The basal 2.9 m are well bedded crinoidal limestones which rest sharply on 4.2 m of calcareous mudstones and muddy limestones of the Worston Shales. This basal part consists of beds of medium and coarse calcarenite packstones that are medium-dark to medium-light grey in colour. The two lowest beds are characterised by conspicuous green patches (probably chlorite) and the three highest include limestone clasts. The fauna includes *Amplexizaphrentis enniskilleni*, cf. *Fasciculophyllum densum*, *F.* cf. *junctoseptatum*, *Rotiphyllum rushianum*, *Dictyoclostus multispiniferus*, *Krotovia spinulosa*, *Rylstonia benecompacta*, *R.* cf. *dentata*, *Zaphrentites parallela* and an indeterminate goniatite. The succeeding bed consists of 3.4 m of massive limestone conglomerate with subangular to subrounded clasts up to 15 cm of medium to medium-light grey wackestones, packstones and grainstones. The matrix comprises medium-light grey wackestone and packstone with locally abundant crinoidal, shell and coral debris. This bed has yielded a Holkerian or Asbian fauna including *Axophyllum vaughani*, *Lithostrotion martini*, *L. sociale*, *Avonia youngiana* and *Plicatifera plicatilis*. The overlying strata in this section comprise 2.1 m of well bedded to lenticular, medium-dark grey calcarenite packstones that contain *Striatifera striata* (suggesting an early Brigantian or latest Asbian age), and *Diphyphyllum furcatum* and *D. lateseptatum* (indicating an early Brigantian age).

On the south-eastern flank of the anticline, the limestone conglomerate passes south-westwards into limestone-with-mudstone. Limestones in the latter subdivision are exposed in Flasby Beck [9488 5683] at Holme Laithe, north-east of Flasby where they comprise well bedded, medium-dark to medium-light grey, fine to coarse calcarenite and calcirudite packstones and grainstones with *Hettonia fallax* and indeterminate zaphrentoids. A thin-section of a packstone-grainstone shows crinoid plates, lithoclasts (wackestone and packstone) and bryozoa as the principal grains. Quartz occurs as an internal replacement of crinoid plates. There is complete matrix neomorphism to spar, and syntaxial overgrowth of crinoid plates.

In a poorly exposed section [9443 5615] in Low Wood, south-west of Flasby Hall, some 5 m of limestone-with-mudstone separate fissile mudstones of the Lower Bowland Shales from interbedded poorly fissile calcareous mudstones with bioturbated muddy limestones at the top of the Worston Shales. They comprise sharp-based beds of partly cherty, medium-dark to medium-light grey calcarenite and calcirudite interbedded with fissile mudstones; limestone clasts are most abundant near the base of individual limestone beds. 0.1 m bed of limestone includes collophane nodules, and a thin-section shows lithoclasts, collophane nodules, crinoid plates, bryozoans and foraminifera to be the principal grains, with a lump of *Girvanella* among the subordinate components. There is complete matrix neomorphism to spar, and pyrite is disseminated throughout.

Lower Bowland Shales (Brigantian)

In the Craven Basin the division of mudstone, siltstone and sandstone that rests on the Pendleside Limestone or, where this is absent, on the Worston Shales, and extends upwards to the Leion Marine Band, is termed Lower Bowland Shales (Figure 15). These strata are broadly analogous to the lower parts of the Bolland Shale of Phillips (1836) and Bowland Shales of Tiddeman (see Hull and others, 1875, and Primary Survey One-Inch Geological Sheet 92NW, published 1892). The Bowland Shales were defined as 'series' by Parkinson (1926). Bisat (1928) divided the series into three 'zones' (P_1, P_2 and E_1) using the included goniatite faunas, and recognised a faunal horizon marked by the incoming of *Eumorphoceras* and *Cravenoceras* as the base of E_1. He used the $P_2 - E_1$ boundary to define 'lower' and 'upper' divisions of the series. Later (1930, 1933) he assigned the lower division (the Lower Bowland Shales of Booker and Hudson, 1926; and Parkinson, 1936) to the upper Viséan, and the upper to the Namurian. This junction, marked specifically by the Leion

Band, has since been accepted (Ramsbottom and others, 1978) as the Dinantian–Silesian boundary and, although there are no major lithostratigraphical reasons for dividing the sequence at this horizon, it is the current practice for this boundary to be represented on Geological Survey maps. The distinction between 'Lower' and 'Upper' Bowland Shales was recognised in the Clitheroe district by Earp and others (1961), but the divisions were combined into a 'Bowland Shale Group' on the one-inch geological map to which their memoir related. Lithostratigraphical criteria were employed by Fewtrell and Smith (1980), and their 'Bowland Shale Formation' or 'Bowland Formation' is equivalent to the 'Bowland Shales' of Tiddeman.

The Lower Bowland Shales are widespread in the basinal area where they are up to 300 m thick (Figure 20). The unit is absent immediately to the south of the Craven Reef Belt near Scaleber Bridge, but thin sequences are present at two localities to the north of the Reef Belt where they rest unconformably on the Malham Formation and Wensleydale Group. Their outcrop generally gives rise to subdued topography, but south-east of the Slaidburn Anticline, intercalated sandstones form prominent features. The sandstones have been previously referred to as Pendleside Grit (Tiddeman *in* Hull and others, 1875; Parkinson, 1926), Pendleside Sandstone (e.g. Earp and others, 1961) and 'Upper' and 'Lower' Pendleside Sandstone (Parkinson, 1936). In view of the complex geometry of these sandstone bodies, a new term, 'Pendleside Sandstones' is preferred, and employed in this account for the sandstones in the Lower Bowland Shales.

In the basin the base of the Lower Bowland Shales is generally transitional from Pendleside Limestone, the boundary being taken at the top of the highest conspicuous limestone bed in the sequence (see Fewtrell and Smith, 1980). This junction is diachronous, and the base is generally of P_{1b} to P_{1c} age though locally it is of P_{1a} age. North of the Reef Belt the overlapping Lower Bowland Shales are of P_{2b-c} age in the Cominco Borehole S3.

The characteristic lithologies of the Lower Bowland Shales are fissile mudstones, silty mudstones and platy weathering calcareous mudstones. Some of the mudstones are micaceous and some contain ironstone nodules. Bivalves and carbonaceous plant fragments are common, and there are several layers rich in goniatites. Many sections include beds of medium-dark grey limestone, mostly sharp-based graded units that vary lithologically from calcirudite (Plate 19f) or calcarenite to laminated or cross-laminated calcisiltite. Some of these limestones are sandy (Plate 19e) and intraclasts of mudstone or calcisiltite occur locally. In places they are slumped, and sole-marks including groove- and prod-casts are recorded. Limestone also occurs as nodules and bullions up to 1 m across and 0.25 m thick. Pebbly or conglomeratic layers are known from several parts of the sequence. The clasts are of light and dark grey limestones and can be matched with lithologies in the marginal reef limestones of the Malham Formation and limestones in the lower part of the Wensleydale Group including the Lower Hawes Limestone.

Sandstones and siltstones are present in the central and south-western areas, and dominate the successions in Newton Gill (Little Newton) and between Slaidburn and Knotts; they are absent north-east of the South Craven Fault

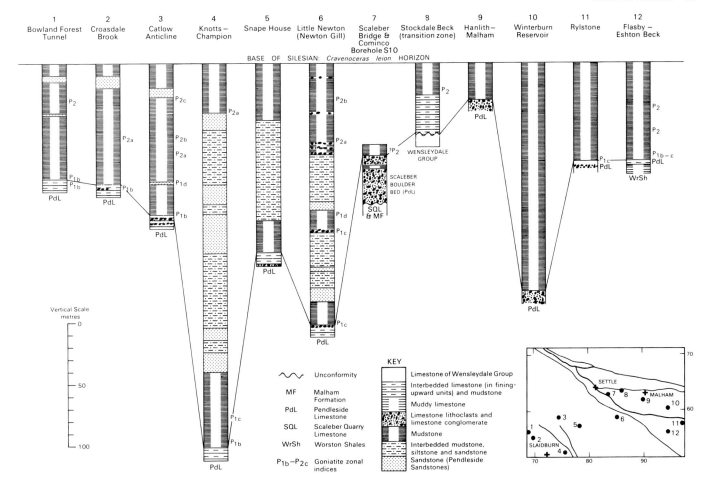

Figure 20 Comparative sections of the Lower Bowland Shales showing faunal horizons. The datum line is the Dinantian–Silesian boundary

system. The sandstones comprise thick- and thin-bedded, fine-grained, siliceous and locally ferruginous varieties. Some contain mudstone clasts and carry sole-marks including groove-casts, flute-casts and load-casts. Instances of slump-folds are recorded, and the upper surfaces of some beds are rippled. Some beds are conspicuously carbonaceous, with comminuted plant debris.

Associated with the Pendleside Sandstones there are local but substantial deposits of interbedded and interlaminated sandstone, siltstone and mudstone referred to here as 'sandstone-with-mudstone'. These beds are typically flaggy and micaceous. The sandstones have sharp bases and tops and occur in beds a few centimetres thick and as laminae within sequences of 'striped-beds'. Some of the siltstones and mudstones may contain ironstone nodules. Where sandy strata are believed to be present in poorly exposed terrain, they are represented on the map as 'sandstone-with-mudstone' even though they may include Pendleside Sandstones.

The distribution of the various lithofacies and the variations in thickness within the district are illustrated in Figure 20. Where possible the succession has been subdivided into the P_1 and P_2 biozones and into the P_{1a} – P_{1d} and P_{2a} – P_{2c} subzones on the basis of the included goniatite faunas (see

Bisat, 1934; and Hudson and Mitchell, 1937).

On the northern limb of the Slaidburn Anticline and in the Catlow Anticline, the Lower Bowland Shales are 90 to 120 m thick, and in the Bowland Forest Tunnel, 94 m are referred to this division (Earp, 1955) with *Goniatites falcatus* (P_{1b}) at the base and the Leion Marine Band at the top. Sandstones and sandy shales are recorded at two levels in P_2. Much of the sequence up to P_{2b} is exposed in the banks of the River Hodder near Collyholme Wood where a thin sandstone of P_{1c-d} age is present. A sandstone of similar age, perhaps 20 m thick and associated with mudstones containing limestone boulders, is exposed in Bottoms Beck and in a tributary south-west of Hesbert Hall. A higher sandstone of P_{2c} age is exposed farther upstream in Bottoms Beck, near Halsteads.

The Lower Bowland Shales are about 300 m thick to the south-east of the Slaidburn Anticline, between Slaidburn and Knotts. Sandy strata, including several substantial, partly lenticular units of sandstone, occupy some 200 m of this sequence between proved faunal bands of P_{1c} and P_{2a} age. The sandstones form prominent features between Lower Edge Farm and Knotts where they are exposed in disused quarries. Together with their associated sandstone-with-mudstone they are well displayed in the stream at Tinklers Farm.

The Lower Bowland Shales are poorly exposed in central parts of the district except in Newton Gill near Little Newton, where 212 m are present from the top of the Pendleside Limestone up to the estimated position of the Leion Band. Here the lowest proved faunas are of P_{1c} age and the highest of P_{2b} age. Sandy strata form two layers: the lower is 5 m thick and is of P_{1c} age; the upper is 45 m thick, and lies between faunal bands of P_{1d} and P_{2a} age. The mudstones contain pebbles or boulders of limestone at intervals throughout; the clasts comprise pale reef lithologies as well as dark varieties matching those in the Wensleydale Group. A boulder of dark grey wackestone with oncolites (Lower Hawes Limestone) is recorded in deposits of P_{1c} age, and a pebble of black chert is recorded higher in the sequence in thin limestone of P_{2a-b} age.

North-east of the South Craven Fault system near Malham the Lower Bowland Shales are unexposed. The mapping suggests, however, that the sequence is exceptionally thin hereabouts, with less than 50 m of strata separating mudstones of proved E_{1b} age (Upper Bowland Shales) in Tranlands Beck, south-west of Malham, from the top of the Pendleside Limestone which is marked by a sinkhole south-west of Kirkby Top. Of this interval, perhaps less than 30 m is referable to the Lower Bowland Shales. Westwards from here in Scaleber Beck, downstream from Scaleber Bridge, the Lower Bowland Shales are overlapped by the Upper Bowland Shales.

In poorly exposed ground around Winterburn Reservoir, the Lower Bowland Shales are about 185 m thick, though neither the base nor the top are seen. Some 7 m of mudstone and limestone, including layers with angular fragments of limestone, were noted on a field map by R. H. Tiddeman from what is now taken to be the upper part of the sequence in a section now submerged.

Sections on the south-eastern flank of the Eshton–Hetton Anticline show the Lower Bowland Shales to be about 80 m thick. At Flasby the basal beds are of P_{1b-c} age, and in Washfold Beck, south of Rylstone, are of probable P_{1c} age. According to Booker and Hudson (1926) the junction hereabouts between the Lower Bowland Shales and their Skelterton (Pendleside) Limestone is markedly diachronous. Strata of P_1 age may be less than 20 m thick at Flasby, and there is no record of sandstone within this sequence.

Immediately south of the Craven Reef Belt, to the northwest of Scaleber Bridge, some 9 m of mudstone referred to the Lower Bowland Shales were proved under rock-head in the Cominco Borehole S10. These mudstones rested sharply on limestone conglomerate, and yielded a possible *Goniatites granosus* indicative of a P_{2a} age. Farther east, in the Cominco Borehole S3, near Stockdale Farm, 43.7 m of Lower Bowland Shales were proved from the Leion Marine Band down to the Wensleydale Group. The sequence yielded *Neoglyphioceras sp.*, indicative of a P_{2b-c} age, and the lowest 26 m are unusual in that they are dominated by limestones, with mudstone restricted to partings and to a few interbeds up to 0.9 m thick. The limestones comprise dark to medium-dark grey muddy calcilutites, calcisiltites and wackestones. Crinoidal and shelly debris is common, and oncolites are present at intervals; slump-structures and graded limestone beds are recorded.

There is a small exposure of Lower Bowland Shales north

Plate 19 Photomicrographs of Pendleside Limestone, Lower Bowland Shales, Gordale Limestone and Scaleber Quarry Limestone.

a. Pendleside Limestone, Brock Thorn Quarry, Slaidburn [7561 5520]. Packstone composed of calcified sponge spicules and ?radiolaria. Field of view 5 mm RSA 2813
b. Pendleside Limestone, Teenley Rock Quarry, Wigglesworth [8160 5720]. Grainstone, unevenly grained, composed of peloids, limestone lithoclasts, crinoid plates and foraminifera. Field of view 5 mm E 51224
c. Pendleside Limestone, Brock Thorn Quarry [7561 5520]. Packstone coquina composed of brachiopod fragments, crinoid plates and bryozoa. Note internal replacement of crinoid plates by silica and the abundant pyrite (black) disseminated throughout. Field of view 5 mm RSA 2814
d. Pendleside Limestone, Croasdale Brook [6998 5503]. Grainstone, unevenly grained, consisting of crinoid plates, peloids, foraminifera and algae (*Koninckopora*). Note micrite envelopes around the crinoid plates. Field of view 5 mm E 60534
e. Lower Bowland Shales, Greenwoods [7540 5219]. Sandy calcarenite (?packstone) composed of foraminifera, crinoid plates and algae (kamaenids) with abundant detrital quartz and feldspar grains. Field of view 5 mm E 60535
f. Lower Bowland Shales, Newton Gill, Hellifield [8502 5867]. Calcirudite composed of limestone lithoclasts and coarse crinoidal debris in a matrix totally replaced by a mosaic of euhedral dolomite. Field of view 5 mm E 51198
g. Gordale Limestone, High Hill [8337 6370]. Replacement dolostone, a mosaic of dolomite euhedra with interstitial quartz. Field of view 3 mm E 60529
h. Scaleber Quarry Limestone, Cominco Borehole S10 [8360 6304] at 91.15 m. Replacement dolostone showing a replacive euhedral mosaic with relic crinoid plates and shell fragment. Field of view 5 mm ARE 1935

of the Middle Craven Fault in the banks [9409 6394] of Cow Gill, west of Bordley Hall. The section shows about 0.5 m of northward-dipping calcareous silty mudstone with calcarous nodules and crinoidal debris, and brachiopods of P age; these beds are overlain, apparently unconformably, by mudstones containing limestone bullions and shells of undeterminable age.

DETAILS

Slaidburn Anticline

Of the sequence of Bowland Shales described by Earp (1955) from the Bowland Forest Tunnel on the north-western limb of the fold, 94 m are here referred to the Lower Bowland Shales. The lowest beds of Earp's sequence (below his Horizon 3) include 'several posts of limestone' up to 0.46 m thick, and are classified as Pendleside Limestone. A 0.3 m sandstone is present in the lower part of P_2, and 7.6 m of sandy shales with thin sandstones are recorded at the top of P_2.

Much of the Lower Bowland Shales sequence is exposed farther north in Croasdale. The lower part, resting on limestone-with-mudstone of the Pendleside Limestone, is seen in the banks [6992 5523 to 6996 5514] of Croasdale Brook, and comprises fissile mudstones and platy-weathering calcareous mudstones. Fauna from an exposure [6987 5516] high on the south-western bank includes *Catastroboceras quadratus*, *Rineceras hibernicum*, *Goniatites granosus* and *Sudeticeras sp.*, indicative of a P_{2a} age. Farther upstream [6987 5534], thick-bedded to massive fine-grained micaceous sandstone with subordinate interlaminated sandstone and siltstone ('striped-

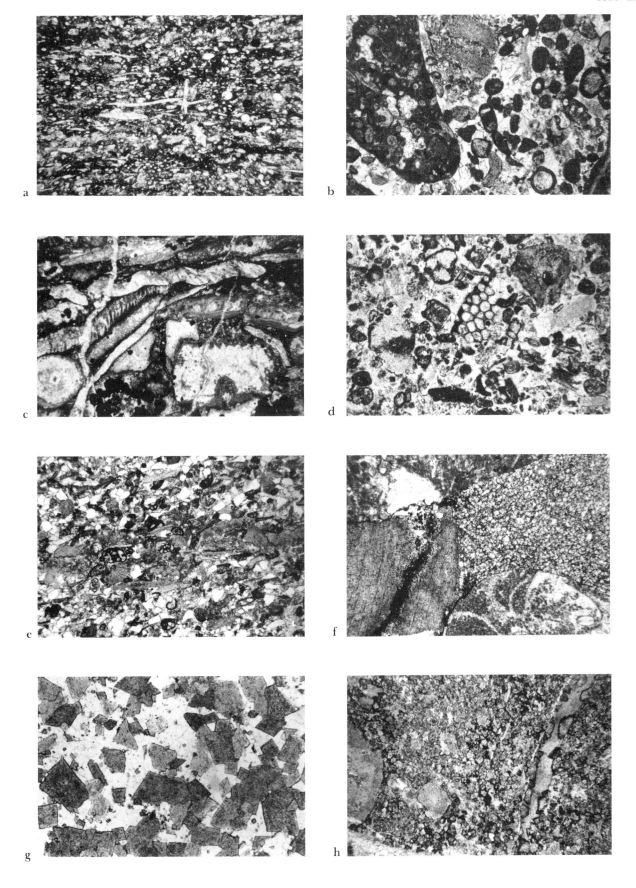

beds') is exposed, forming a unit at least 7 m thick. There are small exposures of sandstone and striped-beds in this part of the sequence in streams farther east towards Stocks Reservoir. In one of these sections [7250 5589], the sandstone is underlain by mudstones and calcareous mudstones with crinoidal laminae and thick beds of calcisiltite; the mudstones have yielded a poorly preserved specimen of *Neoglyphioceras* or *Lyrogoniatites sp.* of probable P_{2b} age.

Beds ranging from P_{2a-b} to the base of the Namurian (indicated by the association of *Posidonia corrugata* and *P. membranacea*) were exposed [7283 5696 to 7290 5666] during the resurvey on the bed of Stocks Reservoir, south of Birch Hill. These strata, which are both tightly folded and faulted, comprise interbedded partly calcareous mudstones and limestones, and the mudstones include layers with crinoidal debris and limestone clasts. The limestones occur in beds up to 0.5 m thick, that range from calcisiltite to coarse calcarenite. They are commonly laminated or cross-laminated and some posts show well defined grading. In part of this section the beds are slump-folded.

Sections in Bottoms Beck and Hesbert Hall Syke, south of Hesbert Hall, expose a sandstone of P_{1b-d} age. Some 16 m are seen, faulted at the top, in Bottoms Beck [7470 5685], and comprise thick- and thin-bedded fine-grained sandstone, partly micaceous and carbonaceous, interbedded with silty mudstone and 'striped-beds'. Sole-marks are recorded, including groove-casts trending N40°W. This sandstone is underlain by mudstone with bullions and boulders of dark, crinoidal limestone, (see Parkinson, 1936, plate 25). The basal mudstones, faulted against the boulder-bearing mudstones described above, have yielded *Goniatites striatus* and *G. spirifer*, indicating a P_{1b} age, at [7463 5667].

In Hesbert Hall Syke the sandstone is about 20 m thick, with 'striped-beds' and silty mudstone dominant towards the base. It rests on fossiliferous mudstones and calcareous mudstones with limestone clasts, and at one exposure [7502 5668] includes a 1.5 m layer with boulders of pale reefal limestone and dark calcisiltite. Above the sandstone there are faulted exposures [7472 5687 and 7489 5684] of mudstone with mostly thin-bedded, laminated and cross-laminated calcisiltites and calcarenites, as well as 2 m of mudstone conglomerate; this latter unit contains shells, corals, nodules and bullions of limestone, and clasts of light grey reefal and dark limestones up to 0.4 m. A higher sandy layer is poorly exposed in the bed [7468 5692] of Bottoms Beck.

Catlow Anticline

The Lower Bowland Shales are best seen in exposures [7517 5955 to 7543 5955] in Dob Dale Beck and its tributaries near Fair Hill. The basal beds have yielded a fauna of P_{1c} age including *Posidonia becheri*, *P. kochi*, *Epistroboceras kathleeni*, *Rineceras luidi*, *Girtyoceras sp.*, *Goniatites elegans* and *Hibernicoceras carraunense*. The lower part of the sequence includes very thin beds of fine grained sandstone, overlain by mudstones with limestones of P_{2a} age (*G. granosus*). Succeeding beds of similar lithologies have yielded P_{2b} faunas including *Posidonia corrugata* and *Sudeticeras splendens*. Higher beds are exposed farther south-west in Dob Dale Beck [7465 5888], where some 40 m of mudstone rest on 7.0 m of thin-bedded, fine-grained sandstone and interbedded micaceous, carbonaceous 'striped-beds'; these in turn overlie 20 m of mudstone with subordinate limestone interbeds. The top part of the latter mudstones has yielded a P_{2c} fauna including *Posidonia corrugata*, *P. membranacea*, *Girtyoceras spp.* and *Lyrogoniatites georgiensis*.

On the north-western limb of the fold near Lamb Hill Farm, the lower part of the Lower Bowland Shales sequence and the Pendleside Limestone appear to be cut out by a north-east-trending strike-fault seen in an exposure [7030 5798] north-west of the farm buildings. The Lower Bowland Shales hereabouts were interpreted by Parkinson (1936, p.322) as resting unconformably on an irregular surface of his Worston Series. The outcrop [7023 5783] that is here regarded as Pendleside Limestone was considered by him to be a contemporaneous sea-stack against which Lower Bowland Shales of P_{2a} age were banked. In view of the structural complexity of this ground and the lack of critical exposure, Parkinson's interpretation cannot be disproved, but a structural explanation of the data is preferred.

Much of the Lower Bowland Shales sequence is exposed [7205 5743 to 7255 5722] in the banks of the River Hodder, east of Collyholme Wood. Two thin beds of fine-grained, siliceous sandstone totalling 16 cm are present [7210 5740] towards the base, with groove-casts trending N45°W. They are overlain by P_{1d} mudstones and 'striped beds', and rest on laminated calcareous mudstones containing 0.35 m of mudstone conglomerate with pale and dark limestone clasts up to 10 cm. A P_{2a} fauna including *Sudeticeras crenistriatum* is recorded at an exposure [7224 5723] 20 m higher in the sequence where there are beds of calcisiltite and calcarenite. Some 20 m above this, an exposure [7233 5722] of mudstone contains *Neoglyphioceras subcirculare* indicative of P_{2b} age. The sequence hereabouts contains a few thin beds of partly laminated limestone ranging from calcisiltite to medium calcarenite, and bearing groove- and prod-casts. There are also limestone bullions up to 1 m across and 0.25 m thick, and 0.25 m of mudstone conglomerate with limestone clasts up to 3 cm across. Interbedded limestones continue into the highest parts of the section where they are locally slumped.

Champion, Knotts

In the area between Slaidburn and Knotts, the Lower Bowland Shales are thicker, and sandstones or sandy strata dominate the sequence between P_{1c} and P_{2a} faunal bands. The lowest beds are exposed in disused quarries and streams in folded and faulted ground south of Knotts. The basal strata are exposed in a gully [7726 5292] south-east of Spring Side where they comprise mudstone and calcareous mudstone with subordinate sharp-based beds of laminated calcisiltite and graded calcarenite. The mudstones have yielded *Posidonia becheri*, *Goniatites* cf. *crenistria* and *Nomismoceras sp.*, indicating a highest P_{1a} age. Farther up this gully [7719 5292] calcareous mudstones yielded a low P_{1c} fauna including *G. elegans*, and mudstones in a gully [7683 5282 and 7680 5282] at Barrow Brow have yielded P_{1b} faunas including *P. becheri*, *Beyrichoceratoides sp.*, *Girtyoceras sp.*, *G. spirifer*, *G. striatus*, *G.* aff. *concentricus* and *G. radiatus*.

The Pendleside Sandstones form prominent features at Knotts and westwards to beyond Anna Land End. They occur as several leaves, that either have short lenticular crops, or crops extending for more than 1 km along strike. One of the best sections is in a disused quarry [7653 5322] west of Spring Side where 7.25 m of thick-bedded to massive fine-grained, siliceous sandstone are exposed, weathered to thin, platy slabs at the top. The sandstone includes pockets of mudstone clasts. The lowest leaf on Stephen Moor is exposed in a disused quarry [7426 5370] where the section comprises 6 m of thin- and thick- (up to 1.20 m) bedded, fine-grained sandstones, with platy weathering at the top. The sandstones have partings or thin beds of micaceous siltstone and 'striped-beds'. A similar lithofacies is exposed in a quarry [7414 5331] north-east of Anna Land End.

Near Tinklers Farm, there are good sections in the Pendleside Sandstones and the associated sandstone-with-mudstone in a stream [7307 5195 to 7357 5242]. The more south-western part of this section shows thin-bedded to flaggy, fine-grained, micaceous sandstones, some of which are rich in plant fragments. These sandstones are interbedded with siltstones, silty mudstones and 'striped-beds', and contain load-casts and groove-casts trending N10°E. The more north-eastern part exposes thick-bedded (up to 0.7 m), fine-grained sandstone in units up to 13 m thick. The sandstones include layers rich in mudstone clasts up to 0.5 m across.

The top of the highest of the local Pendleside Sandstones is exposed in a stream [7540 5220 and 7551 5210] south-east of Champion. Overlying mudstones in this section [7540 5220] have yielded *Posidonia corrugata*, *G.* cf. *granosus* juv., and *Neoglyphioceras sp.* juv., indicating a P_{2a} age. A thin bed of laminated, sandy packstone is present in the succeeding beds. Thin-sections (Plate 19e) show it to be a bioclastic fine to medium calcarenite, with quartz, pyritised foraminifera, kamaenids and crinoid plates as the principal grains in a neomorphic sparry matrix.

Wigglesworth, Little Newton, Otterburn Beck

Little is known of the Lower Bowland Shales in the Ribble valley. Some 10 m of sandstone and shale, here classified as 'sandstone-with-mudstone', are recorded at rock-head in a borehole [7961 5760] near Laddy Green, Wigglesworth, and east of the River Ribble 27.5 m of sandstone and shale are recorded in a bore [8450 5795] near Holme Bridge, Long Preston.

A little farther east, most of the sequence is exposed in Newton Gill [8498 5874 to 8508 5838], north of Little Newton. Faunas from the basal 4 m include *Goniatites elegans* and *G.* aff. *sphaericostriatus*, indicative of a P_{1c} age. Two sandy units are present in this section. The lower one lies 20 m above the base of the sequence and is 53 m thick. It consists of thick- (up to 1.5 m) and thin-bedded, fine- and (subordinate) medium-grained sandstone, locally siliceous, with scattered white mica, carbonaceous plant fragments and mudstone clasts. Interbeds of micaceous and planty siltstones and silty mudstone are present. The fine-grained sandstone occurs both as 20 cm beds with sharp sole-marked bases and as 'striped beds' with flaggy laminae. Sandstone dominates in the lowest 11 m of the unit. These strata are separated from the higher sandy unit by some 18 m of mudstones that are calcareous in part with subordinate laminated calcisiltite, and have clasts of limestone (including pale, reefal varieties and dark wackestones) in their lower part. One boulder of dark wackestone with oncolites is recorded. Faunas from this mudstone interval at one locality [8511 5855] include *Hibernicoceras mediocris*, indicative of a P_{1d} age. The higher sandy unit is 42 m thick, and has 6 m of sandstone at the base. Silty mudstone and siltstone with laminae and beds (up to 15 cm) of fine-grained sandstone are dominant above; subordinate beds (up to 0.6 m) of sandstone are present, one of which is slumped and another fills a channel. The succeeding strata, up to the estimated horizon of the Leion Band, are about 80 m thick, and consist of mudstones and calcareous mudstones with thin beds of partly laminated calcisiltite as well as calcarenite and calcirudite packstones. Boulders and pebbles occur in several layers particularly in the lower part of this interval; they include angular or subangular, pale reefal limestones as well as dark lithologies which can be matched with limestones of the Wensleydale Group. A pebble of chert is also recorded. The fauna from an exposure [8503 5865] in the lower part of the sequence above the higher sandy layer includes *Goniatites granosus* and *Sudeticeras* cf. *crenistriatum*, indicating a P_{2a} age, and collections from higher levels [8502 5869 and 8499 5869] include *Sudeticeras* cf.

splendens and *Neoglyphioceras sp.* of P_{2b} age. A thin-section of calcirudite associated with basal P_{2b} mudstones [8502 5867] shows it to contain diverse limestone clasts (Plate 19f) in a dolomitised matrix. Lithologies represented in the clasts are bioclastic packstone, peloidal grainstone, boundstone and bioclastic wackestone, and there are collophane peloids, *Girvanella* lumps, and a fragment of a *Tabulipora* colony.

Mudstones of P_2 age are exposed farther east in Otterburn Beck [8763 5913 and 8766 5913] where they have yielded *Girtyoceras sp.*, *Neoglyphioceras sp.* and *Sudeticeras sp.* This sequence includes a bed of limestone conglomerate, containing blocks up to 3 m across and overlying 2 m of mudstone [8769 5912] with limestone boulders, derived brachiopods and B_2 goniatites including *Goniatites moorei*.

Eshton – Hetton Anticline

The Lower Bowland Shales are exposed in several sections near Flasby on the south-eastern fold limb. The lowest beds overlie very thin Pendleside Limestone in Flasby Beck [9447 5617 and 9444 5615] south-west of Flasby Hall, and comprise fissile mudstones and calcareous P_{1b-c} mudstones with *Nomismoceras sp.* Mudstones of P_2 age crop out farther upstream [9452 5616], and yield *Neoglyphioceras sp.* about 25 to 30 m above the base. The highest beds, at about the horizon of the Leion Marine Band, contain *Posidonia membranacea horizontalis* and *P. corrugata*, and are exposed in the banks of Flasby Beck [9514 5699], north-east of Flasby. No sandy strata are known in this section.

Just south of the Craven Reef Belt near Settle, supposed Lower Bowland Shales were proved in the Cominco Borehole S10 [8360 6304]. They were drilled from rock-head at 10.87 m to the top of the Pendleside Limestone at 19.38 m, and consist of silty mudstone that is weakly calcareous in part. *Posidonia corrugata* and a possible *Goniatites granosus*, indicating a P_{2a} age, were found 6.33 m above the base of the succession.

Craven Reef Belt (Settle to Malham)

Immediately south of the Middle Craven Fault near Stockdale Farm, Lower Bowland Shales were drilled in the Cominco Borehole S3 [8601 6350] from below the Leion Band at 14.63 m to the Wensleydale Group at 58.52 m. Mudstones occur down to 32.33 m, with layers of muddy crinoidal wackestone in the lowest metre, but below this the sequence is dominated by limestone. Fragments of *Neoglyphioceras* or *Lyrogoniatites* are recorded between 31.47 and 34.59 m, indicating a P_{2b} age. A similar limestone-dominated sequence was proved at the base of the Lower Bowland Shales nearby in the Cominco Borehole S11 [8590 6340], where the beds dip at about 30°. These strata were drilled from 3.05 m to 20.57 m, where the basal limestone bed rests with a sharp but irregular base on probable Malham Formation. Limestones in the upper part of the sequence are partly slumped, and angular limestone clasts are recorded in a crinoidal calcarenite at 19.51 m.   RSA

CHAPTER 4

Upper Carboniferous: Silesian

The main outcrop of Silesian strata, mostly Namurian (Millstone Grit Series) but including some Westphalian (Coal Measures), is in the western part of the district covering the Bowland Block (Figure 2). Early Namurian strata crop out in the Craven Basin principally in the Whelp Stone, Scosthrop and Hetton Common synclines and on Flasby Fell in the south-eastern corner of the district; they also crop out over much of the Craven Reef Belt (Figure 2) and, against the North Craven Fault, at Black Hill and on Threshfield Moor. On the Askrigg Block they form an outlier which caps Fountains Fell. The Westphalian strata form a south-eastward extension of the Ingleton Coalfield, from which coal has been mined in the adjoining Hawes district.

PREVIOUS RESEARCH

The presence of 'Millstone Grit' in the Settle district was noted by Phillips (1836). The Primary Survey undertaken by R. H. Tiddeman from 1871 to 1887 (published at one inch to one mile in 1892) led to a more detailed knowledge of the distribution of these strata and their succession. Tiddeman recognised 'Coal Measures' overlying 'Millstone Grits' in the north-west, forming the eastern part of the Ingleton Coalfield.

The Namurian stratigraphy of the main crop was refined by Holmes and Bisat (1925) who identified goniatite zones in Keasden Beck and other tributaries of the River Wenning. Moseley (1956) carried out a survey of the Namurian strata in the Keasden area and the stratigraphy which he erected provides the basis of the lithostratigraphic classification used during this resurvey.

The early Namurian outcrops of the Craven Basin were studied by Booker and Hudson (1926) in the Eshton–Hetton Anticline; by Parkinson (1936) around the Slaidburn and Catlow anticlines; and by Hudson and Mitchell (1937) in the Skipton Anticline, just beyond the south-eastern corner of this district. These successions were classified in terms of the biozonation established by Bisat (1924, 1928). The early Namurian outcrops over the Craven Reef Belt and northwards to the North Craven Fault were described by Hudson (1930a), who drew attention to the existence of an unconformity at the base of the sequence.

The early Namurian outlier at Fountains Fell lies partly within the adjoining Hawes district; it was described by Dakyns and others (1890) and by O'Connor (1964). The outlier is of particular palaeontological interest, due to the recovery of Namurian goniatites (Hudson, 1941: Black, 1950; O'Connor, 1964) below the base of the Main Limestone, a horizon which is taken as the mappable base of the Namurian elsewhere in northern England (Johnson and others, 1962).

The Ingleton Coalfield was resurveyed in 1934 by J. V. Stephens who recognised several marine bands; his

manuscript maps are held in BGS archives. Ford (1954) published an account of the coalfield and later (1958) reviewed coal-mining in the area.

PALAEOGEOGRAPHY

Throughout the Namurian, sedimentation in Northern England was dominated by a southward-prograding delta. As in the Dinantian, the essential control was the differential subsidence of the various underlying blocks and basins. During the Namurian, however, the 'rift' subsidence which had characterised Dinantian sedimentation was replaced by a more general 'sag' subsidence (Leeder, 1982), and the definition of the Craven Basin became increasingly weak, both in terms of its bounding structures and its sedimentary infill.

Deltaic conditions continued from the late Dinantian, but these were initially restricted to the Askrigg Block, and resulted in the cyclothemic sedimentation of the Wensleydale Group (Hudson, 1924; Moore, 1958). The Namurian of the Craven Basin remained free from deltaic influence until late Pendleian times, when the marine bathymetric basin that had existed since the mid-Dinantian began to be filled with deltaic sediments. By late Pendleian times, delta-top conditions, as indicated by the sedimentary features of the Grassington Grit, temporarily extended from the Askrigg Block into the Craven Basin. Southward progradation of the delta over both the blocks and the basin continued throughout the Silesian, although periodically this was interrupted by marine transgressions.

CLASSIFICATION

In this district the Namurian Series is equated with the strata formerly known as 'Millstone Grit(s)', with the addition of the 'Bowland Shales' that lie above the Leion Marine Band. The Westphalian Series corresponds to those strata known formerly as 'Coal Measures'.

All the Namurian stages (Ramsbottom and others, 1978) with the exception of the Alportian (H_2) have been identified on the basis of their diagnostic goniatite faunas; also the oldest of the Westphalian stages, Westphalian A. These stages are defined in relation to the bases of widespread marine bands. The Namurian stages are divided, also on the basis of diagnostic goniatites, into zones and subzones many of which have been identified in the Settle successions. In parts of the succession where no diagnostic macrofauna has been found, age determinations have been made on the basis of included miospore assemblages, using the classification proposed by Owens and others (1977).

The lithostratigraphical classification partly follows the established nomenclatural practice in the British Silesian of naming only limestones, sandstones, coals and faunal bands and of leaving mudstones and siltstones unnamed. The exceptions are the Upper Bowland Shales, Sugar Loaf Shales and the Caton Shales; and the Pendle Grit and Roeburndale formations both of which include mudstones and siltstones. The classification is given in Figure 21 which also shows the age of the divisions and the characteristic development in the structural units.

The named lithostratigraphical units proposed by Ford (1954) and Moseley (1956) have mostly been retained. The term 'Pendle Grit Formation' has been introduced here in place of the 'Pendle Grit' (Earp and others, 1961), and 'Roeburndale Formation' in place of Moseley's 'Roeburndale Grit Group'.

For descriptive purposes the Silesian succession is divided into eight parts, seven belonging to the Millstone Grit Series (Namurian) and one to the Coal Measures (Westphalian). The first of these comprises the strata of 'Yoredale' type on the Askrigg Block which are here placed in the Wensleydale Group. The second comprises the Pendleian Sugar Loaf Shales and Sugar Loaf Limestone of the Askrigg Block–Craven Basin transition zone. The remaining divisions apply principally to the outcrops on the Bowland Block and in the Craven Basin. RSA,EWJ

MILLSTONE GRIT SERIES (Namurian)

Wensleydale Group (part) (Pendleian, E_1)

A Pendleian succession of siltstone, limestone and sandstone belonging to the Wensleydale Group conformably overlies Dinantian strata as an outlier on Fountains Fell (Figure 14). The base of the Namurian is taken at the top of the Underset Limestone (Brigantian), so that the colour change from Dinantian to Namurian on the Settle 1:50 000 map does not exactly correspond with that on the adjacent Hawes Sheet where the line is drawn at the base of the Main Limestone.

Up to 32 m of siltstones, in part with sandy laminae, separate the Underset Limestone from the Main Limestone; they are largely exposed [8725 7173] in the headwaters of Darnbrook Beck, just within the Hawes district. The basal 5 m of these siltstones are calcareous, platy, in places cherty, and contain the Leion Marine Band[1]. *Cravenoceras leion* was collected [8742 7171] during the resurvey, and previous faunal records from these strata include *Eumorphoceras pseudobilingue* (Hudson, 1941) and *E. tornquisti* (O'Connor, 1964).

1 The marine band nomenclature within the Namurian is informal

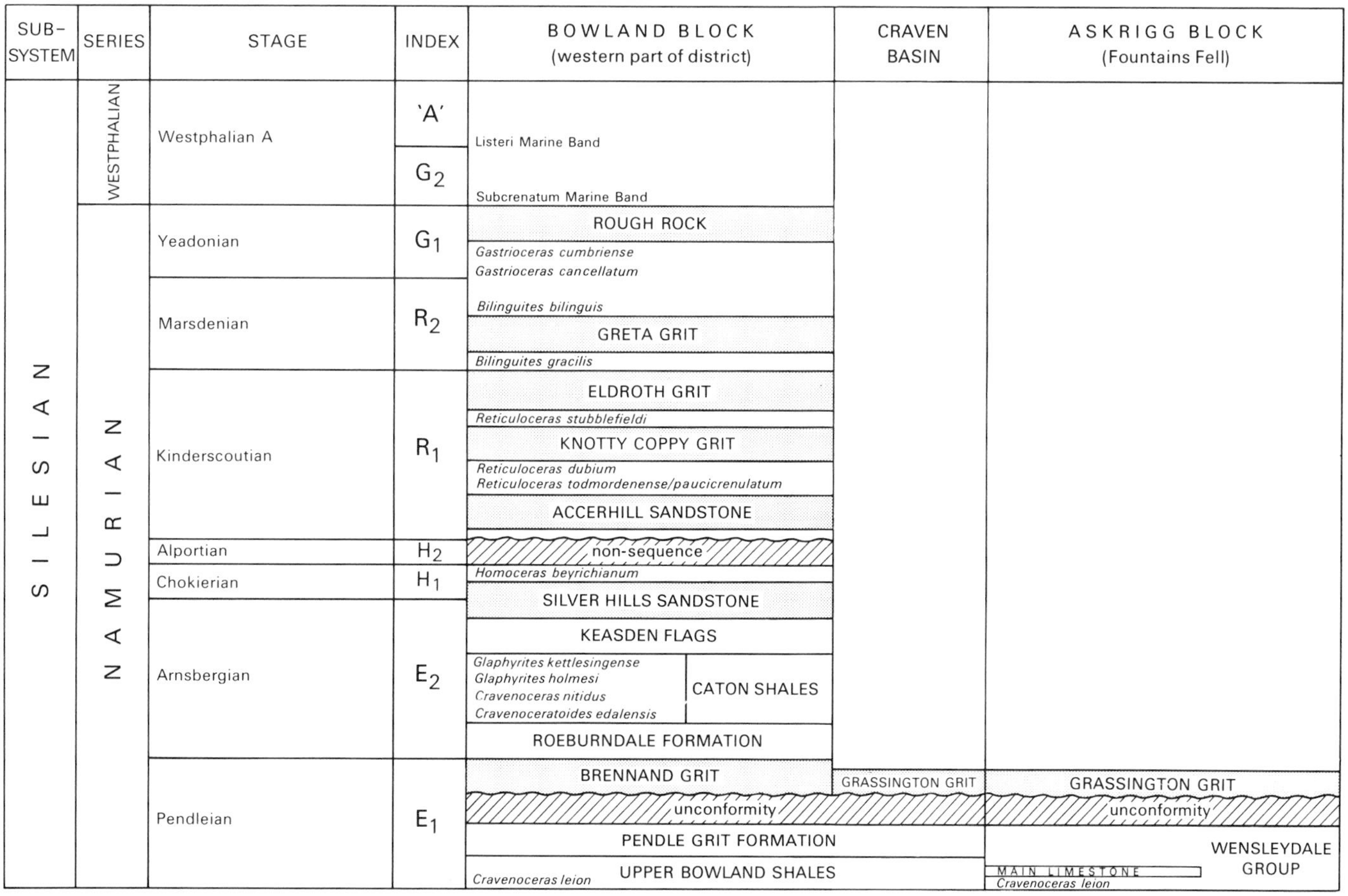

SUB-SYSTEM	SERIES	STAGE	INDEX	BOWLAND BLOCK (western part of district)		CRAVEN BASIN	ASKRIGG BLOCK (Fountains Fell)
S I L E S I A N	WESTPHALIAN	Westphalian A	'A'	Listeri Marine Band			
			G_2	Subcrenatum Marine Band			
	N A M U R I A N	Yeadonian	G_1	ROUGH ROCK			
				Gastrioceras cumbriense			
				Gastrioceras cancellatum			
		Marsdenian	R_2	*Bilinguites bilinguis*			
				GRETA GRIT			
				Bilinguites gracilis			
		Kinderscoutian	R_1	ELDROTH GRIT			
				Reticuloceras stubblefieldi			
				KNOTTY COPPY GRIT			
				Reticuloceras dubium			
				Reticuloceras todmordenense/paucicrenulatum			
				ACCERHILL SANDSTONE			
		Alportian	H_2	non-sequence			
		Chokierian	H_1	*Homoceras beyrichianum*			
				SILVER HILLS SANDSTONE			
		Arnsbergian	E_2	KEASDEN FLAGS			
				Glaphyrites kettlesingense *Glaphyrites holmesi* *Cravenoceras nitidus* *Cravenoceratoides edalensis*	CATON SHALES		
				ROEBURNDALE FORMATION			
		Pendleian	E_1	BRENNAND GRIT		GRASSINGTON GRIT	GRASSINGTON GRIT
				unconformity			unconformity
				PENDLE GRIT FORMATION			WENSLEYDALE GROUP
				Cravenoceras leion	UPPER BOWLAND SHALES	MAIN LIMESTONE *Cravenoceras leion*	

Figure 21   Classification of the Silesian rocks of the Bowland Block, Craven Basin and Askrigg Block

The Main Limestone comprises 8 to 10 m of light grey, thinly bedded and in part cross-bedded, crinoidal calcarenite with disseminated rhombs of dolomite. It contains a sparse brachiopod fauna including *Brachythyris sp.*, *Martinia* aff. *glabra* and trilobite fragments.

Mudstones and siltstones that thin southwards from 26 to 13 m separate the Main Limestone from the Grassington Grit. Here, as elsewhere on the southern part of the Askrigg Block, this variation in thickness results from pre-Grassington Grit erosion (Rowell and Scanlon, 1957). These strata are exposed [8727 7132 to 8739 7138] in the head-waters of Darnbrook Beck. The basal mudstones are pyritic and contain a sparse marine fauna including *Brachythyris sp.*, *Lingula mytilloides* and *L.* cf. *squamiformis*. Thin interbedded sandstones are present in the overlying siltstones.   EWJ

Sugar Loaf Shales and Sugar Loaf Limestone (Pendleian, E_1)

The Sugar Loaf Shales crop out only in the Sugar Loaf Hill area, where they unconformably overlie Brigantian limestone of the Wensleydale Group and underlie the Sugar Loaf Limestone. Although poorly exposed, scattered small outcrops indicate a succession of between 25 and 30 m of mudstone, decalcified siltstone ('plate'), and thin limestone with chert. An outcrop [8371 6366] west of the summit of Sugar Loaf Hill has yielded a fauna including trepostome bryozoa, sponge anchorate basalia ('*Hyalostelia*' *parallela*) and brachiopods including *Buxtonia sp.*, *Pleuropugnoides greenleightonensis* and *Productus concinnus*. This sequence post-dates the late Brigantian strata on High South Bank (Middle Limestone or above). Lithologically and faunally the Sugar Loaf Shales are similar to the beds above the Underset Limestone on Fountains Fell, and a Pendleian age is thus attributed to them.

The Sugar Loaf Limestone is a medium-dark grey, shelly lime-mudstone to wackestone, commonly fenestral, which conformably overlies the Sugar Loaf Shales. The limestone forms a 6 m cap to Sugar Loaf Hill [8375 6368]. A more extensive outcrop occurs 50 m north-east of the hill, where at least 15 m are present, and exposures [8384 6376] here have yielded a rich brachiopod-molluscan fauna, including *Buxtonia sp.*, *Eomarginifera longispina*, *Martinia sp.*, *Phricodothyris sp.*, *Productus concinnus* (abundant), *Schizophoria resupinata* and *Streblochondria anisota*. The limestone is known only from the Sugar Loaf Hill area and from a single small exposure [8581 6354] on High South Bank, which also contains *Productus concinnus*.

The age of the limestone, from the evidence of the underlying strata, is Pendleian. Faunally the limestone is very similar to the Main Limestone, which on the western side of Fountains Fell [860 718] contains abundant *P. concinnus* in association with *Buxtonia sp.*, *Eomarginifera sp.* and *Phricodothyris sp.* There is little lithological similarity, however, between the Sugar Loaf Limestone and the Main Limestone; the latter (on Fountains Fell) being a medium to coarse crinoidal calcarenite. The Sugar Loaf Limestone is thus a unique facies of very restricted lateral extent in a marginal block situation, and is broadly the equivalent of the Main Limestone.   DJCM

Upper Bowland Shales (Pendleian, E_1)

Mudstones up to 240 m thick, termed the Upper Bowland Shales, rest conformably on Lower Bowland Shales in the basinal area, where they are overlain by the Pendle Grit Formation (Figure 22). Their junction with the Lower Bowland Shales has been defined biostratigraphically at the incoming of the goniatite *Cravenoceras leion* (Bisat, 1928), which marks the boundary between Dinantian and Silesian strata (Bisat 1930, 1933). The Upper Bowland Shales belong entirely to the oldest Silesian stage (Pendleian) and the sequence has been divided into zones (E_{1a}, E_{1b} and E_{1c}) defined by distinctive goniatite marker bands (see Hudson and Mitchell, 1937).

Over much of the Craven Reef Belt and northwards to the North Craven Fault, the Upper Bowland Shales rest unconformably on the Malham Formation or Wensleydale Group (Figure 22). In this area, their base is diachronous, and in some sections the basal mudstones are of E_{1c} age. A non-sequence has also been described at the base of the Upper Bowland Shales just south of the Reef Belt at School Share, near Scaleber Bridge (Dixon and Hudson, 1931). On High South Bank south of Stockdale Farm, the Upper Bowland Shales are themselves locally overlapped by the Pendle Grit Formation. The top of the Upper Bowland Shales is an imprecise boundary over much of the crop; the junction is considered to be diachronous, though it is within the E_{1c} Zone.

For descriptive purposes the succession is divided at the highest faunal band, that with *Cravenoceras malhamense*.

Strata up to and including the Malhamense Marine Band

The succession up to the Malhamense Marine Band is 85 to 125 m thick in the basin. To the north of and across the Reef Belt, these strata are thinner or locally absent, as on High South Bank, Stockdale, and at Bark Plantation, Bordley.

The sequence consists mostly of fissile mudstones, and contains ironstone nodules and bands. Some mudstones are partly calcareous, and the calcareous layers locally include beds or laminae of dark grey calcisiltite. Limestone is also recorded as bullions and as thin beds of crinoidal calcarenite packstone. Thin-shelled bivalves including *Posidonia corrugata* and *P. membranacea* are common to abundant in both calcareous and non-calcareous mudstones, and goniatites tend to occur either within or just above the calcareous layers. Plant fragments are also common. Between the Leion and Malhamense marine bands, which respectively mark the bases of E_{1a} and E_{1c}, the succession contains other faunal bands characterised by *Eumorphoceras pseudobilingue* (see Parkinson, 1936, p.318), the incoming of which marks the base of E_{1b}.

West of the River Ribble there are good sections of these strata in Hare Clough Beck at the south-western end of the Catlow Anticline and in Hollow Gill Wood, south of Rathmell. Farther east there are well exposed sequences in tributaries of the River Aire between Malham and Hanlith, including Tranlands Beck, Granny Gill and Cow Close Syke.

Boulders of limestone embedded in mudstone are recorded at several localities, notably at School Share near Scaleber

Bridge (Dixon and Hudson, 1931), where they form lenticular conglomerate units, with clasts mostly of medium-dark grey limestones of the Wensleydale Group, set in a mudstone matrix (Figure 22 and Plate 20). Elsewhere there are clasts of medium-light grey bioclastic wackestone of presumed reefal origin. In some of the more western sections, near Kenibus for example, 2 m of silty coarse-grained sandstone directly underlies the Malhamense Marine Band (Figure 22). This is regarded as a precursor of the succeeding Pendle Grit Formation.

Strata above the Malhamense Marine Band

The succession above the Malhamense Band shows a wide variation in thickness. In the basinal area much of the variation is due to the diachronous nature of the upper boundary of the formation (Figure 22). In the Bowland Forest Tunnel in the extreme west, only 7.6 m of mudstone separate the Malhamense Marine Band from the Pendle Grit Formation, but south of Malham and south-east of Flasby, this interval is some 100 m thick.

Poorly fissile, finely laminated mudstones and silty mudstones characterise this part of the Upper Bowland Shales, and contain plant debris and bands and nodules of ironstone. They are locally micaceous and are generally non-calcareous, though bullions are recorded in the basal beds in some of the more eastern sections including Ellis Gill near Bordley. Goniatites are not recorded above the Malhamense Marine Band; bivalves are common in the basal few metres but are sparse in higher strata. Layers of carbonaceous mudstone with fish-scales occur in some sections west of the River Ribble.

Fine-grained, micaceous sandstone and siltstone are present as laminae towards the top of local sequences, and these are locally sufficiently abundant to form 'striped-beds'. In a few sections sharp-based, channel-fill sandstones also occur. There are no records of limestone clasts in these mudstones; chert pebbles are, however, present near Bark Plantation, Bordley.

There are good exposures of this part of the succession in tributaries of the River Aire east of Malham and in streams on the north-western flank of Flasby Fell. On High South Bank, south of Stockdale Farm and at Bark Plantation, these mudstones locally overlap the lower part of the formation and rest unconformably on either the Malham Formation or

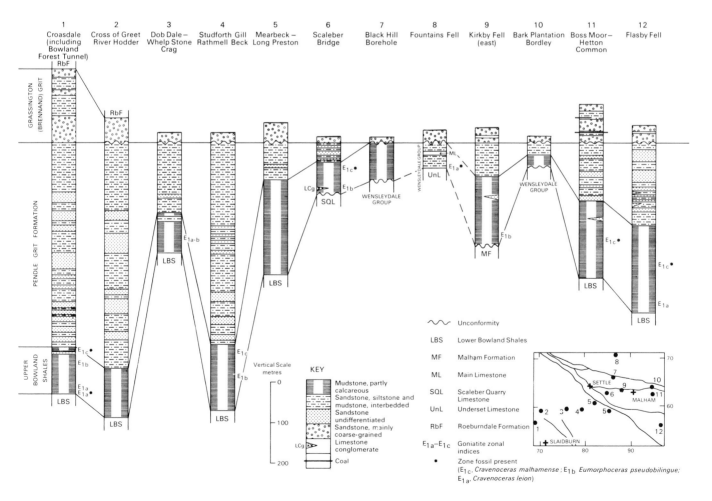

Figure 22 Comparative sections of Pendleian strata including the Upper Bowland Shales, Pendle Grit Formation and Grassington (Brennand) Grit, showing faunal horizons

Wensleydale Group. This unconformable relationship is exposed in potholes near the summit of High South Bank.

DETAILS

West of the River Ribble

In the Bowland Forest Tunnel (Earp, 1955) 110 m of mudstones are referred to this formation. Both the Leion and Malhamense marine bands were proved, as was a band yielding *Eumorphoceras* cf. *pseudobilingue* (E_{1b}) about 73 m above the base. Some 12 m of 'limy mudstones' were recorded at the 'horizon' of the Malhamense Marine Band. This band is exposed [6880 5437] nearby, north of Burn Side, where it has yielded *Posidonia corrugata*, *P. corrugata gigantea*, *P. membranacea* and *Cravenoceras malhamense*, and farther north-east on Low Fell [6935 5506]. In the tunnel 7.6 m of mudstone separate the Malhamense Marine Band and the base of the Pendle Grit Formation; there is a similar interval in a poorly exposed section [6395 5506] on Low Fell.

A high E_{1a} fauna with *P. corrugata* and *Eumorphoceras medusa* was obtained from mudstones and calcareous mudstones in Croasdale Brook [6983 5540]. Upstream [e.g. 6968 5551] calcareous mudstones have yielded *P. corrugata*, *E. pseudobilingue* and *E. sp.* [with a large, beaded venter indicative of an old age form]. A similar fauna was recovered from calcareous mudstones in Phynis Beck [7108 5570], SE of Harkers, where an estimated 70 m of the sequence are fairly well exposed [7097 5577 to 7115 5562].

The strata are well exposed at the south-western end of the Catlow Anticline, particularly in Hare Clough Beck [7016 5712 to 7046 5727], and its tributary gullies. A Marine Band with *Eumorphoceras pseudobilingue* crops out at several localities [e.g. 7047 5715], and has yielded *P. corrugata*, *P. membranacea*, *E. pseudobilingue* and *E. sp.* [old age form with beaded venter]. The Malhamense Marine Band is exposed in Copped Hill Clough [7114 5721] where its fauna includes *P. membranacea*, *Naticopsis consimilis*, *Cravenoceras* cf. *malhamense* and *Kazakhoceras scaliger*. Here it is underlain by at least 1.8 m of coarse-grained, micaceous and feldspathic, silty sandstone, with clasts of mudstone up to 10 cm. This sandstone is also exposed [7122 5709 to 7138 5723] in a stream nearby, and channel-fill, coarse-grained, silty sandstone are present in this part of the sequence in Hare Clough Beck. Some 8 m of mudstones separate the Malhamense Marine Band from the base of the Pendle Grit Formation in Copped Hill Clough.

In the eastern part of the Catlow Anticline the Upper Bowland Shales are probably considerably thicker. Tributaries of Bottoms Beck [7576 5980 to 7579 5978] expose mudstones presumed to overlie the Malhamense Marine Band; these beds include an intercalation of siltstone with laminae and thin beds of fine-grained sandstone carrying sole-marks and containing a slumped layer. The uppermost mudstones [e.g. 7555 5932] are conspicuously laminated and contain ironstone nodules. Similar well laminated, partly micaceous mudstones and silty mudstones at the top of the formation are well exposed [7475 5791 to 7512 5815] in a gully north of Hindley Head; they include [7508 5813] 0.3 m of coarse-grained sandstone with quartz pebbles and intraclasts of mudstone.

A stream section [7734 5750 to 7732 5747] near Studforth Gill gives incomplete exposure of some 70 m of mudstones and calcareous mudstones; these have yielded [7734 5750 and 7732 5747] a E_{1b} fauna including *P. corrugata*, *P. membranacea*, *Eumorphoceras pseudobilingue* and *E. sp.* [with beaded venters]. Farther upstream poorly fissile, laminated, silty mudstones with micaceous laminae, presumed to lie above the Malhamense Marine Band, are exposed [7700 5776 to 7717 5765]; these mudstones, with lenses of coarse-grained, muddy sandstone, rest on a leaf of slumped 'striped-beds', and this in turn on black, carbonaceous mudstone with comminuted plant fragments and fish-scales.

The Pseudobilingue Marine Band and the probable Malhamense Marine Band are recorded in a stream section in Hollow Gill Wood, south of Rathmell. The lowest beds [8029 5839 to 8044 5836] are fissile to platy, calcareous, silty mudstones with coaly plant fragments and poorly preserved bivalves. The higher beds [8004 5851 to 8013 5848] are similar mudstones, with subordinate partly pyritic muddy limestones and layers with goniatites and abundant bivalves; the faunas [8004 5851, 8010 5849 and 8013 5848] include *P. corrugata*, *P. corrugata gigantea*, *E. pseudobilingue* and *E. sp.* [with beaded venters]. The highest beds are mudstones and calcareous mudstones which have yielded [7990 5857 and 7983 5864] *P. membranacea* and *Cravenoceras* cf. *malhamense*.

Upper Bowland Shales crop out at the southern margin of the district south of Champion, where they give rise to prominent scarps (see Earp and others, 1961, p.82) which may be formed by calcareous layers.

Long Preston to Winterburn Reservoir

The Upper Bowland Shales are poorly exposed in the Ribble valley but there is a section [8158 6109 to 8188 6003] in a gully north of Mearbeck. The lowest beds include *P. corrugata* and lie at about the horizon of the Malhamense Marine Band. The top part of the section exposes about 42 m of laminated silty mudstones beneath sandstone of the Pendle Grit Formation.

Partly calcareous mudstones and silty mudstones are impersistently exposed in the headwaters of Newton Gill, north of Newton Moor. The mudstones include ironstone bands and muddy limestones. A fauna of suspected E_{1b} age, including *P. corrugata* and *Eumorphoceras sp.*, was recovered [8558 5896], and *C. malhamense?* has been obtained from a locality [8526 5903] downstream.

A 0.5 m layer of limestone boulders is embedded in mudstones and calcareous mudstones of E_{1a} age in a tributary [8596 6025] of Otterburn Beck, near Crake Moor. Both pale and dark limestone clasts are present, and can be matched respectively with the Malham Formation and Wensleydale Group. The fauna within these mudstones [8599 6024] includes *Eumorphoceras* cf. *pseudocoronula* and *E. sp.* [cf. *tornquisti* group]. Upstream [8581 6050] mudstones and calcareous mudstones have yielded *P. corrugata* and *E. pseudobilingue*.

Mudstones are well exposed farther north-east in Tranlands Beck, south-west of Malham. They are partly calcareous and include small calcareous bullions, thin dark grey limestones and layers of ironstone nodules. Embedded boulders of medium-dark grey crinoidal limestone are recorded [8968 6242] from a northern tributary. The section has yielded [8946 6236 and 8940 6230 to 8931 6227] faunas of E_{1b} age including *P. corrugata*, *P. corrugata elongata* and *Eumorphoceras pseudobilingue*. Farther north near Field Barns, E_{1b} mudstones appear to lap against the Malham Formation. Mudstones exposed in a gully [8897 6295 to 8917 6299] include limestone bullions and 0.3 m of crinoidal packstone; the mudstones have yielded [8897 6296; 8914 6301] *P. corrugata* and *E. pseudobilingue*. These strata lie a few metres above a limestone conglomerate which occurs [8925 6300 to 8930 6298] at the base of the formation and largely consists of boulders of Malham Formation.

There are good exposures of Upper Bowland Shales with E_{1b} faunas in eastern tributaries [9051 6201 to 9074 6190; 9052 6235 to 9085 6199] of the River Aire, south-east of Malham. The sequence comprises mudstones and calcareous mudstones with bullions and beds of medium-dark grey limestone up to 0.7 m thick. The mudstones have yielded [9083 6208] *P. corrugata* and *E. pseudobilingue*. Farther south, near Out Gang, an exposure [9076 6151] of folded calcareous mudstones, with limestones up to 0.5 m thick, yielded *C. malhamense*. In tributaries east of Malham, some 70 m of mudstones above the Malhamense Marine Band are well exposed [9104 6251 to 9110 6230, 9115 6263 to 9164 6250 and 9115 6263 to

Plate 20 Limestone conglomerate (School Share Boulder Bed) in Upper Bowland Shales, Scaleber Bridge [8445 6237]. Limestone boulders rest on an irregular erosion surface in the mudstone. (L 2754)

9150 6276] up to the base of the Pendle Grit Formation. The mudstones are partly silty and micaceous, and generally well laminated; they contain plant fragments and a few laminae and thin beds of sandstone.

Partly calcareous mudstones with bullions are exposed [9424 6058 to 9426 6055] in a western tributary of Winterburn Reservoir, and calcareous mudstones on the eastern shore [9474 6067] of the reservoir yielded *P. corrugata* var. *elongata* and *Eumorphoceras sp.* indicative of an E_{1a-b} age. RSA

Craven Reef Belt (Settle to Malham)

Between Settle and Malham, the Upper Bowland Shales thin out northwards over the Craven Reef Belt, and thicknesses vary markedly (Figure 22). The basal mudstones south-west of Scaleber Bridge are of E_{1a-b} age and rest unconformably on an olistolith block [8401 6240] of Malham Formation limestone. A section [8405 6247] high in the south-eastern bank of Scaleber Beck shows 7 m of mudstones, including muddy limestones and a layer with pale limestone clasts up to 1 cm across; the mudstones yielded *P. corrugata*, *P. membranacea*, *Catastroboceras sp.*, *E. pseudobilingue* and *E. sp.* [with a large beaded venter].

The Upper Bowland Shales are well exposed [8428 6212 to 8460 6234] in a tributary of Scaleber Beck at School Share. This section includes a classic 'boulder bed' locality [8445 6237] (Marr, 1899; Garwood and Goodyear, 1924; Dixon and Hudson, 1931) where the sequence contains lenses of limestone conglomerate up to 5 m thick (Plate 20). The conglomerate comprises boulders (up to at least 3 m across) of medium-dark to dark grey Wensleydale Group limestones; these include crinoidal packstones, oncolitic wackestones, and one with gigantoproductoid brachiopods. The boulders are in a mudstone matrix, and are overlain by some 5 m of bullion-bearing calcareous mudstones which have yielded [8846 6235] *P. corrugata* and *E. pseudobilingue*, indicative of E_{1b}. The section given by Dixon and Hudson recorded a non-sequence in the shales 5.5 m below the boulder bed, but this was not exposed during the resurvey. The break was described as sharp, separating dark non-jointed shales with bullions and limestone clasts (above), from 2.4 m of dark, closely jointed shales with bullions containing *Lyrogoniatites sp.* and *Sagittoceras* cf. *meslerianum*, indicative of P_2.

Just north of the Craven Reef Belt, the Leion Marine Band was proved, apparently resting conformably on Lower Bowland Shales, in the Cominco Borehole S3 [8601 6350]. A fauna between 10.52 and 14.20 m included *P. corrugata*, *Cravenoceras leion* and *E. tornquisti*. South-westwards, however, the formation shows progressive onlap over older formations of the Reef Belt. The Upper Bowland Shales are exposed in a stream [8538 6336] on Low South Bank, south of Stockdale Farm, where laminated mudstones with bullions, plant fragments and ironstone bands, rest on an irregular surface of limestones. The unconformity is also well displayed in potholes [e.g. 8594 6301] near the summit of High South Bank. Locally a section [8544 6300] shows that the Upper Bowland Shales thin out against a limestone palaeocliff, and are overlapped by the Pendle Grit Formation.

The Malhamense Marine Band forms a conspicuous feature [8455 6310 and 8476 6320] on the hillside south of Stockdale Beck, where it has yielded *P. corrugata*, *P. membranacea* and *C. malhamense*. It was also proved as a calcareous layer betwen 40.5 and 45.4 m in the Cominco Borehole S9 [8309 6330] near Preston's Barn; there it overlay some 20 m of mudstones with ironstone bands and nodules, which rested with a sharp, probably faulted, contact on altered limestone of the Malham Formation. The fauna of the band included *P. corrugata*, *P. membranacea*, *C. malhamense* and *Kazakhoceras scaliger*.

Immediately north of the Middle Craven Fault, east of Stockdale Farm, a section [8658 6389] shows that mudstones with bivalves onlap against a contemporaneous southward-facing scarp of Malham Formation, and a similar relationship is recorded [8792 6372] farther east near Pikedaw Hill. In the intervening ground, exposures in potholes [e.g. 8733 6381] on the northern flank of Kirkby Fell show mudstones with scattered bivalves resting with angular unconformity on an irregular surface of Lower Hawes Limestone. A poorly preserved fauna [8719 6369] included *P. corrugata* and *Eumorphoceras?*, and is of possible E_{1b} age.

The Cominco Borehole S6 [8770 6360], drilled on the eastern flank of Kirkby Fell, proved laminated mudstones and silty mudstones with subordinate striped-beds and siltstone for some 60 m below the base of the Pendle Grit Formation at 77.6 m; the Malhamense Marine Band was not penetrated. Similar mudstones are exposed farther east in a gully [8868 6322 to 8884 6326] west of Field Barns; the section includes a bullion layer and at least 0.5 m of sandstone, mostly medium-grained but including coarse-grained, feldspathic layers with quartz pebbles and intraclasts of mudstone.

DJCM,RSA

Bordley to Linton Moor

Between Malham and Bordley the Malhamense Marine Band is the lowest proved faunal band in the Upper Bowland Shales, and the underlying basal mudstones, which here rest unconformably on the Malham Formation and Wensleydale Group, are thus of E_{1b} age. These strata include bullions and abundant bivalves, and are well exposed [9333 6394 to 9350 6397] in Moor Close Gill, the type locality for *C. malhamense*; the Malhamense Marine Band is seen [9308 6379] in a southern tributary of this stream where it has yielded *P. membrancea* and *C. malhamense*. The Malhamense Marine Band, including *P. membranacea*, *Cravenoceras sp.* and *Kazakhoceras hawkinsi*, is also recorded [9453 6384] in Ellis Gill. Here some 50 m of mudstones, capped by a channel sandstone, overlie the band, and include a bullion layer towards its base. Comparable laminated mudstones, with lenses of channel sandstone 1 to 2 m thick, are exposed in gullies near Park House [9385 6347].

At Bark Plantation, the sequence thins over Wensleydale Group relief [948 643], and barely 30 m separate the Pendle Grit Formation from the Wensleydale Group. In a nearby gully [9483 6464] these mudstones include a layer with chert pebbles. Southeastwards, laminated mudstones with ironstone are well displayed [9668 6134 to 9696 6151 and 9692 6172 to 9744 6161] in Hamerton Hill Syke and one of its tributaries. A 2.5 m-thick planty channel-fill sandstone with mudstone clasts lies within the sequence [9743 6161].

Fossiliferous mudstones exposed [9660 6420] in Rowley Beck near Lower Height are taken to represent the Malhamense Marine Band. This locality lies just south of the North Craven Fault, and has yielded *P. corrugata*, *P. membranacea horizontalis*, *Anthracoceras sp.* and *Cravenoceras sp.*

Flasby

To the south of the Eshton–Hetton Anticline, mudstones and calcareous mudstones of E_{1a} age are exposed [9422 5572 to 9424 5554] in the banks of Eshton Beck. The mudstones include beds of limestone and muddy limestone up to 0.4 m thick and limestone bullions up to 1 m across. The fauna of the mudstones [9422 5573] includes *Streblochondria sp.*, *E.* cf. *tornquisti* and *Cravenoceras* cf. *leion*. Similar bullion-bearing mudstones are seen in a stream [9457 5523] in Lord's Wood, where they have yielded *Cravenoceras sp.* and debris of *E. tornquisti*. The Malhamense Marine Band is exposed [9534 5612] upstream, where it comprises 0.5 m of platy limestone and calcareous mudstone resting on barren silty mudstone with ironstone. Its fauna includes *P. corrugata*, *C.* cf. *malhamense* and *Kazakhoceras scaliger*. Farther south-east, in a stream north of Stirton, there are exposures [9713 5338 to 9720 5344] of fissile mudstone presumed to lie above the Leion Marine Band. These mudstones contain a bed of dark grey limestone and boulders of dark limestone, including a coarsely crinoidal variety.

Upper Bowland Shales above the Malhamense Marine Band on Flasby Fell are about 100 m thick and are dominated by laminated mudstones and silty mudstones. They are exposed [9534 5612 to 9580 5625] in a stream north of High Wood. The mudstones are partly micaceous and contain ironstone bands and nodules. They include [9564 5629] 0.5 m of fine-grained channel-fill sandstone. In their upper part there are laminae and thin beds of fine-grained sandstone.

RSA

Black Hill

Mudstones and siltstones with subordinate thin dark grey limestones referable in part to the Upper Bowland Shales occur in the Daw Haw-Black Hill area immediately south of the North Craven Fault. Although this outcrop is largely covered by boulder clay and peat, there are small exposures in and around Cowside Beck [8565 6637] and in Daw Haw Beck [8510 6646]. The sequence was cored in the Black Hill Borehole [8630 6628] where 91 m of siltstones and mudstones were proved beneath the Grassington Grit. This succession, considered to be largely Upper Bowland Shales, overlies an eroded surface of a Wensleydale Group limestone (either the upper part of the Simonstone Limestone or the Middle Limestone). No diagnostic goniatites were found in the borehole, the faunas being restricted to *Lingula*, *Orbiculoidea*, *Posidonia corrugata* and *P. membranacea*, but the faunal aspect suggests an E_1 age. *Cravenoceras leion* (E_{1a}) and *C. malhamense* (E_{1c}), however, have been recorded by Hudson and Cotton (1945) from Daw Haw and Cowside becks. In addition to E_1 goniatites, the stream sections have also yielded *Neoglyphioceras sp.*, *Sudeticeras sp.* and a dimorphoceratid (Hudson and Jackson, 1929), and *Dimorphoceras lunula* and *Sudeticeras sp.* (O'Connor, 1964). Representatives of part of the Lower Bowland Shales are thus present in the Black Hill area, although they are not mappable.

The relation of the Bowland Shales to the Wensleydale Group sequence is difficult to ascertain. Rayner (1953) suggested that the shale succession around Black Hill represents a transitional facies between the Yoredales and Bowland Shales. The contact with the Wensleydale Group is exposed in Cowside Beck [8571 6628], Daw Haw Beck [8510 6646], and [8472 6617] south-east of Cowside Farm, but these sections are unhelpful because the contacts are all faulted. Evidence from the Black Hill Borehole and mapping south of Black Hill, however, suggest unconformity and overlap rather than a lateral passage.

DJCM

Pendle Grit Formation (Pendleian, E_1)

A varied succession of siltstones, silty mudstones and sandstones for which the name Pendle Grit Formation is here introduced, overlies the Upper Bowland Shales. No diagnostic fauna is known, but the formation is taken to be of E_{1c} age from its relations with the Malhamense Marine Band in the Upper Bowland Shales and the Edge or Warley Wise Marine Band (basal E_2) in the overlying strata in the adjoining Bradford and Clitheroe districts (Stephens and others, 1953; Earp and others, 1961). The Pendle Grit Formation equates with the Pendle Top Grit of the Lancaster district (Moseley, 1954, 1962), the Pendle Grit of the Clitheroe district (Earp and others, 1961), and includes the Hanlith Moor Sandstones and Shales of Hudson (1944b).

The Pendle Grit Formation is generally conformable on the Upper Bowland Shales, although locally in the Craven Reef Belt it overlaps these shales to rest on an irregular surface of the Malham Formation. Its base is markedly diachronous, lying as little as 7.6 m above the Malhamense Marine Band in the west, but some 100 m above it in the east. The Pendle Grit Formation is overlain throughout by the Grassington (Brennand) Grit. There are several sections where an unconformity can be demonstrated beneath the Grassington Grit, with some erosion of the Pendle Grit Formation at least on a local scale. Thus on Flasby Fell, where angular discordance at the junction is well displayed, the thickness of the Pendle Grit Formation preserved under the

Grassington Grit ranges from 15 to 240 m. The formation is locally overstepped by the Grassington Grit across the Reef Belt (e.g. south of Stockdale Beck), between the Middle and North Craven faults near Bordley, and south of the Reef Belt near Mearbeck. It is absent at Black Hill and on Fountains Fell, possibly due to non-deposition.

Variations in the thickness of the formation are illustrated in Figure 22. The thickest sequences are west of the River Ribble, with an estimated 550 m on the northern limb of the Catlow Anticline near Cross of Greet Bridge, and 490 m farther south-east between Brayshaw and Rathmell Beck. East of the Ribble sequences in excess of 200 m are exceptional, while across and to the north of the Craven Reef Belt the formation is less than 100 m thick.

The disparity in the thickness of the Pendle Grit Formation preserved on the northern and southern limbs of the Whelp Stone Syncline (Figure 22), about 170 and 490 m respectively, is a combined result of northward sedimentary thinning towards the axial zone of the Catlow Anticline and of pre-Grassington Grit erosion. Marked sedimentary thinning occurs in Gisburn Forest, north-east of Hesbert Hall, where northwards-dipping sandstones wedge out northwards against the base of the formation. These relationships are thought to involve some dislocation on growth faults, though this is unproved. Discordant relationships within the formation are evident in Croasdale and around the Catlow Anticline. They may be a consequence of syn-sedimentary disruption such as mass-movement under gravity, or of tectonic dislocation, or even of intraformational onlap.

Siltstone and silty mudstone are the principal lithologies. They are generally well laminated and micaceous, and include sporadic plant debris and bands or nodules of ironstone. Fine-grained sandstone laminae occur within the siltstone-mudstone sequences, giving a conspicuous striped appearance ('striped beds'). Thin, thick, and massive beds of fine-, medium- or coarse-grained sandstone are also present. Some of the mapped sandstone units comprise individual thick or massive beds; others are amalgamations of beds, with or without interbedded siltstone or mudstone. Some units are laterally persistent, extending for more than 1 km along strike, but others are channel-fill bodies with restricted lenticular crops. The sandstones are mostly micaceous and feldspathic; clasts of mudstone and siltstone are common inclusions, and exceptionally may exceed 15 cm across. Sub-rounded pebbles of quartz are present in some of the medium- and coarse-grained sandstones, and locally are sufficiently abundant to form conglomerate. Tool-marks are conspicuous on many of the thin-bedded sandstones; cross-lamination and rippled tops are additional features. Sole-marks are seldom apparent on the thicker bedded sandstones, though flute casts have been recorded at several localities. In some instances the thick-bedded sandstones have sharp bases that rest on erosion surfaces. Cross-bedding is rare. Slumps are common in the formation west of the River Ribble, especially in the siltstones, mudstones and striped beds in and around the Catlow Anticline.

In the thick succession north-west of Slaidburn, laterally extensive sandstone units, up to 40 m thick, make up much of the lowest 200 to 300 m; they form persistent features on Low Fell, and are well exposed in the River Hodder near Cross of Greet Bridge. These sandstones comprise fine,

medium- and coarse-grained varieties, and some are pebbly. Farther east, near Halsteads, these well bedded sandstones are absent; instead, the lowest 200 m include lenticular channel-fill sandstones which are mostly coarse grained and pebbly, and up to 15 m thick. In the thin sequence between Dob Dale and Whelp Stone Crag, sandstone is present only as minor channel-fill units, and in the much thicker sequence between Brayshaw and Rathmell Beck persistent bedded units characterise only the lowest 130 m; in the higher strata sandstone is a minor component. Within the relatively thin sequences east of the River Ribble, sandstones are mostly well bedded units that form persistent features east of Scaleber Bridge, on The Weets and on Flasby Fell. Fine- and medium- to coarse-grained varieties are typical, some of the coarser units including scattered quartz pebbles.

Details

Croasdale

In the Bowland Forest Tunnel (Earp, 1955), some 335 m of strata between the Upper Bowland Shales and the Warley Wise Grit, were referred to the 'Pendle Grit Group'. Most of this thickness was encountered in the northward drive from Croasdale Shaft [6868 5650]. The uppermost 180 m is dominantly argillaceous but includes a few beds of sandstone. The shales throughout the unit appeared to be non-marine, though no fossils were obtained from them.

The sequence on Low Fell is about 400 m thick, and includes sandstones which form persistent 'hog-back' features. The lowest 140 m are sporadically exposed in a track cutting [6896 5490 to 6920 5489] where they comprise interbedded sandstones, siltstones and mudstones. The sandstones are feldspathic, and include fine- to coarse-grained varieties; some are carbonaceous and some incorporate mudstone flakes. They include thick-bedded and massive units up to 12 m thick. Sole-markings include groove- and flute-casts.

Some of the highest strata of the formation are exposed in a western tributary [6845 5614 to 6859 5603] of Croasdale Brook. They include carbonaceous micaceous siltstones and striped beds with thick- and thin-bedded, fine- to medium-grained sandstones. The sandstones are sharp-based, and include ripple structures, mudstone flake layers, load-, groove- and flute-casts. There are also irregular channel-fill lenses, up to 2 m thick, of coarse-grained, fining-upwards feldspathic sandstone. Cross-lamination, groove-casts and prod-marks indicate a current from N30°E.

Stratigraphic relations at the top of the Low Fell sequence are unclear. Mapping to the north of Hind Slack Rig [6875 5530] suggests that the gently inclined, massive, coarse-grained sandstone exposed in Hind Slack [6868 5582] may overstep more steeply inclined sandstone-bearing strata lower in the sequence.

Catlow Anticline

On the north-western limb of the anticline near Cross of Greet Bridge, over 300 m of interbedded sandstones and siltstones are exposed in the River Hodder and its tributaries [7016 5892 to 7081 5893]. The sequence lies some 70 m above the top of the Upper Bowland Shales. The sandstones are feldspathic, and range from thin-bedded to massive; they are fine to coarse grained, locally pebbly, or even conglomeratic. They include micaceous and carbonaceous varieties, with mudstone clasts, slump structures and load casts. The mapped units are combinations of several beds. In the lowest exposed unit the sandstone beds are up to 1 m thick, and are separated by mudstone or siltstone. Siltstones are well exposed in a southern tributary [7000 5812 to 7014 5846]; they are locally slumped, and include striped beds and thin, sharp-based beds of fine-grained sandstone, some with groove-casts. An additional 165 m of the Pendle Grit Formation are calculated to overlie the exposed sequence at Cross of Greet Bridge, extending to the base of the Brennand Grit, but they are generally poorly exposed. Farther east, in a tributary [7139 6001] west of Hasgill Fell, about 12 m of thick-bedded to massive sandstone are present, apparently in the same part of the sequence. North of Halsteads the formation contains few laterally persistent sandstones. The lowest 200 m comprise partly slumped siltstones and striped beds as seen in Rig Gill Syke [7368 5966 to 7372 5948]. Coarse-grained channel-fill sandstones locally exceeding 150 m in thickness are present on the Halstead Fell [740 599].

A sandstone sheet near Merrybent Hill [708 569] appears to be discordant. It forms a well defined dip-slope, which converges with the base of the formation north-westwards, towards the crest of the Catlow Anticline.

Whelp Stone Syncline

The Pendle Grit Formation is well exposed in a broad outcrop in the core of the Whelp Stone Syncline. The fullest sections are in Long Gill Beck, between Long Gill and Whelpstone Lodge, where some 490 m are present, with laterally persistent sandstone units in the lowest 130 m. For example, west of Long Gill [7825 5840 to 7835 5842] 7 m of thick-bedded sandstone rest on slumped siltstone and silty mudstone with thin beds of sandstone and lenses of silty, pebbly, coarse-grained sandstone. The overlying 90 m are dominated by micaceous planty siltstone and silty mudstone with subordinate interbedded sandstone, and are exposed near Middle Brayshaw [7735 5849 to 7764 5842]. Above this, a further 70 m of micaceous siltstone and silty mudstone are exposed near Higher Brayshaw [7665 5898 to 7713 5858], and are partly slumped, with thin beds of sandstone and calcareous concretions towards the top. About 200 m of strata dominated by siltstone are calculated to complete the sequence to the base of the Brennand Grit at Whelp Stone Crag. Further good sections occur in Rathmell Beck and its tributaries [7871 5964 to 7953 5996]. Instability of the sediments during deposition is well illustrated farther upstream [7931 6020 to 7920 6029], with deformation structures including slumps [7920 6029 to 7931 6020], balled-up sandstone blocks [7940 6005], and debris slides [7940 6005 and 7947 6005].

On the north-western limb of the syncline, north-west of Whelp Stone Crag, the thickness of the Pendle Grit Formation is about 170 m. The sequence here is largely siltstone, though there are a few lenticular outcrops [7576 5944] of presumed channel-fill coarse-grained pebbly sandstone. The outcrops extending for some 2 km SSW from Whelp Stone Crag are dominated by feature-forming lenticular outcrops of sandstone. These sandstones are well exposed in quarries [753 578 and 756 576], where they are thick-bedded to massive, medium and coarse grained and feldspathic. Locally, they include plant debris, quartz pebbles, siltstone and mudstone clasts, and lenses of siltstone and striped beds. Some beds are richly carbonaceous, and some are slump-folded. Observed bedding in these sandstones is inclined generally northwards at 5 to 15°, and individual sandstone lenses appear to wedge out northwards against the base of the formation. In a gully [7512 5815] near Hindley Head the junction of one of the stratigraphically higher sandstones is exposed resting sharply on Upper Bowland Shales.

Settle

East of the River Ribble, siltstones and sandstones of the Pendle Grit Formation are exposed in a gully [8188 6103 to 8214 6101] north of Mearbeck where they rest on the Upper Bowland Shales and are overlain unconformably by the Grassington Grit. The basal 100 m are partly exposed in Bookil Gill Beck. The lowest 30 m

[8430 5946] are thick- and thin-bedded sandstones with subordinate interbedded micaceous silty mudstones and siltstone. The thicker sandstones (up to 1 m) are medium to coarse grained, and the thinner beds, fine to medium grained. The sandstones include load casts, rippled tops and cross-lamination, mudstone pellets and plant debris. The higher part of the section [8441 5953 to 8477 5996] includes 20 m of sandstone, comprising a massive, medium- to coarse-grained 6 m unit that fills a channel in the underlying 14 m unit, which is thick-bedded, medium to coarse grained with interbedded siltstone and mudstone.

The Croft Closes Borehole [8030 6428] near Giggleswick passed through the Brennand Grit and proved the Pendle Grit Formation from 88.7 m below surface to the supposed Upper Bowland Shales at 185.9 m. The sequence comprises interbedded sandstones, siltstones and mudstones. The sandstones are mostly fine and medium grained, commonly striped with layers rich in mica and carbonaceous debris; the siltstones are micaceous and planty; the mudstones are partly silty, with ironstone nodules and contain *Curvirimula sp.* towards the base.

South-eastwards from Settle, sandstones with associated siltstones and striped beds give rise to good scarp features, and are exposed in gullies [8193 6203 to 8249 6180] east of Anley and in disused quarries [8207 6261] farther north. The sandstones include feldspathic, medium- to fine-grained, and micaceous varieties, and some are cross-bedded. There are good sections also in Scaleber Beck, in its tributary south of Scaleber Bridge [8362 6197 to 8392 6241], and in the headwater tributaries [8460 6138 to 8484 6134] of Bookil Gill Beck. The Cominco Borehole S9 [8309 6330], north-west of Preston's Barn, proved sandstone in the basal part of the Pendle Grit Formation from rock-head at 3.9 m to the Upper Bowland Shales at 11.4 m.

On the higher ground between Scaleber Bridge and Rye Loaf Hill, sandstones in the Pendle Grit Formation form scarp features, for example, on High Greet [8527 6237], where they are capped by small outliers of Grassington Grit. On the hillside [8543 6300] above Low South Bank, south of Stockdale Farm, the formation overlaps the Upper Bowland Shales, and rests unconformably on the Malham Formation. The estimated thickness of the formation on the watershed [860 630] SW of Rye Loaf Hill is 20 to 30 m.

Malham, Bordley, Flasby

The formation was proved in the Cominco Borehole S6 [8770 6360] on the eastern flank of Kirkby Fell from the base of a landslip at 11.3 m to the top of the Upper Bowland Shales at 77.6 m. The sequence is dominated by siltstone and silty mudstone, with plant debris, ironstone nodules and fish scales. Interbedded sandstones are mostly fine grained, laminated, planty and micaceous.

The Pendle Grit Formation crops out widely in the upland tract between Aire Head, Malham and Hetton Common Beck. The thickest sequence (about 150 m) is in the core of an eastward-plunging syncline on Hetton Common. The base of the formation is marked by a persistent medium- to coarse-grained sandstone on Hanlith Moor and The Weets. This sandstone, exposed in gullies and quarries [9153 6243 and 9166 6251], is up to 6 m thick with parallel thick and thin beds separated by siltstone. It is succeeded by at least 40 m of siltstone, silty mudstone and fine-grained, flaggy, micaceous sandstone. Sandstones, siltstones and striped beds forming the highest part of the sequence are exposed in a gully [9442 6280 to 9455 6385] near Know Bank.

Mapping around The Weets [9243 6318] suggests that the Pendle Grit Formation is locally overstepped by the Grassington Grit. The same may be true north of Bark Plantation [9511 6463], Bordley.

The formation crops out around Firth Hill Plantation and farther south on Threshfield Moor. There are few good sections, the best being in Rowley Beck, where the basal beds are exposed [9667 6414 to 9693 6417], and its tributaries [9566 6439 to 9578

6448]. Siltstones and silty mudstones are interbedded with fine-grained, flaggy and carbonaceous sandstones. In Rowley Beck they include a 3 m thick, medium- to coarse-grained unit with scattered quartz pebbles, and minor channel-fill bodies of coarse-grained sandstone.

Sheet-like sandstone bodies in the lowest 100 m of the formation form good scarp features on the hillside [9586 5535 to 9626 5556] north-east of Sharp Haw, Flasby Fell. One of these sheets forms a lenticular outcrop [9594 5567] some 25 m above the base, and is presumably a channel-fill sandstone. Beds some 150 m above the base are exposed in a quarry [9610 5662] south-east of Flasby Moor Side, where 2.5 m of thick-bedded, medium-grained sandstone are overlain unconformably by massive, coarse-grained, pebbly Grassington Grit. The former sandstone includes scattered coarse grains and quartz pebbles, and the bed-tops are flaggy or rippled. This sandstone and others in this part of the sequence form strong scarp features on the hillside [9610 5635] to the south.

Grassington (or Brennand) Grit (Pendleian, E_1)

The Grassington Grit (Dakyns, 1892) has its type area to the east of the Settle district. It consists largely of massive to cross-bedded, coarse-grained, pebbly sandstone which gives rise to prominent and persistent scarps (Plate 21). Complete sequences are known only west of the River Ribble between Giggleswick and Croasdale where the sandstone is known as the Brennand Grit (Moseley, 1956), and is overlain by the Roeburndale Formation. Elsewhere, in the outliers on the Askrigg Block (Fountains Fell and Black Hill) and in the outcrops to the the south of the Craven Reef Belt, the Grassington Grit is the youngest preserved Silesian strata, with the possible exception of a drift-covered outcrop on Boss Moor, where a few metres of overlying strata may be present.

The age, definition and regional correlation of the Grassington Grit and Brennand Grit are controversial, and are currently under investigation. Until conclusive evidence is obtained, the Grassington Grit is here considered to be lithostratigraphically continuous with the Lower Howgate Edge Grit of the Hawes district (Rowell and Scanlon, 1957), with the Brennand Grit of the Lancaster and western Settle districts (Moseley, 1954, 1956), with the Warley Wise Grit of the Clitheroe district (Earp and others, 1961), and includes the Kirkby Fell Grits of Hudson (1944b). Moseley (1954) recorded *Eumorphoceras bisulcatum* (E_{2a}) from two closely spaced marine bands (Tarnbrook-Wyre Marine Beds) overlying the Brennand Grit, and *Cravenoceras cowlingense* from one, probably the higher, of these bands. Earp and others (1961) recorded *E. bisulcatum* from the Warley Wise (Edge) Marine Band, above the Warley Wise Grit, but no marine strata are recorded from strata immediately above the Grassington Grit in the Settle district. In the adjoining Pateley Bridge district, however, the Cockhill Limestone (Marine Band) overlies the Grassington Grit, and contains *C. cowlingense* and *E. bisulcatum*. Yates (1962) described three distinct varieties of *E. bisulcatum* from separate marine bands, and suggested that the faunas from the Tarnbook-Wyre Marine Beds could be correlated with those from the Cockhill Limestone because both contain *E. bisulcatum grassingtonense*, the earliest variety of the species. This suggestion supports the equivalence of the Brennand and Grassington grits, and the placing of these units within the Pendleian, though Ramsbottom (1974) has speculated that the *C. cowlingense* horizon lies between the Pendle Grit (Formation) and

the Warley Wise Grit, thus placing the Warley Wise Grit (and its equivalents) in the Arnsbergian.

An unconformity at the base of the Grassington Grit is inferred in many parts of the outcrop (Figure 22). Across and to the north of the Craven Reef Belt and at Mearbeck, south of Settle, the Grassington Grit oversteps the Pendle Grit Formation onto Upper Bowland Shales or early Pendleian Wensleydale Group. Angular discordance is particularly apparent on Flasby Fell (Mundy and Arthurton, 1980), where the unconformity is irregular, and Pendle Grit Formation sandstones form ridges over which the Grassington Grit thins.

West of River Ribble, the Brennand Grit is generally 80 to 90 m thick, though exceptionally it attains a maximum of about 220 m in Croasdale (Figure 22). A complete sequence of 86.4 m was proved in a borehole at Croft Closes, near Giggleswick. On Bloe Greet and at Reeves Edge in Croasdale, the sandstone is split into three leaves; the lowest of these, probably the equivalent of the Lower Brennand Grit of Moseley (1954), is itself split by impersistent, soft-weathering partings.

The unit is well exposed in the headwaters of the River Hodder where its lower part is massive or very crudely cross-bedded. Cross-bedding becomes pronounced upwards, the foresets inclined generally towards the south-east. The uppermost 10 to 20 m comprise planty siltstone and sandstone, with ganister and rootlet layers. Farther east near Knotteranum, and on Whelp Stone Crag, channel-fill bodies of coarse-grained pebbly sandstone locally form the basal part of the unit. These ribbon-like bodies are aligned approximately N–S and display eastward-dipping, tabular foresets; the main scarp is either broken or subdued where it intercepts these bodies.

At Whelp Stone Crag, on the ground west of Giggleswick village, and in many of the outliers south and east of Settle there are two or more leaves, the lowest of which commonly gives rise only to an impersistent feature. On Boss Moor, there are three leaves, with intervening planty siltstone, coal and coaly mudstone. The thickest coal, known as the Caton (or Skirethorns) Coal, lies between the two lower leaves; it is up to 0.9 m thick and has been worked extensively south of the Middle Craven Fault. On Flasby Fell, where two leaves are preserved, the sandstone is stained red, presumably a consequence of Permo-Triassic weathering.

DETAILS

Croasdale – Far Costy Clough

The Brennand Grit is well exposed, except for its basal part, in Far Costy Clough, in the headwaters of the River Hodder. The lowest beds are seen in a quarry [6948 5955] where there are at least 12 m of massive, wedge cross-bedded, coarse-grained, partly pebbly sandstone, with mudstone and siltstone as clasts and lenses up to 1 m thick. The stream section [6902 5950 to 6936 5950] exposes higher parts of the sequence which is mostly strongly cross-bedded, medium- and coarse-grained, pebbly sandstone (Figure 22). The scale of the cross-bedding reduces upwards, and the foresets are inclined generally to the ESE. At the top of the section, coarse-grained, cross-bedded sandstone is overlain by 0.5 m of thin-bedded sandstones with plant debris and rootlets. Farther upstream another section [6866 5923] at the top of the unit shows 10.5 m of thick- and thin-bedded, planty, fine-grained sandstones, siltstones and striped beds, with two rootlet layers.

Southwards across Bloe Greet to Reeves Edge in Croasdale, the Brennand Grit splits into three leaves. On Bloe Greet the lowest of these includes a slack, and forms a strong 70 m scarp known as Bloe Greet Breast [694 584]. Well defined cross-bedding is recorded only at the top of this leaf, but is prominent in the higher leaves. At Reeves Edge [687 574], the lowest leaf includes complex, soft-weathering partings which locally increase its thickness to more than 100 m. It is here succeeded by a slack, calculated to contain 65 m of strata, and two upper leaves of 20 and 15 m separated by a 30 m slack. The lowest leaf extends north-eastwards in a lobe-like outcrop [698 581] on the south-eastern side of Near Costy Clough; the sandstone of this crop appears to be strongly unconformable on the Pendle Grit Formation.

An unconformity is apparent at the base of an outlier of the presumed Brennand Grit farther south [6950 5691] on the north-eastern flank of Croasdale. Here, gently inclined massive, coarse-grained, pebbly sandstone and conglomerate rest on siltstone inclined to the west at some 30°.   RSA

Bowland Knotts – Whelp Stone Crag

The formation forms a prominent south-facing escarpment between Bowland Knotts [722 602] and Rock Cat Knott [741 609]; to the north there is an extensive, largely drift-covered dip-slope. At Green Knots [732 603] south-east of Knotteranum, a lobe of channel-fill sandstone protrudes southwards from the escarpment. It appears to have a planar base which, taking the regional dip into account, lies at a level below the base of the main escarpment. Tabular foresets are inclined eastwards at 18 to 27°.

To the east of the Catlow Anticline, gently inclined Brennand Grit is preserved in a number of outliers including Scoutber Crag and Whelp Stone Crag where the sequence is at least 25 m thick. The oldest beds form prominent but impersistent north-trending ribs on the north-western side of the crag [7610 5945], with easterly dipping tabular foresets. The ribs are overlapped [7613 5935] by a scarp-forming sheet of cross-bedded sandstone and conglomerate, generally 10 to 15 m thick but much thinner over the ribs; the foresets of this sheet are inclined to the south-east. At the north-eastern end of the crag, a higher leaf of cross-bedded sandstone and conglomerate is preserved. A quarry [7639 5946] exposes a 9 m sec-tion, with tabular foresets inclined to the south-east in the lower part, and small-scale cross-bedding above.   EWJ, RSA

Giggleswick – Settle – Kirkby Fell

The Brennand Grit is well exposed in crags and quarries to the west of Giggleswick, where it is split into several leaves. West of Giggleswick School, poorly cross-bedded pebbly sandstones in the lower part of the sequence form a scarp [8080 6405] some 15 m high, and in a quarry [8074 6410] farther west, 8 m of massive coarse-grained pebbly sandstone fill a channel in cross-bedded sandstone. The uppermost 15 m of the formation form a strong scarp east of Croft Closes with large-scale cross-bedding in the lower part and small-scale towards the top [8048 6473]. A water borehole [8030 6428] south-east of Croft Closes proved almost the full sequence of the Brennand Grit from rock-head at 2.3 m to the top of the Pendle Grit Formation at 88.70 m. The sandstones here are mostly medium- and coarse-grained, feldspathic, and with sparse to abundant quartz pebbles. They include clasts of mudstone and siltstone and plant debris, and contain a few thin interbeds of mudstone and siltstone. There is a rootlet horizon recorded in mudstone at 30.0 m depth.

There are many exposures of the Grassington Grit to the south and south-east of Settle where the outcrop is repeated by faulting. The formation is about 65 m thick and divided into two or three, locally four, leaves [8237 6270 to 8264 6210]; cross-bedding foresets are inclined generally between south-west and south-east. The Grassington Grit forms an outlier at Mearbeck where it dips WSW at 5 to 6° [818 609]; it rests with marked unconformity on the Pendle Grit Formation, exposed in a gully to the north. A similar unconformity is apparent at the base of an outlier of the grit at Little Harestones [846 620], south-east of Scaleber Bridge.

Two leaves are preserved on Rye Loaf Hill and Kirkby Fell. The lower forms a locally impersistent feature up to 12 m high, and comprises crudely bedded, coarse-grained pebbly sandstone with mudstone clasts that is cross-bedded at the top. It is separated from the upper leaf, which is up to 18 m thick on Rye Loaf Hill [8642 6331], by a 5 m slack. Fragments of coal in head deposits on the southern bank [8647 6382] of Stockdale Beck may be derived from this slack.

Plate 21   Brennand Grit, Cold Stone, Catlow Fell [7116 6077]. Well developed cross-stratification in the upper part of the sandstone. (L 2857)

The Weets – Boss Moor – Threshfield Moor

Eastwards from Malham, the lower leaf of the Grassington Grit is preserved in several outliers, the remnants of a sheet dipping gently to the east or south-east at up to 6°, between The Weets and Park House. Mapping indicates that the formation oversteps the Pendle Grit Formation onto Upper Bowland Shales near Weets Top [9256 6320].

Farther east, two leaves form strong features around Lainger House. The lower leaf, estimated to be 15 m thick and comprising cross-bedded, coarse-grained pebbly sandstone, is exposed in gullies [9474 6310 to 9480 6323 and 9480 6271 to 9489 6274]; the succeeding slack includes a coal, formerly worked from bell pits, which appears to thin out [9474 6310] north-westwards. The upper leaf is some 12 m thick, and is lithologically similar to the lower.

On Boss Moor and Threshfield Moor, where the thickness of the formation is 110 m, there are three leaves. The lowest forms a locally impersistent feature, and in Hamerton Hill Syke [9671 6223] it is 12 m thick, with cross-bedded foresets inclined between south and west. On the scarp farther east [9701 6227] this leaf is 18 m thick, and recorded foresets are mostly inclined to the south. The succeeding slack includes the Caton (or Skirethorns) Coal, which has been worked extensively from bell pits over Boss Moor, and from the shafts of the abandoned Threshfield Colliery [9733 6285]. The section on the abandonment plan shows the coal to be 0.9 m thick, overlain by 0.9 m of shale and ironstone, and this in turn by 15.9 m of sandstone (middle leaf). Dumps from the various workings include planty, micaceous mudstone. The middle leaf, from 20 to 50 m thick, is seen in Hamerton Hill Syke [9664 6231 to 9672 6227] and in quarries [9554 6210 and 9564 6193] on Boss Moor; its top part is well exposed in Lainger Beck [9534 6284 to 9561 6320]. Cross-bedded foresets are generally inclined between west and south-east. Above the middle leaf, the succession is poorly exposed, and a 20 m interval is presumed to consist largely of mudstone and siltstone, though a thin coal, coaly mudstone, and planty siltstone are recorded near the base in Lainger Beck [9527 6279]. The highest leaf, some 20 m thick, is poorly exposed in pits [9573 6277] south-east of Lainger House, where coarse-grained pebbly sandstone has been quarried, and near Hamerton Hill Syke [9657 6220] where medium- to fine-grained sandstone has been dug. The mapping suggests that this leaf may be locally capped by mudstone in the drift-covered ground north of Boss Moor.

Northwards from the Middle Craven Fault near Firth Hill Plantation the basal relationship of the lowest leaf of the Grassington Grit is complex. South of the plantation, coarse-grained pebbly sandstone appears to be banked against a contemporaneous scarp of fine- to medium-grained sandstone of the Pendle Grit Formation [e.g. 9600 6365].

A borehole [9721 6380] near Lower Height proved the following sequence in the lowest two leaves of the Grassington Grit: 7.6 m of 'grit' under rock-head; underlain by 0.6 m of coal on 2.5 m of 'shale'; underlain by 24.9 m of 'grit'; resting on 6.1 m of 'shale with grit' (Pendle Grit Formation).

Flasby Fell

The Grassington Grit is preserved in outliers on Flasby Fell where it is red-stained. In Crag Wood, it has two leaves forming a strong double feature, and is well exposed [9570 5504 to 9580 5509] south-west of Sharp Haw. The lower leaf comprises about 20 m of massive, cross-bedded, coarse-grained pebbly sandstone with foresets inclined to the west. Above an unexposed 10 m slack, the upper leaf comprises at least 30 m, and possibly as much as 45 m, of similar sandstone. Two leaves in a 35 m sequence are preserved on Rough Haw [963 559], one of three outliers which appear to be the remnants of a sheet inclined to the north at about 4°. In a more northern outlier, the sandstone rests with unconformity on more steep-

ly inclined Pendle Grit Formation [9610 5635], and thins abruptly from 22.5 to about 6 m over a sandstone rib in the underlying sequence.   RSA

Black Hill, Fountains Fell

The formation forms an outlier on Black Hill on the downthrow side of the North Craven Fault, and a disused quarry [8640 6630] exposes medium-grained, feldspathic sandstone, with cross-bedding foresets dipping SSE. The Black Hill Borehole [8630 6628] proved 14.5 m of the formation resting on Upper Bowland Shales mudstones and siltstones.

Farther north, an outlier of the Grassington Grit occurs on Fountains Fell, where it is known also as the Lower Howgate Edge Grit (Rowell and Scanlon, 1957), and lies unconformably on Pendleian siltstones of the Wensleydale Group. The coarse-grained, feldspathic sandstone with quartz pebbles is up to 50 m thick, and is split into two leaves by siltstones that contain seatearths and thin coals. Only the 20 m thick lower leaf crops out within the district. It is graded towards the top and is capped by a ganister [e.g. 8694 7052]. The overlying siltstones and the upper leaf crop out in the Hawes district to the north.   DJCM, EWJ

Roeburndale Formation, Caton Shales to top of Silver Hills Sandstone (Arnsbergian, E₂)

The term Roeburndale Formation is introduced to replace 'Roeburndale Grit Group' (Moseley, 1954, 1956). It denotes a prograding deltaic sequence of interbedded siltstones and sandstones; the sandstones are collectively referred to as Roeburndale Sandstones. The base and top of the formation are taken at the boundaries Moseley (1956) used to define his group in the Keasden area, respectively at the top of the Brennand Grit and at the base of the Caton Shales. There are few natural sections and none extends through the formation. The thickness ranges from 90 m near Settle to about 500 m on Burn Moor. No age-diagnostic fauna is known, although the formation is placed in the E_{2a} Subzone of the Arnsbergian Stage on the evidence of its position, beneath the Edalensis Marine Band (basal E_{2b}) in the overlying Caton Shales and above the Tarnbrook-Wyre Marine Beds (Moseley, 1954) which contain *Eumorphoceras bisulcatum* of E_{2a} age.

Laminated siltstones occur at the base of the sequence, and a graded fluviatile sandstone with a ganister cap is present at the top. The middle part comprises interbedded siltstones and turbiditic sandstones. In the thinnest sequence, between the South Craven and Lawkland faults near Settle, there are no turbiditic sandstones. Between Rome and Keasden Beck, there are two such sandstones totalling 60 m in the 200 m succession. West of Keasden Beck, on Burn Moor, the formation consists mostly of turbiditic sandstones, but a delta-top sandstone overlain by a seatearth and coal has also been identified within the succession. The coal probably correlates with the Smeer Hall Coal of the Lancaster district which is known to occur progressively lower in the Roeburndale Formation towards the east (Moseley, 1954). To the north of Burn Moor near Mewith, the sandstone at the top of the formation is over 100 m thick and contains several seatearths. Locally, in this part of the district, this sandstone is overlain by up to 30 m of laminated silty sandstones that form a ridge rising above the presumed delta top and are interpreted as levee or overbank deposits.

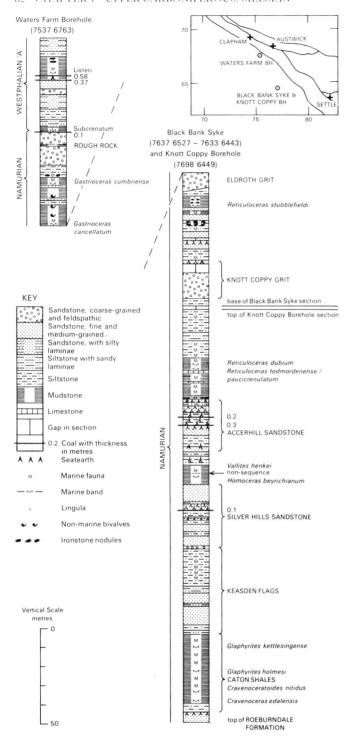

Figure 23 The Silesian successions in Black Bank Syke, and the Knott Coppy and Waters Farm boreholes

The term Caton Shales was used by Slinger (1936) for 'the calcareous shales of the 1in. Geological Survey map, containing goniatites of late E_2 age . . . .' on Caton Moor, near Lancaster, overlying the Roeburndale Grit, and it is here used in this sense. The shales are fissile, marine, silty mudstones with an abundant fauna of goniatites and bivalves. The mudstones are dark grey, bituminous and pyritic in part, and they contain septarian nodules and thin beds of argillaceous limestone. The Caton Shales are 40 m thick in the Knott Coppy Borehole (Figure 23), and similar thicknesses are calculated at crop. Their stratigraphy was first described by Holmes and Bisat (1925) from sections in Keasden Beck and Kettles Beck. Moseley (1956) divided the succession into lower and upper parts using the goniatite subzones. Generally the shales includes four goniatite horizons, all of E_{2b} age: *Cravenoceratoides edalensis*, *Ct. nitidus*, *Glaphyrites holmesi* and *Gl. kettlesingense*. An exception occurs near Mewith where the shales are less than 1 m thick, and only the Holmesi Marine Band is present. The thinning is believed to occur over a ridge formed by a major delta distributary in the underlying Roeburndale Formation.

Some 60 m of mostly sandy, micaceous, well laminated siltstone, referred to as the Keasden Flags (Moseley, 1956), overlie the Caton Shales (Figure 23), though in the Knott Coppy Borehole the sequence is only 45 m thick. There are thin sandstone interbeds, and locally, laterally impersistent, irregular bodies of sandstone. The division is best exposed in Kettles Beck, Dub Syke, Keasden Beck and Meregill Beck. Scattered plant fragments occur throughout and a sparse marine fauna, including brachiopods and bivalves, is present.

The succeeding Silver Hills Sandstone (Moseley, 1956) is mostly thick- and thin-bedded, medium- to coarse-grained, and includes a conglomerate at the base. It is generally in two leaves, separated by siltstone which contains a coal and seatearth near its base. In the Knott Coppy Borehole (Figure 23), the leaves are each about 13 m thick and the intervening siltstone 8 m; similar thicknesses are present in Kettles Beck. The Silver Hills Sandstone thickens north-east of the Lawkland Fault, where the width of its outcrop and the dip indicate that it is up to 90 m thick, with no evidence of the siltstone parting.

DETAILS

West of Settle, the base of the Roeburndale Formation is exposed in a glacial drainage channel [7976 6396] south-west of Croft Closes, where it rests conformably on the ganister cap of the Brennand Grit. The basal siltstones yielded miospores of the TK Zone which correlate approximately with the E_2 goniatite zone (Owens and others, 1977). The sandstone at the top of the succession is seen in exposures [7986 6551 to 8008 6540] on the downthrow side of a fault, and the top surface is covered with concentric corrugations of the marine trace-fossil *Zoophycos*. It is overlain by 0.15 m of ochreous, clay-seatearth which separates it from the succeeding Caton Shales.

The formation is extensively drift-covered between Rome and Keasden Beck. Turbiditic sandstones form prominent ridges [7812 6260 to 7850 6267 and 7828 6280 to 7845 6286] west of Rome. The lower sandstone is syndepositionally deformed; thinner beds are slumped and folded, and many bedding planes are curved. The siltstones are exposed in the glacial drainage channels now occupied by Storth Gill and its tributaries [790 630]. The following section, through some 90 m of the upper part of the formation is seen in Kettles Beck [7426 6250 to 7460 6322]:

	Thickness m
Base of Caton Shales	
Sandstone with ganister at top	2.0
Siltstone; laminated, with septarian nodules	27.0

Siltstone with sandstone interbeds	10.0
Siltstone; locally with sandstone interbeds	13.0
Sandstone with siltstone interbeds	11.0
Siltstone	2.7
Sandstone; graded turbidite succession (base unexposed)	25.2

A section [7259 6260] in Cowsen Gill, a tributary of Keasden Beck, exposes 0.1 m of coal resting on a siltstone-seatearth which overlies a weakly bedded sandstone. Overlying the coal, 0.2 m of silty mudstone contains *Lingula mytilloides*, and passes upwards into laminated micaceous siltstone (0.8 m) that is overlain by 4 m of well bedded quartzose sandstone with a white-weathering ganister at the top. These beds are all placed in the Roeburndale Formation, and this is the only locality in the district where a marine fauna has been found within the formation. The coal is tentatively correlated with the Smeer Hall Coal of the Lancaster district. The succession exposed in Keasden Beck and its tributaries [7209 6285 to 7239 6539] is similar to that seen in Kettles Beck; 50 to 90 m of siltstones with a few sandstone interbeds separate thick-bedded turbiditic sandstones from the overlying 40 m thick delta-top sandstone. A 0.15 m coal occurs 5 m below the top of the latter, but no seatearth is present below the coal, suggesting that it is a float coal. The top of the sandstone [7239 6539] contains vertical rootlets and subhorizontal *Stigmaria* root stocks.

To the west of Keasden Beck exposure is poor, but there are generally good scarp features. Parts of the succession are exposed in Barclay Gill Syke and Outlaw Gill on the east side of Burn Moor. The thicker sandstones locally form crags, for example at Cat Stones [696 642], Fox Holes [699 628], Ravens Castle [693 613] and on Lythe Fell [688 622]. A thin (0.05 m) coal in Outlaw Gill [7102 6345] rests on 0.1 m of laminated mudstone with coal streaks in an interbedded succession of sandstone and siltstone. It may correlate with the Smeer Hall Coal, but no seatearth is present, suggesting that it too is a float coal.

The delta-top sandstone at the top of the succession is exposed in Keasden Beck [7172 6661], Ratten Syke [7133 6691] and Bloe Beck [7033 6740]. A 0.15 m coal lies within the sandstone at the last locality, and coal was recorded in Ratten Syke during the Primary Survey but the section is now obscured. Near Mewith the delta-top sandstone is overlain by laminated sandy siltstones which are exposed in Badger Ford Beck [6924 6711 to 6926 6814] and have been recorded in a nearby borehole [6909 6774]. The Roeburndale Formation succession in the borehole is:

	Depth m
Boulder Clay and weathered silty sandstones	to 15.6
Mudstone and siltstone; sandy, laminated	to 35.4
Sandstone; mostly fine-grained, quartzose	to 48.8
Sandstone; coarse-grained, thickly bedded, pebbly at base	to 53.4
Sandstone; fine-grained ganister	to 56.0
Mudstone-seatearth	to 58.0
Sandstone; mostly coarse-grained, with ganister at top	to 69.5
Sandstone; reverse-graded	to 77.7
Mudstone-seatearth	to 78.4
Sandstone; feldspathic, graded	to 88.4
Sandstone; with siltstone partings to base of borehole	at 116.7

The Knott Coppy Borehole [7698 6449] (Figure 23) proved the following goniatite horizons in the Caton Shales (in metres above the base of the Caton Shales):

4.30	*Posidonia corrugata, Anthracoceras sp.*
5.56 – 8.58	*Cravenoceratoides edalensis* E_{2b1} horizon *P. corrugata, Selenimyalina variabilis, Anthracoceras*
	sp., Brachycycloceras scalare, Glaphyrites subplicatus and *Ct. edalensis*
8.60 – 10.50	*P. corrugata, S. variabilis, Anthracoceras sp., Eumorphoceras bisulcatum* s.l.
10.57 – 10.73	*Cravenoceratoides nitidus* E_{2b2} horizon *P. corrugata, Anthracoceras sp.* and *Ct. nitidus*
10.93 – 18.45	*Obliquipecten sp., P. corrugata, S. variabilis, Euphemites sp., Anthracoceras glabrum, Anthracoceras tenuispirale, Kazakhoceras sp.* and *Elonichthys sp.*
19.17 – 21.50	*Glaphyrites holmesi* E_{2b2} horizon *Obliquipecten sp., P. corrugata, Anthracoceras sp.* and *Gl. holmesi*
22.30 – 33.20	*P. corrugata, S. variabilis, A. glabrum* and *Metadimorphoceras sp.*
33.25 – 35.80	*Glaphyrites kettlesingensis* E_{2b2} horizon *Lingula mytilloides, Phestia sharmani, P. corrugata, S. variabilis, Cycloceras rugosum, A. glabrum* and *G. kettlesingensis*
35.80 – 40.35	*P. corrugata, S. variabilis, A. glabrum* and *Metadimorphoceras sp.*

The Caton Shales are exposed in Kettles Beck [7460 6322 to 7457 6368], but the section is faulted and the succession incomplete: 0.3 m of limestone containing *Cravenoceratoides nitidus* occurs 5.1 m above the base of the unit [7461 6326 and 7455 6347]. The section in Keasden Beck [7241 6541 to 7142 6734] is also discontinuous and faulted, and the shales rest [7241 6541] on an irregular surface of ganister at the top of the Roeburndale Formation. The 0.3 m limestone with *Ct. nitidus* occurs some 5 m above the base [7244 6546].

Near Mewith the Caton Shales are less than 1 m thick, and are exposed in Badger Ford Beck [6913 6769 to 6926 6810]. A section [6916 6776] reveals 0.2 m of silty mudstone, overlain by a 0.3 m bed of bituminous limestone that contains *Anthracoceras sp., Gl. holmesi* and pectinoids.

The Knott Coppy Borehole penetrated 45 m of Keasden Flags consisting of laminated sandy siltstone with 23 m of sandstone at the base, and a sparse fauna including *Orbiculoidea sp., Liralingula wilsoni, Rugosochonetes sp., Dunbarella carbonarius* and *Anthraconeilo sp.* was recorded. The most complete natural section occurs in Kettles Beck where some 60 m of laminated siltstones are exposed between a faulted contact with Caton Shales [7457 6368] and the base of the Silver Hills Sandstone [7485 6410]. Elsewhere, laterally impersistent sandstones occur within the siltstones and are exposed in Keasden Beck [7243 6573 and 7250 6561] and in Dub Syke [7293 6557 and 7299 6563].

Some 34 m of strata classified as the Silver Hills Sandstone were penetrated by the Knott Coppy Borehole (Figure 23). At the base, there is 1.1 m of conglomerate with subrounded ironstone and siltstone clasts in a coarse-grained feldspathic sandstone matrix. The unit is in two leaves: there is a general fining upwards in the lower leaf and the lowest 2 m of sandstone in the upper leaf is bioturbated by horizontal *Planolites* tubes and vertical spreite. A similar succession is present in Kettles Beck, although exposure is discontinuous. Here [7485 6410], the basal conglomerate rests on an eroded surface of Keasden Flags; it is about 1 m thick and contains pebbles and cobbles of sandstone and derived ironstone nodules in a friable sandstone matrix. Overlying the conglomerate are 3.3 m of channel-fill sandstones; some beds have conglomerate at their bases, and syndepositional faults with displacements of up to 0.3 m are present in this unit. The strata separating the two leaves of sandstone crop out in Kettles Beck [7493 6425 to 7499 6473]; a section in them [7502 6448] exposes 0.2 m of coal overlying 0.25 m of clay-seatearth; the base of the coal occurs 1.35 m below the base of the upper leaf of sandstone.

Top of Silver Hills Sandstone to top of Rough Rock (Chokierian, H_1; Kinderscoutian, R_1; Marsdenian, R_2 and Yeadonian, G_1)

The Silver Hills Sandstone is overlain by 17 m of mudstone and siltstone in the Knott Coppy Borehole (Figure 23). A non-sequence 6 m above the base of these beds cuts out the Alportian strata. *Homoceras beyrichianum*, diagnostic of the H_{1b} Subzone, lies below the non-sequence, and Kinderscoutian R_{1a} strata with *Vallites henkei* are present above.

The overlying Accerhill Sandstone (Moseley, 1956) is mostly fine-grained and well bedded, and contains much ganister, interbeds of siltstone and seatearth, and two thin coals. It is best exposed east of the Holm Fault, near Accerhill Farm. Here, and in the Knott Coppy Borehole where it is 28 m thick, the sandstone is in three leaves separated by siltstone partings (Figure 23). The only evidence of thickness variation in the district occurs northeast of the Lawkland Fault where 40 m are calculated to be present from the width of the outcrop and the dip of the strata.

Some 50 m of mudstones and siltstones overlie the Accerhill Sandstone. The lowest 20 m of these are fossiliferous, dark grey, silty mudstones, calcareous in part and containing thin beds of limestone. There is a gradational passage upwards into paler grey, sandy, micaceous, laminated siltstones, which contain ironstone nodules, plant fragments and a sparse marine fauna. Parts of this succession are exposed in stream sections between Black Bank and Craven Ridge, and all except the top few metres were proved in the Knott Coppy Borehole. Kinderscoutian (R_{1a}) goniatites were recorded from the basal part of the succession by Moseley (1956), and the Todmordenense/Paucicrenulatum and Dubium marine bands, of R_{1a} to R_{1b} age, have been identified in the Knott Coppy Borehole.

These beds are succeeded by the Knott Coppy Grit (Moseley, 1956), a mostly thick-bedded, coarse-grained feldspathic sandstone with a sharp base. The top 5 m of the sandstone are thin-bedded, graded, medium- and fine-grained, and capped by ganister. The sandstone forms a south-facing scarp between Blaithwaite and Black Bank, where it is about 20 m thick.

The Knott Coppy Grit is overlain by 30 to 35 m of interbedded sandstones, mudstones and siltstones in Black Bank Syke (Figure 23). The sandstones are fine- to medium-grained, thin-bedded or laminated, and the mudstones are micaceous, well laminated, and some contain a sparse brachiopod-bivalve fauna. The top 10 m of strata comprise dark grey, fissile mudstones that pass gradationally upwards into laminated, sandy, micaceous siltstones. At the base, the mudstones contain the Stubblefieldi Marine Band, and in higher beds *Lingula* is abundant.

The succeeding 50 to 60 m thick Eldroth Grit (Moseley, 1956) is a thick-bedded, coarse-grained, feldspathic sandstone that contains rounded quartz pebbles and coaly wood fragments. Its base, exposed in Black Bank Syke (Figure 23), rests sharply on the underlying siltstone, and the grit forms a prominent ridge between Clapham Station and Green Close on Newby Moor.

The outcrops of the strata overlying the Eldroth Grit are mostly drift-covered. Their stratigraphy is based on the suc-cession established in the Ingleton area (Ford, 1954) to the north-west of the district, and the upper part of the succession was proved in the Waters Farm Borehole, near Austwick (Figure 23). The ages of mudstones and siltstones in isolated exposures have been determined from their included miospore assemblages, using the classification proposed by Owens and others (1977).

The Eldroth Grit is separated from the overlying Greta Grit by some 15 m of dark grey, fissile mudstones and the basal part of this sequence contains the Gracile Marine Band which defines the base of the Marsdenian Stage (R_2). These mudstones are exposed in the extreme north-west of the district, in Fowgill Beck, south-west of Nutgill Farm. In Nut Gill, the upper part of this succession comprises sandy, micaceous, laminated siltstones that pass gradationally upwards into medium-grained sandstone at the base of the Greta Grit.

The Greta Grit (Ford, 1954) is about 40 m thick in Nut Gill and Aspland Beck, where it is a locally reddened, thickly bedded, coarse-grained, pebbly feldspathic sandstone; near the top it is graded and there is a cap of ganister. A 0.1 m coal overlies the grit in Aspland Beck where the succeeding strata comprise sparsely fossiliferous (bivalves and *Lingula*) silty mudstones which pass upwards into 8 m of fine- to medium-grained sandstone. The sandstone is ganisteroid in part and in turn is overlain by laminated micaceous siltstone.

The upper part of the Greta Grit also crops out south-west of Eldroth, where it is overlain by dark grey mudstone which passes upwards into laminated micaceous siltstone. Near the base of the mudstone the Bilinguis Marine Band contains an abundant and varied marine fauna and indicates the R_{2b} Subzone of the Marsdenian Stage. The marine band is tentatively correlated with the *Lingula* band that overlies the Greta Grit in Aspland Beck and in the Ingleton area (Ford, 1954). No other marine faunas are known between the Greta Grit and the Cancellatum Marine Band which defines the base of the Yeadonian Stage. This band is present in the Settle district and also in the Ingleton area where it occurs about 35 m above the top of the Greta Grit (Ford, 1954). Mudstones containing this marine band were the oldest strata encountered in the Waters Farm Borehole (Figure 23), where some 20 m of mudstone and siltstone separate it from the succeeding Cumbriense Marine Band. This later marine band was found near Tewit Hall during the resurvey and is the only known exposure of Yeadonian strata in the district.

The Rough Rock, which lies 10 m above the base of the Cumbriense Marine Band in the Waters Farm Borehole, comprises some 17 m of mostly thick-bedded, coarse-grained, feldspathic sandstone. Seatearths, the highest one being overlain by 0.1 m of coal, are present towards the top of the sandstone, which is immediately overlain by the Subcrenatum Marine Band, the base of which defines the base of the Westphalian.

Details

The Knott Coppy Borehole (Figure 23) provides the only continuous section through the mudstones and siltstones that overlie the Silver Hills Sandstone. The 6 m of mudstone below the non-sequence (see above), contain the Beyrichianum Marine Band, with *Lingula sp.*, *Anthraconeilo sp.*, *Selenimyalina sp.* and indeterminate orthocones in addition to the definitive goniatite. The basal 2.1 m above the non-sequence contain a fauna of R_{1a} age including *Myalina sp.*, indeterminate orthocones, *Vallites henkei*, indeterminate dimorphoceratids, *Sargentina sp.*, indeterminate ostracods and fish debris. The precise age of the fauna is uncertain although it predates the Todmordenense Marine Band. No variation in lithology was detected across the non-sequence, although the faunas clearly demonstrate the hiatus and the absence of Alportian strata.

The Knott Coppy Borehole also provides the only complete section through the Accerhill Sandstone. The siltstone interbeds split the sandstone into three leaves; the 2.7 m-thick lower leaf is separated by 5.5 m of siltstone from the 7.8 m-thick middle leaf which in turn is separated by 3.4 m of strata from the 8.2 m upper leaf. The siltstone separating the middle and upper leaves contains a 0.15 m coal, 1.85 m above the base, and passes gradationally upwards into the overlying sandstone. Abundant productoids are present 0.1 m below the top of the upper sandstone leaf.

There are small exposures [7650 6375 and 7673 6381] of the sandstone west of Accerhill, and the second locality has yielded poorly preserved crinoid and brachiopod fragments. The interbedded siltstones in the succession have been recorded from a borehole [7648 6376] south of Hewith.

North-east of the Lawkland Fault, the Accerhill Sandstone is exposed in numerous old diggings [7877 6586 and 7917 6540] in the south-westward facing dip-slope. A section [7888 6572] of the top of the sandstone extends into overlying siltstone.

All but the highest 5 m of beds between the Accerhill Sandstone and the Knott Coppy Grit were penetrated by the Knott Coppy Borehole, which provides the only continuous section through this part of the sequence in the district (Figure 23). The lowest 21 m comprise silty mudstones, much of which is calcareous; these pass upwards into siltstones that form the upper 30 m of the succession. The mudstones contain an abundant and varied fauna including the Todmordenense/Paucicrenulatum and Dubium marine bands.

There are 13 m of the silty mudstones below the Todmordenense/Paucicrenulatum Marine Band, the lowest 8 m of which contain a sparse fauna including crinoid ossicles, *Eolissochonetes sp.*, *Lingula mytilloides*, *L. straeleni*, *Orbiculoidea sp.*, *Productus carbonarius*, cf. *Anthraconeilo sp.*, cf. *Microptychus sp.* and *Archaeocidaris sp.*. A 6 cm-thick limestone is present 1.5 m above the base of the mudstones, and the basal 15 mm of this limestone is a calcilutite with *Girvanella*-like algal nodules up to 15 mm diameter and the upper part is a crinoidal calcirudite. The upper 5 m of mudstones contain interbeds of limestone (crinoidal, calcarenite wackestones and crinoidal, calcirudite packstones), and the highest 2 m contain a more abundant and varied fauna including crinoid ossicles, chonetoid fragments, *Crurithyris sp.*, *Eolissochonetes sp.*, *Lingula squamiformis*, *L. straeleni*, *Anthraconeilo taffiana*, *Caneyella sp.*, *Phestia sp.*, *Retispira sp.*, *Parametacoceras pulchrum*, *Homoceratoides varicatus*, *Coleolus sp.*, *Cavellina sp.* and *Youngiella sp.* These marine fossils either represent an early part of the Todmordenense Marine Band or belong to a lower marine band in the R_{1a} Subzone.

The Todmordenense/Paucicrenulatum Marine Band is 3.85 m thick, and its base is 13.32 m above the base of the mudstones. In addition to the index goniatites, the marine band contains crinoid ossicles, *Lingula mytilloides*, *L. squamiformis*, *Orbiculoidea sp.*, *Caneyella squamula*, *Dunbarella rhythmica*, 'Modiola' *sp.*, *Posidonia obliquata*, *Sanguinolites sp.*, *Metadimorphoceras sp.*, *Reticuloceras* aff. *adpressum* (early form), *Vallites sp.*, *Cavellina sp.* and cf. *Shleesha sp.* One specimen of *R. paucicrenulatum* possesses jaws within the body chamber and is the first record of goniatite jaws from the R_1 of the British Namurian. Barren mudstone, 0.7 m thick, separates the Todmordenense/Paucicrenulatum and the Dubium marine bands, and apparently there is no non-marine phase separating the two.

The Dubium Marine Band is 5.95 m thick and its base is 17.87 m above the base of the mudstones; the highest 2.25 m of the band occurs in siltstone. The fauna includes crinoid ossicles, *Crurithyris sp.*,

Lingula squamiformis, *Orbiculoidea* cf. *phillipsi*, *Anthraconeilo taffiana*, *Caneyella squamula*, *Dunbarella rhythmica*, *Nuculopsis gibbosa*, 'Modiola' *sp.*, *Lithophaga sp.* (juv.), *Phestia attenuata*, *P. sharmani*, *Posidonia obliquata*, *Sanguinolites v-scriptus*, *Girtyspira sp.*, *Microptychus sp.*, aff. *Mourlina sp.*, *Retispira striata*, *Straparollus* cf. *amaenus*, *Kioniceras sp.*, *Catastroboceras kilbridense*, *Parametacoceras pulchrum*, *dimorphoceratids*, *Homoceratoides sp.*, *Reticuloceras adpressum*, *R. dubium*, *R. sp.* (*paucicrenulatum* group), *Vallites sp.*, *Cavellina sp.*, *Kirbyella sp.*, *Youngiella sp.*, *Coleolus sp.* and *Serpulites stubblefieldi*. Some *R. dubium* specimens occur as solid casts, and this is thought to be the first record of their preservation in this form.

The silty mudstones pass upwards into siltstones which form the uppermost 30 m of the succession. The siltstones are micaceous, sandy and laminated, bioturbated in part and contain a sparse marine fauna. In the 12 m of strata above the Dubium Marine Band, this includes *Rhizodopsis sauroides*, *Teichichnus sp.*, *Dunbarella sp.*, *Nuculopsis sp.* and *Retispira sp.*; in addition subvertical, cylindrical burrows occur at intervals. In the uppermost 14 m, indeterminate chonetoids, *Crurithyris sp.*, *Eolissochonetes sp.*, *Productus carbonaria*, *Coleolus sp.*, *Nuculopsis sp.* and indeterminate pleurotomarian gastropods are present. Fossiliferous mudstones and limestones at this level are exposed at several localities [e.g. 7631 6415; 7648 6415; 7728 6428 and 7822 6435] between Black Bank and Craven Ridge, in Kettles Beck [7489 6598] and Cow Gill [7421 6599].

The Knott Coppy Grit forms a prominent south-facing scarp between Black Bank [7640 6443] and Blaithwaite [7805 6476], and is exposed in Black Bank Syke [7633 6445 to 7630 6466], where it has a sharp base and rests, apparently conformably, on laminated, sandy, micaceous siltstones (Figure 23). The basal 13 m of the grit here comprise thick-bedded, coarse-grained feldspathic sandstone, and individual beds are cross-bedded, with foresets dipping to the NNE. The overlying 5 m of strata are unexposed. Above the gap there is 1.5 m of medium-grained, thinly bedded sandstone with carbonaceous debris, some beds having ripple-laminated tops. A siltstone parting separates these from the succeeding 0.3 m ganister which caps the grit. In a disused quarry [7697 6459] at Knott Coppy, 12.5 m of the grit are exposed.

The strata separating the Knott Coppy Grit and the Eldroth Grit comprise an interbedded succession of sandstone, siltstone and mudstone that are well exposed in Black Bank Syke [7630 6466 to 7634 6512]. The basal part of 1 m of siltstone that overlies the Knott Coppy Grit is calcareous and contains a fauna including *Rugosochonetes* cf. *hindi*, *Euphemites sp.*, *Paleyoldia macgregori*, *Orbiculoidea nitida*, orthotetoids, *Lingula mytilloides*, *Coleolus* cf. *carbonarius*, *Prothyris* cf. *carbonaria*, *Spiriferellina sp.* and *Reticuloceras sp.* This fossiliferous siltstone is overlain by 14 m of sandstone with siltstone interbeds and partings, and the top sandstone beds contain a sparse spiriferoid fauna. The succeeding 4.2 m of mudstones are fossiliferous near the base with *Lingula mytilloides*, *Orbiculoidea sp.*, *Productus sp.* and *Rugosochonetes hindi*; towards the top they contain laminae and nodules of ironstone. Thin-bedded sandstones follow, and are in turn overlain by 1.5 m of fossiliferous mudstone that contains *Lingula mytilloides*, orthotetoids, *Serpuloides carbonarius*, *Euphemites sp.*, *Aviculopecten intestitalis*, *Schizodus axiniformis* and *Streblochondria sp.* The succeeding 1.2 m of sandstone is thick-bedded ganister. It is overlain by 6.0 m of mudstone with the Stubblefieldi Marine Band. The fauna of this band is most abundant in the basal 1 m and includes *Paraconularia sp.*, *Hyalostelia sp.*, *Planolites sp.*, *Crurithyris sp.*, *Lingula mytilloides*, *Orbiculoidea nitida*, *Rugosochonetes sp.*, *Anthraconeilo laevirostrum*, nuculoid, *Myalina* cf. *peralata*, *Paleyoldia macgregori*, *Posidonia obliquata*, *Brachycycloceras sp.*, *Reticuloceras stubblefieldi*, ostracods, crinoid columnals and fish spines; upwards it becomes impoverished and is dominated by *Lingula sp.*. The mudstones pass gradationally upwards into laminated siltstones, and up to 5 m are exposed in the stream section. The Eldroth Grit rests discordantly on an erosion surface cut into the siltstone.

The sandstones and siltstones from the base of the Eldroth Grit to the top of Rough Rock are poorly exposed in the drift-covered ground between Eldroth and Newby Moor, immediately south-west of the Lawkland Fault. The succession is calculated from the available outcrop data to be about 190 m thick; only a small part of it is exposed or has been proved in boreholes.

The base of the Eldroth Grit is exposed in Black Bank Syke [7634 6513], where it rests discordantly on a low-relief erosion surface cut in the underlying siltstones. Some 15 m of lithologically uniform feldspathic sandstone are exposed downstream. Along strike to the east of the stream-section, the grit forms an escarpment on the south side of Lawkland Hall Wood [7721 6545 to 7790 6532]; 7 m of cross-bedded sandstone with SSW-dipping foresets are exposed in a disused quarry [7735 6540], and 14 m of the grit are present in a crag [7784 6544] towards the eastern end of the escarpment. West of the Holm Fault, the Eldroth Grit is poorly exposed in a north-west-trending escarpment on Newby Moor [705 700 to 731 682].

The Greta Grit is exposed in Nutgill Beck [6931 7049 to 6923 7074] and Aspland Beck [6970 7080 to 6923 7074], north of Nutgill Farm. In the former stream section the base of the grit overlies laminated sandy siltstones. Thin- and medium-bedded, fine- and medium-grained sandstones, with some seatearths, lie near the base of the grit which mainly consists of thick-bedded, cross-bedded, coarse-grained, feldspathic sandstone with quartz pebbles. Much of the grit is reddened and friable. In Aspland Beck, the coarse grit is capped by a ganister which, in turn, is succeeded by 2.5 m of silty mudstone that is coaly at the base and contains a few *Lingula*. Well bedded, medium-grained sandstone, 1.4 m thick, with coaly plant fragments overlies the silty mudstone, and this is followed by a further 3 m of micaceous silty mudstone with plant debris and a sparse *Lingula*-bivalve fauna. The marine mudstones are overlain by fine- to medium-grained sandstone, that is thickly bedded at the base and thinly bedded upwards; they are the youngest strata exposed in the stream section. No goniatites were found, and it is uncertain whether the marine incursions represent the Bilinguis Marine Band or an earlier one.

A section [7575 6480] north-west of Black Bank, on the downthrow side of a SSW-trending fault, exposes thick-bedded, medium-grained, quartzose sandstone with a ganister cap. By comparison with the section exposed in the River Greta (Ford, 1954) the sandstone has been identified as the Greta Grit. The dark grey mudstones overlying this sandstone contain an abundant and varied fauna including the Bilinguis Marine Band, indicative of the R_{2b} Zone of the Marsdenian Stage. Fossils identified from the marine band include *Productus sp.*, *Anthraconeilo sp.*, *Caneyella rugata*, *Dunbarella speciosa*, *Bilinguites bilinguis* and indeterminate ostracods.

The Waters Farm Borehole [7537 6763] provides a continuous section through the Yeadonian strata. The Cancellatum Marine Band is at least 2.35 m thick, but its base was not penetrated in the borehole. In addition to the definitive goniatite, the fauna includes *Lingula mytilloides*, *Dunbarella sp.*, *Edmondia sp.* (juv.), *Posidonia sp.*, turreted gastropod spat, indeterminate orthocones, *Agastrioceras carinatum*, anthraceratids, *Gastrioceras branneroides*, *G. crencellatum*, *G. sp.* aff. *branneroides* and indeterminate ostracods. In the overlying 7.85 m of mudstone, non-marine faunas are present 1.95 m above the base and in the top 0.1 m; *Carbonicola lenicurvata* and *Carbonita sp.* occur in the lower bed, and *Anthraconaia bellula*, *Carbonicola aff. lenicurvata*, *C. pseudacuta* and *Geisina arcuata* in the upper. The succeeding 3.15 m of siltstone with sandstone laminae pass up into 0.8 m of thin-bedded sandstone. This is overlain by 4.3 m of pale grey mudstone with a non-marine fauna including *Anthraconaia sp.* (juv.), *Carbonicola lenicurvata*, *C. aff. pseudacuta* and *Naiadites aff. hibernicus* 0.95 m to 1.35 m above base. Dark grey mudstones, 1 m thick, with disarticulated *Lingula mytilloides* follow, and are overlain by 1.45 m of silty sandstone with, near the base, a non-marine fauna of *Naiadites hibernicus*, *Geisina arcuata*, *Spirorbis sp.* and *Rhizodopsis sp.*. Dark grey mudstones, 5.8 m thick, containing the Cumbriense

Marine Band overlie the sandstone. The fauna of this band includes *Crurithyris sp.*, *Lingula mytilloides*, *Anthraconeilo sp.*, *Dunbarella sp.*, *Posidonia sp.*, *Donaldina sp.*, *Coleolus sp.* (juv.), anthracoceratoids, *Gastrioceras crenulatum*, *G. sp.* aff. *crenulatum*, *G. cumbriense*, *Homoceratoides sp.*, conodont debris and fish debris including *Rhadinichthys sp.* Some 4.4 m of laminated siltstone separate the mudstones from the overlying Rough Rock, a coarse-grained, feldspathic sandstone 17.10 m thick. The sandstone includes 1.05 m of siltstone and a 0.3 m bed of off-white clay-seatearth 9.95 m and 16.50 m respectively above the base. The sandstone is capped by 0.3 m of ganister on which rests 0.1 m of earthy coal.

During the resurvey the Cumbriense Marine Band was identified in Goat Gap Syke [7163 6997] near Tewit Hall; the fauna includes *Lingula mytilloides*, *Caneyella multirugata*, *Dunbarella cf. elegans*, *Posidonia sp.*, *Anthracoceratites sp.*, *Gastrioceras crenulatum*, *G. cumbriense*, *Homoceratoides sp.*, conodont debris and scales of *Rhadinichthys sp.*.

COAL MEASURES (Westphalian)

Strata of Westphalian A (Langsettian of Owens and others, 1985) age are confined to the Ingleton Coalfield (Ford, 1954), which extends into the extreme north-western part of the district, and to a faulted outlier south of Austwick that was discovered during the resurvey. Up to 150 m of Coal Measures are preserved conformably overlying the Namurian, and the basal 50 m of the succession were proved in the Waters Farm Borehole.

The thickness of the Westphalian marine bands in the Waters Farm Borehole (Figure 23), and the goniatite-pectinoid faunas they contain, are indicative of a basinal environment (N. J. Riley, personal communication). The Subcrenatum Marine Band contains species that show it was deposited on the periphery of the basin; however, these do not belong to the marginal benthonic facies which is preserved in strata to the east of the district, at Knaresborough (Burgess and Cooper, 1980) and at Winksley (Institute of Geological Sciences, 1976).

The succession in the Ingleton Coalfield (Ford, 1954) can be correlated with successions on the southern flanks of the Craven Basin. Comparison of strata within the *Anthraconia lenisulcata* and *Carbonicola communis* non-marine bivalve zones of the Bradford (Stephens and others, 1953) and Clitheroe (Earp and others, 1961) districts suggests a gradual southward deepening of the depositional basin. Although there is little outcrop data, there is no evidence to indicate that the strata preserved in the Ingleton Coalfield were deposited in a basin isolated from that in which the more southerly Coal Measures accumulated.

DETAILS

In the Waters Farm Borehole [7537 6763] the Subcrenatum Marine Band, which defines the base of the Westphalian, comprises 2 m of dark grey mudstone with the following fauna: *Lingula mytilloides*, *Anthraconeilo laevirostrum*, *Posidonia sp.*, *Schizodus sp.*, *Retispira sp.* and *Gastrioceras subcrenatum*. Laminated, micaceous siltstones (9.76 m) overlie the marine band, and in turn are succeeded by 14.79 m of bioturbated sandstone. A 0.37 m coal (cannel and dirt) occurs above the sandstone and is overlain by 2.37 m of mudstone-seatearth with 0.58 m of bright coal. The coal is succeeded by mudstones (3.53 m) of the Listeri Marine Band, the fauna of which includes *Lingula mytilloides*, *Caneyella multirugata*, *Dunbarella papyracea*, *Myalina sp.*, *Posidonia gibsoni*, *Gastrioceras circumnodosum* and *G. listeri*.

The overlying 5.69 m of silty mudstones contain nodules and thin beds of ironstone but are unfossiliferous. These are overlain by siltstone (2.30 m) which passes gradationally upwards into sandstone (7.75 m) that contains siltstone laminae and interbeds.   EWJ

CHAPTER 5

Quaternary

It is likely that ice-sheets occupied the district on several occasions during the Quaternary, but the last glaciation during late Devensian times (c.26 000–10 000 years BP) was so intense that it destroyed practically all evidence of earlier Pleistocene events and their deposits. Only within Victoria Cave, Settle, are older deposits known; these contain mammalian faunas dated at, or slightly older than, 114 000 to 135 000 years BP, the Ipswichian interglacial episode. Other pre-Devensian deposits may remain undetected, but are likely to be very limited in extent.

Ice entered the area from the north during the late Devensian and profoundly modified the terrain. Its deposits are dominated by an extensive sheet of boulder clay or till which extends up to about 490 m above OD, above which there are broad swathes of head which may be partly contemporaneous with the till. On the higher ground the boulder clay is patchy, and could be interpreted as a dissected older till, were it not that its upward limit is commensurate with the limits established for the late Devensian ice-sheet farther north and south along the western slopes of the Pennines (Evans and others, 1968; Arthurton and Wadge, 1981). The lower ground is extensively blanketed by till that forms a drumlin-field. The orientation of the drumlins establishes the direction of movement of the ice (Figure 24). Much of the ice emanated from an ice-dome situated in the Mallerstang area at the head of Wensleydale (Raistrick, 1930) and entered the district southwards down Ribblesdale and moved south-eastwards along the higher reaches of Airedale (Tiddeman, 1872). Some ice entered from the north-west, down Chapel le Dale, Kingsdale and Lunedale. The two ice-streams were probably accompanied by subglacial melt-waters for, in the Ribble valley in particular, the till is associated with gravel, sand, and laminated silt and clay.

The erosional effects of the ice are less apparent, though the solid rocks in the cores and on the flanks of some of the drumlins appear to have been shaped by moving ice, and scouring of the limestone outcrops north of Malham facilitated the formation of some of the finest of the surface karst landforms within the British Isles (Plate 7).

Towards the close of the Devensian the climate ameliorated and the ice-sheet began to decay; fluvial activity became increasingly dominant. Meltwaters confined in subglacial streams eroded channels in the underlying superficial deposits or solid rock. A well developed system of channels is present in Malham Formation limestones around Malham Tarn; particularly impressive are those on the escarpment at Malham Lings, notably at Gordale Scar (Plate 23) and Malham Cove. In the western part of the district, channels of another system are incised into Silesian strata between Rathmell and Bowland Knotts; some of these cross the present-day watershed. Sand and gravel deposits are associated with the channel systems, many with well defined landforms including eskers and kames, as well as broader sheets.

It is hard to separate the processes of deposition and erosion in the late Devensian from those of the Flandrian; the dividing-line is taken conventionally at 10 000 years BP, but few of the deposits contain datable material. Accumulation of silts and peats seems to have been continuous in Malham Tarn since late Devensian times (Pigott and Pigott, 1959), and this may well be true of other upland tarns and of some of the lowland lakes (Raistrick, 1930, 1933) that formed in depressions left when the ice melted. The landslips, river terrace deposits and alluvium probably similarly range from the latest Devensian to the Flandrian, while the extensive tracts of upland peat are certainly of Flandrian age.   EWJ,RSA

BOULDER CLAY (TILL)

The deposits of boulder clay are composed of ill sorted rock fragments, from pebbles to boulders, set in a matrix ranging from sandy clay to clayey sand. Much of the debris is of local derivation, largely Carboniferous limestones and sandstones with some Lower Palaeozoic clasts from the Craven Inliers. The locally derived fragments are most obvious towards the base of the boulder clay. Thus the basal till in stream-gullies west of Malham contains blocks of calcareous mudstone derived from the Upper Bowland Shales bedrock, while coarse-grained pebbly sandstone debris extend south-eastwards from a crag of Grassington Grit at Rough Haw. Erratics from beyond the Pennines are rare and indicate the dominance of local ice.

An extensive sheet of boulder clay covers much of the lower ground. It masks all but the most prominent solid features, and is locally more than 20 m thick. Over much of the uplands, however, the boulder clay forms only a patchy veneer. Indeed it is absent above about 490 m above OD over the highest ground in the district on Fountains Fell and Knowe Fell. The extensive drapes of head deposits above this height suggest that the upward limit of the boulder clay closely approximates to the margin of the ice-sheet against the Pennine flanks.

A major drumlin-field fills much of the Craven Lowlands, the 'whale-back' mounds being typically 20 to 30 m high, 400 to 700 m long and 200 to 300 m wide. Most of the drumlins are formed of boulder clay, though some contain lenses of gravel and others are moulded on solid features that have been shaped by the ice. Their orientation, shown in Figure 24 (see also Raistrick, 1930), suggests that ice funnelled into the district from the north and north-west, and then bifurcated with one mass of ice moving southwards and one south-eastwards.

In the Ribble valley between Settle and Hellifield the boulder clay contains many intercalations of sand, gravel, silt and clay, the latter laminated in places. The resultant

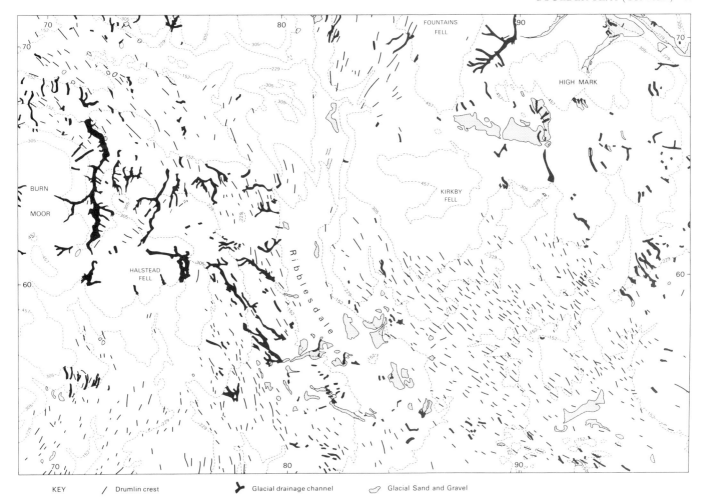

KEY   / Drumlin crest   Glacial drainage channel   Glacial Sand and Gravel

Figure 24   Glacial features of the Settle district

deposit, here referred to as the Ribble Drift Complex, attains at least 54 m in thickness, and occupies a tract of country with subdued relief about 3.5 km wide within which drumlins are largely absent (Figure 25). Presumably this tract indicates an area of subglacial drainage and ponding in which glaciofluvial deposition was significant. Sands, gravels and silts underlie boulder clay along the valley of Winterburn Beck and have been proved in association with boulder clay in the Aire valley south-east of Gargrave.

Details

West of the River Ribble

A sheet of boulder clay, commonly more than 10 m thick, occupies much of the River Wenning catchment area in the north-west. It thins out against the limestone escarpment north of Clapham and Austwick, and is thin or absent over Burn Moor and the watershed at Bowland Knotts. Many of the present-day streams, such as Keasden Beck, flow in gullies cut through the sheet into solid rock. Drumlins are a feature of the Wenning valley, their crests trending NW–SE. Lower Palaeozoic erratics are conspicuous in sections in Keasden Beck and its tributaries, on Clapham Moor, and on Giggleswick and Gisburn commons. Boreholes [753 681 and 781 672] south of Austwick proved gravel, apparently as lenses, within the boulder clay.

On the west side of Crummack Dale, north of Austwick, are the famous Norber erratics (Kendall and Wroot, 1924) (Plate 22). These blocks of Austwick Formation sandstones and siltstones have been plucked from outcrops [770 704] north-west of Sowerthwaite Farm, glacially transported, and strewn over the limestone pavements on Norber [767 700].

Drumlins typify the south-western part of the district, where up to 32.9 m of boulder clay have been proved in boreholes [e.g. 7804 5582]. The drumlins trend generally N–S, although in the extreme south-west they swing NE–SW; their relief becomes subdued towards the southern boundary of the district between Knotts and Paythorne. Lower Palaeozoic clasts are conspicuous in sections in Tosside Beck [7810 5399], and are recorded near Rathmell, on Stephen Moor, and in a roadside cut [7372 5712] in Gisburn Forest. Sections [7296 5542 and 7338 5577] in boulder clay on the shore of Stocks Reservoir show an abundance of limestone and mudstone debris apparently of local derivation. Lenses of sand and silts are recorded at the base of a section [7268 5780] in boulder clay in Hasgill Beck, and in a stream [7980 5462 to 7986 5454] near Coar's Farm up to 1 m of weathered boulder clay rests on up to 1.5 m of laminated silt, the latter resting in turn on boulder clay.

East of the River Ribble

The solid geology north of Stainforth and in much of Silverdale is masked by drumlins which are orientated NNE–SSW. Boulder clay covers much of the ground to the south of Malham and extends

Plate 22 Glacial erratic, Norber [767 700]. Block of Austwick Formation, plucked by ice from outcrop in Crummack Dale 1 km to the north, rests on Malham Formation limestone. (A 7599)

beyond the southern boundary of the district. In this ground, the drumlins have a consistent NW–SE trend and the thickest proved boulder clay is 23.8 m in a borehole [9234 5865] at Cowper Cote. Natural sections of up to 12 m are seen in meander scars of the principal streams, for example in Otterburn Beck [8909 5723], in the River Aire [9082 5752], and in Eshton Beck [9268 5821 and 9448 5514]. Lower Palaeozoic erratics are common between Settle and Long Preston, but have not been noted farther east, with the exception of a large block of Lower Palaeozoic siltstone in a gully [9657 6142] on Linton Moor. The occurrence of Lower Palaeozoic erratics in Wharfedale was recorded by Dakyns (1872) and Garwood and Goodyear (1924), and taken by these workers as evidence of a concealed Lower Palaeozoic inlier in Upper Wharfedale or Lower Littondale (Raistrick, 1931). Lower Palaeozoic rocks were proved, however, at 90.12 m below surface in the Chapel House (Outgang Laithe) Borehole 1.5 km south of Kilnsey (Murray, 1983).

Sections [9375 6182] on Hetton Common and Flasby Fell [9721 5502] show locally derived drift, free from limestone clasts, overlying boulder clay in which limestone blocks and boulders are conspicuous. From their field relations, the limestone-free deposits are believed to have been glacially derived rather than formed by solifluction. On Flasby Fell, they extend southeastwards as a 'tail' from Rough Haw, with the ground surface strewn with blocks of Grassington Grit. A detached raft of Grassington Grit [9640 5565] some 90 m long is incorporated in this deposit.

Stratified deposits lie within the boulder clay north of Hetton, and a section [9601 5994] in a gully near Fleets House shows 3 m of sand, gravel, silt and clay overlain and underlain by boulder clay. Calcreted coarse gravel underlies boulder clay in the western banks of the valley of Winterburn Beck [9378 5950]. In a tributary [9341 5954], 1.5 m of boulder clay overlies 3.5 m of faulted and contorted sand, gravel and silt.

In the Ribble valley between Wigglesworth and Hellifield, the boulder clay is intercalated with stratified sediments forming a deposit at least 54 m thick and referred to here as the Ribble Drift Complex. The stratigraphy of this laterally variable deposit was established by boreholes on a proposed dam-site at Arnford (Figure 25). The stratified sediments comprise sand and gravel, and laminated silt and clay with stony layers.

Natural sections in the complex are few, the best [8457 5555] being in the banks of the Ribble, where stoneless clay is exposed, and in a man-made cut [8523 5632 and 8533 5638] near Hellifield. A section in a 6 m-high meander scar [8350 5781] at Long Preston, near the northern limit of the complex, shows irregular layers of boulder clay, sand and silt with cemented gravel at the base. An adjacent borehole [8335 5795] proved boulder clay with intercalations of sand and silt to 10.19 m. It is overlain locally by glacial sand and gravel, and incised by late-glacial and post-glacial drainage channels, notably the River Ribble itself.

A laterally variable succession of glacial sediments was proved by boreholes in the Aire valley near Inghey Bridge, south-east of Gargrave (Figure 25). Some of the sand and gravel and laminated silt and clay proved may be lacustrine and of late or post-glacial age, for according to Raistrick (1929) ice melt-waters formed 'a lake in the valley around Skipton, impounded by the terminal moraine of the Aire glacier at Cononley'.

GLACIAL SAND AND GRAVEL

In addition to the sand and gravel associated with boulder clay, there are other deposits of sand and gravel (here termed Glacial Sand and Gravel, though they may include glaciofluvial and fluvioglacial components), that post-date the accumulation of boulder clay but pre-date the establishment of the present-day drainage regime.

The distribution of the Glacial Sand and Gravel at surface is shown on Figure 24. The principal deposits lie in Ribblesdale, in the Aire valley at Gargrave, and in the valley of the River Skirfare (Littondale). An extensive sheet also occurs near Malham Tarn. Some of these deposits have distinctive esker and kame landforms. Sinuous eskers, up to a kilometre long, are a feature of the ground between Wigglesworth and Halton West, where they consist largely of sand with a veneer of clayey sand and gravel or stony clay. The kames form irregular, mounds of gravel such as those around Malham Tarn (Clark, 1967; Clayton, 1981). In places they pass into terrace deposits of gravel and sand, locally pocked with kettleholes, such as those overlying the glacial deposits of the Ribble Drift Complex south-west of Hellifield. The sand and gravel deposits that flank the alluvium and river terrace deposits of the River Aire at Gargrave and the River Skirfare have also been placed in this catagory.

Details

In the north-west of the district, there are mounds of sand and gravel [728 700] north-east of Newby, three kame-like mounds [706 688, 710 685 and 710 684] on Newby Moor, and a well defined esker [712 612] extending for 0.3 km in the headwaters of Keasden Beck. In the south-west, kames are present on the north-eastern side of Croasdale Brook where one section [6999 5534] shows 1 m of silty gravel resting on 5 m sand. Farther south there are mounds, up to 5 m high, composed mainly of sand in the valley of Eller Beck, near Pages, where a temporary section [6998 5279] showed 1.5 m of medium gravel resting unconformably on 1.4 m of laminated, medium- and fine-grained sand.

The principal deposits of Glacial Sand and Gravel in Ribblesdale lie to the south of Long Preston. They include a suite of mounds, including eskers, extending from Town Moor, Wigglesworth, to Halton West. Sand is exposed on the eskers at the eastern end of the tract [8358 5432 and 8380 5442], and is recorded in a temporary

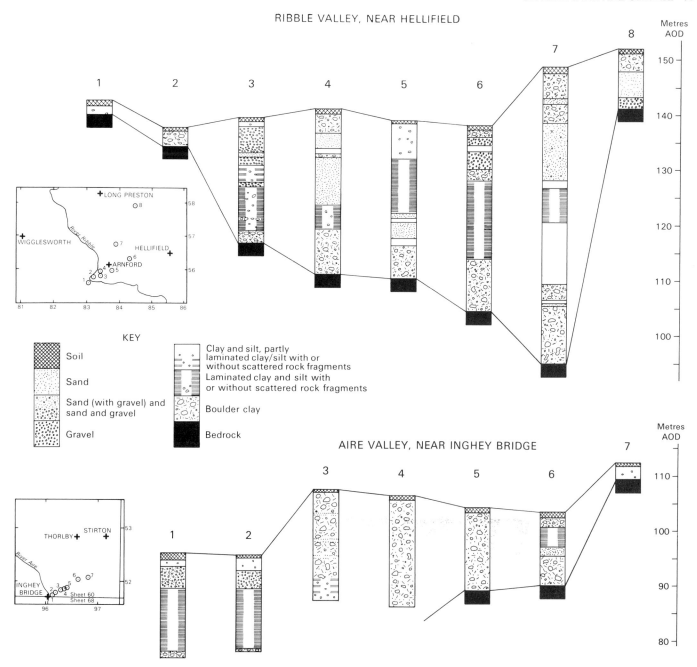

Figure 25 Boreholes in the glacial deposits of the Ribble and Aire valleys

section at Pikeber [8030 5617]. Generally these features are covered with a veneer of stony clay.

Younger deposits, mainly of gravel, form terraced, fan-shaped spreads where the valleys of Wigglesworth Beck and Long Preston Beck reach the floodplain of the Ribble valley. A stream-bank section [8403 5801] east of Long Preston shows 7.5 m of coarse gravel, and the log of a borehole [8094 5695] near Wigglesworth records sand and gravel to a depth of 19.8 m. Two deposits of Glacial Sand and Gravel overlie the Ribble Drift Complex south-west of Hellifield. The older of these has been worked [8465 5639] near Gallaber, and its surface is pitted by kettleholes at Pan Beck Plantation [8471 5565]; the younger forms a terraced surface [849 555] at a lower level. Both are clearly at least partly fluvioglacial in origin.

A deposit of gravel, with abundant limestone and subordinate sand, extends eastwards and westwards from Malham Tarn. Its irregular upper surface commonly contains kettleholes, and there is an esker-like ridge [897 657 to 900 658] east of Low Trenhouse. Farther north-east, gravel is widespread in the valley of the River Skirfare west of Hawkswick, and sections [9503 7070] show a predominance of limestone clasts in a matrix of sand or silty sand. This deposit forms mounds near Arncliffe Cote, and includes an esker [9445 7050] lying subparallel to the trend of the valley. There is another ridge [9391 7082] aligned along the foot of limestone cliffs near Blue Scar; there are limestone blocks within the deposit and it may be a lateral moraine. Gravel, with limestone clasts ranging from angular coarse-grained sand-sized fragments to rounded pebbles and boulders set in a sandy matrix, forms extensive spreads on the north-western flanks of Cowside Beck [9181 7070] and Cote Gill [9385 6965]. North-west of Yew Cogar Scar, the glacial gravel is deeply gullied; the deposits may be a ground moraine.

Fluvioglacial gravel (included within the Glacial Sand and Gravel) forms flattish ground flanking the alluvium of the Aire valley around Gargrave, the best exposures [9325 5398 and 9302 5385] being in Gargrave village south of the river. Boreholes [e.g. 9368 5430] sited on the alluvium east of the village penetrated up to 21.3 m of sand and gravel before entering boulder clay, and all but the uppermost few metres of this deposit are likely to be of glacial origin.

GLACIAL DRAINAGE CHANNELS

Meltwaters from the decaying ice-sheet collected in subglacial streams that incised well defined channels in the underlying boulder clay and bedrock. The channels may extend over several kilometres, are typically 50 to 100 m wide, and range from 0 to 30 m deep. Their distribution is shown in Figure 24. The most impressive ones are cut into solid rock, and these are particularly common in the high

Plate 23   Glacial drainage channel in Malham Formation, Gordale Scar [914 640]. (L 2704)

limestone country around Malham Tarn especially between the North and Middle Craven faults. The best examples are the Watlowes dry valley, along which the Pennine Way is routed, that terminates in the amphitheatre of Malham Cove, and the channel now occupied by Gordale Beck [914 640] (Frontispiece and Plate 23). They are also well developed west of the River Ribble on the eastern flanks of the Bowland Fells, as for example one [775 600] north of Cockley Bank, west of Rathmell, which is cut in the Pendle Grit Formation. Some channels now form major valleys, notably those in Keasden Beck and Cowside Beck (north of Malham); others are cut into interfluves, and run either directly downslope or are oblique to the contours as on the western flank of Ribblesdale near Rathmell. Indeed, some straddle present-day watersheds, such as the channel [865 665] between Knowle Fell and Black Hill. The channels generally trend subparallel to the direction of ice-movement as indicated by the orientation of the drumlins (Figure 24), and examples of such an alignment are seen in the channels west of Stocks Reservoir, west of Rathmell, north of Stainforth and east of Winterburn Reservoir.

Channel-floor profiles generally show a consistent direction of fall. However, some profiles are humped, implying that the meltwater flowed uphill under hydrostatic pressure. There are examples [7770 5939, 9511 6081 and 8867 6800] near Cockley Bank west of Rathmell, north-west of Hetton, and north-west of Malham Tarn. The floors of many of the channels are covered by peat. In others, for example the channel [9607 6100] near Fleets House north of Hetton, streams have modified the original channel form, either by erosion or by the deposition of alluvium or glacial gravel. The intimate association of the glacial channels with some of the sand and gravel suggests that the two are partly coeval, indicating erosional and depositional regimes of the same meltwater streams. This association is clearly displayed between the channels west of Rathmell and the eskers between Wigglesworth and Halton West.

HEAD

Deposits of head, consisting of poorly consolidated silty and sandy clay with mainly angular fragments of sandstone, siltstone and mudstone, are widespread in the upland Namurian outcrops. They are mostly thin (less that 1 m), however, and have been mapped only in a few places. They are considered to have formed by solifluction under periglacial conditions.

Head drapes the solid rocks above the local upper limit of boulder clay (about 490 m above OD) over much of the highest ground of the district on Fountains Fell and Knowe Fell. The deposit, which is largely covered by peat, consists of angular blocks of sandstone and fragments of siltstone in a matrix of sandy clay. An impersistent apron of head including blocks of Brennand Grit is present around Whelp Stone Crag [76 59]. Similar aprons, with embedded angular blocks of sandstone, flank scarps [750 537] of Pendleside Sandstone west of Knotts. In the west of the district, there is a veneer of head, beneath a cover of peat on Burn Moor and Bowland Knotts.

SCREE

Aprons of scree are present below some of the larger limestone scars and cliffs, especially those in the upper part of the Cove Limestone. They occur below Robin Proctor's Scar [763 697], in the valley of Clapham Beck, north of Austwick, below Giggleswick Scar [803 653], and in the Ribble valley [825 667] south of Stainforth. East of Ribblesdale there are deposits below scars [898 640] at Malham Cove, and others [895 673] north-east of Malham Tarn, as well as in Cowside Beck [e.g. 915 702 and 972 679] near Kilnsey Crag. Sandstone scree is uncommon, but some occurs [767 616] on Giggleswick Common under the scarp of the Brennand Grit.

CAVE DEPOSITS

Cave deposits have yielded mammalian bones and artifacts at several sites along the outcrop of the Malham Formation (Kendall and Wroot, 1924; Raistrick, 1933; King, 1974). The most important locality is Victoria Cave [8383 6504], in the Gordale Limestone north-east of Settle. Tiddeman (1873–1878) recorded two distinct cave-earths within it, separated by laminated clay. The Lower Cave Earth was truncated by boulder clay at the mouth of the cave, and thus pre-dates the late Devensian. Mammalian bones recovered from it include straight-tusked elephant, rhinoceros, hippopotamus and hyaena—an assemblage regarded by Sutcliffe (1960) as a typical late Pleistocene 'hippopotamus fauna', as assigned by him to the warmest part of the Ipswichian interglacial. Tiddeman regarded the overlying laminated clay as having a glacial origin, and recorded bones of arctic fox and grizzly bear at the base. The Upper Cave Earth included Neolithic and Romano-British cultural remains. Excavations by Lord in 1937 revealed unweathered mammalian remains within the Lower Cave Earth, and these were covered by a layer of calcite flowstone (Gascoyne and others, 1981). Samples of this flowstone, analysed by the ^{230}Th/^{234}U dating method, gave ages of between 135 000 ± 8000 and 114 000 ± 5000 years BP; the 'hippopotamus fauna' is about this age, or slightly older.

Neolithic pottery has been recovered from a number of caves, notably Attermire Cave [8417 6416] and Jubilee Cave [837 655], while Neolithic remains, including that of a child in a stalagmite grave, are recorded from Douky Bottom Cave (Dowkerbottom Hole) [951 689] on Hawkswick Clowder; Romano-British remains are also recorded from this latter locality (King, 1974).

Workings [9722 6486 and 9742 6437] at Skythorns Quarry near Wood Nook have revealed small caves and fissures in the Cove Limestone filled with partly bedded brown sand and clayey silt. Similar deposits are known in the reef limestone of the Malham Formation exposed in Swinden Quarry north-east of Rylstone.

PEAT AND LACUSTRINE DEPOSITS

A blanket of peat up to about 3 m thick is widespread over the gentler slopes and plateaux of Fountains Fell and the uplands of the western part of the district. The blanket peat generally rests on head or boulder clay. In many places it is being eroded either along gullies or more extensively, as on parts of Bloe Greet where locally only isolated 'haggs' remain. Some gully sections show that the peat contains a layer of birch roots and twigs at its base, and examples occur [6854 5959] on Bloe Greet, [7003 6266] on Burn Moor and at Reca Bank Moss [733 623] on Austwick Common. A similar 'forest' layer in blanket peat on the northern Pennines has been dated by pollen analysis as early Boreal (about 9000 years BP) (Johnson and Dunham, 1963). In a few places the blanket peat has been dug for fuel, as on Crutchenber Fell [724 602].

Peat is also present in poorly drained hollows on high and low ground alike, where it is commonly associated with lacustrine deposits. Deposits are common in hollows within drumlin-fields, in kettleholes in Glacial Sand and Gravel, and on the floors of glacial drainage channels, for example those between Cockley Bank and Long Gill [78 59]. It also occurs in 'mosses' with lacustrine associations both on low ground, as at Austwick Moss [76 66], Studfold Moss [80 69] near Swarth Moor and White Moss [792 547], and in the upland area north-east of Settle, at Attermire [841 648] and Tarn Moss at Malham Tarn, where up to 2 m of peat are exposed on the shore of the tarn [8895 6673]. Pigott and Pigott (1959) have proved up to 10 m of interbedded peat, marl and clay at Tarn Moss, and at least 6 m lie under the bed of the tarn itself; these deposits have accumulated continuously since late glacial times.

Deposits of presumed lacustrine origin, including silt and clay (some of which is laminated), peat and shell marls, are present in the Ribble valley between Settle and Long Preston. There is an extensive terrace of peat a metre or two above the floodplain [814 584] near Rake Head Laithe, and more limited tracts [824 587] border it west of Long Preston. The recovery of a skull of 'Bos primigenius' under some 3 m of silt and peat hereabouts was recorded by Raistrick (1933). Farther north, near Gildersleets, up to 7 m of laminated silt and clay have been proved under alluvial sand and gravel in boreholes [809 622] sited on the floodplain. An excavation some 2 m deep 'in the (Settle) lake edge near Settle', proved about 1 m of peat, with a stone celt at the base, overlying sand with bones of deer (Raistrick, 1933). A dug-out canoe was recovered in 1863 from the lacustrine silts of the now drained Giggleswick Tarn [806 646]. The 'Settle Lake' was drained by a post-glacial channel cut into the Ribble Drift Complex at Arnford and into the Worston Shales at Deep Dale [831 557] (Raistrick, 1930).

A deposit of shell marl is recorded under peaty soil in the banks of an ephemeral pond [8507 5699] north-west of Hellifield. South-east of Hellifield, near Tenley Plantation, 0.3 m of contorted laminated clay of presumed lacustrine origin is exposed [8650 5560]. Near Kendal Hill a tributary [8950 5744] of Otterburn Beck exposes a marginal lacustrine sequence: 0.6 m of peat overlies 0.3 m of stony clayey sand on sandy clay; these beds rest on 0.15 m of organic silty clay which overlies 0.4 m of shell marl. Nearby [8953 5735], the base of this peat layer contains boulders, wood and the bones of Bos taurus (identified by Dr P. L. Armitage) which are not older than 6000 years BP. Raistrick (1933) described further sections in supposed lacustrine deposits, seen during the construction of a railway bridge across part of his 'Skipton Lake'; these revealed 'a very great thickness of laminated clay' overlain by sands and gravels containing bones.

RIVER TERRACE DEPOSITS, ALLUVIAL FANS AND ALLUVIUM

Post-glacial deposits of sand, gravel and silt are associated with the more mature streams and rivers within the district. Where these deposits form the present-day flood plain they have been classified as alluvium; where they form terraced surfaces above the level of the flood plain they have been classified as river terrace deposits. In some instances the distinction between the two categories, is poor, as is the distinction between some river terrace deposits and certain fluvioglacial terraces.

River terrace deposits, consisting largely of medium to coarse gravel, occur up to about 4 m above normal stream level in the valleys of Croasdale Brook and the River Hodder. Similar terraced deposits are present in Otterburn Beck. In Ribblesdale, a gravel terrace, 2.5 m above the floodplain at Gildersleets near Settle, appears to grade into the alluvium downstream near Rathmell. Terraced gravels are also present in many places along the banks of Bond Beck and Tosside Beck, south of Tosside, where the terraces lie up to 3 m above normal stream level. It is possible that these streams are incised along earlier glacial drainage channels, and that the terraced gravels are fluvioglacial or glacial.

Alluvial fan deposits are usually present where tributary streams enter the principal valleys, notably in Ribblesdale between Settle and Long Preston, in the Aire valley, north of Airton, and in the valley of Bordley Beck.

Alluvium is extensive in the Ribble valley between Settle and Long Preston, in parts of Otterburn Beck, in Eshton Beck and along the River Aire. In the catchments of the Wenning south of Clapham and the Aire around Bank Newton, the alluvium forms extensive spreads within drumlin fields. Peat is associated locally with the alluvium, as at Eshton Tarn [918 576] and Austwick Moss [761 666].

CALCAREOUS TUFA

Deposits of calcareous tufa are present around springs and in streams at several localities, notably at the waterfall [9152 6402] below Gordale Scar where they form a screen below the cascade (Kendall and Wroot, 1924; Pentecost, 1981). There is another deposit in Gordale Beck at Janet's Foss [9118 6332]. Tufa is also present around a spring that issues from the Kilnsey Limestone on the west bank of the Ribble [8163 6673] near Stainforth, and at Mealey Bank [8258 6320], south-east of Settle where it contains abundant gastropods. It is also occurs at a seepage [7726 5368] from Worston Shales on the south-eastern bank of Barn Gill, Slaidburn, and another [7349 6994] from boulder clay north-west of Clapham. Small deposits of marly tufa with gastropods are present around springs [9092 5531] in the Aire valley east of Coniston Cold, and others [9603 5838] adjoining Hetton Beck, south of Hetton.

LANDSLIPS

Localised slope-failures under gravity were probably initiated in late glacial and post-glacial times; some are still active. Both rotational and superficial slips occur. The former are commonest in the alternating lithologies of the Silesian, but also occur in boulder clay. The superficial slips are largely restricted to boulder clay; they displace smaller volumes of material than do the rotational slips, and several take place along the rock-head surface.

In Croasdale [692 566] a rotational slip in the Pendle Grit Formation extends downslope for some 750 m. Farther north, on Lamb Hill Fell, there are several smaller slips in the Roeburndale Formation [688 595, 689 594 and 691 595]. On the eastern slopes of Kirkby Fell [880 635], where the failures involve the Grassington Grit, the Pendle Grit, the Upper Bowland Shales, and a veneer of boulder clay, there seem to have been two distinct phases of movement. Rotational slips are also present in the Pendle Grit Formation and the Upper Bowland Shales farther east on the western flank of Bordley Beck [943 633], and on the north-west of Flasby Fell at High Wood [957 558] where the twin back-scar is known as Dead Eyes. A large rotational landslip within boulder clay has taken place in drumlin terrain on the east side of Ribblesdale [820 695] near Helwith Bridge.

Superficial slips in boulder clay occur along many streams, notably Keasden Beck [e.g. 72 63], Croasdale [6922 5603 to 6967 5568], Hasgill Beck [692 566], and on the northern flank of Cowside Beck [830 673] near Catrigg Force, Stainforth. They also occur on steep boulder clay slopes, including the flanks of some drumlins, as for example the one [7385 5485] near Rain Gill, Slaidburn. The laminated silts and clays that crop out in the Ribble valley near Hellifield show evidence of failure by flow or creep that is manifest in a characteristic bulge to the lower part of the slope-profile; the section [8511 5516] west of Halton Bridge is typical.

LIMESTONE DISSOLUTION

The subaerial dissolution of limestone is an important erosive process. Its rate in post-glacial times can be gauged by the pillars of limestone that stand up well above the surrounding pavement level where the rock is protected by large impermeable Lower Palaeozoic erratics. This is well seen at Norber, north of Austwick (Kendall and Wroot, 1924) (Plate 22). More general are the fretted limestone pavements, of which those above Malham Cove are particularly well known examples (Plate 7). These pavements comprise limestone slabs (clints) separated by rectilinear fissures (grikes), developed along joint-sets (Kendall and Wroot, 1924; Sweeting, 1974).

Dolines and shake-holes owe their origin to a combination of subaerial dissolution and groundwater activity. The district includes the largest dolines (large closed depressions) in the country (O'Connor and others, 1974). They lie near Langcliffe Scar [844 650], near Flock Rake [92 68], on High Mark [935 681], on Hawkswick Clowder [946 690], and on Kilnsey Moor [945 672] (see Moisley, 1955). The dolines lie variously on the outcrops of the Gordale, Lower Hawes, Upper Hawes and Gayle limestones. O'Connor and others

(1974) considered that they probably began to form in late Tertiary times, and have gradually enlarged since then; according to Sweeting (1974) they may represent large pothole-type features that were initiated along former limestone – shale junctions. Once established the floors of the dolines may have preferentially subsided because the hollows collected surface drainage and had a cover of wet soil (Clayton, 1966).

Shake-holes are much smaller funnel-shaped pits that are common where limestones have a thin impermeable covering of shales or boulder clay. Groundwater widens the joints in the limestone and removes the finer material from the cover which then gradually collapses above points where dissolution is greatest. Shake-holes are commonest in the north of the district on outcrops of the Malham Formation and limestones within the Wensleydale Group. Where profuse they are useful in defining solid and drift geological lines. On the lower ground in the south of the district, they are present on the outcrops of the Chatburn Limestone, the Thornton Limestone, some of the better jointed limestones within the Worston Shales, and the limestone conglomerate in the Pendleside Limestone.

Much dissolution takes place well underground, and its documentation in the district is profuse. Details of the various cave-systems produced and followed by subterranean streams, their origins and their evolution lie outside the scope of this work. The subject is covered by Smith and Atkinson (1977) and in a compilative work by Waltham (1974).   RSA

CHAPTER 6

Structure

The principal named structural elements of this district are the **'Askrigg Block'** (Hudson, 1938), earlier termed the 'Rigid Block' (Marr, 1921), and the **'Craven Basin'** (Hudson, 1933). The latter has also been termed the 'Bowland Basin' (Ramsbottom, 1974), the 'Bowland Trough' (Kent, 1974), and the 'Craven Lowlands' (Wilmore, 1910). The junction of these two elements lies between the **North Craven Fault** and the Craven Reef Belt, just south of the **Middle Craven Fault** (Figure 26); and this tract is here referred to as the 'transition zone'. In addition, a third element, for which the name **'Bowland Block'** is introduced, occupies much of the western part of the district; its boundary with the Askrigg Block is taken at the South Craven Fault and its boundary with the Craven Basin is drawn, on the evidence of Bouguer gravity anomaly data, on a line extending WSW from Settle. This line (Figure 26) indicates the upper margin of the basin slope as derived from the gravity data (Figures 34 and 35); it is not feasible, however, to determine the precise position of the basin margin from the geophysical results. The structural differentiation between the Craven Basin and the blocks was established in late Devonian to early Dinantian times. The extent to which the boundaries of these structural elements were determined by earlier basement fractures is speculative. The 'E–W Craven Fault Belt' has, however, been suggested as a possible line of (earlier) Devonian transcurrent faulting (Tegerdine and others, 1981).

It is probable that Lower Palaeozoic rocks underlie all parts of the district, including the Craven Basin and the Bowland Block, but their existence has been established only on the Askrigg Block, where they crop out in the Craven Inliers (Figure 3). Throughout most of Lower Palaeozoic time, the south-west-trending Iapetus Ocean separated England (on the edge of a 'European' continental lithospheric plate) from an 'American' plate which included Scotland (Phillips and others, 1976; Moseley, 1978). The ocean narrowed as oceanic crust was subducted beneath the European continental plate, during the Ordovician. Ingleton Group sediments were deposited on the margin of the 'European' continent, and were tightly folded in a pre-Ashgill deformation episode associated with tectonism on the margin of the 'European' continent. The deformed Ingleton Group forms part of a belt of magnetic basement rocks (Bott, 1961, 1967), named the Furness-Ingleborough-Norfolk Ridge by Wills (1978). The ridge lies on the north-eastern margin of the English Microcraton (Wills, 1978) (Figure 27). Erosion, in the Llanvirn–Caradoc interval, preceded the onlap of shelf sediments onto the ridge in the Ashgill.

Geosynclinal sedimentation dominated late Ordovician and Silurian times. During the Wenlock sediments derived from the 'European' continent entered the trough on the southern side of the Furness-Ingleborough-Norfolk Ridge. In the Ludlow, sediments with an 'American' provenance crossed the ridge as the geosynclinal development migrated southwards. In the orogenic episode associated with the collision of the two continental plates and the formation of the Caledonian continent at the close of the Silurian, the late Ashgill and Silurian rocks were deformed in open folds. Subsequently granite plutons were emplaced in the new Caledonian continent; these include the Wensleydale Granite (400 ± 10 Ma) in the adjoining Hawes district (Bott, 1967; Dunham, 1974a).

The interval from end-Silurian to early Dinantian times is largely unrepresented in the preserved sedimentary successions of northern England. From ?late Devonian to early Dinantian times, however, the region formed part of an intracratonic rift-province, with several fault-bounded rift basins (including the Craven Basin) in which thick sedimentary sequences accumulated (Johnson, 1967; Leeder, 1982). The basins formed as a result of crustal stretching. Some of these more buoyant areas are known to be underlain by end-Silurian granite plutons: the Askrigg Block is one such area (Bott, 1967; Wills, 1978).

The rift province lay within a shear-zone during the Dinantian. The shearing was probably the expression in the British Isles of right-lateral transform faulting affecting the Canadian Maritimes which lay to the south-west at that time (Dewey, 1982). Lateral displacements in the Lower Palaeozoic basement which may have resulted from such shearing have been proposed as the cause of much of the deformation of the Carboniferous strata of the Craven Basin (Arthurton, 1984). This deformation includes the establishment of the Ribblesdale Fold Belt (Earp and others, 1961), which comprises an *en-échelon* set of south-west-trending, mostly asymmetrical, close to open anticlines with broad intervening synclines that extends for over 80 km in a WSW–ENE tract up to 25 km wide. The Carboniferous cover of the Askrigg Block was not affected by this folding, and has remained comparatively undisturbed up to the present-day (Plate 26).

During the Silesian the 'rift' subsidence was replaced by 'sag' subsidence (Leeder, 1982). The Craven Basin was subjected to major uplift during the late Silesian, and became deeply eroded before the deposition of Permian and Triassic sediments, remnants of which are preserved resting unconformably on mid-Dinantian strata near Clitheroe (Earp and others, 1961) and on Westphalian strata near Ingleton (Ford, 1954).
EWJ,RSA

STRUCTURE OF LOWER PALAEOZOIC ROCKS

Askrigg Block

The Ingleton Group (Arenig), which underlies the younger Ordovician and Silurian rocks of the Craven Inliers, is deformed in tight to isoclinal north-west-trending folds (Leedal and Walker, 1950) of Llanvirn to Caradoc age. The

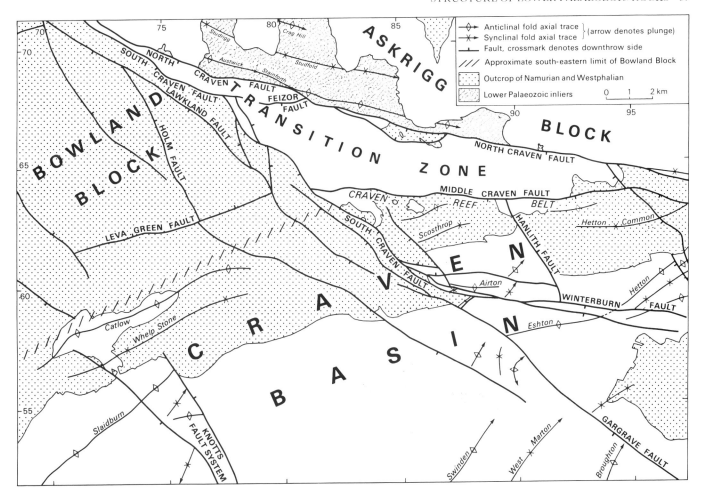

Figure 26 Structural features of the Settle district

folding pre-dates the depositon of the Ashgill Norber Forma-tion, which overlies the group unconformably. In the Chapel le Dale Inlier the axial planes of the isoclinal folds dip at 70° to the south-west (Leedal and Walker, 1950); a horizontal section through the south-western part of this inlier indicates that the folds have wavelengths of about 250 m and amplitudes of about 300 m. In Ribblesdale the Ingleton Group is poorly exposed and, apart from one second order fold-pair in the railway cutting south of Horton station, ap-pears to dip uniformly to the SSW at about 70°. The In-gleton Group forms part of the Furness-Ingleborough-Norfolk Ridge (Wills, 1978) which behaved as a rigid, positive element influencing subsequent sedimentation and controlling the later Lower Palaeozoic structural evolution (Figure 27).

The younger Ordovician and Silurian rocks of the inliers are deformed against the ridge of Ingleton Group rocks in close and open ESE-plunging folds of end-Silurian age; an axial planar cleavage is associated with this deformation (Plate 24). There are three major fold axes within the district (Figure 3). The Studrigg–Studfold Syncline is flanked to the north by the Crummack Anticline and to the south by the Austwick Anticline. All of the folds plunge ESE at 10 to 12°. The anticlines bring Ordovician strata to crop in the western part of the main inlier and at Crag Hill.

Minor folds, with amplitudes of up to 100 m, occur within the envelopes of the major folds and have a similar axial trend; these are best displayed in the more competent lithostratigraphical units, notably the Crag Hill Limestone [803 711] and the Austwick Formation, although they affect all parts of the Lower Palaeozoic succession. Examples of these minor folds in the Austwick Formation are seen in Ar-cow Wood Quarry [813 706]; also in exposures [776 704] north-west of Wharfe and [815 685 to 815 678] in the Ribble valley south of Sherwood House. The amplitudes and wave-lengths of the minor folds show a general decrease nor-thwards, compatible with the view that the ridge formed by the Ingleton Group behaved as a rigid element during the end-Silurian deformation. North-east of Dry Beck Farm [815 714] there is a set of ten parallel ESE-plunging folds within 600 m; their axes become more closely spaced and the amplitude decreases northwards.

The WNW-trending, subvertical, axial planar cleavage associated with the end-Silurian deformation occurs in all the younger Ordovician and Silurian rocks. It is most intense in argillaceous lithologies, particularly where these are weakly bedded as in the Sowerthwaite and Crummack formations. In calcareous lithologies, such as the Arcow Formation, the cleavage is crenulate with widely spaced, parallel 'master' planes. Refraction of the cleavage occurs where there are

Figure 27 Major features of early Ordovician palaeogeography

contrasts in lithology; this is well developed in the turbidite sandstone-siltstone succession of the Austwick Formation (Plate 24).   EWJ

STRUCTURE OF CARBONIFEROUS ROCKS

Askrigg Block

The structure of the Dinantian rocks of the Askrigg Block within the district is that of a broad half-dome, elongated WNW–ESE and bounded to the south by the North Craven Fault (see Dunham, 1959) (Figure 28). The highest regional dips are 7°, near the eastern margin.

The axis of the warp lies within a kilometre or so of the North Craven Fault; strata forming the southern 'limb' are seen at Norber near Austwick and on Malham Moor in the east. In the latter area a synclinal axis lies parallel to, and within 100 to 150 m of, the North Craven Fault. The existence of this syncline suggests that there may have been a compressional episode in the history of the fault, and that the latter may formerly have had a northward throw hereabouts.

In the western part of the block, few faults cut the Carboniferous strata. Farther east there is a group of WNW-trending faults with throws of up to 20 m on Knowe Fell and a group of north-east-trending mineralised fractures with displacements of up to a few metres on the high ground between Cowside and Kilnsey Moor. Some of the latter terminate northwards against an east–west fault-zone which extends from Nab End to Hawkswick, and includes the

mineralised Davy Rake. The trends of the joints in the limestones of the block and the transition zone were mapped by Wager (1931); he interpreted deviations from the regional trends in the vicinity of the North and Middle Craven faults as indicators of lateral displacement on those faults.

Continuous regional subsidence of the Askrigg Block during the Dinantian is implied by the absence of major non-sequences within the mid- and late Dinantian succession. The rate of subsidence, however, was not uniform across the block. In general it reduced southwards as shown, for example, by the thinning of early Brigantian strata from the northern parts of the block towards the North Craven Fault (Burgess and Mitchell, 1976; Dunham and Wilson, 1985).

Uplift of the southern part of the block (including that part of the block within this district) occurred in Pendleian times, before the accumulation of the Grassington Grit (Chubb and Hudson, 1925; Rowell and Scanlon, 1957; Wilson, 1960; Dunham and Wilson, 1985). The uplift and subsequent erosion was greatest in the Greenhow area of the adjoining Pateley Bridge district, where around Greenhow Quarry the entire Wensleydale Group is cut out under the Grassington Grit. On Fountains Fell the base of the grit rests on strata a short distance above the Main Limestone.   EWJ,DJCM,RSA

Plate 24 Cleavage in Austwick Formation, near Wharfe [777 700]. Contrasting competencies of the interbedded sandstones and siltstones refract the end-Silurian–early Devonian cleavage. (L 2352).

Transition zone

The stratigraphically and structurally complex transition zone is bounded to the north by the North Craven Fault which downthrows the Malham Formation southwards by as much as 160 m, and to the south, arbitrarily, by the Craven Reef Belt (Figure 26). It includes the Middle Craven Fault, and is bounded to the west by the South Craven Fault. The major faults of this zone were collectively named the 'Craven Faults system' by Phillips (1836).

The general structure of the Carboniferous strata between the North and Middle Craven faults is illustrated in Figure 28. In broad terms the central part of this fault block is structurally analogous to the southern part of the Askrigg Block. It comprises an elongate half-dome with an east-trending axis just to the north of the Middle Craven Fault. The culmination of this warp [85 64] lies south of Settle Scar.

North-west of Settle, the structure is a gentle WNW-plunging syncline which is cut by many north-west-trending faults, and is truncated to the west by the South Craven Fault. Farther north, the Feizor Fault marks the southern limit of a northward-dipping fault-slice between the North and South Craven faults which extends WNW to Clapham and beyond. To the north-east of Malham, the Dinantian strata up to and including the Simonstone Limestone are disposed in a gentle ENE-plunging syncline, much complicated by NW-trending faults.

The Middle Craven Fault, termed the Attermire Fault by Marr (1899), has an irregular east-west trace, the irregularity being partly accounted for by its southerly hade which approaches 45° [824 641] on the eastern slopes of Ribblesdale, north-east of Settle. The fault has a southward throw. In Stockdale it throws the Malham Formation some 300 m and the top of the Chapel House Limestone about 400 m; there may thus be some mid-Dinantian movement (Figure 28). Here it is split into two major fractures; the southern one does not displace the Bowland Shales and the northern fracture is mineralised with quartz-rock [862 637].

South of the Middle Craven Fault, the structure of the Dinantian rocks is poorly known. A gentle anticline, with an axis approximately coincident with the Craven Reef Belt, is manifest in the Silesian cover (Figure 26). It affects the Grassington Grit on Rye Loaf Hill and Kirkby Fell, and east of The Weets it plunges gently eastwards. The underlying Bowland Shales and Pendle Grit Formation are more strongly folded, although this effect may be due partly to sedimentary draping and differential compaction over the reef belt. The existence of the anticline in the underlying Dinantian strata remains unproved but is favoured in this account. The absence of evidence of southward-inclined Dinantian rocks led Hudson (1930a) to speculate on the presence of a substantial southward-throwing fault to the south of the reef belt.

The elongate fault block **between the North and Middle Craven faults** is cut by two sets of minor faults of small hade. One of these comprises south-west-trending, locally mineralised faults with throws of up to a few metres only as, for example [850 643] on Settle Scar. The other, by far the dominant set, comprises faults with a preferred NW-trend, and with throws exceptionally up to 90 m, as at Attermire Scar [844 642]. Some of this set carry oreshoots and quartz mineralisation [843 643 and 943 643]. Some of the NW-trending faults throw down to the south-west, others to the north-east. The fault slices form stepped zones, as in Bordley Beck, horsts, as on Warrendale Knotts [833 642], and grabens, such as those near Bordley [925 645], and [933 645] near New Houses. Some cut across the entire main fault block: others are less persistent; for example, at Gordale Scar [916 640] faults die south-eastwards short of the Middle Craven Fault.

Similar north-west-trending faults extend south-eastwards from the Middle Craven Fault, displacing the limestones of the Craven Reef Belt. On High South Bank, south of Stockdale, such faults displace the Malham Formation and the early Wensleydale Group, but not the overlying Pendleian rocks [e.g. 8548 6318 and 8608 6316] thus suggesting late Brigantian movement.

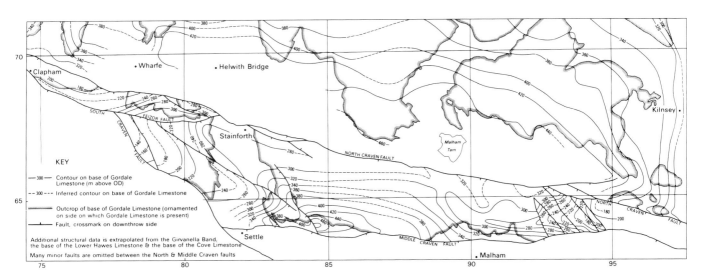

Figure 28 Structure of the Askrigg Block and transition zone. Contours are on the base of the Gordale Limestone

Plate 25 Upper Bowland Shales unconformably overlying Lower Hawes Limestone, Kirkby Fell, Malham [8733 6381]. Demonstrating onlap of basinal facies onto the Askrigg Block during the Pendleian. (L 2752)

Plate 26 Sub-Carboniferous unconformity, Combs Quarry, Foredale [800 701]. Sub-horizontal Kilnsey Formation rests on an erosion surface cut in steeply dipping Horton Formation. (L 2360)

Tectonic history of the transition zone

The North and Middle Craven faults were regarded by Wager (1931) as tear-faults, which, along with the Ribblesdale folds, were caused by post-Westphalian (Hercynian) compressive forces. A history of Dinantian movement on the faults was recognised, however, by Tiddeman (1889, 1891); and Hudson (1930a, 1933, 1944b) described movements during a late Dinantian to early Namurian interval on the Middle Craven Fault and, by implication, on the North Craven Fault also.

The influence of the **North Craven Fault** on early Dinantian sedimentation is not known. Movement along it predating the Grassington Grit is suggested by the contrasting Brigantian to early Pendleian sequences in the Black Hill area south of the fault and on Fountains Fell and Knowe Fell to the north. The unconformable relationship at the base of the Upper Bowland Shales south of the fault (Plate 25) suggests the possibility of a down-north movement as a precursor to the southwards late Brigantian to early Pendleian collapse; which created a fault-scarp against which the Bowland Shales accumulated. Subsequent (post-Pendleian) down-south movement is indicated by the present respective dispositions of the Grassington Grit on Black Hill and Fountains Fell.

The **Middle Craven Fault** has a long history of movement; a gentle anticline [858 637] flanking the fault to the north in Stockdale suggests that some of this movement was compressional. Arundian–Holkerian displacement is inferred from the abrupt southward thickening of the Kilnsey Formation (equated with the Scaleber Quarry and Scaleber Force limestones), as proved in the Stockdale Farm Borehole and Cominco boreholes S1, S2, S5 and S10 (Figure 29). Down-north movement at the beginning of the Brigantian is implied by the local thickening of the oncolite-bearing part of the Lower Hawes Limestone on Great Scar [e.g. 858 642], north of the fault, and by the condensed nature of the Wensleydale Group to the south on High South Bank and in Cominco Borehole S8 (Figure 29). The onset of this movement was accompanied by the introduction of limestone debris from the Craven Reef Belt into the basin as debris-flows and gravity slides, to become incorporated in the limestone conglomerates of the Pendleside Limestone.

Much greater down-south displacements occurred on both branches of the Middle Craven Fault in Stockdale during the late Brigantian; Bowland Shales of P_2 age rest unconformably on Malham Formation and early Brigantian limestones of the Wensleydale Group south of the faults. Farther east Bowland Shales (probably Upper) onlap against a contemporaneous south-facing (Middle Craven) fault-scarp [8656 6384] of Malham Formation near Rye Loaf Hill and at Pikedaw Hill [8792 6372] (Hudson, 1944b) (see also Plate 25). At Sugar Loaf Hill, the late Brigantian displacement did not produce a fault-scarp, and a Yoredale facies, comprising the Sugar Loaf Shales and Limestone, was established south of the fault in the early Pendleian (Figure 29).

The structure of the Upper Bowland Shales north of the Middle Craven Fault at Moor Close Gill, east of Malham, is synclinal, and implies local Pendleian or post-Pendleian down-north movement on the fault; possible synsedimentary displacement is suggested by an angular unconformity [9308 6379] within the Upper Bowland Shales. East of Bordley Beck intra-Pendleian movement is indicated by the onlap of Grassington Grit against a contemporaneous south-facing (Middle Craven) fault-scarp [960 637] of a sandstone within the Pendle Grit Formation near Firth Hill Plantation. The Pendleian movement on the Middle Craven Fault may have been contemporaneous with the folding or warping implied elsewhere by the unconformity at the base of the Grassington Grit. Post-Pendleian displacement on the fault is indicated by the disposition of the Grassington Grit of Rye Loaf Hill

and on Threshfield Moor, where the Grit is thrown down to the south by up to 80 m.

The late Brigantian (early Pendleian) tectonic phase, implicit in the stratigraphical relationships across the Middle and North Craven faults, also produced the set of north-west-trending faults, as was recognised by Hudson (1930a). These faults post-date the early Brigantian rocks (up to the Simonstone Limestone at least), but pre-date the onlap of the Bowland Shales which, in Stockdale, commenced in P_2 (late Brigantian) times. The displacements led to the establishment of considerable topographic relief along the Craven Reef Belt, so that parts of the belt, such as those to the north of Scaleber Bridge and under the eastern part of Kirkby Fell, became deeply buried whereas other parts, such as High South Bank (south of Stockdale Farm) and The Weets, remained barely covered.

In the Bordley area there is evidence of repeated movements on these north-west-trending faults, both pre-dating and post-dating the Upper Bowland Shales. For example, early displacement on a fault at Lee Gate House [927 645] led to the preservation, under Bowland Shales cover, of the Wensleydale Group up to the top of the Hardraw Scar Limestone to the north-east; to the south-west only the Lower Hawes Limestone is preserved. A subsequent reversal of movement on this fault has resulted in the fault-slice containing the fuller sequence now being a horst.

The pattern of the north-west-trending faults has been interpreted as a product of divergent dextral wrenching on the North and Middle Craven faults, the transition zone having been one of transtension during the late Brigantian (Arthurton, 1984). This interpretation is compatible with the

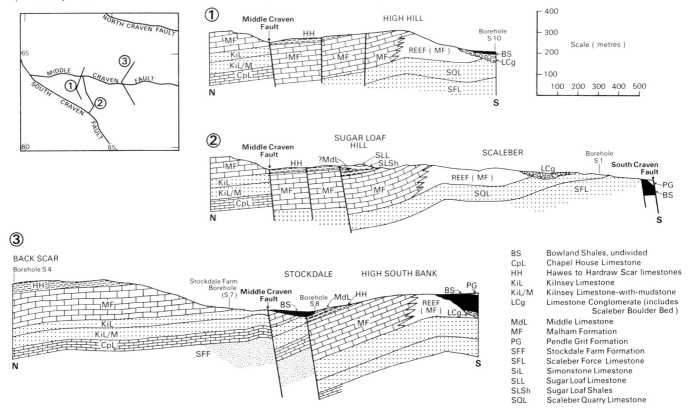

Figure 29 Sections across the Middle Craven Fault and Craven Reef Belt

evidence of major late Brigantian rift displacement on the North and Middle Craven faults. Dextral movement of unspecified age along the Craven faults was earlier claimed by Westoll (in discussion to Moseley and Ahmed, 1967).

DJCM, RSA

Craven Basin

The part of the Craven Basin that lies within the district comprises a Dinantian to Pendleian sedimentary succession up to at least 4 km thick. In contrast to their age counterparts on the Askrigg Block, these strata are strongly folded, and the folds form part of the system of Ribblesdale folds (Phillips, 1836) known also as the Ribblesdale Fold Belt (Earp and others, 1961), with fold axes trending generally SW–NE (Figure 26). The folds include six major anticlines, named the Catlow, Slaidburn, Swinden (Sawley–Gisburn–Swinden), Broughton, Airton and Eshton–Hetton anticlines. These names are already established in the literature (Wilmore, 1910; Hudson and Dunnington, 1944; Ramsbottom, 1974, fig. 17; Arthurton, 1983). The Catlow Anticline, formerly regarded as part of the Sykes Anticline (Parkinson, 1936; Hudson and Mitchell, 1937; Moseley, 1962; Ramsbottom, 1974), is periclinal, and the remainder of the anticlines plunge north-eastwards. The anticlines are separated by broad synclines. The latter include the West Marton Syncline (Earp and others, 1961) and the Whelp Stone, Scosthrop and Hetton Common synclines, new names introduced in this account (Figure 26).

The rocks of the basin are cut by the important north-west-trending South Craven Fault system (Figure 26) (Hudson and Mitchell, 1937; Hudson and Dunnington, 1944), whose components include the South Craven Fault at Scaleber Beck (Hudson, 1930a), and the Winterburn and Gargrave faults farther south-east (Booker and Hudson, 1926; Hudson and Dunnington, 1944). In the south-west, they are cut by the Knotts Fault System (Figure 26), a name introduced by Arthurton (1984) for a group of faults extending north-westwards from the Anna Lane Tear Fault of the Clitheroe district (Earp and others, 1961).

Chevron folds with wave-lengths of the order of 10 to 20 m affect parts of the basinal outcrop; in most instances these small-scale folds occur demonstrably within fault-zones, notably the Knotts and South Craven fault systems (Figure 30).

The **Catlow Anticline** extends for some 10 km near the inferred north-western margin of the Craven Basin (Figure 26). The anticline is an asymmetrical pericline; its north-western limb is the steeper and is locally vertical. The fold culmination lies toward the western end of the structure, north of Kenibus. Strata up to and including the Pendle Grit Formation are strongly folded; the Brennand Grit, which forms outliers resting unconformably on the Pendle Grit Formation across the eastern nose of the fold, appears to be unaffected, implying that this fold had formed by late Pendleian times. Similarly, at the western closure of the fold the Brennand Grit to the south of Near Costy Clough is less steeply dipping than the underlying Pendle Grit Formation. There is a structural discordance between the fold [7072 5820] near Lamb Hill Farm and the enveloping Worston Shales, which implies the possible existence of an unconformity at the base of the Worston Shales.

To the east of Catlow, the main anticline carries an *en échelon* set of second-order periclinal folds along its crest. The axes of these subtend angles of about 25° with the main axial trace. The subsidary folds are known to affect strata up to and including the Lower Bowland Shales of P_{1b} age.

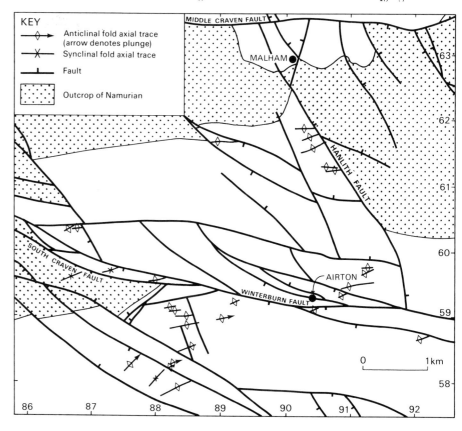

Figure 30 Minor folds around Airton in the Craven Basin

The Catlow Anticline is cut by several WNW- and NNW-trending faults, for example one 200 m east of Catlow which displaces the outcrop of limestone conglomerate at the top of the Pendleside Limestone by some 400 m. In this instance the folding is either partly contemporaneous with, or post-dates the faulting; differences in lateral displacement resulting from the tight folding in the Pendleside Limestone to the north-east of the fault [7206 5846] compared with the more open flexures to the south-west have been accommodated along the fault. Farther north-east near Higher Clough, north-west-trending faults are associated with NNE-trending chevron folds in the Pendleside Limestone. A stream section [7310 5887], normal to the bedding strike, exposes five anticlinal axes over 90 m. Similar chevron folds of various trends affect the Worston Shales in the River Hodder at Lock Bridge [7138 5844], and in a tributary stream nearby [7135 5836].

The existence of a north-east-trending reverse strike-fault is inferred on the north-western limb of the Catlow Anticline near Lamb Hill Farm. The fault is believed to juxtapose the Bowland Shales and Worston Shales [7030 5798] in a gully north-west of the farm.

The field relations between the Bowland Shales and the Pendleside Limestone at the south-western closure of the anticline in Hare Clough Beck are obscure. Parkinson (1936, 1964) claimed that gently dipping Bowland Shales of high P_2 age almost surrounded breccia (Pendleside Limestone) dipping at 'varying angles up to 90°'. The explanation subscribed to here involves a conjectural ENE-trending fault on which much of the tight folding in the Pendlesdie Limestone was accommodated.

The **Slaidburn Anticline** is asymmetrical, with a steep, locally vertical, north-western limb. The culmination of the fold lies south-west of Slaidburn. North of Slaidburn the plunge is north-eastwards at about 10°. Chatburn Limestone is exposed in the core of the fold which affects strata up to and including the Pendle Grit Formation. The unconformable relationship of a knoll-reef limestone at the base of the Worston Shales to the Thornton Limestone [7176 5320] near Holmehead Bridge (Plate 10) is evidence of at least local uplift during the late Chadian (Arthurton and Jones, 1980; Arthurton, 1984). The field relations along the Thornton Limestone – Worston Shales boundary suggest that on the south-eastern limb of the fold the Thornton Limestone is progressively cut out towards the south-west.

North-east-trending strike-faults affect the core of the fold near Pain Hill, and were encountered in the Bowland Forest Tunnel (Earp, 1955) in the Chatburn Limestone. One of the faults figured by Earp is a reverse structure throwing to the north-west. Another low-angle, reverse strike-fault is exposed farther north in the north-western limb [6970 5549] in the Upper Bowland Shales of Croasdale Brook.

Several north-west- to NNW-trending faults cut the Slaidburn Anticline, particularly its north-western limb. These faults are regarded as belonging to the Knotts Fault System. Some of them have a wrench component of displacement; thus a fault zone [706 552] near Croasdale House produces a dextral outcrop shift of some 400 m in steeply inclined Pendleside Limestone. Fine-grained limestones in this part of the fold limb are locally affected by closely spaced jointing which produces a conspicuous lineation on weathered surfaces; the jointing recorded on the shore of Stocks Reservoir [7242 5515], near Black House, trends N110°E.

Chevron folds with north-east-trending axes are present in the outcrops of the Worston Shales, Pendleside Limestone and Lower Bowland Shales in the north-western limb of the Slaidburn Anticline, where they are cut by the Knotts Fault System. In a section [7455 5670] in Bottoms Beck, chevron folds in the Pendleside Limestone are truncated north-eastwards against one of the faults; strata to the north-east of that fault are free from such folds. Similar chevron folds in Pendleside Limestone are exposed on the shore [7228 5551] of Stocks Reservoir, near Hollins House; and in the Worston Shales in Croasdale Brook [7028 5498], near Croasdale House. At this latter locality the chevron fold axes trend between N10°E and N60°E, and mostly plunge towards the north-east; the folds have wave-lengths of 10 to 15 m. North-east-trending chevron folds in Lower Bowland Shales were recorded in a temporarily exposed section [7289 5682] on the bed of Stocks Reservoir, near Birch Hill. ENE-trending minor folds of low amplitude, with wave-lengths in the range 50 to 100 m, affect sandy strata in the Lower Bowland Shales on the south-eastern limb of the Slaidburn Anticline in the stream [7314 5201 to 7352 5239] south-west of Tinklers Farm.

Towards the southern margin of the district, the **Knotts Fault System** comprises a 1 km-wide zone of WNW-trending fractures that separates southward dipping Bowland Shales (including Pendleside Sandstones) from northward dipping Worston Shales. The strata in individual fault slices are inclined variously to the west and southwest, but in one slice the Pendleside Limestone and Lower Bowland Shales are deformed in north-east-trending chevron folding.

Within this district, the **Swinden Anticline** is a symmetrical open fold that plunges north-eastwards at 10 to 20°. The closure is cut by faults belonging to the South Craven Fault system at Coniston Cold (see Hudson and Dunnington, 1944). The **Broughton Anticline** similarly plunges to the north-east, but is a tighter, asymmetrical fold; the more steeply dipping north-western limb is inclined at up to 70° at Clints Delf [9292 5175].

The **South Craven Fault system** extends south-eastwards from Settle across the Craven Basin. Near Orms Gill Green it divides into the east-trending Winterburn Fault and the south-east-trending Gargrave Fault; both of these are themselves complex fault zones.

Between Settle and Orms Gill Green the system throws down to the south-west. One of the principal faults, the South Craven Fault (Hudson, 1930a), is exposed [8392 6242] in Scaleber Beck, south-west of Scaleber Bridge; sandstones of the Pendle Grit Formation are thrown down against the Scaleber Force Limestone. The latter is overlain unconformably by an allochthonous block of reef-limestone (Malham Formation), and this in turn by Upper Bowland Shales of E_{1a} age. This unconformity is a consequence of down-south movement on the fault in the late Asbian to early Pendleian interval. The sequence proved in the nearby Cominco Borehole S10 [8360 6304] suggests that the movement on the fault was of P_2 age or earlier; the oldest datable strata above the unconformity are Lower Bowland Shales that contain a possible *Goniatites granosus*.

To the south-west of Scaleber Bridge, the South Craven Fault system affects a belt of country some 2 km wide. Most of the faults throw to the south-west, repeating the outcrop of the Grassington Grit in step-like scarps including Peart Crags [825 624], Hunter Bark [829 612] and Cleatop Park [822 612]. It is possible that some of these faults are listric-faults which formed at the margin of a Silesian basin that thickens abruptly south-westwards across a South Craven hinge-line. The relationship between the Grassington Grit and the underlying Pendle Grit Formation is demonstrably unconformable at the south-western margin of the fault belt [82 61] near Mearbeck. Here the Grit is gently folded about a north-west-plunging axis, and the Pendle Grit Formation is more tightly folded along an ENE-trending axis [821 610].

Farther south-east, the members of the fault system that cut the Upper Bowland Shales [e.g. 8593 6030] in a stream section south-east of Crake Moor are reverse faults, hading north-east at up to 65°. A weak east–west-trending fold deforms the Pendle Grit Formation downstream [8596 6010], and ENE chevron folds (wave-length about 20 m) affect the Worston Shales [8672 6033] in a stream section some 700 m to the east.

The **Winterburn Fault** is exposed [8700 5986] in a stream at Orms Gill Green, where muddy limestones, near the top of the Worston Shales, are thrown south-westwards against the Thornton Limestone. Between Orms Gill Green and Otterburn to the south-east the fault slices are complexly folded.

The general structure to the south of the Winterburn Fault at Airton Green is synclinal about an ENE-trending axis, but this syncline does not extend to the north of the fault. Similarly the major Eshton–Hetton Anticline to the north-east of the **Gargrave Fault** at Otterburn has no apparent extension to the south-west of the fault, where stream sections [88 58] expose Worston Shales with subsidiary folding about axes plunging to the north-east. Similarly subsidiary folding, though about axes which plunge to the WSW in limestones within the Worston Shales, is exposed to the north of the Gargrave Fault [884 588] in Otterburn Beck. In a tributary farther north [8827 5908] near Park House east-trending chevron folds are present in the Worston Shales.

Southerly throws on the Winterburn Fault and some of its branches at Airton repeat the Thornton Limestone outcrop in the Aire valley [9026 5964 to 9041 5915]. Tight, ENE-trending chevron folds are present in the Worston Shales in this part of the Winterburn Fault zone, for example in the River Aire [9042 5912], and in a cutting [9090 5934] at Calton.

The course of the Winterburn Fault across the Eshton–Hetton Anticline is ill defined but a zone of dolomitisation in the Thornton Limestone [940 588 and 947 587] is believed to indicate a northern branch. On Flasby Fell, Pendleian displacement on another branch of the Winterburn Fault, exposed [9558 5766] in Hetton Beck, is believed to have been partly responsible for the north-west-trending folds which affect strata up to and including the Pendle Grit Formation [961 564]. The overlying Grassington Grit has not been involved in this folding, which is thus of E_{1c} age (Mundy and Arthurton, 1980).

The course of the **Gargrave Fault** is also ill defined, although that of one of its branches north-east of Bell Busk is marked by a fault-scarp in the Thornton Limestone [911 568].

Both the **Swinden** and the **Broughton** anticlines die north-eastwards against the Gargrave Fault zone. The closure of the Broughton Anticline faces an escarpment of the Grassington Grit on Flasby Fell across the fault to the north-east. The closure of the Swinden Anticline faces the southern limb of the Eshton–Hetton Anticline at Bell Busk. Here, however, there is an intervening pericline [90 56] with an arcuate axial trace, concave towards the east, within the fault zone.

The **Airton Anticline** is a complex fold with an arcuate axial trace, north-west-trending near Orms Gill Green but swinging to the north-east, north of Airton. The anticline is truncated to the south by the Winterburn Fault and is cut by many of its branches. The Thornton Limestone is extensively dolomitised in the vicinity of these faults. North of Airton, the fold plunges to the north-east and its limit is defined on the eastern side of the Aire valley by the postulated north-west-trending **Hanlith Fault** which accomodates the juxtaposition, east of Hanlith, of Upper Bowland Shales with *Cravenoceras malhamense* [9076 6150] and the Pendleside Limestone. Both are deformed by west-trending chevron folds that are particularly well displayed in disused quarries [9062 6123] in the Pendleside Limestone, where their axial planes are inclined at 65° to the south.

The **Eshton–Hetton Anticline** is an asymmetrical ENE-trending fold with dips of up to 72° recorded in its steep northern limb. The structure is cut obliquely by the Winterburn Fault and associated fractures, and it is truncated to the west by the Gargrave Fault. To the north of the Winterburn Fault it comprises two anticlines with subparallel axes which plunge towards the ENE; the northern one of these is on the same line as the elongate outcrop of marginal reef limestone (Malham Formation) at Swinden, north-east of Rylstone, and is largely within the adjoining Pateley Bridge district.

The Dinantian succession in the western part of the Eshton–Hetton Anticline contains evidence of contemporaneous uplift and faulting. The unconformity at the base of the Worston Shales, exposed [9139 5636] at Haw Crag Quarry and penetrated in the Throstle Nest Borehole [9166 5660], indicates substantial erosion of the axial zone of the fold, which has removed not only the Hetton Beck Limestone but a substantial thickness of the Thornton Limestone as well. The presence of reef limestone debris in the limestone conglomerate above the unconformity points to the former presence of knoll-reefs in the axial zone, although no authochthonous vestige remains. The Worston Shales thicken abruptly south-westwards along the strike in this part of the fold limb, a thickening that is believed to reflect contemporaneous displacement on the Gargrave Fault.

·The **Scosthrop** and **Hetton Common synclines** preserve Namurian strata between the Craven Reef Belt and the Airton and Eshton–Hetton anticlines respectively. The Scosthrop Syncline is poorly exposed and little is known of its detailed structure. The Hetton Common Syncline is cut by north- to north-west-trending faults. On Hetton Common the folded Upper Bowland Shales and Pendle Grit Formation plunge eastwards, and the structure tightens at least as far as Bordley Beck. The Grassington Grit forms gently dipping outliers on Hetton Common and is more openly folded. A late Pendleian phase of folding is inferred from this relationship.

Tectonic history of Craven Basin

The history of folding and faulting in the Craven Basin is controversial. Turner (1936) regarded the basin as a minor geosyncline in Carboniferous times; its subsequent eversion (into the Ribblesdale Fold Belt) was apparently a repetition in miniature of what he considered to be the earlier history of the region, the fold belt constituting a 'posthumous Caledonide range'. Wager (1931) contended that the Ribblesdale folds were produced by post-Westphalian to pre-Permian compression. Moseley (1962) regarded the folding of the Sykes Anticline (in the adjoining Lancaster district) as post-dating the Pendle Grit (Formation). Hudson and Mitchell (1937), however, claimed three phases of Dinantian folding in the Skipton Anticline (in the adjoining Bradford and Pateley Bridge districts), in addition to a 'post-Millstone Grit (Namurian)' phase.

Rift subsidence continued in the Craven Basin throughout the Dinantian and into the Silesian, until Pendleian times at least. All the major stratigraphical units of the basin up to the Pendle Grit Formation either thin out completely or are drastically reduced in thickness across the transition zone. The basin succession is at least some 4 km thick compared with a maximum of 0.6 km for the equivalent succession on the Askrigg Block.

Wager (1931) considered that the dextral displacements on the North and Middle Craven faults were a result of the same compressive forces that produced the Ribblesdale folds. Conversely, Westoll (in discussion, Moseley and Ahmed, 1967) regarded the folds in the basin as the results of dextral displacements along the faults, the South Craven Fault forming a splay in relation to such movement. If there is a genetic relationship between the North and Middle Craven faults and the Ribblesdale folds, then the late Dinantian to early Namurian age established for the faults by Hudson (1930a) would apply also to the folds. The argument favouring an interrelationship between folds and faults in the basin was developed by Arthurton (1984); he regarded the Ribblesdale Fold Belt as having formed between late Chadian and Pendleian times, in response to regional east–west dextral shear, and considered that the folds in the Carboniferous cover formed as a result of wrench displacement on fractures in the Lower Palaeozoic basement.

The South Craven Fault was regarded by Hudson (1930a) as 'definitely post-Carboniferous in age', and by Wager (1931) as 'entirely post-Permian and therefore unconnected with the Hercynian compression'. Later, Hudson and Mitchell (1937) reasoned that the lack of structural continuity across the 'South Craven Fault' (Gargrave Fault) at the western end of the Skipton Anticline was due either to an intimate connection between folding and faulting, or to a considerable lateral component on the fault. The former option would imply the possibility of Dinantian movement on the fault, and would also involve some lateral displacement.

Detailed knowledge of the early Dinantian succession (up to and including the Thornton Limestone) is, however, restricted to small outcrops in the cores of the 'Ribblesdale' anticlines, and is probably insufficient to allow stratigraphical generalisations over the whole basin to be made. Nevertheless, the succession includes shallow-water sedimentary indicators at various levels, implying that sedimentation broadly kept pace with subsidence during the early Dinantian. In late Chadian times this equilibrium between subsidence and sedimentation was not maintained; in most parts of the basin the overlying succession, up to and including the Pendle Grit Formation, contains sedimentary indicators of deposition in a basin of substantial bathymetric contrasts. Widespread shallow-water to emergent conditions were only re-established over block and basin alike in late Pendleian times, as shown by the fluviatile character of the Grassington (Brennand) Grit.

There are stratigraphical indications in the basin to suggest that the rift subsidence was interrupted by additional tectonic events, at least from late Chadian times onwards. Episodes of folding within the basin are indicated both by the lateral variation in thickness and facies, notably in the Worston Shales, the Lower Bowland Shales and the Pendle Grit Formation, and by angular unconformities within local sequences. This is most clearly demonstrated by the unconformity at the base of the Worston Shales in the Eshton–Hetton Anticline. The depth of Arundian erosion of the Thornton Limestone on the south-eastern limb at Haw Crag increases towards the fold axis, illustrating that the anticline was established by the early Dinantian. The unconformity at the base of the Worston Shales in the Slaidburn Anticline provides further evidence of local uplift in the basin, in this instance of late Chadian age.

Brigantian tectonism in the basin is implied by the thickness variations of the Lower Bowland Shales and the included Pendleside Sandstones. The axial zone of the Slaidburn Anticline formed a hinge to a rapidly subsiding area with thick sedimentary accumulation to the south-east around Champion and Knotts; a thick sequence also occurs to the north of the Eshton–Hetton Anticline at Winterburn Reservoir. The South Craven Fault may also have been active at this time, for the Pendleside Sandstones and associated sandy strata are some 100 m thick to the south of the fault at Newton Gill but appear to be absent to the north.

The effects of intra-Namurian folding are most marked in the Pendle Grit Formation (Pendleian), notably in the Catlow Anticline, though it is unclear whether the thinning of the formation over the anticlinal crest is the result of differential subsidence associated with folding or of subsequent pre-Grassington Grit erosion. Folding in the Pendle Grit Formation which pre-dates the Grassington Grit at Flasby Fell is considered to be related to displacement on fractures associated with the Winterburn Fault. Pendleian movement on the South Craven Fault system is also demonstrated by the unconformable relationship between the Grassington Grit and the Pendle Grit Formation near Mearbeck.

Folding and faulting that post-date the accumulation of the Grassington Grit are indicated by the present disposition of the Grit. Generally, the folding, whether representing one or more epidsodes, is weak compared with the structures in the succession up to and including the Pendle Grit Formation. The faulting, however, for example that in the Grassington Grit in the South Craven Fault system south-east of Settle, was substantial.

The genesis and age of the minor folds which affect the basin succession below the Grassington Grit have been discussed by Arthurton (1983, 1984). *En échelon* chevron folds in the early Dinantian strata of the Skipton Anticline were shown to have formed as a result of dextral displacement within the axial zone of the (pre-existing) major anticline. Similarly he considered the *en échelon* subsidiary folds on the crest of the Catlow Anticline to have been established as a result of similar displacement within the axial zone. In this latter instance none of the minor folds is known to affect strata younger than the Lower Bowland Shales, and it is thus possible that these folds are of Brigantian age. The chevron folds which are associated with the Knotts and South Craven fault systems (Figures 26 and 30) are also regarded as having formed by wrenching in cover sediments, translated from wrench displacement on fractures at depth.

Recent movement has occurred on the South Craven Fault system. Versey (1948) recorded a seismic event known as the Skipton (or Settle) Earthquake, which occurred in 1944. He regarded the epicentre as 'in all probability' lying along the Gargrave Fault. Damage was caused to a bridge and subsurface drains along the (unspecified) 'mapped line of this fault'.   RSA

Bowland Block

The Bouguer gravity anomaly contours of the western part of the district indicate the existence of a gravity 'high' extending WSW from Settle. Anomaly values fall sharply to the south-east of the 'high' (across a zone termed the 'Bowland Line' in Figure 35) and more gradually to the NNE. Interpretation of these anomalies (Chapter 8) has led to the postulation of the existence of Lower Palaeozoic rocks at shallow depths immediately north of the Catlow Anticline, with Carboniferous or similar rocks thickening abruptly to the south-east, and gradually to the NNE.

The interpretation of the structure to the south-east of the gravity 'high' is in accord with the existence of the thick Dinantian to early Namurian succession that has been established there at crop; the interpretation of the structure to the north of the 'high' is supported by the observed structure of the Silesian succession at crop, but there is no direct evidence of the nature of the presumed underlying Dinantian succession. There is, however, indirect stratigraphical evidence of the existence of a Dinantian block succession in this area, and this, together with the gravity interpretation, has led to the postulation of a 'Bowland Block', extending northwards from the gravity 'high' to the Askrigg Block (Figure 26).

Although the South Craven Fault system runs between the two blocks, there is no evidence that it acted as a block–basin hinge in the Dinantian north-west of Settle. On the contrary, between Feizor and Giggleswick there is no indication of any block-marginal Dinantian facies comparable with those of the Craven Reef Belt adjacent to the South Craven Fault. Thus it is assumed that the block Dinantian succession extends south-west of the South Craven Fault, continuing onto the Bowland Block.

This assumption is supported by exposures in the western part of the Craven Basin, particularly by the nature and distribution of the limestone conglomerate component of the Pendleside Limestone (late Asbian to early Brigantian). This conglomerate extends southwards as far as Knotts [77 53]; the thickest known sequences (42 m), however, are in the northernmost outcrop in the Catlow Anticline. Here the conglomerates include allochthonous blocks of reef limestone which are considered to be the proximal derivatives of a contemporaneous reef-belt, analogous to, and probably an extension of, the Craven (Settle–Malham) Reef Belt. Such a reef belt is presumed to extend along the Bowland Line, the geophysically defined southern margin of the Bowland Block.

Silesian strata are present on the Bowland Block and dip to the north at about 10°. They are cut by faults with a preferred north-west trend, and generally with throws of less than 100 m, although the Holm Fault is known to throw 250 m to the north-east [759 640] west of Black Bank. The greatest thickness of Westphalian strata in the district is preserved in a down-faulted block between this fault and the Lawkland Fault. Silesian strata are also cut by faults with an easterly trend. The most significant of these is the Leva Green Fault [796 639 to 711 615] which throws almost 200 m to the north [790 636], south of Craven Ridge. This fault trends ENE, parallel to the postulated south-eastern margin of the Bowland Block; the projected eastward continuation of the fault coincides with the Middle Craven Fault (although the throw of the latter is to the south). Westphalian strata are preserved against the South Craven Fault system which marks the northeastern boundary of the Bowland Block. The fault system here comprises two main faults, both throwing down to the south-west, the South Craven Fault and the Lawkland Fault. The Namurian strata exposed within the fault-zone between Clapham and Giggleswick dip southwestwards at up to 60°; this suggests that these strata were once folded into a south-west-facing monocline which was faulted along the hinge-zone by subsequent movements between the Bowland and Askrigg blocks.

The sedimentology of, and thickness variations within, the Namurian succession indicate intra-Namurian tilting of the Bowland Block to the west. The greatest movement occurred early in the Arnsbergian during deposition of the Roeburndale Formation; it thickens westwards from 90 m [76 64] near Giggleswick to some 200 m [78 63] north of Birchshaw Rocks, and increases to about 500 m west of Keasden Beck. The westward thickening continues in the Lancaster district where the formation attains 650 m (Johnson, 1981). The uniform thickness of the succeeding Caton Shales in the district indicates that the tilting later in the Arnsbergian was minimal; however, Moseley (1954) describes a slight westward thickening of the shales in the Lancaster district, demonstrating that it had not ceased.

Post-Westphalian to pre- (or intra-) Permian displacement down to the south-west on the South Craven Fault system is suggested by the presence of supposed Permian conglomerate (brockram) resting unconformably on Westphalian strata near Ingleton, in the adjoining Hawes district. The clasts in the conglomerate are mainly of Dinantian limestone; these are presumed to have been derived from a contemporaneous fault-scarp to the north which formed the margin of the Askrigg Block. A further, post-Permian, throw to the south-west is indicated by the present faulted disposition of the conglomerate.   EWJ,RSA

CHAPTER 7

Mineralisation

There is no active metalliferous mining in the district but, in the past, mineralised fractures and caverns in the Dinantian limestones of the Askrigg Block have been exploited. Lead, copper and zinc minerals have been won from veins in the Malham–Kilnsey area, and calamine and ochre have been extracted from caverns near Pikedaw Hill, west of Malham. Elsewhere in the district few mineral deposits have been worked.

The mineralisation and history of mining in the Malham–Kilnsey area have been researched by Raistrick (1938, 1953, 1954 and 1973). Legend has it that mining was carried out in the monastic period under the control of Fountains Abbey, but according to Raistrick (1938, 1953) such claims are unfounded, as extant monastic records show that early mining was confined to Greenhow Hill, Wensleydale and Mashamshire. The discovery of a coin (dated from 1272 to 1327) in spoils at Cold Streak Mine near Arncliffe (Hawes district) testifies to the possibility of some mining nearby during the monastic period.

Mining began in the Malham–Kilnsey area during the 17th Century, initially for copper ores and later for lead and zinc. The activity was intermittent, and ceased in about 1880; production was greatest between 1750 and 1830. Some of the copper and most of the lead ore were smelted locally near Malham Tarn and at Kilnsey. Smithsonite from the the Pikedaw Calamine Mine was sold for brass-making to the Cheadle Brass Company, and was also used, along with ochre from the mine, in a small local paint industry.

Cominco S.A. undertook a programme of mineral exploration in the district between 1966 and 1970. They drilled several boreholes close to the Middle Craven Fault east of Settle, looking for an 'Irish-style' sulphide body but had no success. The 'Institute of Geological Sciences' Mineral Reconnaissance Programme included a survey of the Craven Basin (Wadge and others, 1983); it comprised geophysical surveys (Chapter 8), a ground geochemical survey, and a limited drilling programme. Targets for lead-zinc mineralisation in the district were investigated along the Middle Craven Fault between Malham and Settle, on Threshfield Moor and Hetton Common, and at Orms Gill Green, How Hill and Copter Syke. However, no significant mineral deposits were identified. An account of the mineralisation of the northern part of the district (Askrigg Block) is given in Dunham and Wilson (1985); the reader is referred to that volume for a review that includes historical and genetic aspects of the mineralisation.

VEIN-MINERALISATION

Vein-mineralisation in the district is most notable in the Gordale Limestone and lower limestones of the Wensleydale Group of the Askrigg Block, where it is localised in the High Mark area (Figure 31) and adjacent to the Middle Craven Fault (Figure 32) between High Hill and Pikedaw Hill. Elsewhere in the district surface exposures reveal little vein-mineralisation of importance.

Details

Askrigg Block and transition zone

The only mineralised fractures recorded in Lower Palaeozoic strata are veinlets, containing small amounts of sphalerite with some chalcopyrite and pyrite, that occur in the axial region of a minor anticline in laminated siltstones of the Horton Formation in Dry Rigg Quarry [8001 6940].

Most occurrences, however, lie in the Dinantian rocks. In the Kilnsey Moor–High Mark–Dew Bottoms area (Figure 31), most of the veins trend north-east; they are generally narrow and are analogous to the Derbyshire 'Scrins', many being little more than mineralised major joints. From Great Clowder northwards to Blue Scar (Figure 31) the veins trend east–west and ENE; here they include wider veins such as the Davy Rake. The east–west trend continues in the Knipe Scar area (Figure 31), where the veins form the southern part of the Middlesmoor Vein Complex centred in the Hawes district. The host rocks of these veins are the upper part of the Gordale Limestone and the Wensleydale Group limestones up to the Hardraw Scar Limestone; most are in the Hawes and Gayle limestones. Galena was the principal ore mined (Table 1) although the amount extracted was probably small. Sphalerite, chalcopyrite, and the secondary minerals malachite and smithsonite occur in the spoils. Gangue minerals are dominated by baryte and calcite, and fluorite occurs in the Knipe Scar and some of the High Mark veins.

Between High Hill and Pikedaw Hill (Figure 31), adjacent to the Middle Craven Fault, south-east-trending veins are present in the Grizedales area and at Ben Scar. Narrow veins, such as those between Settle Scar and Back Scar, commonly have the north-east trend of the High Mark group. Minor east–west veins occur along the Middle Craven Fault, for example at Crutching Close [8613 6370], and on associated faults at Pikedaw Hill [8840 6365]. The host rock ranges from the Gordale Limestone up to the Hardraw Scar Limestone. In addition to galena (with secondary anglesite and cerrusite), chalcopyrite (with secondary malachite and azurite) and zinc minerals (largely secondary smithsonite) occurred in sufficient quantities to be mined particularly in the south-east-trending veins. Gangue minerals of these veins included baryte and calcite but, unlike the High Mark Veins, they contained abundant quartz and lacked fluorite.

South of the Middle Craven Fault near High Hill, trials have been made in small south-east-trending veins in dolomitised Hawes and Gayle limestones (Figure 32). The spoil yields galena, smithsonite, baryte and quartz. On High South Bank small veins trend both south-east and ENE (Figure 32); galena, malachite and baryte are present in their spoils. These veins are again hosted by Wensleydale Group limestones (Hawes to Hardraw Scar) close to a zone of widespread silicification. Further details of the High Mark and High Hill–Grizedales veins are given in Table 1.

In the North–Middle Craven fault area beyond the main Settle–Malham mineralised tract, there are a few small workings and trials, for example in the vicinity [918 636] of Great Knott near Malham and west of the River Ribble between Reisber Scar [8116 6609] and Blackriggs Quarry [7923 6610].

Craven Basin and Bowland Block

Small veins of quartz and calcite, containing chalcopyrite and sphalerite, are present in dolomitised and silicified Thornton Limestone on the east bank [8695 5993] of Orms Gill. Limestones within the Worston Shales contain feeble veins of sphalerite in the banks [9043 5910] of the River Aire, near Airton. Sphalerite is also present with calcite in a vein on the south bank [8895 6094] of Kirkby Beck, west of Kirkby Malham. Galena occurs in an irregular vein, up to 1 cm wide, in a limestone olistolith in Worston Shales at Fogger Rook [8928 5526].

On the north-western limb of the Slaidburn Anticline, small veins containing sphalerite and calcite occur in partly dolomitised Pendleside Limestone exposed in a gully [7185 5543] near Hollins House. Malachite and calcite are present in a vein trending N330°E [7221 5552] in dolomitised Pendleside Limestone on the shore of Stocks Reservoir.

In the Catlow Anticline fluorite and calcite are present in a vein trending N010°E that cuts limestone conglomerate of the Pendleside Limestone in a stream [7504 5950] south of Fair Hill.

Sphalerite and galena have been recorded from a vein worked by pits and opencuts [7407 5937 to 7417 5924] near Halsteads. At How Hill [7457 5941 to 7462 5970] dolomitised and silicified limestone conglomerate (Pendleside Limestone) contains traces of sphalerite and possible smithsonite concentrated along joints. Also in the Catlow Anticline, the upper part of the Pendleside Limestone in Nursery Beck [7486 5962] near Fair Hill, contains sphalerite veinlets. Sphalerite together with calcite occurs in small veins [7192 5709] associated with faults trending N310°E in Upper Bowland Shales near Collyholme Wood.

Higher in the Namurian sequence a vein [7269 6380 to 7280 6375] trending N295°E in sandstone of the Roeburndale Formation, south of Dovenanter End, was worked from a shaft; traces of galena and silicified sandstone are present in the spoil. Baryte and calcite were recorded by the Primary Survey on a fault trending N010°E in Roeburndale Formation siltstones and sandstones exposed in a beck [7086 6697] near Mewith Head. Traces of galena and pyrite are present in calcite-filled joints in sandy siltstones within the Accerhill Sandstone, at a depth of 72.9 to 73.0 m in the Knott Coppy Borehole [7698 6449].

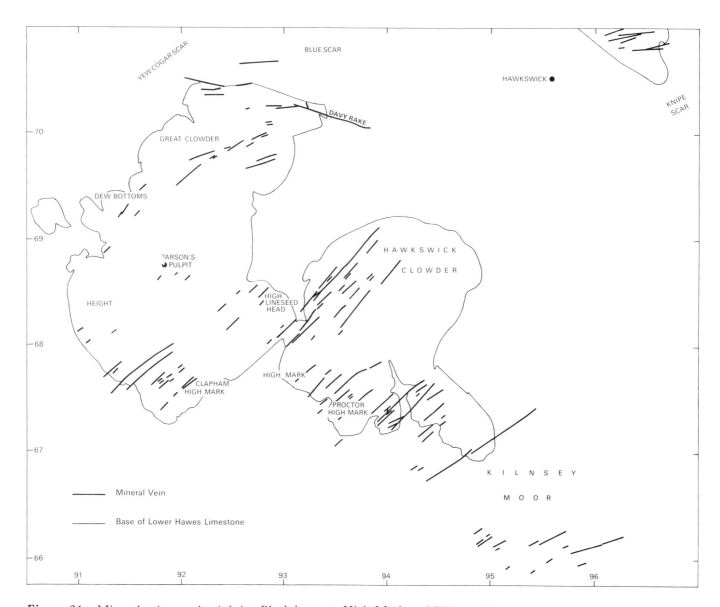

Figure 31 Mineral veins on the Askrigg Block between High Mark and Kilnsey Moor

Table 1 Mineralogy of vein groups in the High Mark and High Hill–Pikedaw Hill areas, with nature of host and wall rock alteration indicated

Vein group	Principal ore mined	Host rock	Ore minerals		Gangue	Wall rock alteration
			Primary	Secondary		
Kilnsey Moor Veins	Pb	Gordale Limestone	Galena*	Malachite	Baryte* Calcite*	
High Mark Vein Complex [Flock Rake to Barstows Kilnsey Moor]	Pb	Hardraw Scar Limestone Gayle Limestone Hawes Limestone Gordale Limestone	Galena* Chalcopyrite Sphalerite	Malachite	Baryte* Calcite* Fluorite Quartz	minor dolomitisation
Blue Scar–Low Cote Moor Veins, including Davy Rake	Pb	Gayle Limestone Hawes Limestone Gordale Limestone	Galena* Chalcopyrite	Smithsonite	Baryte* Calcite*	
Hawkswick–Knipe Scar Veins [Southern extension of Middlesmoor Vein complex, Hawes distrct]	Pb	Gayle Limestone Upper Hawes Limestone	Galena*		Baryte* Calcite* Fluorite*	
Pikedaw–Grizedales Veins	Cu Pb Zn	Hawes Limestone Gordale Limestone	Galena* Sphalerite	Azurite* Malachite* Anglesite Smithsonite*	Quartz* Baryte* Calcite* Aragonite Pyrite	Extensive silicification
Little Scar–Great Scar Veins	Pb	Hawes Limestone Gordale Limestone	Galena*	Malachite	Baryte*	
Settle Scar–Back Scar Veins	Pb	Hardraw Scar Limestone Gayle Limestone Hawes Limestone Gordale Limestone	Galena*	Malachite	Baryte*	
Ben Scar–Attermire Scar Veins	Pb	Gordale Limestone	Galena* Chalcopyrite	Anglesite Cerussite Azurite Malachite Smithsonite	Quartz* Baryte* Calcite* Witherite Pyrite	Silicification and minor dolomitisation
High Hill Veins	Pb	Gayle Limestone Hawes Limestone	Galena*	Smithsonite	Baryte* Quartz	Extensive dolomitisation and minor silicification
High South Bank Veins	Pb	Hawes–Hardraw Scar Limestone Gordale Limestone	Galena*	Malachite	Baryte*	Silicification

* denotes principal minerals present. For locations see Figures 31 and 32.
Information from this survey and BGS records, with inclusion of data from Raistrick, 1938.

DISSEMINATED MINERALISATION

This mineralisation includes disseminated metasomatic replacement by primary sulphide minerals, presumably related to the main phase of vein-mineralisation, together with small void and veinlet infilling by secondary minerals. Minor disseminated sphalerite and chalcopyrite, with secondary minerals smithsonite, malachite and azurite, occur in dolomitised and silicified Dinantian limestones in the High Hill–Scaleber area. Disseminated galena and pyrite are present in Ordovician strata of the Austwick–Ribblesdale inlier.

Details

At High Hill an exposure [8300 6350] of replacement dolostone in reef limestone contains disseminated chalcopyrite with secondary malachite and azurite; smithsonite is present in small cavities and veinlets in dolomitised reef limestone nearby (Wadge and others, 1983). On the east bank [8414 6272] of Scaleber Beck sphalerite is present over a small area in cherty Scaleber Quarry Limestone near its contact with the Scaleber Boulder Bed; the zinc content of the limestone has been estimated at up to 8 to 10 per cent (Wadge and others, 1983). Downstream, near Scaleber Bridge, an exposure [8413 6258] of partly silicified Scaleber Quarry Limestone contains traces of smithsonite filling small cavities (Wadge and others, 1983).

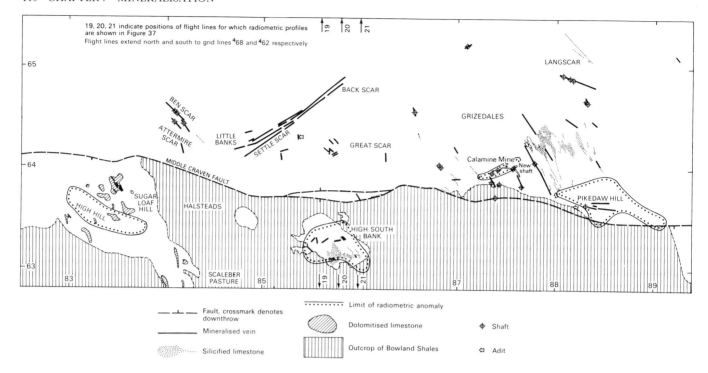

Figure 32   Mineralisation features of the transition zone between High Hill and Pikedaw Hill

In the Norber Formation (Ordovician) on the south side of Wharfe Gill [7814 6910], an impure limestone is patchily dolomitised and contains disseminated galena. At Douk Ghyll [8139 7237], just within the Hawes district, disseminated galena with pyrite occurs in the 6 m of siliceous conglomerate at the base of the Norber Formation.

CAVERN DEPOSITS

An unusual deposit of a smithsonite (calamine) sediment, geopetally filling a cavern system known as the Pikedaw Calamine Mine, was discovered during copper mining in 1788 and was worked until 1830. A comprehensive account of the deposit and the mine are given by Raistrick (1954). In 1806 a shaft was sunk into the centre of the cavern system to avoid the difficult access through the copper workings and to aid extraction. This shaft [8757 6400] (referred to as the 'new shaft'), rediscovered in 1944 (Gemmel and Myers, 1952), lies close to the Malham–Settle bridleway.

The smithsonite occurred in chambers, referred to by the miners as the 104 yard, 44 yard and 84 yard (according to their length); the deposit was 0.9 to 1.8 m deep. In the 84 yard cavern the smithsonite was sealed under a stalagmite floor. Dunham and Wilson (1985) estimated that up to 15 000 tons of smithsonite may have been present in the caverns, and that total production for the years of mining was 5000 tons. Remnants of the smithsonite sediment are still present between boulders on the cavern floor and filling cavities adjacent to the main caverns. It varies in colour from creamy white to buff, and consists of flakes and platelets ranging from 0.25 to 4 mm in diameter; XRD analysis of six samples of this sediment by Mr B. Humphreys confirmed the smithsonite composition.

Limonite (ochre), filling cavities, was worked at about the same time as the calamine. The main deposit occurred at Twinbottom Scar, some 210 m north-east of the Calamine Mine 'new shaft'. According to Raistrick (1954) the deposit occupied a cavity developed along a bedding plane; the limonite, some 0.6 to 0.9 m thick, was extracted from an area about 91 m long and 18 to 27 m wide.

LIMESTONE REPLACEMENT

The replacement of limestone by dolomite and or silica is evident locally in the Dinantian limestones of both the Askrigg Block and the Craven Basin, particularly in the transition zone. Although most of this replacement postdates the intra-Carboniferous faulting episodes, there has also been some minor early diagenetic replacement. Bedded dolomicrites in the 'mixed laminites' of the Chapel House Limestone, for example (Plate 4d), are interpreted as originating from penecontemporary dolomitisation in a supratidal environment. Chert, confined to certain lithostratigraphical units (i.e. Thornton Limestone, Pendleside Limestone, Hardraw Scar Limestone), was an early replacement. Allied with its formation is the small-scale silica replacement that occurs throughout the basinal Dinantian limestones. This silicification replaces bioclasts internally, particularly crinoid plates and shell fragments, with mosaic and chalcedonic quartz (see Plates 9e, f and 19c).

Later, metasomatic replacement of the Dinantian limestones occurs as wall-rock alteration adjacent to mineral veins, and accompanies zones of shearing and faulting. Larger replacement bodies, some crudely concordant with the bedding, are commonly directly associated with mineralised fractures, as for example in the silicified

Plate 27 Malham Formation limestone replaced by silica, Great Scar, Settle [8687 6376]. Irregular replacement bodies in Gordale Limestone. (L 2756)

limestone at High South Bank (Figure 32 and Plate 27); elsewhere however, some of the replacement dolostones (e.g. Smearsett Scar), do not appear to be linked to any particular fracture, although they occur in areas adjacent to faulted ground. Fluids responsible for the replacement probably migrated from the fractures along favourable horizons.

Dolomitisation and silicification of the Pendleside Limestone in the How Hill area, and elsewhere along the outcrop, are joint controlled and not always associated with faulting. The most extensive alteration occurs in limestone beneath the Bowland Shales contact; replacement of the limestone in such areas may have been caused by the shales impeding the flow of silica- and magnesium-bearing fluids. It is significant that the large areas of replacement adjoining the Middle Craven Fault (Figure 32), have strong structural controls, and are confined to ground where Bowland Shales overlap.

Silicification and dolomitisation occur together in places producing mixed replacement zones (e.g. How Hill). However, one phase is usually dominant or even exclusive of the other; for example, close to the Middle Craven Fault, the replacement between Grizedales and High South Bank (Figure 32) is dominated by silicification, whereas replacement bodies farther west at High Hill and Scaleber are dominated by dolomitisation.

Evidence from replacement bodies in the Pikedaw Hill–Grizedales area suggests that the silicification may have been later than the dolomitisation, for petrographic sections from zones of silicification [8795 6375] west of Pikedaw Hill show that quartz commonly pseudomorphs dolomite rhombs. The same relationship was also suggested by Wadge and others (1983) for the replacements at How Hill.

Details

The most conspicuous area of exposed surface replacement dolostone occurs in the High Hill–Scaleber area (Figure 32) be-

tween the Middle and South Craven faults; several lithostratigraphical units are affected including the Scaleber Quarry Limestone, Gordale Limestone, marginal reef limestone, Hawes Limestone and the Scaleber Boulder Bed. The dolostone is buff to light brown, compact or vughy, crossed by small calcite veins, and contains subordinate quartz which generally lines the vughs. The form of the dolomite replacement varies from strongly discordant to crudely concordant. Discordant replacement is well exposed at Scaleber and on the south side of High Hill. An example at the latter locality has a dyke-like outcrop [8316 6338 to 8323 6322], some 190 m long by 45 m wide. The discordant replacements are aligned north-west–south-east or NNW–SSE, parallel to the dominant fracture-trends in the area. Larger, crudely concordant replacements [8337 6370] occur just north of High Hill, west of Sugar Loaf Hill. Here the dolomite occupies an exposed area of some 4.3 hectares, but is divided into irregularly shaped masses, with areas up to 1.65 hectares. The replacement dolostone at the above localities includes both euhedral (Plate 19g) and subhedral mosaics. Where partial replacement occurs, remnants of the previous limestone fabric are clearly discernible (Plate 19h). Mr Humphreys reports that the dolostones from this area are composed of ferroan dolomite, which commonly shows the curved crystal faces and cleavages and the sweeping extinction indicative of hydrothermal 'saddle' dolomite (Radke and Mathis, 1980). The dolomite fabrics are commonly overprinted by patchy dedolomitisation, and the rock altered to non-ferroan calcite.

Weak silicification occurs in the High Hill–Scaleber area affecting the Scaleber Quarry Limestone [8413 6258], reef limestone of the Malham Formation [8333 6340], and Hawes Limestone [8355 6369].

Large areas of silica replacement occur adjacent to the Middle Craven Fault between High South Bank and Grizedales (Figure 32). In the Grizedales area the silicification occurs in the Gordale, Hawes and Gayle limestones, is strongly discordant, and forms parallel sets of dyke-like masses with a preferred NW–SE orientation (Plate 27). Some of the silicification occurs as wall-rock alteration of mineral veins, but along other fractures the replacement is present without the vein mineralisation. The discordant masses locally coalesce to form replacive zones of irregular outline. Between these replacive bodies silicification along joints is common.

More isolated silicified fractures, also with a NW–SE orientation, occur in the Langscar area [8832 6509] to the north-east of Grizedales, and also farther west [8700 6408] towards Great Scar. Close to the Great Scar area [8689 6376] silicification also occurs near to and on the Middle Craven Fault; it is particularly well developed at Crutching Close [8613 6370] where a compact quartz-rock is exposed.

On High South Bank (Figure 32), silicification in the Gordale Limestone occurs both in discordant dyke-like bodies with a NW–SE orientation [e.g. 8600 6310] and as a crudely concordant replacement which covers some 1.6 hectares.

The silicified limestone in the High South Bank–Grizedales area forms crags and ridges. The rock is dark brown, and replacement varies from partial to total (described by Orme, 1974, as quartzose limestone and quartz rock respectively). Unaltered pods of limestone within silicified zones generally contain abundant disseminated bipyramidal quartz euhedra. Weathering of the silicified limestone generally leaches any unaltered limestone, producing a porous 'rottenstone'. Mr Humphreys has examined thin-sections of the silicified limestone near Pikedaw Hill; he reports complex fabrics involving quartz-rhombs, doubly terminated euhedra, quartz laths, mosaic quartz and microcrystalline granular quartz; the crystals have calcite inclusions, commonly in discrete zones. Although dolomite is rare in these rocks, the presence of quartz rhombs, similar rhombs filled by limonite and calcite, and rhombic voids, attest to its former occurrence.

Between the Middle and North Craven faults, partial and complete stratiform dolomitisation affects the basal 20 m of the Gordale Limestone at Smearsett Scar [8000 6788] and an exposure [7964 6810] north-west of the Scar at a slightly higher stratigraphical level. Crudely stratiform dolomite replacement locally affects the Cove Limestone in crags [8118 6744] WNW of Little Stainforth, where surface weathering has caused partial disaggregation of the dolostone.

Crudely concordant dolomitisation also occurs near the Malham Formation–Kilnsey Formation boundary in Stainforth railway cutting [8226 6671 to 8233 6637]. Dolomitised limestone at a similar stratigraphical level was proved in the Lower Winskill Borehole [8259 6670] between 88.0 and 129.0 m below surface. Also in this borehole, grainstones in the Chapel House Limestone are partly to wholly dolomitised over 34 m (178.0 to 212.0 m depth). Stratiform replacement by dolomite of Chapel House Limestone is exposed [8183 6709] in the River Ribble south of Stainforth Force, but is confined to a bed 1.7 m thick. Small areas of replacement dolostone occur in the Lower Hawes Limestone on the South Craven Fault scarp [7872 6651] at Common Scars (Giggleswick Scar).

North of the North Craven Fault dolomitisation is conspicuous in the Skythorns quarries where exposures [e.g. 9720 6495, 9730 6487 and 9730 6458] show discordant to poorly concordant replacement dolostones up to 25 m thick in the Cove Limestone. Adjacent to the fault in Gordale Beck [910 658] grainstones of the Chapel House Limestone are heavily dolomitised, and in the Chapel House Borehole [9726 6647], some 2.2 km north of the North Craven Fault, these limestones are totally dolomitised over a thickness of 11 m (69.0 to 80.0 m depth).

In the Craven Basin, the Thornton Limestone intermittently shows discordant dolomitisation associated with minor silicification over a 3 km tract WNW of Airton. The replacement occurs in grainstones immediately north of, and within 1 km of, the South Craven–Winterburn faults and is exposed in stream sections and crags [8695 5996 to 8703 5990, 8683 6021 to 8692 6000 and 8729 5989] north-west, north and east of Orms Gill Green, in quarries [8887 5961 and 8902 5965] near Low Scarth Barn, and also [8944 6010 and 8953 6017 to 8957 6015] near Dykelands, Kirkby Malham.

On the north-western limb of the Slaidburn Anticline, the Pendleside Limestone is partly dolomitised in exposures [7221 5552 to 7230 5556] on the shore of Stocks Reservoir and in a gully [7185 5543] near Hollins House. Limestone conglomerate of the Pendleside Limestone in the Catlow Anticline shows minor dolomitisation and silicification, as in the River Hodder [7192 5751] near Collyholme. At How Hill near Halsteads, limestones of the Pendleside Limestone are replaced [7457 5941 to 7462 5970] near their contact with the Lower Bowland Shales, and dolomitised and silicified limestone stand out as ribs and crags over a distance of some 400 m on the eastern side of the hill. The Pendleside Limestone is extensively replaced by silica in White Syke [7047 5830] near Lamb Hill Farm.

ORIGIN AND AGE OF MINERALISATION

Lead-zinc-fluorite-baryte mineralisation in the southern Askrigg Block, as in the Alston Block and the South Pennine (Derbyshire) Orefield, belongs to a low temperature hydrothermal form of mineralisation known as the 'Mississippi Valley' type (Heyl, 1969; Heyl and others, 1974). Temperatures of the hydrothermal fluids, based on fluid-inclusion studies of fluorite from the Grassington and Upper Wharfedale area (Rogers, 1978), are between 92 and 160°C. In the Settle district, fluorite is present only in the Knipe Scar and some of the High Mark veins that lie along the western margin of the fluorite zone. The rest of the Askrigg Block within the district lies in the lower temperature baryte and calcite zones (Dunham, 1934; Dunham and Stubblefield, 1945; Dunham and Wilson, 1985). The fluid-inclusion studies also indicate that the mineralising hydrothermal fluids were hypersaline brines, six times more saline than sea-water (Rogers, 1978; Dunham and Wilson, 1985; see also Sawkins, 1966). The origin and mobilisation of the mineralising fluids is still a matter of conjecture, numerous mechanisms having been suggested (see summary in Dunham, 1974b; Dunham and Wilson, 1985). A current view (Rogers, 1978) is that they originated as heated brines which were expelled from the Craven Basin into the fractured Carboniferous strata of the Askrigg Block.

No precise age for the primary mineralisation is available. The lead isotope dates of Moorbath (1962) are now discredited, and more recent age determinations of galena from Greenhow and Skyreholme (Mitchell and Krouse, 1971) are considered to be unrealistic since anomalous Joplin-type radiogenic lead is involved. On stratigraphical grounds, Dunham and Wilson suggested a Stephanian to Thuringan (Zechstein) interval for the main pulse of hydrothermal mineralisation.

The production of the secondary minerals, in an oxidation zone affected by vadose meteoric waters, is a much later phase. The depths of the oxidation zone in parts of the Askrigg Block indicate that the controlling water table was appreciably lower than at present, and this led Dunham and Wilson to suggest that the secondary mineralisation took place during a drier climate sometime before the Pleistocene, though the smithsonite sediment of the Pikedaw Calamine caverns is almost certainly a Quaternary deposit. They also speculated that this sediment was either derived directly from a massive smithsonite deposit or represents a direct precipitate from carbonated waters carrying zinc. DJCM

CHAPTER 8

Geophysical investigations

Regional gravity and aeromagnetic surveys have been carried out in the district; Bouguer gravity anomaly variations yield information on the larger geological structures, although the Craven faults are only partially defined. An area considerably greater than that of the Settle district (Figure 33) has been selected to provide a setting for the regional geophysical interpretation; this is referred to here as the 'Settle region'.

In addition to the regional surveys, a detailed airborne geophysical survey using magnetic, electromagnetic and radiometric methods was carried out in 1973 in the Askrigg Block–Craven Basin transition zone as part of the Survey's Mineral Reconnaissance Programme (Wadge and others, 1983). Other parts of this programme in the Craven Basin included a detailed ground geophysical survey at How Hill, Halsteads, and a seismic reflection survey across the South Craven Fault near Hellifield.

PHYSICAL PROPERTIES OF ROCKS

The densities of the main rock types within the Settle region are summarised in Table 2. For the purposes of interpreting the gravity data a broad distinction is made for the Carboniferous sediments between higher density limestones and lower density shales and sandstones, with the known older basement rocks having a density similar to, or greater than, the limestones. The change within the Carboniferous sequence is considered to occur at the base of the Namurian on the Askrigg Block and at the base of the Worston Shales in the Craven Basin.

There is little contrast between the densities of the Dinantian calcareous sediments and the various underlying basement rocks, although the Ingleton Group rocks encountered in the Beckermonds Scar Borehole (Figure 33) (Wilson and Cornwell, 1982) have a particularly high value. These rocks are also exceptional in that they are the only known examples of magnetic rocks within the Settle region and have an average susceptibility of 0.031 SI units, equivalent to a magnetite content of about 1 per cent.

Although the Carboniferous sediments are typically too weakly magnetised to produce detectable magnetic anomalies, high sensitivity measurements have shown that the Dinantian limestones retain a weak, but consistent, remanent magnetisation which has been investigated intensively to provide information on palaeomagnetic field directions (Turner, 1975a; Turner and Tarling, 1975; Turner and others, 1979; Palmer and others, 1985), and the origin of the magnetisation (Turner, 1975b). Samples from various limestone units, including the Great Scar Limestone (partly equivalent to the Malham Formation), the Pendleside and the Chatburn limestones, were examined by Turner and Tarling (1975) and found to have remanent magnetisations with intensities of 0.3 to 2.0×10^{-3} A/m, apparently due to

depositional magnetite. The directions of magnetisation of these sediments are consistent with the conclusion that the British Isles were located near the palaeo-Equator in Dinantian (Lower Carboniferous) time (Turner and Tarling, 1975). Turner and others (1979) subsequently showed that the magnetisations of Dinantian limestones from the Craven Basin were complex, with some rocks being remagnetised before Permo-Carboniferous folding. The palaeomagnetic results for the Pendleside Limestone were found to be different from those for the Draughton Limestone, despite the geological evidence for the contemporaneity of these two units (Hudson and Mitchell, 1937). Addison and others (1985) described how the magnetic properties of the Pendleside Limestone could have been affected by dolomitisation and silicification.

Velocity determinations carried out on samples of Dinantian strata from boreholes near Settle gave an average value of 6.1 ± 0.3 km/s for a predominantly limestone sequence. This is near the maximum value recorded during seismic reflection surveys in the same area (see below), the lower survey values probably being more indicative of a greater proportion of argillaceous rocks than massive limestone; Banks and Gurbuz (1984) reported a value of 5.25 km/s for Lower Carboniferous limestones, based on long seismic refraction profiles. They also reported a velocity of 5.98 km/s for Ordovician sediments (Ingleton Group), very similar to the average value of samples of the pre-Carboniferous basement rocks in the Beckermonds Scar Borehole, and a lower velocity (5.64 km/s) for Silurian rocks.

REGIONAL GRAVITY SURVEYS

The Bouguer gravity anomaly data for the Settle region are based on BGS surveys carried out at various times, and include a resurvey of the area around the Craven faults initially described by Whetton and others (1956). Elevation control for most of the gravity stations was provided by Ordnance Survey bench marks and spot heights; for a few stations on the moorland of the Askrigg Block, tacheometric or barometric levelling was made. The density of 2.58 Mg/m^3 used for the Bouguer correction is a compromise value, and could be excessive for areas of thick Namurian sediments and possibly too low for areas of massive limestone; however, this figure was found to be reasonable for the Askrigg Block. The Bouguer anomalies shown in Figures 33 and 34 include recent data additional to that shown in the published 1:250 000 scale maps, mainly the Lake District sheet (Institute of Geological Sciences, 1977).

The Bouguer anomaly values vary between − 10 mGal and + 14 mGal and there is no simple contour pattern (Figure 33). The northern margin of the map truncates a series of Bouguer anomaly lows which are separated from an oval-shaped low centred south-west of Westhouse [66 73] by an elongated south-east-trending zone of high Bouguer anomaly values closing near Settle. Another zone of high values trends towards the north-east from near the south-western extremity of the region. A broad area of low Bouguer anomaly values in the extreme south-east of the region is interrupted by a few low-amplitude ENE-trending anomalies.

Many of the main features of the Bouguer gravity anomaly map have been described and interpreted by Whetton and others (1956) and Wadge and others (1983). In the latter publication, a residual Bouguer anomaly map of the Craven Basin area was presented in which a regional westward increase of about 0.2 mGal/km was removed from the observed gravity data in order to emphasise anomalies of more local origin.

In the original geophysical survey of the Askrigg Block – Craven Basin transition zone ('Craven faults area'), Whetton and others (1956) ascribed the Bouguer anomaly low centred over the Askrigg Block to low-density, acid crystalline rocks of probable Precambrian age. The absence of a clear Bouguer anomaly over the Craven faults was also commented on, and the northward decrease in anomaly values appearing near Malham [90 68] was interpreted as being due to the rise of 'Ingletonian/Precambrian' rocks with a density lower than the Lower Palaeozoic sediments farther south. The Bouguer anomaly low over the Askrigg Block, represented in part along the northern margin of Figure 33, was later described by Bott (1961) and Myers and Wardell (1967) as being caused by a granitic intrusion in the pre-Carboniferous basement, and this interpretation subsequently was proved to be correct by the Raydale Borehole (Dunham, 1974a). The main central cupola of this intrusion, known as the Wensleydale Granite, is responsible for the Bouguer anomaly low near Kidstones [94 82], but the concealed intrusion probably continues at greater depth both westwards and eastwards, giving rise to the lows on Gayle Moor [79 82] and near Horsehouse [SE 05 82]. The Bouguer

anomaly gradients flanking the central low are particularly pronounced around and to the east of the Beckermonds Scar Borehole [864 802] where the main magnetic anomalies also occur (Figure 36), suggesting that the magnetite-bearing sediments may have a particularly large density contrast with the granite.

The zone of high Bouguer anomaly values extending from Casterton Fell [66 80] to an area east of Settle [84 64] is terminated to the south-west along much of its length by the pronounced gradient associated with the western part of the South Craven Fault system. The zone of high values appears to be associated with Ingleton Group rocks (especially those of Chapel le Dale) rather than with the upper Ordovician and Silurian sediments of Ribblesdale, although this is not strongly supported by the density data (Table 2), (see Bott *in* discussion of Whetton and others, 1956). Such an association would suggest that Ingleton Group rocks also form the basement beneath the high lying east of Settle [84 64], and possibly also beneath the area of high values south-west of the South Craven Faults system in the Forest of Bowland area (Figure 33).

The sharp change in Bouguer anomaly values across the western part of the South Craven Fault System is caused by the juxtaposition of Silesian strata and the higher density Dinantian and underlying basement rocks of the Askrigg Block. The amplitude of the step-like anomaly reaches a maximum of about 8 mGal near Ingleton [69 74] (Figure 33) where the gradient has a value of 4.0 mGal/km. This combination of amplitude and gradient values implies a near-surface (less than 0.7 km) source for the anomaly, and it is apparent that the isolated Westphalian basin forming the Ingleton Coalfield (Ford, 1954) contributes to the anomaly. The positions of the minimum Bouguer anomaly values suggest that the greatest thickness of low density strata occurs about 2.5 km south-west of the South Craven Fault. The elongated low extending north-westwards from near Settle is ascribed to thick Namurian strata and to the Westphalian

Table 2 Density values for the main rock types of the Settle region

Rock type	Density (Mg/m^3)	Number of sites sampled
Carboniferous		
Silesian		
Westphalian	2.45 (Assumed value)	
Namurian sandstones	2.42[2]*	
	2.39[2]	3
Dinantian		
Limestones	2.69[1,2]	4
Lower Bowland Shales	2.54[2]*	
Silurian		
Various lithologies	2.70*	
'Sandstones and flags' (siltstones)	2.74[2]	2
Mudstones	2.75[1]	3
Ordovician		
Tuffs and limestones	2.70[2]	2
Ingleton Group		
'Slates and grits' (sandstones)	2.68[3] (average)	unrecorded
'Slates'	2.67[2]	1
'Grits' (sandstones)	2.68[2]	1
Sandstones and siltstones (Beckermonds Scar Borehole)	2.78[1]	1

* Value derived from density traverse results
1 BGS data (including Wilson and Cornwell, 1982)
2 Whetton and others (1956)
3 Bott *in* Whetton and others (1956)

strata whose extension from the Ingleton Coalfield to near Austwick has been established in the Waters Farm Borehole during the resurvey.

The section of the South Craven Fault system east of Settle (AA′ of Figures 33 and 34) has no associated distinctive Bouguer anomaly feature, indicating that the rocks on either side of the faults have no large-scale density contrast. Detailed gravity observations within the area of the seismic survey (see below), however, revealed local variations of up to 1 mGal amplitude, some of which appear to be due to near-surface density changes across the fault-lines (Wadge and others, 1983).

In the south-eastern part of the region (Figure 33) the Bouguer anomaly map for the main part of the Craven Basin shows generally ENE-trending contours, with local highs corresponding broadly with anticlines in the Carboniferous

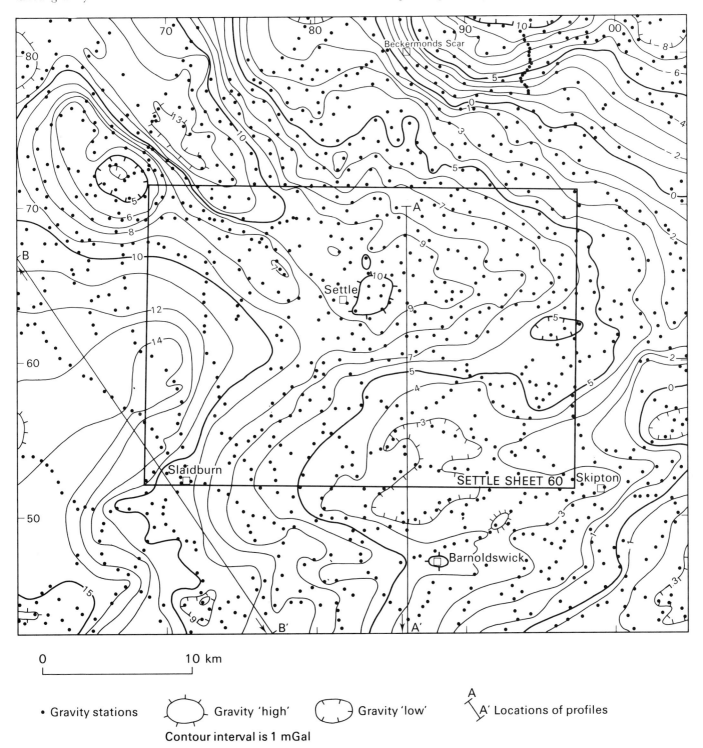

Figure 33 Bouguer gravity anomaly map of the Settle region

rocks. The amplitudes of these anomalies depend both upon the presence of Dinantian limestones in the cores of the folds and upon the size of the anticlines. Structures which are particularly well marked include the Skipton, Skyreholme, Eshton–Hetton and Thornton anticlines.

Although many of the minor variations on the Bouguer gravity anomaly map appear to reflect known geological structures, there are several difficulties in quantitatively interpreting these geophysical data to provide, for example, vertical sections. The main problem is the comparatively low amplitude of the anomalies compared with errors which might be introduced by the use of an incorrect density values for the main geological divisions. In addition the data available (Tables 2 and 3) are not sufficient to rule out the possibility of lateral density variations related to changes in lithostratigraphy.

THEORETICAL MODEL OF THE CRAVEN BASIN

The major structure of the Craven Basin can be examined using the Bouguer gravity data. Figure 34 shows two profiles, AA′ and BB′ (see Figure 33 for location), extending beyond the boundaries of the Settle region.

Profile AA′ extends southwards from the Askrigg Block across the Craven Basin to the Holme Chapel Borehole [8609 2878], where a Lower Palaeozoic basement of metamorphosed slates was proved at 1.7 km below OD. This borehole is situated on an east–west elongated Bouguer anomaly high, despite the considerable thickness (1.48 km) of lower-density Westphalian and Namurian strata proved there. These latter rocks have the effect of reducing the Bouguer anomaly value by about 12 mGal, using densities given in Table 2. As a basement geophysically similar to that in the Holme Chapel Borehole also occurs at the northern end of the profile in the Austwick-Ribblesdale Inlier, the background Bouguer anomaly needs to be reduced northwards to produce a consistent level for interpretative pur-

poses. In Profile AA′ a simple linear decrease has been assumed. The model shown in the lower part of the section has a gravity effect which, when added to the observed profile, produces values which are similar to the smooth background field shown in Figure 34.

The most interesting aspect of the model is the necessity for introducing low-density rocks in the area of the Craven Basin to produce a satisfactory interpretation. In Profile AA′ it has been assumed that these rocks form a downward extension of the basin, and include, in their upper part, the thick Dinantian sequence proved in the Swinden Borehole (Table 3). It is impossible from the gravity evidence alone to define the base of the Carboniferous, or even to decide if the underlying low-density rocks form part of the sedimentary basin fill; a granitic body, for example, could produce a similar gravity effect, although this is considered unlikely in such a basinal setting (Chapter 6). An alternative approach to the interpretation is to postulate the existence, beneath areas with high Bouguer anomaly values, of basement rocks with a density greater than 2.70 Mg/m^3. This could have the effect in Figure 34 of reducing the thickness of the unknown rocks with a density of 2.60 Mg/m^3, but a considerable thickness of Lower Palaeozoic and older sediments would still remain beneath the basin. The northern margin of this concealed basin coincides, fortuitously, with the South Craven Fault (Profile AA′ in Figure 34), and the southern margin coincides approximately with the edge of the Namurian basin. The interpretation of this latter margin is dependent upon the density adopted for the Namurian; for example, increasing the density would have the effect of reducing the thickness of low-density sediments required in the deep basin.

The second profile (BB′ in Figure 34) extends northwestwards from the Holme Chapel Borehole to the southeastern extremity of the Lake District where Lower Palaeozoic strata crop out. A linear background field between these two localities has again been assumed, and the model shown has been derived in the same way as Profile

Table 3 Density, porosity and velocity values for individual sites or boreholes (BH) in the Settle region. The Holme Chapel Borehole lies to the south of the area shown in Figure 33, but the logging results are relevant to the Settle district

Age	Lithology	Site grid reference (SD)	No. of Samples	Density Mg/m³		Effective porosity %	Saturated velocity km/s
				Saturated	Grain		
Carboniferous							
Namurian	Grit	847 601	2	2.45	2.66	12.7	3.84
	Various (Holme Chapel BH)	861 288					4.05[1]
Dinantian	Limestone	981 612	3	2.69 ± .01	2.70 ± .01	1.0 ± 0.3	6.54 ± 0.14
	Limestone (Chatburn)	756 437	5	2.70 ± 0	2.70 ± .01	0.3 ± 0.3	
	Various (Swinden No.1 BH)	860 505	—	2.61[1]	—	—	4.40[1]
	Various (Holme Chapel BH)	861 288	—				4.82[1]
Lower Palaeozoic							
Ludlow	Mudstone	814 696	3	2.76 ± .01	2.77 ± 0	0.5 ± 0.1	5.84 ± 0.24
	Mudstone	811 692	3	2.77 ± .01	2.77 ± 0	0.4 ± 0.2	6.02 ± 0.59
	Mudstone	815 692	2	2.71	2.78	3.7	5.70
Undifferentiated	Slates (Holme Chapel BH)	861 288					5.01[1]

[1]Data from geophysical borehole logs

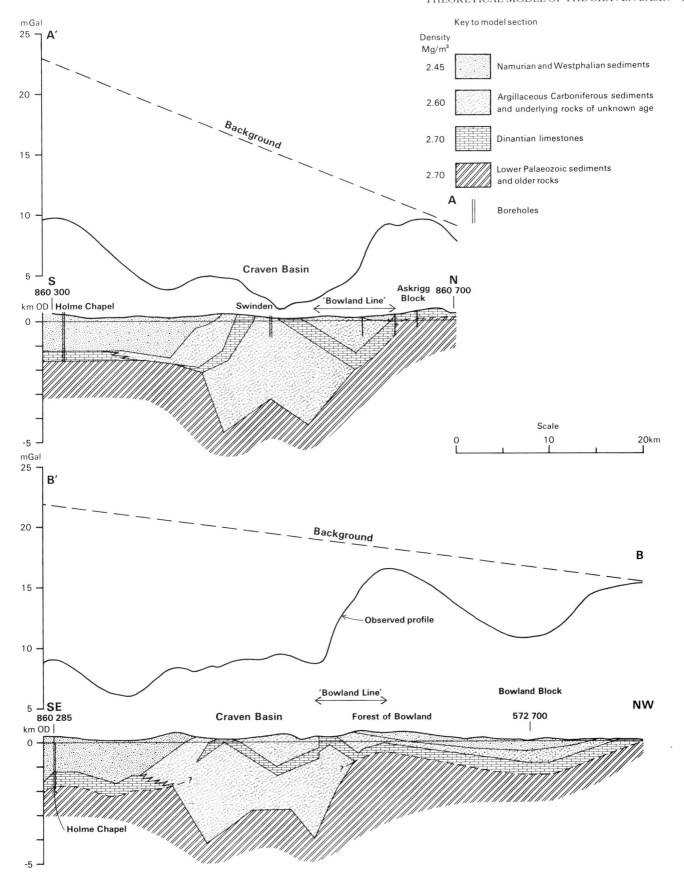

Figure 34 Bouguer anomaly profiles and theoretical models in the Settle region

AA′. The pronounced 'step' in Bouguer anomaly values near the Forest of Bowland provides stronger evidence for a density change at depth than is the case in Profile AA′, as it coincides with a structural high (the Slaidburn Anticline) in Carboniferous sediments. This Bouguer anomaly feature can be traced across the Settle region, reappearing on Profile AA′ near the position of the South Craven Fault system, and is believed to represent the gravity effect of a major ?pre-Carboniferous boundary, here named the 'Bowland Line' (Figure 35). It is tentatively suggested that the Middle Craven and North Craven faults may represent a response in the Carboniferous cover to movement on the Bowland Line.

The change in Bouguer anomaly values along the Bowland Line can be reproduced by the gravity effect of an inclined density boundary sloping down to the south or south-east. Although it cannot be located precisely from the gravity evidence, the position of the Bowland Line on Figure 35 has been taken at the approximate upper edge of the slope.

AEROMAGNETIC SURVEYS

The Settle region was included in the national aeromagnetic survey in 1958. Total magnetic field measurements were made at a mean terrain clearance of 305 m (1000 ft) along east–west flight lines 2 km apart, and north–south tie lines 10 km apart. The contoured data, shown in Figure 36, were published on the 1:250 000 scale map series, mainly the Lake District sheet (Institute of Geological Sciences, 1978).

The aeromagnetic map is dominated by the east–west elongated belt of positive anomalies across its northern edge and the associated gradient to the south. This gradient terminates in the magnetic low trending to the ENE in the southern part of the region, but to the east the values rise again.

The magnetic anomalies over the the Askrigg Block were first described by Bott (1961), who interpreted them as being due to magnetic pre-Carboniferous basement rocks flanking and draping the concealed Wensleydale Granite. The source of the anomaly at Beckermonds Scar [85 81] was subsequently drilled and proved to be magnetite-bearing sediments comparable in other ways to the Ingleton Group (Wilson and Cornwell, 1982). The presence of magnetite on this scale in Lower Palaeozoic sediments is unusual, and there has been discussion (in Wilson and Cornwell, 1982) as to whether it is a primary or secondary constituent. The magnetic sediments at Beckermonds Scar probably continue around the margin of the granite and give rise to the anomaly [91 78] east of Raisgill; they may extend westwards as far as Ribblehead [75 79], although the anomaly there is larger and is more remote from the concealed granite. The isolated anomaly in Coverdale [SE 02 79] is probably caused by a pipe-like body or isolated block of magnetic material.

The anomalies over the Askrigg Block indicate magnetic material at a depth of a few hundred metres, probably at the basement surface and part of a 200 km-long belt of magnetic anomalies extending from the Lake District to The Wash, the Furness-Ingleborough-Norfolk Ridge of Wills (1978). Part of the extension into the Lake District is just visible in the north-western corner of Figure 36, but the source material is considerably deeper there, the increase in depth

occurring along the line of the Dent Fault.

The magnetic gradient at the southern margin of the Askrigg Block anomalies indicates the presence of magnetic material dipping southwards to a considerable depth, perhaps as much as 8 to 12 km. It is probable, therefore, that the Craven Basin is underlain by a great thickness of Carboniferous and older sediments; the ENE-trend of the contours south-west of Slaidburn [70 50] suggests a structural trend similar to that of the Carboniferous at surface. The Craven Basin magnetic low is terminated in the east by south-trending contours, which indicate a rise in the magnetic basement that culminates north of Leeds, 25 km east of Skipton.

SEISMIC SURVEYS

In an attempt to determine the nature of the deeper part of the Craven Fault system, particularly the structure south of the Middle Craven Fault, a set of profiles was recorded, using the seismic reflection method, as part of the Survey's Mineral Reconnaissance Programme (Wadge and others, 1983, figs. 9–14). The results are of particular interest because very few reflection data are available for Lower Carboniferous sediments in Britain. The survey comprised three profiles, two in a north–south direction and one on an east–west tie-line, with a combined length of 8.9 km. On parts of the profiles clear reflectors were observed with arrival times of between 0.1s and 0.6s. As the average velocities derived from the seismic data are about 4 to 5 km/s, the reflecting horizons lie at depths down to 1.3 km, and include the Pendleside Sandstones, the Pendleside Limestone and possibly the base of the Worston Shales. Folds indicated on the seismic sections correlate well with those observed at surface, but the major structure of the South Craven Fault is not very apparent, perhaps because of the poor quality of the data in the northern parts of the two north–south profiles.

The structure of the upper crust in the northern part of the district has been investigated on a broader scale by seismic refraction surveys making use of quarry blasts as energy sources (Banks and Gurbuz, 1984). The survey results indicate structures that are similar to those predicted from the geological evidence. A refracting layer with a relatively high velocity of 6.2–6.3 km/s, at depths of about 3 km beneath the southern margin of the Askrigg Block, is interpreted as the more deeply buried part of the Ingleton Group.

ASKRIGG BLOCK–CRAVEN BASIN TRANSITION ZONE SURVEY

An airborne survey of the transition zone formed part of the Survey's Mineral Reconnaissance Programme (Wadge and others, 1983). It was carried out by helicopter along a total of 940 km of north–south flight lines spaced 200 m apart, between Settle and Pateley Bridge. Electromagnetic, magnetic and radiometric systems were employed (Burley and others, 1978) within the Settle district as shown in Figure 35.

Plots of the magnetic data reflect the regional anomaly pattern described above, and show no features of local interest.

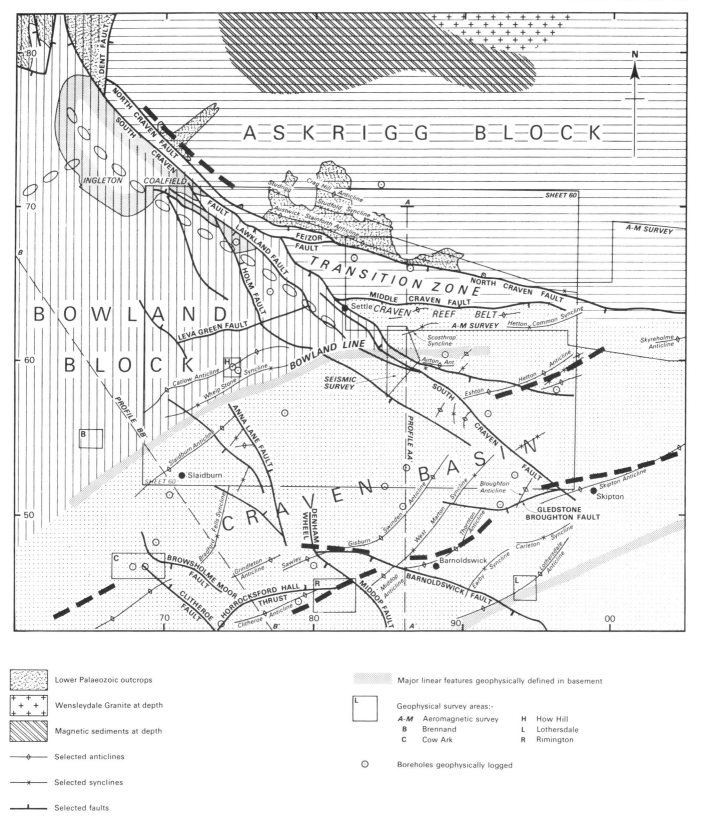

Figure 35 Summary map of geophysical features of the Settle region

Contours of the electromagnetic (EM) response show a number of features which are related to the local stratigraphy. In particular, the contact between the limestones of the Malham Formation and Wensleydale Group and the mudstones of the Bowland Shales is picked out at several localities between Settle and Threshfield Moor; there is a significant background response from the shales but the limestone offers little response. This effect is clearly seen along the line of the Middle Craven Fault west of Pikedaw Hill, near Malham, where mudstones and limestones are in faulted contact; and on the marginal reef limestones east of Malham which are onlapped by the mudstones. Along the line of the North Craven Fault the EM contours pick out the mudstone–limestone contact north-west of Threshfield Moor [950 645] and the faulted northern boundary of the Bowland Shales west of Black Hill [860 660].

The EM response of the Bowland Shales is locally intensified at a number of localities, and most of these anomalies were followed up with ground EM surveys. Examples occur at Linton Moor [975 620] and at Hetton Common [935 623]. The former anomaly probably occurs because the dip in the shales is locally higher against the flank of the reef limestone at Swinden, north-east of Rylstone, so providing a

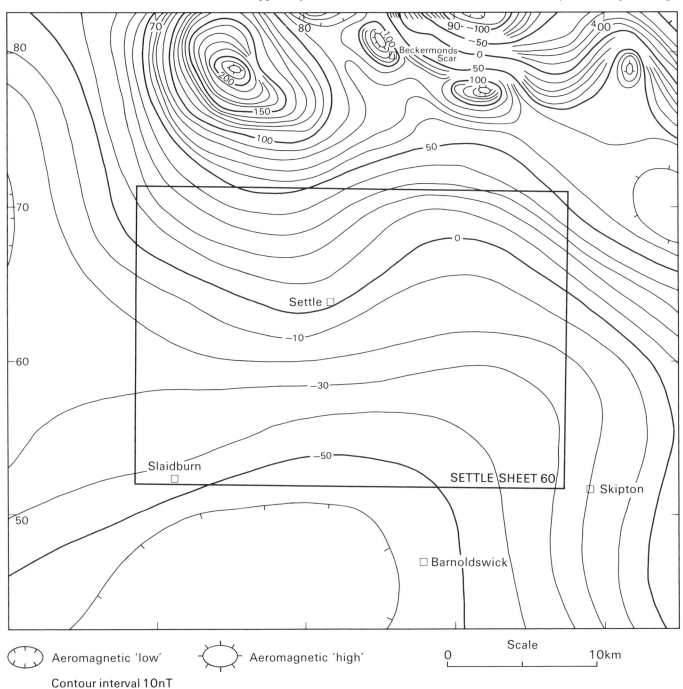

Figure 36 Aeromagnetic map of the Settle region

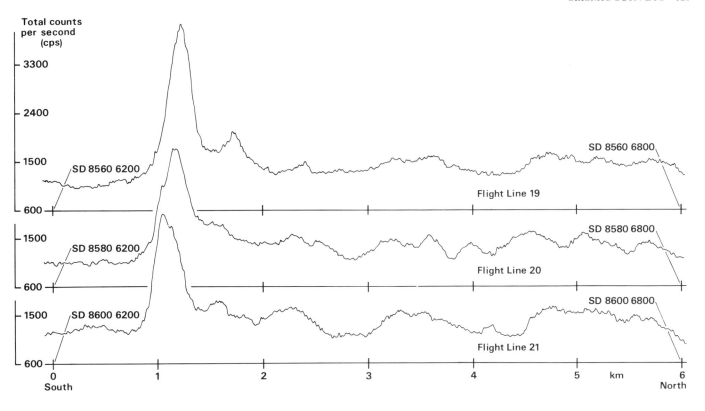

Figure 37   Airborne radiometric profiles east of Settle, showing the anomaly over High South Bank

more effective coupling between the bedding and the vertical-loop EM system employed in the airborne survey. The anomaly at Hetton Common cannot be explained by the known geology, for it trends east–west, cutting across the local strike. Its existence was confirmed by a ground EM survey, and further interest is provided by a series of geochemical stream sediment (panned concentrate) anomalies for Ba and Zn in Whetstone Gill; these anomalies do not continue upstream from the geophysical anomaly.

The airborne radiometric profiles across much of the survey area are irregular, and suggest that the data are not diagnostic of rock type. This may be because true response differences between rock types are obscured by the effects of variable drift cover. Data published by Ponsford (1955) indicate that the Bowland Shales can be expected to demonstrate an enhanced radioactivity and the purer Lower Carboniferous limestones notably low radioactivity. However, in the present area the most significant anomalies occur over limestones.

Three of the more prominent anomalies have been followed up with ground radiometric and soil sampling surveys (Wadge and others, 1983). The strongest anomaly occurs at High South Bank [856 632] over partially silicified Gordale Limestone (Figures 32 and 37) where it grades into a marginal reef facies (see Chapter 3). Other anomalies occur at High Hill [834 634], again over the Gordale Limestone (locally dolomitised) where it grades into reef facies; at Pikedaw Hill [884 637], also over the Gordale Limestone and close to an area of extensive silicification; and north of Kirkby Fell [875 640], over the Lower Hawes Limestone. With the exception of High Hill, the anomalies coincide with the sites of abandoned workings in Pb-Zn-Cu mineralisation (Figure 32). The anomalies are most readily seen on the total counts gamma spectrometer profile (Figure 37); in all cases the main response is in the part of the spectrum associated with uranium.

Subsequent ground surveys showed these radiometric anomalies to be very localised, with peak values declining abruptly over a few metres. At High South Bank, for example, the source of the anomaly appears to be concentrated in a 20 m wide east–west zone, with peak count rates of 150 μR/hr against a background of 10 μR/hr. Across this zone, soil samples collected on the same grid are anomalous for uranium, and are also significantly anomalous for Pb, Zn and Cu.

Insufficient data are available from the soil samples from High Hill and Pikedaw Hill to determine whether the same association of uranium and base metal mineralisation occurs at those localities.

The cause of these uranium concentrations remains unidentified. Peacock and Taylor (1966) showed that radiometric anomalies in Carboniferous limestones of similar age and setting at Castleton (Derbyshire) and Swinden (immediately east of the Settle district) [983 615] are caused by uraniferous collophane. Airborne radiometric data show anomalies at Swinden (though these are less prominent than those described above), over part of the Swinden reef limestone, and over nearby areas of Pendleside Limestone (the basinal equivalent of the Gordale and Cove limestones). Chemical analyses presented by Peacock and Taylor showed the concentrations of uranium in the rocks sampled to be closely related to the quantity of P_2O_5, suggesting that the presence of the uranium is indirectly due to the presence of impurities in the limestone related to changes in the depositional environment. In contrast, the association of uranium on High South Bank with concentrations of base metals suggests a hydrothermal origin, possibly involving scavenging of U from the base of the Cove Limestone (see below) by ascending fluids.

A geochemical drainage survey of the Craven Basin, carried out as part of the Mineral Reconnaissance Programme (Wadge and others, 1983), identified groups of stream sediment anomalies which were followed up with detailed soil sampling and/or geophyscial surveys to identify the source of the mineralisation. The only one of these survey locations within the district is at How Hill, near Halsteads in the Catlow Anticline, though a number of other locations lie close to the boundary of the district (Figure 35).

The survey at How Hill was intended to provide information on the structure of the rocks around the mineralised limestone exposed approximately 400 m north-east of Halsteads, and to test for the presence of any related sulphide mineralisation at depth. Induced polarisation (IP), apparent resistivity, and VLF-electromagnetic methods (Burley and others, 1978) were employed along a series of traverses approximately 100 m apart, to cover an area of approximately 1 km². The results are discussed in detail elswhere (Wadge and others, 1983). Briefly, the resistivity data identify the contact between the Pendleside Limestone and the overlying Lower Bowland Shales, and in places show this contact to be steep, and possibly faulted. Apparent resistivities for the mudstones range from about 20 Ωm to about 200 Ωm, and for the limestones from about 500 Ωm to about 3000 Ωm; the variable cover of drift probably accounts for the wide range of values observed over these two principal rock types. The VLF-EM data also identify the mudstone–limestone contacts, and support the interpretation of the resistivity data. The IP data show no significant anomalies and no clear pattern of background response which might be related to rock type. Weak anomalies occur in places over the exposed limestones but there is no indication that these rocks carry substantial mineralisation at depth.

BOREHOLE GEOPHYSICS

Geophysical measurements have been made in eleven boreholes in the Settle district. They comprise gamma-ray logs of six boreholes drilled as part of the Survey's assessment of limestone resources in the Craven Lowlands (Harrison, 1982) and in the Settle and Malham area (Murray, 1983); gamma-ray and IP apparent resistivity logs in two boreholes at How Hill, Halsteads, drilled as part of the Mineral Reconnaissance Programme (Wadge and others, 1983); and more comprehensive suites of logs run by a commercial contractor in boreholes at Lower Winskill, Black Hill and Knott Coppy. All of these borehole sites are indicated on Figure 35.

Perhaps the most interesting feature to be observed occurs in the Silverdale Borehole [8435 7143], just outside the district, and Lower Winskill Borehole [8259 6670], where the gamma-logs identify a radioactive horizon at approximately

the junction of the Cove Limestone and Kilnsey Limestone (Figure 38). Murray (1983) attributed these anomalies to phosphatic fossil debris, but the chemical analyses presented show no significant increase in P_2O_5 content of the limestones across the anomaly. Samples from the anomalous zone show a uranium content of 20 ppm, so that if the U/P_2O_5 relationship suggested by Peacock and Taylor (1966) were to hold, a P_2O_5 content of approximately 0.5 per cent would be expected. Association of the uranium with a particular stratigraphical level suggests a syngenetic origin, and Bell (1963) noted that syngenetic uranium is invariably contained within impurities adventitiously deposited with the host sediments. The possibility that this uranium has been partially re-mobilised, and deposited locally in reef limestones in the Settle – Malham area, has been noted above.

JDC, ADE

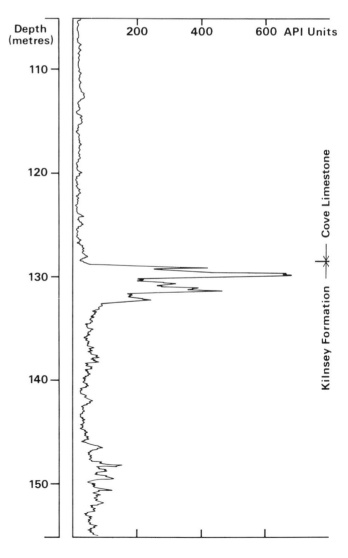

Figure 38 Gamma ray log for part of the Lower Winskill Borehole, showing response from uranium-rich limestones at the top of the Kilnsey Formation

APPENDIX 1

Six-inch geological maps and photographs

Six-inch geological maps

Six-inch geological maps included wholly or in part in the area of 1:50 000 Geological Sheet 60 are listed, with the dates of survey. The surveying officers were R. S. Arthurton, E. W. Johnson, L. C. Jones and D. J. C. Mundy. All maps are available for public reference at the library of the British Geological Survey at Keyworth, Nottingham, and with the exception of those marked with an asterisk, can be bought as dyeline copies. All lie within the 100-km National Grid square SD.

*65 NE	Croasdale Fell	RSA	1979
*65 SE	Dunsop Bridge	RSA	1979
*66 NE	High Bentham	EWJ	1978
*66 SE	Lythe Fell	EWJ	1978
*67 SE	Ingleton	EWJ	1978
75 NW	Catlow	RSA	1978
75 NE	Whelp Stone Crag	RSA	1978
75 SW	Slaidburn	RSA	1978–9
75 SE	Knotts	RSA	1979
76 NW	Clapham and Keasden	EWJ	1976–78
76 NE	Austwick	EWJ, DJCM	1976–79
76 SW	Bowland Knotts	EWJ	1978–79
76 SE	Black Bank and Wham	EWJ	1978
*77 SW	Ingleborough	EWJ	1978
*77 SE	Crummack Dale	EWJ, DJCM	1976–80
85 NW	Long Preston	DJCM, RSA	1977
85 NE	Hellifield	RSA	1977
85 SW	Paythorne	LCJ	1979
85 SE	Nappa	LCJ	1979
86 NW	Stainforth	DJCM, EWJ	1976–80
86 NE	Malham Tarn	EWJ, DJCM	1976–81
86 SW	Settle	DJCM, RSA	1977–80
86 SE	Kirkby Malham	DJCM, RSA	1976
*87 SW	Horton in Ribblesdale	EWJ	1976
*87 SE	Fountains Fell	EWJ	1976
95 NW	Airton	RSA	1976–77
*95 NE	Hetton	RSA	1977
95 SW	Gargrave	LCJ	1978
*95 SE	Skipton	LCJ	1978
96 NW	High Mark	LCJ, DJCM	1976
*96 NE	Kilnsey	LCJ	1977
96 SW	Gordale	DCJM, RSA	1976
*96 SE	Threshfield	RSA	1976
*97 SW	Arncliffe	LCJ	1977
*97 SE	Kettlewell	LCJ	1977

Geological photographs

Copies of photographs illustrating the geology of the Settle district are deposited for reference in the library of the British Geological Survey at Keyworth and at the BGS Information Office in the Geological Museum, Exhibition Road, London SW7 2DE. The majority of these belong to the L Series and were taken at the time of resurvey; the remainder belong to the earlier A series. The photographs depict details of the lithostratigraphy, particular geological features and also general views and scenery. Black and white prints and slides can be supplied at a fixed tariff and colour prints and transparencies are also available for all photographs.

APPENDIX 2

List of boreholes

The main borehole records for the district are listed by six-inch maps. Copies of these records may be obtained from the Keyworth office of the British Geological Survey at a fixed tariff. Each entry in the list shows first the permanent record number and location of the borehole, and then its stratigraphical range. Borehole names used in this account are shown in bold type. An asterisk indicates that borehole cores are curated by the British Geological Survey.

66 NE 3   [6909 6774]
Badger Ford Bridge, High Bentham
Roeburndale Formation

75 NW 2   [7469 5952]
How Hill No.1, Halsteads*
Pendleside Limestone
(Details published in Wadge and others, 1983)

75 NW 3   [7469 5962]
How Hill No.2, Halsteads*
Pendleside Limestone
(Details published in Wadge and others, 1983)

75 NW 4   [7460 5960]
How Hill No.3, Halsteads*
Pendleside Limestone
(Details published in Wadge and others, 1983)

75 NE 7   [7622 5760]
Dickinson's Heights, Tosside
Pendle Grit Formation

75 NE 12 [7794 5661]
Snape House, Tosside*
Pendleside Limestone
(Details published in Harrison, 1982)

75 SW 1   [7029 5123] (Clitheroe district)
Blue Butts Farm, Slaidburn*
Thornton Shales-with-Limestone including knoll-reef limestone
(Details published in Harrison, 1982)

76 NE 9   [7870 6722]
Feizor*
Wensleydale Group (?Simonstone – Upper Hawes Limestones)
(Details published in Murray, 1983)

76 NE 11   [7537 6763]
Waters Farm, Austwick*
Westphalian 'A' (including Listeri Marine Band)—Namurian (to the Cancellatum Marine Band)

76 SE 16   [7698 6449]
Knott Coppy, Eldroth*
Namurian strata above Accerhill Sandstone—Roeburndale Formation

85 SW 5   [8471 5194]
Dobbers Quarry, Paythorne*
Thornton Shales-with-Limestone including knoll-reef limestone
(Details published in Harrison, 1982)

85 SE 16   [8606 5301]
High Laithe, Nappa*
Thornton Limestone – Thornton Shales-with-Limestone
(Details published in Harrison, 1982)

86 NW 4   [8259 6670]
Lower Winskill*
Cove Limestone (Malham Formation) – Chapel House Limestone
(Details published in Murray, 1983)

86 NE 2   [8630 6628]
Black Hill*
Grassington Grit – Gordale Limestone (Malham Formation)

86 SW 3   [8030 6428]
Croft Closes, Giggleswick
Grassington Grit – Upper Bowland Shales

86 SW 5   [8421 6275]
Cominco S1, Scaleber Bridge*
Scaleber Boulder Bed (Pendleside Limestone) – Scaleber Force Limestone

86 SW 6   [8491 6345]
Cominco S2, Low Barn, Stockdale Beck*
Malham Formation – Scaleber Force Limestone

86 SW 7   [8309 6330]
Cominco S9, Preston's Barn, Settle*
Malham Formation including marginal reef limestone – Scaleber Force Limestone

86 SW 8   [8360 6304]
Cominco S10, Preston's Barn, Settle*
Lower Bowland Shales – Scaleber Force Limestone

86 SE 1   [8601 6350]
Cominco S3, Rye Loaf Hill, Stockdale*
Upper Bowland Shales – Kilnsey Limestone

86 SE 2   [8606 6470]
Cominco S4, Great Scar, Stockdale*
Hardraw Scar Limestone (Wensleydale Group) – Gordale Limestone (Malham Formation)

86 SE 3 [8701 6432]
Cominco S5, Grizedales*
Hardraw Scar Limestone (Wensleydale Group) – Gordale Limestone (Malham Formation)

86 SE 4   [8770 6360]
Cominco S6, Kirkby Fell*
Pendle Grit Formation – Upper Bowland Shales

86 SE 5   [8590 6340]
Cominco S11, Rye Loaf Hill, Stockdale*
Lower Bowland Shales – Malham Formation

86 SE 6   [8541 6378]
Stockdale Farm (Cominco S7), Stockdale*
Kilnsey Limestone (Kilnsey Formation) – Stockdale Farm
Formation

86 SE 7   [8562 6352]
Cominco S8, Stockdale*
Middle Limestone (Wensleydale Group) – Chapel House
Limestone

86 SE 8   [8867 6031]
High Ings Barn, Airton*
Thornton Limestone – Thornton Shales-with-Limestone
(Details published in Harrison, 1982)

87 SE 9   [8435 7143] (Hawes district)
Silverdale*
Gayle/Upper Hawes limestones (Wensleydale Group) – Horton
Formation (Silurian); including Malham Formation, Kilnsey For-
mation and Chapel House Limestone
(Details published in Murray, 1983)

95 NW 4   [9309 5703]
St. Helen's Well, Eshton
Thornton Limestone

95 NW 7   [9166 5660]
Throstle Nest, Eshton*
Worston Shales including 'Haw Crag Boulder Bed' – Thornton
Limestone
(Details published in Harrison, 1982)

95 NE 1   [9629 5813]
Park Laithe, Rylstone*
Limestone within Worston Shales including Hetton Beck
Limestone – Thornton Limestone
(Details published in Harrison, 1982)

95 NE 2   [9553 5896]
Grimes Gill Syke, Hetton
Thornton Limestone

95 SW 30   [9346 5259]
Butterhaw, Gargrave*
Worston Shales – Thornton Limestone
(Details published in Harrison, 1982)

96 NE 1   [9726 6647]
Chapel House, Kilnsey*
Kilnsey Formation – Horton Formation (Silurian); including
Kilnsey Limestone, Kilnsey Limestone-with-mudstone and
Chapel House Limestone
(Details published in Murray, 1983)

96 SE 19   [9721 6380]
Lower Height, Threshfield
Grassington Grit – Pendle Grit Formation

REFERENCES

ADDISON, F. T., TURNER, P. and TARLING, D. H. 1985. Magnetic studies of the Pendleside Limestone: evidence for remagnetization and late-diagenetic dolomitization during a post-Asbian normal event. *J. Geol. Soc. London*, Vol.142, 983–994.

ARTHURTON, R. S. 1983. The Skipton Rock Fault—an Hercynian wrench fault associated with the Skipton Anticline, northwest England. *J. Geol.*, Vol.18, 105–114.

— 1984. The Ribblesdale fold belt, NW England—a Dinantian–early Namurian dextral shear zone. 131–138. in HUTTON, D. H. W. and SANDERSON, D. J. (editors). Variscan tectonics of the North Atlantic region. *Spec. Publ. Geol. Soc. London*, No.14. 270 pp.

— and JONES, L. C. 1980. Revision of the Dinantian stratigraphy of the Craven Basin, N. England. *Geol. Mag.*, Vol.117, 613–614.

— and WADGE, A. J. 1981. Geology of the country around Penrith. *Mem. Geol. Surv. G.B.*, Sheet 24. 177 pp.

BANKS, R. J. and GURBUZ, C. 1984. An investigation of the crustal structure of north-west England using quarry blasts as seismic sources. *Proc. Yorkshire Geol. Soc.*, Vol.45, 19–25.

BELL, K. G. 1963. Uranium in carbonate rocks. *Prof. Pap. U.S. Geol. Surv.*, No.474-A. 29 pp.

BISAT, W. S. 1924. The Carboniferous goniatites of the north of England and their zones. *Proc. Yorkshire Geol. Soc.*, Vol.20, 40–124.

— 1928. The Carboniferous goniatite-zones of England and their continental equivalents. *C. R. Cong. Strat. Carb., Heerlen*, 117–133.

— 1930. On *Cravenoceras leion* sp. nov., the basement goniatite of the Namurian, Upper Carboniferous. *Trans. Leeds Geol. Assoc.* Pt.20, 28–32.

— 1933. The phylogeny of the North of England goniatites. 255–260. in The geology of the Yorkshire Dales. *Proc. Geol. Assoc.*, Vol.44, 227–269.

— 1934. The goniatites of the *Beyrichoceras* zone in the north of England. *Proc. Yorkshire Geol. Soc.*, Vol.22, 280–309.

BLACK, W. W. 1950. The Carboniferous geology of the Grassington area, Yorkshire. *Proc. Yorkshire Geol. Soc.*, Vol.28, 29–42.

— 1954. Diagnostic characters of the Lower Carboniferous knoll-reefs in the north of England. *Trans. Leeds Geol. Assoc.*, Vol.6, 262–297.

— 1958. The structure of the Burnsall-Cracoe district and its bearing on the origin of the Cracoe knoll-reefs. *Proc. Yorkshire Geol. Soc.*, Vol.31, 391–414.

— and BOND, G. 1952. The Yoredale succession in the northern flank of the Skyreholme Anticline, Yorkshire. *Proc. Yorkshire Geol. Soc.*, Vol.28, 180–187.

BOND, G. 1950a. The Lower Carboniferous reef limestones of northern England. *J. Geol.*, Vol.58, 313–329.

— 1950b. The nomenclature of the Lower Carboniferous 'reef' limestones in the north of England. *Geol. Mag.*, Vol.87, 267–278.

— 1950c. The Lower Carboniferous reef limestones of Cracoe, Yorkshire. *Q. J. Geol. Soc. London*, Vol.105, 157–188.

BOOKER, K. M. and HUDSON, R. G. S. 1926. The Carboniferous sequence of the Craven Lowlands south of the reef limestones of Cracoe. *Proc. Yorkshire Geol. Soc.*, Vol.20, 411–438.

BOTT, M. H. P. 1961. Geological interpretation of magnetic anomalies over the Askrigg Block. *Q. J. Geol. Soc. London*, Vol.97, 481–495.

— 1967. Geophysical investigations of the northern Pennine basement rocks. *Proc. Yorkshire Geol. Soc.*, Vol.36, 139–168.

BOUMA, A. H. 1962. *Sedimentology of some flysch deposits; a graphic approach to facies interpretation.* 168 pp. (Amsterdam: Elsevier.)

BURGESS, I. C. and COOPER, A. H. 1980. The Farnham (IGS) Borehole near Knaresborough, North Yorkshire. *Rep. Inst. Geol. Sci.*, No.80/1, 12–17.

— and HOLLIDAY, D. W. 1979. Geology of the country around Brough-under-Stainmore. *Mem. Geol. Surv. G.B.*, Sheet 31. 131 pp.

— and MITCHELL, M. 1976. Viséan lower Yoredale limestones on the Alston and Askrigg blocks and the base of the D₂ Zone in northern England. *Proc. Yorkshire Geol. Soc.*, Vol.40, 613–630.

BURLEY, A. J., CORNWELL, J. D. and TOMBS, J. M. C. 1978. Geophysical field techniques for mineral exploration. *Miner. Reconnaissance Programme Rep. Inst. Geol. Sci.*, No.20, 26 pp.

CHARSLEY, T. J. 1984. Early Carboniferous rocks of the Swinden No.1 Borehole, west of Skipton, Yorkshire. *Rep. Br. Geol. Surv.*, No.84/1, 5–12.

CHISHOLM, J. I., MITCHELL, M., STRANK, A. R. E., COX, F. C. and HARRISON, D. J. 1983. A revision of the stratigraphy of the Asbian and Brigantian limestones of the area west of Matlock, Derbyshire. *Rep. Inst. Geol. Sci.*, No.83/10, 17–24.

CHUBB, L. J. and HUDSON, R. G. S. 1925. The nature of the junction between the Lower Carboniferous and the Millstone Grits of north-west Yorkshire. *Proc. Yorkshire Geol. Soc.*, Vol.20, 257–291.

CLARK, R. H. 1967. A contribution to glacial studies of the Malham Tarn area. *Field Studies*, Vol.2, 479–491.

CLAYTON, K. M. 1966. The origin of the landforms of the Malham area. *Field Studies*, Vol.2, 359–384.

— 1981. Explanatory description of the landforms of the Malham area. *Field Studies*, Vol.5, 389–423.

CONIL, R., GROESSENS, E. and PIRLET, H. 1977. Nouvelle charte stratigraphique du Dinantien type de la Belgique. *Ann. Soc. Géol. Nord.*, Vol.96, 363–371.

COPE, F. W. 1940. *Daviesiella Llangollensis* (Davidson) and related forms; morphology, biology and distribution. *J. Manchester Geol. Assoc.*, Vol.1, 199–231.

DAKYNS, J. R. 1872. On the glacial phenomena of the Yorkshire uplands. *Q. J. Geol. Soc. London*, Vol.28, 382–388.

— 1892. The geology of the country between Grassington and Wensleydale. *Proc. Yorkshire Geol. Soc.*, Vol.12, 133–144.

— TIDDEMAN, R. H., GUNN, W. and STRAHAN, A. 1890. The geology of the country around Ingleborough, with parts of the Wensleydale and Wharfedale. *Mem. Geol. Surv. U.K.* (New Series, Sheet 50). 103 pp.

DEWEY, J. F. 1982. Plate tectonics and the evolution of the British Isles. *J. Geol. Soc. London*, Vol.139, 371–412.

DIXON, E. E. L. and HUDSON, R. G. S. 1931. A mid-Carboniferous boulder-bed near Settle. *Geol. Mag.*, Vol.68, 81–92.

DONOVAN, S. K. and PAUL, C. R. C. 1985. Coronate echinoderms from the Lower Palaeozoic of Britain. *Palaeontology*, Vol.28, 527–543.

DOUGHTY, P. S. 1968. Joint densities and their relation to lithology in the Great Scar Limestone. *Proc. Yorkshire Geol. Soc.*, Vol.36, 479–512.

— 1974. Davidsonina (Cyrtina) septosa (Phillips) and the structure of the Viséan Great Scar Limestone north of Settle, Yorkshire. *Proc. Yorkshire Geol. Soc.*, Vol.40, 41–47.

DUNHAM, K. C. 1934. The genesis of the North Pennine ore deposits. *Q. J. Geol. Soc. London*, Vol.90, 689–720.

— 1959. Epigenetic mineralization in Yorkshire. *Proc. Yorkshire Geol. Soc.*, Vol.32, 1–29.

— 1974a. Granite beneath the Pennines in North Yorkshire. *Proc. Yorkshire Geol. Soc.*, Vol.40, 191–194.

— 1974b. Epigenetic minerals. 293–308 in RAYNER, D. H. and HEMINGWAY, J. E. (editors). The geology and mineral resources of Yorkshire. *Occas. Publ. Yorkshire Geol. Soc.*, No.2, 405 pp.

— and STUBBLEFIELD, C. J. 1945. The stratigraphy, structure and mineralization of the Greenhow mining area, Yorkshire. *Q. J. Geol. Soc. London*, Vol.100, 209–268.

— and WILSON, A. A. 1985. The geology of the Northern Pennine Orefield, Volume 2. *Econ. Mem. Br. Geol. Surv.*, Sheets 40, 41 and 50, and parts of 31, 32, 51, 60 and 61, New Series. 246 pp.

DUNHAM, R. J. 1962. Classification of carbonate rocks according to deposited texture. 108–121 in HAM, W. E. (editor). Classification of carbonate rocks. *Am. Assoc. Petrol. Geologists*, Mem.1, Tulsa.

EARP, J. R. 1955. The geology of the Bowland Forest Tunnel, Lancashire. *Bull. Geol. Surv. G.B.*, No.7, 1–12.

EARP, J. R., MAGRAW, D., POOLE, E. G., LAND, D. H. and WHITEMAN, A. J. 1961. Geology of the country around Clitheroe and Nelson. *Mem. Geol. Surv. G.B.*, Sheet 68. 346 pp.

EDEN, R. A., ORME, G. R., MITCHELL, M. and SHIRLEY, J. 1964. A study of part of the margin of the Carboniferous Limestone 'massif' in the Pin Dale area of Derbyshire. *Bull. Geol. Surv. G.B.*, No.21, 73–118.

EVANS, W. B., WILSON, A. A., TAYLOR, B. J. and PRICE, D. 1968. Geology of the country around Macclesfield, Congleton, Crewe and Middlewich. *Mem. Geol. Surv. G.B.*, Sheet 110. 328 pp.

FEWTRELL, M. D. and SMITH, D. G. 1980. Revision of the Dinantian stratigraphy of the Craven Basin, N.England. *Geol. Mag.*, Vol.117, 37–49.

— RAMSBOTTOM, W. H. C. and STRANK, A. R. E. 1981. Carboniferous. 15–69 in JENKINS, D. G. and MURRAY, J. W. (editors). *Stratigraphical atlas of fossil foraminifera*. 310 pp. (Chichester: Ellis Horwood for British Micropalaeontological Society.)

FORD, T. D. 1954. The Upper Carboniferous rocks of the Ingleton Coalfield. *Q. J. Geol. Soc. London*, Vol.110, 231–265.

— 1958. Mining in the Ingleton Coalfield. *Colliery Guardian*, Vol.197, 347–352.

FURNESS, R. R., LLEWELLYN, P. G., NORMAN, T. N. and

RICKARDS, R. B. 1967. A review of Wenlock and Ludlow stratigraphy and sedimentation in N.W. England. *Geol. Mag.*, Vol.104, 132–147.

GARWOOD, E. J. and GOODYEAR, E. 1924. The Lower Carboniferous succession in the Settle district and along the line of the Craven faults. *Q. J. Geol. Soc. London*, Vol.80, 184–273.

GASCOYNE, M., CURRANT, A. P. and LORD, T. C. 1981. Ipswichian fauna of Victoria Cave and the marine palaeoclimatic record. *Nature, London*, Vol.294, 652–654.

GEMMELL, A. and MYERS, J. O. 1952. *Underground adventure.* 20 pp. (Clapham: Dalesman and London: Blandford.)

GEORGE, T. N., JOHNSON, G. A. L., MITCHELL, M., PRENTICE, J. E., RAMSBOTTOM, W. H. C., SEVASTOPULO, G. D., and WILSON, R. B. 1976. A correlation of Dinantian rocks in the British Isles. *Spec. Rep. Geol. Soc. London*, No.7, 87 pp.

HARRISON, D. J. 1982. The limestone resources of the Craven Lowlands. Description of parts of 1:50 000 geological sheets 59, 60, 61, 67, 68 and 69. *Miner. Assess. Rep. Inst. Geol. Sci.*, No.116, 103 pp.

HEYL, A. V. 1969. Some aspects of genesis or zinc-lead-barite-fluorite deposits in the Mississippi Valley, USA. *Trans. Inst. Min. Metall.*, Vol.78B, 148–160.

— LANDIS, G. P. and ZARTMAN, R. E. 1974. Isotopic evidence for the origin of Mississippi Valley—type mineral deposits. *Econ. Geol.*, Vol.69, 992–1006.

HICKS, P. F. 1959. The Yoredale rocks of Ingleborough, Yorkshire. *Proc. Yorkshire Geol. Soc.*, Vol.32, 31–43.

HILL, D. 1938. A monograph of the Carboniferous rugose corals of Scotland. *Palaeontogr. Soc. Monogr.*, Part 1, 1–78, pls 1–2.

HOLLAND, C. H. 1985. Series and stages of the Silurian System. *Episodes*, Vol.8, 101–103.

HOLMES, J. and BISAT, W. S. 1925. Goniatite zones in the Keasden Beck area. *Naturalist*, 307–312.

HUDSON, R. G. S. 1924. On the rhythmic succession of the Yoredale Series in Wensleydale. *Proc. Yorkshire Geol. Soc.*, Vol.20, 125–135.

— 1927. A mid-Avonian reef limestone and conglomerate in the Craven Lowlands. *Geol. Mag.*, Vol.64, 503–511.

— 1930a. The Carboniferous of the Craven Reef Belt; and the Namurian unconformity at Scaleber, near Settle. *Proc. Geol. Assoc.*, Vol.41, 290–322.

— 1930b. The age of the 'Lithostrotion arachnoideum' fauna of the Craven Lowlands. *Proc. Leeds. Philos. Lit. Soc.*, (Sci. Sect), Vol.2, 95–101.

— 1932. The pre-Namurian knoll topography of Derbyshire and Yorkshire. *Trans. Leeds. Geol. Assoc.*, Vol.5, 49–64.

— 1933. The scenery and geology of north-west Yorkshire. 228–255 in The geology of the Yorkshire Dales. *Proc. Geol. Assoc.*, Vol.44, 227–269.

— 1938. The general geology and the Carboniferous Rocks. 295–330 in The geology of the country around Harrogate. *Proc. Geol. Assoc.*, Vol.49, 295–352.

— 1941. The Mirk Fell Beds (Namurian E$_2$) of Tan Hill, Yorkshire. *Proc. Yorkshire Geol. Soc.*, Vol.24, 259–289.

— 1944a. The Carboniferous of the Broughton Anticline, Yorkshire. *Proc. Yorkshire Geol. Soc.*, Vol.25, 190–214.

— 1944b. A pre-Namurian fault-scarp at Malham. *Proc. Leeds Philos. Soc.*, (Sci. sect.) Vol.4, 226–232.

— 1949. The Carboniferous of the Craven Reef Belt at Malham, Yorkshire. *Abstr. Proc. Geol. Soc. London*, No.1447, 38 – 41.

— and COTTON, G. 1945. The Lower Carboniferous in a boring at Alport, Derbyshire. *Proc. Yorkshire Geol. Soc.*, Vol.25, 254 – 330.

— and DUNNINGTON, H. V. 1944. The Carboniferous rocks of the Swinden Anticline, Yorkshire. *Proc. Geol. Asoc.*, Vol.55, 195 – 215.

— and JACKSON, J. W. 1929. *Goniatites spiralis* in a section near the North Craven Fault, Settle district. *Naturalist*, 57 – 58.

— and MITCHELL, G. H. 1937. The Carboniferous geology of the Skipton Anticline. *Summ. Prog. Geol. G.B.*, (for 1935), Part 2, 1 – 45.

HUGHES, T. McK. 1902. Ingleborough. Part 2. Stratigraphy. *Proc. Yorkshire Geol. Soc.*, Vol.14, 323 – 343.

— 1907. Ingleborough. Part 4. Stratigraphy and palaeontology of the Silurian. *Proc. Yorkshire Geol. Soc.*, Vol.16, 45 – 74.

HULL, E., DAKYNS, J. R., TIDDEMAN, R. H., WARD, J. C., GUNN, W. and DE RANCE, C. E. 1875. The geology of the Burnley Coalfield and of the country around Clitheroe, Blackburn, Preston, Chorley, Haslingden and Todmorden. *Mem. Geol. Surv. U.K.*

INGHAM, J. K. 1966. The Ordovician rocks of the Cautley and Dent districts of Westmorland and Yorkshire. *Proc. Yorkshire Geol. Soc.*, Vol.35, 455 – 505.

— and RICKARDS, R. B. 1974. Lower Palaeozoic rocks. 29 – 44 in RAYNER, D. H. and HEMINGWAY, J. E. (editors). The geology and mineral resources of Yorkshire. *Occas. Publ. Yorkshire Geol. Soc.*, No.2, 405 pp.

— McNAMARA, K. J. and RICKARDS, R. B. 1978. The Upper Ordovician and Silurian rocks. 121 – 145 in MOSELEY, F. (editor). The geology of the Lake District. *Occas. Publ. Yorkshire Geol. Soc.*, No.3, 284 pp.

INSTITUTE OF GEOLOGICAL SCIENCES. 1976. IGS Boreholes 1975. *Rep. Inst. Geol. Sci.*, No.76/10, 47 pp.

INSTITUTE OF GEOLOGICAL SCIENCES. 1977. 1:250 000 series Bouguer gravity anomaly map, Lake District Sheet 54°N 04°W. Keyworth: Institute of Geologcal Sciences.

INSTITUTE OF GEOLOGICAL SCIENCES. 1978. 1:250 000 series Aeromagnetic anomaly map, Lake District Sheet 54°N 04°W. Keyworth: Institute of Geological Sciences.

JEFFERSON, D. P. 1980. Cyclic sedimentation in the Holkerian (Middle Viséan) north of Settle, Yorkshire. *Proc. Yorkshire Geol. Soc.*, Vol.42, 483 – 503.

JOHNS, C. 1906. On the Carboniferous basement beds at Ingleton. *Geol. Mag.*, Vol.3, 320 – 323.

— 1908. Some undescribed faults in the Settle – Malham area. *Proc. Yorkshire Geol. Soc.*, Vol.16, 393 – 402.

JOHNSON, E. W. 1981. A tunnel section through a prograding Namurian (Arnsbergian, E_{2a}) delta, in the western Bowland Fells, north Lancashire. *Geol. J.*, Vol.16, 93 – 110.

JOHNSON, G. A. L. 1967. Basement control of Carboniferous sedimentation in northern England. *Proc. Yorkshire Geol. Soc.*, Vol.6, 175 – 194.

— and DUNHAM, K. C. 1963. The geology of Moor House. *Monogr. Nature Conservancy* No.2, 182 pp.

— HODGE, B. L. and FAIRBURN, R. A. 1962. The base of the Namurian and of the Millstone Grit in north-eastern England. *Proc. Yorkshire Geol. Soc.*, Vol.33, 341 – 362.

KENDALL, P. F. and WROOT, H. E. 1924. *The geology of Yorkshire.* 2 Volumes, xxii + 995 pp. Printed privately. Vienna.

KENT, P. E. 1974. Structural history. 13 – 28 in RAYNER, D. H. and HEMINGWAY, J. E. (editors). The geology and mineral resources of Yorkshire. *Occas. Publ. Yorkshire Geol. Soc.* No.2, 405 pp.

KING, A. 1974. A review of archaeological work in the caves of north-west England. 182 – 200 in WALTHAM, A. C. (editor). *The limestones and caves of north-west England.* 477 pp. (Newton Abbott: David and Charles for The British Cave Research Association.)

KING, W. B. R. 1932. A fossiliferous limestone associated with the Ingletonian beds at Horton-in-Ribblesdale, Yorkshire. *Q. J. Geol. Soc. London*, Vol.88, 100 – 111.

— and WILCOCKSON, W. H. 1934. The Lower Palaeozoic rocks of Austwick and Horton-in-Ribblesdale, Yorkshire. *Q. J. Geol. Soc. London*, Vol.90, 7 – 31.

LEEDAL, G. P. and WALKER, G. P. L. 1950. A restudy of the Ingletonian Series of Yorkshire. *Geol. Mag.*, Vol.87, 57 – 66.

LEEDER, M. R. 1982. Upper Palaeozoic basins of the British Isles — Caledonide inheritance versus Hercynian plate margin processes. *J. Geol. Soc. London*, Vol.139, 479 – 491.

LEIGHTON, M. W. and PENDEXTER C. 1962. Carbonate rock types. 33 – 61 in HAM, W. E. (editor). Classification of carbonate rocks. *Am. Assoc. Petrol. Geologists*, Mem.1, Tulsa.

MARR, J. E. 1887. The Lower Palaeozoic rocks near Settle. *Geol. Mag.*, (n.s.) Dec.3, Vol.4, 35 – 38.

— 1899. On limestone-knolls in the Craven district of Yorkshire and elsewhere. *Q. J. Geol. Soc. London*, Vol.55, 327 – 358.

— 1921. On the rigidity of north-west Yorkshire. *Naturalist*, 63 – 72.

McCABE, P. J. 1972. The Wenlock and Lower Ludlow strata of the Austwick and Horton-in-Ribblesdale Inlier of north-west Yorkshire. *Proc. Yorkshire Geol. Soc.*, Vol.39, 167 – 174.

— and WAUGH, B. 1973. Wenlock and Ludlow sedimentation in the Austwick and Horton-in-Ribblesdale Inlier, north-west Yorkshire. *Proc. Yorkshire Geol. Soc.*, Vol.39, 445 – 470.

METCALFE, I. 1981. Conodont zonation and correlation of the Dinantian and early Namurian strata of the Craven Lowlands of northern England. *Rep. Inst. Geol. Sci.*, No.80/10, 1 – 70.

MILLER, J. and GRAYSON, R. F. 1972. Origin and structure of the lower Viséan 'reef' limestones near Clitheroe, Lancashire. *Proc. Yorkshire Geol. Soc.*, Vol.38, 607 – 638.

— — 1982. The regional context of Waulsortian Facies in northern England. 17 – 33 in BOLTON, K., LANE, H. R. and LeMONE, D. V. (editors). Symposium on the palaeoenvironmental setting and distribution of the Waulsortian facies. 202 pp. (El Paso, Texas: El Paso Geological Society and the University of Texas.)

MITCHELL, R. H. and KROUSE, H. R. 1971. Isotopic composition of sulfur and lead in galena from the Greenhow-Skyreholme area, Yorkshire, England. *Econ. Geol.*, Vol.66, 243 – 251.

MOISLEY, H. A. 1955. Some karstic features in the Malham Tarn district. *Ann. Rep. Council for Prom. Field Studies* (1953 – 1954) (1955), 33 – 42.

MOORBATH, S. 1962. Lead isotope abundance studies on mineral occurrences in the British Isles and their geological significance. *Philos. Trans. R. Soc. London*, A, Vol.254, 295 – 360.

MOORE, D. 1958. The Yoredale series of Upper Wensleydale and adjacent parts of north-west Yorkshire. *Proc. Yorkshire Geol. Soc.*, Vol.31, 91 – 148.

MOSELEY, F. 1954. The Namurian of the Lancaster Fells. *Q. J. Geol. Soc. London*, Vol.109, 423 – 454.

— 1956. The geology of the Keasden area, west of Settle, Yorkshire. *Proc. Yorkshire Geol. Soc.*, Vol.30, 331 – 352.

— 1962. The structure of the south-western part of the Sykes Anticline, Bowland, West Yorkshire. *Proc. Yorkshire Geol. Soc.*, Vol.33, 287 – 314.

— 1978. The geology of the English Lake District—an introductory review. 1 – 16 in MOSELEY, F. (editor). The geology of the Lake District. *Occas. Publ. Yorkshire Geol. Soc.*, No.3, 284 pp.

— and AHMED, S. M. 1967. Carboniferous joints in the north of England and their relation to earlier and later structures. *Proc. Yorkshire Geol. Soc.*, Vol.36, 61 – 90.

MUNDY, D. 1978. Reef communities. 157 – 167 in McKERROW, W. S. (editor). *The ecology of fossils.* 384 pp. (London: Duckworth.)

MUNDY, D. J. C. 1980. Aspects of the palaeoecology of the Craven Reef Belt (Dinantian) of North Yorkshire. Unpublished Ph.D. thesis, University of Manchester.

— and ARTHURTON, R. S. 1980. Field meetings: Settle and Flasby. *Proc. Yorkshire Geol. Soc.*, Vol.43, 32 – 36.

MURRAY, D. W. 1983. The limestone and dolomite resources of the country around Settle and Malham, North Yorkshire (with notes on the hard-rock resources of the Horton-in-Ribblesdale area). Description of parts 1:50 000 of geological sheets 50 and 60. *Miner. Assess. Rep. Inst. Geol. Sci.*, No.126. 31 pp.

MYERS, J. O. and WARDELL, J. 1967. The gravity anomalies of the Askrigg Block south of Wensleydale. *Proc. Yorkshire Geol. Soc.*, Vol.36, 169 – 173.

NEVES, R., GUEINN, K. J., CLAYTON, G., IOANNIDES, N. and NEVILLE, R. S. W. 1972. A scheme of miospore zones for the British Dinantian. *C. R. 7 mr Congr. Int. Stratigr. Geol. Carbonif.*, Krefeld 1971, Vol.1, 347 – 353.

O'CONNOR, J. 1964. The geology of the area around Malham Tarn, Yorkshire. *Field Studies*, Vol.2, 53 – 82.

— WILLIAMS, D. S. F. and DAVIES, G. M. 1974. Karst features of Malham and the Craven Fault Zone. 395 – 409 in WALTHAM, A. C. (editor). *The limestones and caves of north-west England.* 477 pp. (Newton Abbott: David and Charles for The British Cave Research Association.)

O'NIONS, R. K., OXBURGH, E. R., HAWKESWORTH, C. J. and MACINTYRE, R. M. 1973. New isotopic and stratigraphical evidence on the age of the Ingletonian: probable Cambrian of northern England. *J. Geol. Soc. London*, Vol.129, 445 – 452.

ORME, G. R. 1974. Silica in the Viséan limestones of Derbyshire, England. *Proc. Yorkshire Geol. Soc.*, Vol.40, 63 – 104.

OWENS, B., NEVES, R., GUEINN, K. J., MISHELL, D. R. F., SABRY, H. S. M. Z. and WILLIAMS, J. E. 1977. Palynological division of the Namurian of northern England and Scotland. *Proc. Yorkshire Geol. Soc.*, Vol.41, 381 – 398.

— RILEY, N. J. and CALVER, M. A. 1985. Boundary stratotypes and new stage names for the early and middle Westphalian sequences in Britain. *Compte Rendu Dixième Congrès International de Stratigraphie et de Géologie du Carbonifère,* Madrid 1983, Vol.4, 461 – 472.

PALMER, J. A. PERRY, S. P. G. and TARLING, D. H. 1985. Carboniferous magnetostratigraphy. *J. Geol. Soc. London*, Vol.142, 945 – 955.

PARKINSON, D. 1926. The faunal succession in the Carboniferous Limestone and Bowland Shales at Clitheroe and Pendle Hill (Lancashire). *Q. J. Geol. Soc. London*, Vol.82, 188 – 249.

— 1936. The Carboniferous succession in the Slaidburn district, Yorkshire. *Q. J. Geol. Soc. London*, Vol.92, 294 – 331.

— 1957. Lower Carboniferous reefs of northern England. *Bull. Am. Assoc. Petrol. Geol.*, Vol.41, 511 – 537.

— 1964. The relationship of the Bowland Shales to the Pendleside Limestone in the Clitheroe, Slaidburn and Sykes anticlines. *J. Geol.*, Vol.4, 157 – 166.

PEACOCK, J. D. and TAYLOR, K. 1966. Uraniferous collophane in the Carboniferous Limestone of Derbyshire and Yorkshire. *Bull. Geol. Surv. G.B.* No.25, 19 – 32.

PENTECOST, A. 1981. The tufa deposits of the Malham district, North Yorkshire. *Field Studies*, Vol.5, 365 – 387.

PHILLIPS, J. 1828. On a group of slate rocks ranging east-south-east between the rivers Lune and Wharfe, near Kirkby Londsale to near Malham. *Trans. Geol. Soc.*, series 2, 3, 1 – 19.

— 1836. *Illustrations of the geology of Yorkshire,* Part 2. *The Mountain Limestone District.* xx + 253 pp. (London: John Murray.)

PHILLIPS, W. E. A., STILLMAN, C. J. and MURPHY, T. 1976. A Caledonian plate tectonic model. *J. Geol. Soc. London*, Vol.132, 579 – 609.

PIGOTT, M. E. and PIGOTT, C. D. 1959. Stratigraphy and pollen analysis of Malham Tarn and Tarn Moss. *Field Studies*, Vol.1, 84 – 101.

PONSFORD, D. R. A. 1955. Radioactivity studies of some British sedimentary rocks. *Bull. Geol. Surv. G.B.*, No.10, 24 – 44.

RADKE, B. M. and MATHIS, R. L. 1980. On the formation and occurrence of saddle dolomite. *J. Sediment. Pet.*, Vol.50, 1149 – 1168.

RAISTRICK, A. 1929. Some Yorkshire glacial lakes. *Naturalist*, 209 – 212.

— 1930. Some glacial features of the Settle district, Yorkshire. *Proc. Univ. Durham Philos. Soc.*, Vol.8, 239 – 251.

— 1931. The glaciation of Wharfedale, Yorkshire. *Proc. Yorkshire Geol. Soc.*, Vol.22, 9 – 30.

— 1933. The glacial and post-glacial periods in West Yorkshire. 263 – 269 in The geology of the Yorkshire Dales. *Proc. Geol. Assoc.*, Vol.44, 227 – 269.

— 1938. Mineral deposits in the Settle-Malham district, Yorkshire. *Naturalist*, 119 – 125.

— 1953. The Malham Moor Mines, Yorkshire, 1790 – 1830. *Trans. Newcomen Soc.*, Vol.26, 69 – 73.

— 1954. The calamine mines, Malham, Yorkshire. *Proc. Univ. Durham Philos. Soc.*, Vol.11, 125 – 130.

— 1973. *Lead mining in the mid-Pennines.* 172 pp. (Truro: Bradford Barton.)

RAMSBOTTOM, W. H. C. 1973. Transgressions and regressions in the Dinantian: a new synthesis of British Dinantian stratigraphy. *Proc. Yorkshire Geol. Soc.*, Vol.39, 567 – 607.

— 1974. Dinantian. 47 – 73 in RAYNER, D. H. and HEMINGWAY, J. E. (editors). The geology and mineral resources of Yorkshire. *Occas. Publ. Yorkshire Geol.*, No.2, 405 pp.

— and MITCHELL, M. 1980. The recognition and division of the Tournaisian Series in Britain. *J. Geol. Soc. London*, Vol.137, 61 – 63.

— CALVER, M. A., EAGAR, R. M. C., HODSON, F., HOLLIDAY, D. W., STUBBLEFIELD, C. J. and WILSON, R. B. 1978. A correlation of Silesian rocks in the British Isles. *Spec. Rep. Geol. Soc. London*, No.10, 82 pp.

RASTALL, R. H. 1906. The Ingletonian Series of West Yorkshire. *Proc. Yorkshire Geol. Soc.*, Vol.16, 87–100.

RAYNER, D. H. 1946. A D_2 coral bed near Settle. *Trans. Leeds. Geol. Assoc.*, Vol.6, 14–25.

— 1953. The Lower Carboniferous rocks in the north of England: a review. *Proc. Yorkshire Geol. Soc.*, Vol.28, 231–315.

— 1957. A problematical structure from the Ingleton rocks, Yorkshire. *Trans. Leeds Geol. Assoc.*, Vol.7, 34–42.

REYNOLDS, S. H. 1894. Certain fossils from the Lower Palaeozoic rocks of Yorkshire. *Geol. Mag.* (n.s.) Dec.4, Vol.1, 108–111.

RHODES, F. H. T., AUSTIN, R. L. and DRUCE, E. C. 1969. British Avonian (Carboniferous) conodont faunas and their value in local and intercontinental correlation. *Bull. Br. Mus. (Nat. Hist.) Suppl.*, No.5, 1–313.

RICKARDS, R. B. 1970. Age of the Middle Coldwell Beds. *Proc. Geol. Soc. London*, No.1663, 111–114.

— 1978. Silurian. 130–145 in MOSELEY, F. (editor). The geology of the Lake District. *Occas. Publ. Yorkshire Geol. Soc.*, No.3, 284 pp.

ROGERS, P. J. 1978. Fluid inclusion studies on fluorite from the Askrigg Block. *Trans. Inst. Min. Metall.*, Vol.87B, 125–131.

ROWELL, A. J. and SCANLON, J. E. 1957. The relation between the Yoredale Series and the Millstone Grit on the Askrigg Block. *Proc. Yorkshire Geol. Soc.*, Vol.31, 79–80.

SAWKINS, F. J. 1966. Ore genesis in the north Pennine Orefield in the light of fluid inclusion studies. *Econ. Geol.*, Vol.61, 385–401.

SCHWARZACHER, W. 1958. The stratification of the Great Scar Limestone in the Settle district of Yorkshire. *Liverpool, Manchester, Geol. J.*, Vol.2, 124–142.

SEDGWICK, A. 1852. On the Lower Palaeozoic rocks at the base of the Carboniferous chain between Ravenstonedale and Ribblesdale. *Q. J. Geol. Soc. London*, Vol.8, 35–54.

SLINGER, F. C. 1936. Millstone Grit and glacial geology of Caton Moor, near Lancaster (Abstract). *Rep. Br. Assoc. Blackpool 1936*, 345.

SMITH, D. I. and ATKINSON, T. C. 1977. Underground flow in cavernous limestones with special reference to the Malham area. *Field Studies*, Vol.4, 597–616.

SOMERVILLE, I. D. 1979. Minor sedimentary cyclicity in late Asbian (Upper D_1) limestones in the Llangollen district of North Wales. *Proc. Yorkshire Geol. Soc.*, Vol.42, 317–341.

— and STRANK, A. R. E. 1984a. Discovery of Arundian and Holkerian faunas from a Dinantian platform succession in North Wales. *Geol. J.*. Vol.19, 85–104.

— — 1984b. The recognition of the Asbian/Brigantian boundary fauna and marker horizons in the Dinantian of North Wales. *Geol. J.*, Vol.19, 227–237.

SOPER, N. J. and HUTTON, D. H. W. 1984. Late Caledonian sinistral displacements in Britain: implications for a three-plate collision model. *Tectonics*, Vol.3, 781–794.

STEPHENS, J. V., MITCHELL, G. H. and EDWARDS, W. 1953. Geology of the country between Bradford and Skipton. *Mem. Geol. Surv. G.B.*, Sheet 69, 180 pp.

STEVENSON, I. P. and GAUNT, G. D. 1971. Geology of the country around Chapel en le Frith. *Mem. Geol. Surv. G.B.*, Sheet 99, 444 pp.

STRANK, A. R. E. 1981. Foraminiferal biostratigraphy of the Holkerian, Asbian and Brigantian stages of the British Lower Carboniferous. Unpublished PhD. Thesis, Manchester University.

SUTCLIFFE, A. J. 1960. Joint Mitnor Cave, Buckfastleigh. *Trans. Torquay Nat. Hist. Soc.*, Vol.13, 1–26.

SWEETING, M. M. 1974. Karst geomorphology in north-west England. 46–78 in WALTHAM, A. C. (editor). *The limestones and caves of north-west England.* 477 pp. (Newton Abbot: David and Charles for The British Cave Research Association.)

TEGERDINE, G. D., CAMPBELL, S. D. G. and WOODCOCK, N. H. 1981. Transcurrent faulting and pre-Carboniferous Anglesey. *Nature, London*, Vol.293, 760.

TIDDEMAN, R. H. 1872. On the evidence for the ice-sheet in North Lancashire and adjacent parts of Yorkshire and Westmoreland. *Q. J. Geol. Soc. London*, Vol.28, 471–491.

— 1873–8. Reports of Victoria Cave Exploration Committee. *Rep. Br. Ass. Adv. Sci.*

— 1889. On concurrent faulting and deposit in Carboniferous times in Craven, Yorkshire, with a note on Carboniferous reefs. *Rep. Br. Assoc. (Newcastle)*, 600–603.

— 1891. Physical history of the Carboniferous rocks in upper Airedale. *Proc. Yorkshire Geol. Soc.*, Vol.11, 482–492.

TURNER, J. S. 1936. The structural significance of the Rossendale Anticline. *Trans. Leeds Geol. Assoc.*, Vol.5, 157–160.

TURNER, P. 1975a. Palaeozoic secular variation recorded in Pendleside Limestone. *Nature, London*, Vol.257, 207–208.

— 1975b. Depositional magnetization of Carboniferous limestones from the Craven basin of northern England. *Sedimentology*, Vol.22, 563–581.

— and TARLING, D. H. 1975. Implications of new palaeomagnetic results from the Carboniferous System of Britain. *J. Geol. Soc. London*, Vol.131, 469–488.

— METCALFE, I. and TARLING, D. H. 1979. Palaeomagnetic studies of some Dinantian limestones from the Craven Basin and a contribution to Asbian magnetostratigraphy. *Proc. Yorkshire Geol. Soc.*, Vol.42, 371–396.

VARKER, W. J. and SEVASTOPULO, G. D. 1985. Dinantian conodonts. 167–189 in AUSTIN, R. L. and HIGGINS, A. C. (editors). *A stratigraphical index of British conodonts.* 263 pp. (Ellis Horwood for British Micropalaeontological Society.)

VAUGHAN, A. 1905. The palaeontological sequence in the Carboniferous Limestone of the Bristol area. *Q. J. Geol. Soc. London*, Vol.61, 181–305.

VERSEY, H. C. 1948. *Geology and scenery of the countryside round Leeds and Bradford.* ix + 94pp. (London: Murby.)

WADGE, A. J., BATESON, J. H. and EVANS, A. D. 1983. Mineral reconnaissance surveys in the Craven Basin. *Mineral Reconnaissance Programme Rep. Inst. Geol. Sci.*, No.66. 100 pp.

WAGER, L. R. 1931. Jointing in the Great Scar Limestone of Craven and its relation to the tectonics of the area. *Q. J. Geol. Soc. London*, Vol.87, 392–424.

WALKDEN, G. M. 1972. The mineralogy and origin of interbedded clay wayboards in the Lower Carboniferous of the Derbyshire Dome. *Geol. J.*, Vol.8, 143–160.

WALTHAM, A. C. 1971. Shale units in the Great Scar Limestone of the southern Askrigg Block. *Proc. Yorkshire Geol. Soc.*, Vol.38, 285–292.

— 1974. The geomorphology of the caves of north-west England. 79–105 in WALTHAM, A. C. (editor). *The limestones and caves of north-west England.* 477 pp. (Newton Abbot: David and Charles for The British Cave Research Association.)

WHETTON, J. T., MYERS, J. O. and WATSON, I. J. 1956. A gravimeter survey in the Craven district of north-west Yorkshire. *Proc. Yorkshire Geol. Soc.*, Vol.30, 259–287.

WILLIAMSON, I. A. 1958. Field meetings along the North Craven Fault. *Proc. Geol. Assoc. London*, Vol.70, 210–216.

WILLS, L. J. 1978. A palaeogeographic map of the Lower Palaeozoic floor below the cover of Upper Devonian, Carboniferous and later formations. *Mem. Geol. Soc. London*, No.8, 36 pp.

WILMORE, A. 1910. On the Carboniferous Limestone south of the Craven Fault (Grassingon-Hellifield district). *Q. J. Geol. Soc. London*, Vol.66, 539–585.

WILSON, A. A. 1960. The Carboniferous rocks of Coverdale and adjacent valleys in the Yorkshire Pennines. *Proc. Yorkshire Geol. Soc.*, Vol.32, 285–316.

— and CORNWELL, J. D. 1982. The Institute of Geological Sciences borehole at Beckermonds Scar, North Yorkshire. *Proc. Yorkshire Geol. Soc.*, Vol.44, 59–88.

WOLFENDEN, E. B. 1958. Paleoecology of the Carboniferous reef complex and shelf limestones in north-west Derbyshire, England. *Bull. Geol. Soc. Am.*, Vol.69, 871–898.

YATES, P. J. 1962. The palaeonotology of the Namurian rocks of Slieve Anierin, Co. Leitrim, Eire. *Palaeontology*, Vol.5, 355–443.

FOSSIL INDEX

GENERAL INDEX

Italic figures refer to tables or illustrations

BRITISH GEOLOGICAL SURVEY

Keyworth, Nottingham NG12 5GG

Murchison House, West Mains Road,
Edinburgh EH9 3LA

The full range of Survey publications is available
through the Sales Desks at Keyworth and
Murchison House. Selected items are stocked by
the Geological Museum Bookshop, Exhibition
Road, London SW7 2DE; all other items may be
obtained through the BGS London Information
Office in the Geological Museum. All the books
are listed in HMSO's Sectional List 45. Maps are
listed in the BGS Map Catalogue and Ordnance
Survey's Trade Catalogue. They can be bought
from Ordnance Survey Agents as well as from
BGS.

*The British Geological Survey carries out the geological
survey of Great Britain and Northern Ireland (the latter as
an agency service for the government of Northern Ireland),
and of the surrounding continental shelf, as well as its
basic research projects. It also undertakes programmes of
British technical aid in geology in developing countries as
arranged by the Overseas Development Administration.*

*The British Geological Survey is a component body of the
Natural Environment Research Council.*

Maps and diagrams in this book use topography
based on Ordnance Survey mapping

HER MAJESTY'S STATIONERY OFFICE

HMSO publications are available from:

HMSO Publications Centre
(Mail and telephone orders)
PO Box 276, London SW8 5DT
Telephone orders (01) 622 3316
General enquiries (01) 211 5656
Queueing system in operation for both numbers

HMSO Bookshops
49 High Holborn, London WC1V 6HB
  (01) 211 5656 (Counter service only)
258 Broad Street, Birmingham B1 2HE
  (021) 643 3740
Southey House, 33 Wine Street, Bristol BS1 2BQ
  (0272) 264306
9 Princess Street, Manchester M60 8AS
  (061) 834 7201
80 Chichester Street, Belfast BT1 4JY
  (0232) 238451
71 Lothian Road, Edinburgh EH3 9AZ
  (031) 228 4181

HMSO's Accredited Agents
(see Yellow Pages)

And through good booksellers